DECOLONIZED CLINICAL SUPERVISION AND LEADERSHIP

This book offers a roadmap to applying anti-oppressive theories, frameworks, and concepts to clinical social work supervision and leadership practice. It introduces anti-oppressive practice, Critical Race Theory, empowerment practice, transgender and critical gender studies, DEI/DEIPAR, critical Black studies, queer studies, and intersectionality, alongside other concepts. Offering practical guidance, reference, skill-building, and critical self-reflection tools, it is ideal for courses in social work supervision, leadership, diversity, and community practice, as well as self-reference for practitioners. Structured to be easily referenced and adapted, this work also incorporates skill-building and reflection activities to promote interaction across a variety of learning contexts.

NATHANIEL L. CURRIE is a scholar-practitioner specializing in the trauma experiences of Black and Brown identified men, anti-oppressive social work practices, and gender and orientation diversity. His clinical community-based participatory research explores the psychosocial intersection of trauma and HIV, along with other health disparities experienced by Black and Brown men.

DECOLONIZED CLINICAL SUPERVISION AND LEADERSHIP

A Social Work Perspective

EDITED BY

NATHANIEL L. CURRIE

Clark Atlanta University

Shaftesbury Road, Cambridge CB2 8EA, United Kingdom

One Liberty Plaza, 20th Floor, New York, NY 10006, USA

477 Williamstown Road, Port Melbourne, VIC 3207, Australia

314–321, 3rd Floor, Plot 3, Splendor Forum, Jasola District Centre, New Delhi – 110025, India

103 Penang Road, #05-06/07, Visioncrest Commercial, Singapore 238467

Cambridge University Press is part of Cambridge University Press & Assessment, a department of the University of Cambridge.

We share the University's mission to contribute to society through the pursuit of education, learning and research at the highest international levels of excellence.

www.cambridge.org
Information on this title: www.cambridge.org/9781009440561

DOI: 10.1017/9781009440585

© Cambridge University Press & Assessment 2026

This publication is in copyright. Subject to statutory exception and to the provisions of relevant collective licensing agreements, no reproduction of any part may take place without the written permission of Cambridge University Press & Assessment.

When citing this work, please include a reference to the DOI 10.1017/9781009440585

First published 2026

Cover image: Cyrus Nelson, *Tribe of Many Colors* mixed media on canvas, 2019

A catalogue record for this publication is available from the British Library

A Cataloging-in-Publication data record for this book is available from the Library of Congress

ISBN 978-1-009-44056-1 Hardback
ISBN 978-1-009-44053-0 Paperback

Cambridge University Press & Assessment has no responsibility for the persistence or accuracy of URLs for external or third-party internet websites referred to in this publication and does not guarantee that any content on such websites is, or will remain, accurate or appropriate.

For EU product safety concerns, contact us at Calle de José Abascal, 56, 1°, 28003 Madrid, Spain, or email eugpsr@cambridge.org

Contents

List of Figures — *page* xiv
List of Tables — xv
List of Contributors — xvi
Preface — xxiii
Acknowledgments — xxv

Introduction: Decolonized Clinical Supervision and Leadership: The Necessity of Now, An Introduction — 1
Gary Bailey

PART I CONTENT KNOWLEDGE AND APPLICATION

1 Decolonizing Social Work Practice and Clinical Supervision: Beginning the Process — 9
Nathaniel L. Currie

2 Utilizing Anti-Oppressive Lens in Social Work Supervision — 32
Nathaniel L. Currie, Ashley Wolfe, Darrin E. Wright, Jack Burke, Gisela Martinez, Gavin Meade, Jad-Évangelo Nasser, and Aydin Olson-Kennedy

3 DEIPAR *(dee-per)* Supervision: Leadership and Power-Sharing — 81
Jacqueline T. Dyer

4 If-Then Antiracism Heuristics: Integration of Critical Race Theory in Clinical Praxis — 106
Adriana Aldana and Michelle Zaragoza

5 The Process of Decolonizing Supervision and Leadership (It Do Take Nerve) — 131
Ann Marie Garran, Nathaniel L. Currie, Jack Burke, Rebecca "Bex" Lisenbee, Gavin Meade, and Adrianna N. Taylor

6 Transforming Leadership and Supervision through the
   Integration of Anti-Oppressive Practices   161
   Christina Crow Cruz

7 Anti-Oppressive and Intersectional Mental Health Practice in
   Psycholegal and Other Interdisciplinary Collaborative Settings   180
   Lindsey Sank Davis and Melanie Robinson Findlay

PART II LEADERSHIP AND SYSTEMS PRACTICE

8 Dismantling Systems That Traumatize and Oppress:
   A Comprehensive Approach   205
   Ann Marie Garran, Nathaniel L. Currie, and Jad-Evangelo Nasser

9 Conducting Community-Based Participatory Research
   Using a Lens of Anti-Oppression: Insights into
   Everyday Application   231
   Natalie D. Crawford

10 Combined Use of Servant Leadership Principles and Afrocentric
   Perspective Principles as Framework to Decolonize Social
   Institutions' Commitment to Well-being and Inclusion   239
   Darrin E. Wright

11 Liberation as Praxis for Antiracist, Anti-Oppressive
   Approaches to Higher Education and Social Work
   Using a BlackCrit Lens   251
   Frederick V. Engram Jr.

12 Reversing the Curse: Liberatory Models for Black Leaders and
   Clinical Supervisors in the Family Separation System   263
   *Sherri Y. Simmons-Horton, Shawna Marie Aarons-Cooke,
   and Tanya Rollins*

13 Supervision and Leadership Impact and Overlap on
   Communities   293
   Nathaniel L. Currie, Jenny Jones, and Larry L. Scott-Walker

Glossary: Terms and Definitions for Anti-Oppressive Practice   313
Further Reading: Anti-Oppressive and Decolonial Resources Unlocked 338
Index   343

Detailed Contents

List of Figures	*page* xiv
List of Tables	xv
List of Contributors	xvi
Preface	xxiii
Acknowledgments	xxv

Introduction: Decolonized Clinical Supervision and Leadership: The Necessity of Now   1
Gary Bailey
This introduction sets the tone for this text by describing the need to further embed anti-oppressive practice and leadership in social work education and education across the helping professions, in that it creates a text that demonstrates sound and innovative application of decolonial lenses, anti-oppressive lenses, and empowerment practice in clinical supervision and social work leadership. Dr. Bailey urges the reader to understand that the process of decolonization within the helping professions is a process across systems, environments, and over time toward liberation.

PART I CONTENT KNOWLEDGE AND APPLICATION

1 Decolonizing Social Work Practice and Clinical Supervision: Beginning the Process   9
Nathaniel L. Currie
In this chapter, the concept, necessity, call to action, and process of decolonial and anti-oppressive clinical supervision is discussed. Functions of clinical supervision are innovated and updated. Practice strategies and implementation are offered for all levels and experiences of clinical supervision. By design, subsequent chapters will overlap, deep dive, and offer multiple practice views of several concepts offered in this chapter.
Boxes 1.1 and 1.2 by Nathaniel L. Currie

2 Utilizing Anti-Oppressive Lens in Social Work Supervision 32
Nathaniel L. Currie, Ashley Wolfe, Darrin E. Wright, Jack Burke, Gisela Martinez, Gavin Meade, Jad-Évangelo Nasser, and Aydin Olson-Kennedy
In this chapter, multiple anti-oppressive and liberative lenses are reviewed and discussed as applications to anti-oppressive decolonial clinical social work supervision and leadership practice. This chapter includes both a review of the theory or practice lens and an emphasis on application to practice. By design, subsequent chapters will overlap, deep dive, and offer multiple practice views of several concepts offered in this chapter.
Boxes 2.1 and 2.2 by Nathaniel L. Currie

3 DEIPAR *(dee-per)* Supervision: Leadership and Power-Sharing 81
Jacqueline T. Dyer
This chapter unpacks the DEIPAR social justice framework, which accounts for intersectionality, power, and antiracism, in relation to supervision, leadership, and power-sharing. The discussion of antiracism details the connection between racism, colonialism, and anti-Blackness, to create clarity regarding the colonial dynamics and hierarchy of supervision. Building on these connections, a pathway is provided for developing socially just power-sharing using the DEIPAR framework in the context of supervision. Opportunities for application of the practice are given.
Box 3.1 by Gisela Martinez and Jacqueline T. Dyer

4 If-Then Antiracism Heuristics: Integration of Critical Race Theory in Clinical Praxis 106
Adriana Aldana and Michelle Zaragoza
Social work's fundamental roots in social justice and human rights have fostered an urgent call for social workers to actively engage in antiracist social work practice. However, social workers face the challenge of translating theoretical concepts into concrete antiracist practices and interventions. This chapter aims to provide one approach social workers may adopt to integrate Critical Race Theory (CRT) in clinical settings. Introducing the practice tool of CRT-informed "if-then" heuristics, we focus on translating three CRT tenets into antiracism praxis recommendations: Social Construction of Race, Racism as Ordinary, and Intersectionality. We briefly describe each tenet's theoretical contributions, introduce its related heuristic, and propose its implications for clinical practice. We also include considerations for clinical supervision and antiracist

organizational leadership. Presenting a table summary of the CRT-informed "if-then" heuristics, corresponding reflexive questions, and a case vignette activity, we offer social workers several practical tools to guide efforts toward an antiracism praxis.
Box 4.4 by Adriana Aldana and Michelle Zaragoza

5 The Process of Decolonizing Supervision and Leadership
   (It Do Take Nerve)   131
   Ann Marie Garran, Nathaniel L. Currie, Jack Burke, Rebecca "Bex" Lisenbee, Gavin Meade, and Adrianna N. Taylor
   This chapter furthers and advances the decolonial process discussed in previous chapters by providing a deeper understanding of the totality of anti-oppressive practice and its embedding into direct clinical work through the clinical supervision process. Special attention is paid to complementary theories and concepts (e.g., the cycle of socialization, relational-cultural theory, building allyship, dismantling racism, inclusive supervision and followership, etc.) that strengthen anti-oppressive decolonial supervision and leadership practice.
   Box 5.1 by Gavin Meade and Jack Burke

6 Transforming Leadership and Supervision through the
   Integration of Anti-Oppressive Practices   161
   Christina Crow Cruz
   This chapter continues the integration of anti-oppressive principles into established supervision and leadership, highlighting the importance of addressing issues of oppression at the micro, mezzo, and macro levels for effective and ethical practice. The role of intersectionality and power dynamics is discussed, and strategies to integrate anti-oppressive principles into practice are outlined. Suggestions for promoting equity and social justice in leadership are provided. Ethical considerations in anti-oppressive leadership, including confidentiality and intersectionality, navigating power dynamics, and addressing ethical dilemmas, are explored. The importance of self-reflection in professional development is emphasized, and approaches to implementing anti-oppressive practices at the organizational level are offered. Additionally, common challenges are discussed, as well as strategies to address resistance and seize opportunities for growth and innovation. This anti-oppressive approach will help equip leaders and supervisors with the knowledge and tools necessary to enhance their practice, support supervisees, and drive organizational change through an anti-oppressive lens.
   Box 6.1 by Christina Crow Cruz

7 Anti-Oppressive and Intersectional Mental Health Practice in
Psycholegal and Other Interdisciplinary Collaborative Settings   180
Lindsey Sank Davis and Melanie Robinson Findlay
Clinical social workers, psychologists, counselors, and other mental health professionals play key roles in a variety of systems, many of which have a history of systematically marginalizing and disadvantaging people of color (POC), sexual and gender minorities (SGM), immigrants and refugees, individuals with disabilities, and other historically oppressed individuals and groups. While the mental health disciplines all require some training in diversity and multiculturalism, graduate-level mental health training varies widely in the extent to which it addresses systemic inequities and builds the capacities of practitioners to disrupt and repair the harm caused by these historical patterns of oppression. This chapter explores this area of focus and practice guidance in embedding anti-oppressive and intersectional concepts into mental and behavioral health practice.
Box 7.1 by Lindsey Sank Davis and Melanie Robinson Findlay

PART II LEADERSHIP AND SYSTEMS PRACTICE

8 Dismantling Systems That Traumatize and Oppress:
A Comprehensive Approach   205
Ann Marie Garran, Nathaniel L. Currie, and Jad-Évangelo Nasser
In this chapter, the intersection of systemic inequality, oppression, and trauma are explored. This chapter outlines the deep historical and contemporary roots of oppression and trauma, explores the multifaceted impact on individuals and communities, and suggests practical strategies for dismantling these systems, all with an eye toward long-term healing and justice.
Boxes 8.1 and 8.2 by Adrianna N. Taylor

9 Conducting Community-Based Participatory Research Using
a Lens of Anti-Oppression: Insights into Everyday Application   231
Natalie D. Crawford
Community-based participatory research (CBPR) must be rooted in anti-oppressive practices that promote equity, power-sharing, and community autonomy, ultimately contributing to the dismantling of systemic racism and the advancement of health equity. Social work leadership and practice are prime locations to incorporate and

support CBPR as a mechanism to strengthen processes, intervention, policy creation, and community strategies.
Box 9.1 by Justin C. Smith

10 Combined Use of Servant Leadership Principles and Afrocentric Perspective Principles as Framework to Decolonize Social Institutions' Commitment to Well-being and Inclusion 239
Darrin E. Wright
To decolonize social institutions (i.e., political, criminal justice, educational, and economic systems), a more profound commitment to inclusion and well-being will require a reimagining of the embedment of antiracist and anti-oppressive paradigms. Various social institutions, either inherited or created to meet the needs and aspirations of the formerly colonized, have faltered and failed under the pressures of neo-colonialism and structural racism, and have manifested in their various forms as structural adjustment programs, outsourcing, privatization of human services, and the rise of non governmental organizations (NGOs). There is an urgent need for new and innovative research on the subject of producing a brave and adaptable generation of leaders who understand the value of servant leadership principles coupled with the principles of the Afrocentric Perspective as a framework to create social policies and engage in leadership practices that are sensitive to the needs of Black, Indigenous, and People of Color (BIPOC) and other oppressed groups, in general, as a conceptualization of a praxis of decoloniality. This chapter will address how these two approaches can contribute to the reinvigoration of upcoming leaders committed to serving BIPOC and other oppressed and marginalized groups.

11 Liberation as Praxis for Antiracist, Anti-Oppressive Approaches to Higher Education and Social Work Using a BlackCrit Lens 251
Frederick V. Engram Jr.
Liberation as a praxis for the helping professions is a tool of resistance aimed at increasing cultural awareness and trauma-informed approaches to engaging with marginalized populations. This approach requires each of us in the helping professions to interrogate our own relationships with anti-Blackness, white supremacy, and bigotry. For effective advocates to do the good work of helping people, there must be a disassociation from white supremacy and white supremacist ideologies. Liberation as a praxis is the only way.

12   Reversing the Curse: Liberatory Models for Black Leaders and
     Clinical Supervisors in the Family Separation System   263
     Sherri Y. Simmons-Horton, Shawna Marie Aarons-Cooke, and Tanya Rollins
     In this chapter, the authors provide critical analysis of the child welfare system as the basis for cultivating the necessary reflection and action among supervisors, leaders, and practitioners to co-create truly anti-oppressive approaches to supervision and leadership. Utilizing a Black Critical Race Theory/BlackCrit lens (applying the principles of Critical Race Theory exclusively to the unique and significantly marginalized experiences of Black people), the authors interrogate the oppressive practices and motivations of historic and modern child welfare systems across the United States that are disproportionately harmful to Black children and families. Motivated to foster hope and facilitate systems change, the authors utilize case studies to support skills development in anti-oppressive supervision and leadership, while reimagining the potential for an antiracist child empowerment and support system for Black children and families. Readers are invited to embrace tools and skills that digress from strategies informed by white supremacy and social control. Ultimately, strategies presented in the chapter lay a foundation for rebuilding and reimagining supportive processes that preserve families and children.
     Box 12.1 by Shawna Marie Aarons-Cooke, Box 12.2 by Tanya Rollins, and Box 12.3 by Nathaniel L. Currie

13   Supervision and Leadership Impact and Overlap
     on Communities   293
     Nathaniel L. Currie, Jenny Jones, and Larry L. Scott-Walker
     This chapter explores the many ways social work supervision and leadership practice engage with and overlap with/within communities through anti-oppressive work. Focuses include utilizing supervision and leadership to engage communities, facilitative leadership, transitional leadership and succession planning, connecting and utilizing the arts in community empowerment, messaging, and liberative movement.
     Box 13.1 by sarah bricke and Box 13.2 by Larry L. Scott-Walker

Glossary: Terms and Definitions for Anti-Oppressive Practice   313
Further Reading: Anti-Oppressive and Decolonial Resources Unlocked   338
    Nathaniel L. Currie

In the further reading, a beginning bank of anti-oppressive, decolonial, and antiracist readings, tools, guides, and community organizations is provided. Practitioners, leaders, community organizers, lay people/folx, and students will find easy access to resources and curriculum to build a more just, cohesive, and liberative practice and community.

Index 343

Figures

1.1	Community building through outreach at NAESM, Inc., Atlanta, Georgia	page 27
2.1	Prism of intersectional oppression	56
5.1	The Cycle of Socialization	135
5.2	Camp Wediko, 2024	153
9.1	Side portrait of happy young Black man looking at cellphone	236
12.1	Integrated model of supervision and leadership	286
13.1	*Community ii* by Langston Allston	294
13.2	*3 Kings*	310

Tables

2.1	Questioning metaphors in social work discourse	*page* 37
2.2	Harmful metaphors in social discourse and public policy	40
4.1	Antiracism heuristics, corresponding CRT tenets, and practice implications	109
10.1	Ten concepts specific to the Afrocentric Perspective	246
11.1	Dimensions of anti-Blackness within the helping professions	261

Contributors

SHAWNA MARIE AARONS-COOKE, DSW, MSW, LCSWR
Blanton-Peale Institute & Counseling Center, Practitioner
Dr. Aarons-Cooke is an executive leader in social services with 20 years of experience supporting children and families. Her career spans child welfare, inpatient psychiatry, adolescent health, youth development, as well as community mental health and substance use treatment. She is committed to anti-oppressive, trauma-informed, and trauma-responsive systems of care.

ADRIANA ALDANA, PHD, MSW
California State University Dominguez Hills, Associate Professor
Dr. Aldana (she/ella) is an associate professor in the Department of Social Work at California State University, Dominguez Hills. Her scholarship examines how participatory action research approaches build youths' capacity for antiracism. She also teaches and writes on the application of Critical Race Theory in social work practice.

GARY BAILEY, DHL, MSW, ACSW
Simmons University, Assistant Dean, Associate Professor
Dr. Bailey is the MSW Program Director at the Simmons University School of Social Work, Boston, Massachusetts. He is also a professor of practice in Simmons Schools of Social Work and Nursing and Health Sciences. He was the assistant dean for community engagement and social justice at the College of Social Sciences, Policy and Practice at Simmons University. Bailey has devoted his career to sharing his deep knowledge, expertise, and leadership in the fields of social work, public health, youth education, and affordable housing. He is former president of the International Federation of Social Workers and the first person of color to hold this post.

Tables

2.1	Questioning metaphors in social work discourse	*page* 37
2.2	Harmful metaphors in social discourse and public policy	40
4.1	Antiracism heuristics, corresponding CRT tenets, and practice implications	109
10.1	Ten concepts specific to the Afrocentric Perspective	246
11.1	Dimensions of anti-Blackness within the helping professions	261

Contributors

SHAWNA MARIE AARONS-COOKE, DSW, MSW, LCSWR
Blanton-Peale Institute & Counseling Center, Practitioner
Dr. Aarons-Cooke is an executive leader in social services with 20 years of experience supporting children and families. Her career spans child welfare, inpatient psychiatry, adolescent health, youth development, as well as community mental health and substance use treatment. She is committed to anti-oppressive, trauma-informed, and trauma-responsive systems of care.

ADRIANA ALDANA, PHD, MSW
California State University Dominguez Hills, Associate Professor
Dr. Aldana (she/ella) is an associate professor in the Department of Social Work at California State University, Dominguez Hills. Her scholarship examines how participatory action research approaches build youths' capacity for antiracism. She also teaches and writes on the application of Critical Race Theory in social work practice.

GARY BAILEY, DHL, MSW, ACSW
Simmons University, Assistant Dean, Associate Professor
Dr. Bailey is the MSW Program Director at the Simmons University School of Social Work, Boston, Massachusetts. He is also a professor of practice in Simmons Schools of Social Work and Nursing and Health Sciences. He was the assistant dean for community engagement and social justice at the College of Social Sciences, Policy and Practice at Simmons University. Bailey has devoted his career to sharing his deep knowledge, expertise, and leadership in the fields of social work, public health, youth education, and affordable housing. He is former president of the International Federation of Social Workers and the first person of color to hold this post.

List of Contributors   xvii

SARAH BRICKE, MFA
University of California San Diego, PhD Student
Bricke (she/her) is a transdisciplinary scholar and practitioner. Her practice is invested in/merges research, materials, and modes of production in ways that trouble dominant narratives and overturn existing orders and structure, investing in radical processes of rethinking, reembodying, and reimagining. bricke holds an MFA from the School of the Art Institute of Chicago. She is currently pursuing a PhD in Art History, Theory, and Criticism at the University of California, San Diego.

JACK BURKE, MA
William James College, PsyD Student
Mr. Burke is a doctoral student in clinical psychology at William James College. He serves as president-elect on the Society for Personality Assessment graduate student board. He also serves as a predoctoral fellow at Clinical Alliance Services in Cambridge, Massachusetts.

NATALIE D. CRAWFORD, PHD, MPH
Emory University, Associate Professor
Dr. Crawford is an associate professor in Behavioral, Social and Health Education Sciences in the Rollins School of Public Health at Emory University. She serves as the co-director of the Prevention and Implementation Sciences Core in the Center for AIDS Research (CFAR) at Emory. Trained in social epidemiology, she received her PhD and MPH in epidemiology from Columbia University's Mailman School of Public Health. Dr. Crawford completed her postdoctoral training at the University of Michigan as a Robert Wood Johnson Health and Society Scholar. She graduated from Spelman College, where she trained in women's studies and biochemistry. Her NIMH-supported research examines the impact of structural interventions in pharmacies on reducing racial inequities in HIV. She is currently advancing the implementation science of HIV prevention services in pharmacies in the US Southeast.

CHRISTINA CROW CRUZ, DSW, MSW, LCSW
Simmons University, Adjunct Professor
Dr. Crow Cruz (she/her) is a dedicated social worker and public health advocate with over 20 years of experience working to close the healthcare gap through nonprofit leadership and social programs both nationally and internationally. Her expertise includes social innovation, diversity, equity, and inclusion (DEI), health equity, education, and clinical social work.

NATHANIEL L. CURRIE, DSW, MSW, LCSW
Clark Atlanta University, Assistant Professor

Dr. Currie (he/him) is a scholar-practitioner specializing in the trauma experiences of Black and Brown identified men and queer identified people; anti-oppressive social work practice and leadership; and gender and orientation diversity. His clinical, community-based participatory research explores the psychosocial intersection of trauma and HIV and other health disparities experienced by Black/Brown men. Dr. Currie is a full-time faculty member at the Whitney M. Young Jr. School of Social Work, Clark Atlanta University. Dr. Currie maintains a robust community-based clinical practice and an anti-oppression focus graduate clinical internship program at NAESM, Inc. in Atlanta, Georgia. Dr. Currie holds a Doctor of Social Work degree from the University of Pennsylvania.

JACQUELINE T. DYER, PHD, MSW, LICSW
Simmons University, Program Director, Associate Professor

Dr. Dyer is the program director and associate professor of practice of the Doctorate of Social Work Program at Simmons University, Boston. She has been a social worker for more than 30 years in direct practice and in leadership, in private practice, community outreach, advocacy, program development, and in academia.

FREDERICK V. ENGRAM JR., EDD
Fairleigh Dickinson University, Assistant Professor

Dr. Engram is an assistant professor of higher education at Fairleigh Dickinson University. He is the author of *Black Liberation through Action and Resistance: MOVE* (2023, Rowman & Littlefield). He is also a widely requested public speaker on the topics of CRT, Black joy, and social justice-related initiatives.

ANN MARIE GARRAN, PHD, MSW
University of Connecticut, Associate Professor

Dr. Garran's scholarship focuses on organizational responses to racism, microaggressions, and psychological safety in higher education and beyond. She is widely published and is co-author of *Racism in the United States: Implications for the Helping Professions, 3rd ed.* (Springer). Her work is known nationally and internationally.

JENNY JONES, PHD, MSW, ACSW
Clark Atlanta University, Dean, Professor

Dr. Jones has over 25 years of experience in higher education. A former child protective services worker, outpatient family therapist, and therapeutic foster care supervisor, Dr. Jones has devoted her professional life to serving and researching the needs of children and families. Her research interests in the child welfare service systems include supervision and organizational culture and its impact on service delivery and child well-being; HIV/AIDS and child welfare; and financial capability and asset building, which considers the integration of financial and economic principles and interventions in direct practice with low-income families.

REBECCA "BEX" LISENBEE, DSW, MSW, LCSW, PMH-C
Community-Based Practitioner, University of Oklahoma, Assistant Professor
Dr. Lisenbee is a medical social worker specializing in maternal/child health, and is a trauma therapist trained in culturally responsive interventions. Lisenbee is a co-conspirator for change surrounding racial and gender disparities in healthcare and is passionate about decolonized education in social work.

GISELA MARTINEZ, DSW, MSW, LCSW-C
Community-Based Practitioner
Dr. Martinez is a scholar-practitioner with over 15 years of experience supporting Latine immigrant families in the southeastern US She has devoted her career to addressing mental health disparities in the Latine immigrant community, particularly among recently arrived youth and reunified families.

GAVIN MEADE, MA
William James College, PsyD Student
Mr. Meade is a doctoral student in clinical psychology at William James College. He is a Child and Adolescent Mental Health Initiative (CAMHI) Fellow. He is also the current director of Camp Wediko at the Home for Little Wanderers, Hillsboro, New Hampshire, and advanced practicum intern at Judge Baker Children's Center in Boston, Massachusetts.

CYRUS NELSON, BFA
Artist
Cyrus Nelson is an Atlanta-based artist who sees his compositions as unions of textures, shapes, patterns, and colors that speak to the soul. From his artistic use of creativity in the field of interactive design to his most recent mixed-media paintings, he expresses his love for form and movement. He finds inspiration in relationships, travel, music, art, and family.

JAD-ÉVANGELO NASSER, MA
J-É Cultural Consulting LLC, Global Inclusion & Cross-Cultural Specialist
Mr. Nasser is a multilingual inclusion specialist with over 12 years of global experience in diversity, equity, and inclusion (DEI); cross-cultural communication; and media work and scholarship. He holds a master's degree in Media Studies: Digital Storytelling from the Parsons School of Design – The New School. He is an award-winning filmmaker for his piece *Once Upon a Color*, available on Prime Video, a TEDx speaker, and co-chair at the LGBTQ Institute at the National Center for Civil and Human Rights.

AYDIN OLSON-KENNEDY, DSW, MSW, LCSW
California State University Fullerton, Adjunct Professor
Dr. Olson-Kennedy has over 15 years of experience providing mental health care for transgender adolescents, adults, and their families, specializing in supporting parents of transgender children of all ages. Informed by critical intersectional theories, Dr. Olson-Kennedy focuses on depathologizing transgender identities and developing anti-oppressive, intersectional clinical praxis.

MELANIE ROBINSON FINDLAY, PSYD, MSW, LICSW
Boston College, Adjunct Professor
Dr. Robinson Findlay is a licensed independent clinical social worker and postdoctoral fellow in clinical psychology at Salem Hospital. She is also in private practice in Boston, Massachusetts. Dr. Robinson Findlay is an adjunct professor at Boston College, Bridgewater State University, and Simmons University Schools of Social Work in Massachusetts.

TANYA ROLLINS, MSW
University of Houston, PhD Student
Ms. Rollins retired from the child welfare system after 30 years. She worked in several divisions, including investigations, intake, training, and disproportionality. She is a PhD student researching aspects of the child welfare system. She advocates for change and believes research on systems should include those working in systems.

LINDSEY SANK DAVIS, PHD
William James College, Assistant Professor
Dr. Sank Davis is a licensed clinical and forensic psychologist, an assistant professor at William James College, and a part-time instructor at Harvard University. She runs the Race and Gender Justice Lab at William James College and maintains a private practice in Massachusetts.

List of Contributors

SHERRI Y. SIMMONS-HORTON, PHD, MSW
University of New Hampshire, Assistant Professor
Dr. Simmons-Horton is an assistant professor in the University of New Hampshire Social Work Department and a core faculty instructor in the Women and Gender Studies Department. She has over 25 years of experience in child welfare. Her research focuses on crossover youth, structural inequities across child welfare and juvenile systems, and empowerment of Black youth through an anti-oppressive lens.

LARRY L. SCOTT-WALKER
Georgia State University, Graduate Student
Mr. Scott-Walker (he/him) is a Baltimore native dedicated to empowering Black same gender loving (SGL) men through nearly two decades of community organizing. He co-founded Safe Space at Morehouse College and THRIVE SS Inc. in Atlanta, Georgia, where he assisted in creating nationally replicated models. A widely published poet, spoken word artist, Scott-Walker is pursuing his MA in Africana Studies, with a focus on community empowerment, at Georgia State University.

JUSTIN C. SMITH, MS, MPH
Harvard University T.H. Chan School of Public Health, DrPH Student
Mr. Smith is a public health practitioner with over 20 years of experience in working toward health equity for communities of color, with a specific emphasis on addressing HIV among Black gay men. A former member of the Presidential Advisory Council on HIV/AIDS, Smith is currently the director of the Campaign to End AIDS at Atlanta's Positive Impact Health Centers. He is currently a Doctor of Public Health student at the Harvard T.H. Chan School of Public Health.

ADRIANNA N. TAYLOR, DSW, MSW, LCSW
Metropolitan State University of Denver, Assistant Professor
Dr. Taylor is a mama, clinician, assistant professor, and veteran military social worker. Her practice focuses on Black women healing through narrative and somatic practices. Her academic focus is on interrogating and creating anti-oppressive curriculum and developing supervision programming related to grants/certification. Her deep heart's cry is to expand the next generation of social workers.

ASHLEY WOLFE, DSW, MSW, LCSW, PPSC
University of the Pacific, Adjunct Professor
Dr. Wolfe is a proud social worker who serves as a high school mental health therapist, organizational leader, clinical supervisor, and social

work educator. Her research interests include identity-centered social emotional learning, cognitive linguistics and social work, suicide prevention in adolescents, and supporting families and communities after a suicide.

DARRIN E. WRIGHT, PHD, MSW, LMSW
Fayetteville State University, Associate Dean, Associate Professor
Dr. Wright is an associate professor and associate dean in social work at Fayetteville State University in Fayetteville, North Carolina. He formerly held the position of director of practicum education at Clark Atlanta University. Having worked in academia for almost 20 years, Dr. Wright has held several leadership roles in social work education both nationally and internationally.

MICHELLE ZARAGOZA, MSW, LCSW
University of California Berkeley, PhD Student
Ms. Zaragoza (she/ella) is a PhD student in social welfare at the University of California, Berkeley. Her research interests include Latinx youth and families, immigration and mental health, and arts-based research. She also operates a small private practice offering somatic-based mental health services, consulting, and clinical supervision.

Preface

In 2021 I designed and created a doctoral course for a university for their newly launched Doctor of Social Work (DSW) program. The course, *Decolonized Clinical Supervision and Management*, which later became *Decolonized Clinical Supervision and Leadership*, came out of the necessity (1) to provide a formal course to teach advanced clinical supervision to students with already established social work practice experience, and (2) to teach and demonstrate how to utilize anti-oppressive lenses across clinical leadership. The course saw several iterations and became quite popular among students. Some of the learning moments for me, as the course creator, developer, and one of the instructors, were that students would often note that this was their first formal supervision course, despite holding formal supervision roles. Most students, many of whom were advanced clinicians in practice, had learned clinical supervision on the job and, as we discuss in this text, their supervision training was largely geared toward the needs of the agency or practice of their employment, and often merged administrative and management functions. Clinical supervision and leadership were often blended with or subsumed by these administrative and management responsibilities. This, for me at the time, demonstrated a clear lack of formal university education in clinical supervision practice and a clear lack of sanctity of the clinical supervision process in agency practice. We also learned that while students were excited to learn or further their knowledge of anti-oppressive lenses, they struggled to understand their application – especially in agencies and systems that were devoted to status quo practices. Lastly, we learned that this education (advanced clinical supervision, clinical leadership, and anti-oppression) was inherently limited – that Master of Social Work programs rarely offered supervision courses, and of the 500,000 social workers in practice in the United States, few are likely to return to universities to train in these areas.

Initially, when I would state these concerns in class with our doctoral students, I would offer the idea that they, as clinical supervisors and the holders of this advanced practice knowledge, perhaps had a duty to engage as many supervisees and practicum students into this material and instruction as a contribution to the profession of social work and to the communities we, as social workers, serve, as well as part of the professional development process. But wait – there's more! Even if this were to occur in abundance, we could never reach as many social workers and professional helpers as we would need to see a major shift in how we build, advance, and protect the practice of clinical supervision. I believed at that time – and still do today – that we need to create materials, specific for social work and professional helping, that could reach many more practitioners and so many more communities. This collection of writings and materials is just that.

This text was designed with the reader – the learner – in mind. It was designed to engage multiple and diverse perspectives, cover various angles, and explore nuances. It is designed to teach all the senses and all types of leaders. Each of the chapters, essays, case vignettes, practice activities, and resource banks is designed to interact and overlap – to be in conversation with each other and with you, the reader. To elicit practice dialogue, to offer practice guidance, and to create leadership strategy. It is not meant to be the sole provider, but a contribution to a larger body of clinical practice works that already exist. It is my hope that my colleagues, friends, former students, community leaders and activists, and I have put together a text that will enhance your professional practice and clinical leadership, and those who depend on you for these services. Thank you for taking this journey with us.

Acknowledgments

To the many fine social work scholars, practitioners, educators, and leaders, many of whom have contributed to this text, who continue to make the profession and practice of social work strong, rigorous, impactful, innovative, global, present and future focused, and necessary.

And to the many fine practitioners of social work practice who guided my professional growth and clinical development in clinical supervision and beyond, including Mr. Ray Walden, MSW, LCSW, at South End Community Health Center, Boston; Ms. Desiree Williams, MSW, LICSW, at District of Columbia Department of Child and Family Services; Ms. Laura Torres, MSW, LCSW-C, at Johns Hopkins Community Health, Baltimore, who was a superb clinical supervisor and community practitioner and who made practicing social work fun and interesting again when I was burning out and almost wanted to leave the profession; Ms. June Crenshaw at The Wanda Alston Foundation, Washington, DC, who believed in my intelligence and abilities and taught me how to trust in my capabilities, and who has been my teacher, mentor, and friend, personally and in our overlapping community leadership; Dr. Natalie D. Crawford at Emory University who has taken me under her wing, and has been a stellar research mentor, colleague, and friend; and to the dozens, maybe hundreds, of past and present supervisees, graduate students, and doctoral students that have been under my tutelage and professional guidance, who continue to teach and shape my practice today.

To my students, colleagues, and fellow leaders who understand the urgency of now, who continue to push social work practice to be all the things it says it is, and who continue to innovate the profession; and to the countless people empowered by the profession of social work every day, **you are all my inspiration in the work and in this book**; thank you to all of the supreme contributors to this text, your time and expertise made this text possible.

And finally, to my mother, Ms. Myrian Currie-Bergeron (November 4, 1943–April 19, 2019), who taught me that education is the only thing you can earn and achieve that cannot be taken from you; that education and care are the great equalizers; who fostered my love for reading; and who was a mother, grandmother, friend, social worker, leader, guide, and wise elder to so many souls, human, animal, and spirit, and whose truth and love inspires to this day.

INTRODUCTION

Decolonized Clinical Supervision and Leadership
The Necessity of Now, An Introduction

Gary Bailey

> Decolonization, as we know, is a historical process: that is to say it cannot be understood, it cannot become intelligible nor clear to itself except in the exact measure that we can discern the movements which give it historical form and content.
> —Franz Fanon, *The Wretched of the Earth* (1963, p. 36)

In the ever-evolving social work landscape, the pursuit of equitable, just, and more effective practices remains at the forefront of the profession's collective and critical consciousness. Freire, in his book *Pedagogy of the Oppressed and Education for Critical Consciousness* (2000 [1970]), described critical consciousness as "*a sociopolitical educative tool that engages learners in questioning the nature of their historical and social situation,*" or, as Freire notes, "learning how to read the world." Social work, by its very nature, should be focused on helping develop practitioners who are able to "read the world" and are committed to working with marginalized communities to challenge systemic injustices and foster environments where historically disenfranchised individuals and communities can thrive.

Currie's book emerges from the critical need to reassess, redefine, and revolutionize clinical supervision and leadership through the lenses of decolonization and anti-oppressive practice (AOP). As the world changes, so too must the frameworks and methodologies that underpin social work practice, many of which were developed based on a biased worldview and individual perspectives.

Decolonization and anti-oppressive practice are not merely theoretical constructs; they are urgent calls to action. Decolonization involves dismantling the lingering remnants of colonial power structures that pervade many aspects of contemporary life, including social work. It demands active engagement in recognizing and challenging the ways in which colonial histories and ideologies continue to influence policies, practices, and perspectives. AOP, on the other hand, is a commitment to identifying, confronting, and dismantling various forms of oppression that exist within society.

Tuck and Yang, in "*Decolonization is not a metaphor*," make a powerful and compelling point about the absence of Indigenous voices being central in discussions of decolonization:

> [Y]et, we have observed a startling number of these discussions make no mention of Indigenous peoples, our/their struggles for the recognition of our/their sovereignty, or the contributions of Indigenous intellectuals and activists to theories and frameworks of decolonization . . . . We, at least in part, want others to join us in these efforts, so that settler colonial structuring and Indigenous critiques of that structuring are no longer rendered invisible. (2012)

Together, these lenses offer a powerful framework for transforming clinical supervision and leadership in social work. Clinical supervision and leadership are foundational to the effectiveness and ethical grounding of social work practice. Effective supervision provides social workers with the support, guidance, and reflection necessary to navigate the complexities of their work, ensuring that they remain grounded in ethical principles and best practices.

Leadership, meanwhile, sets the tone for organizational culture, policy implementation, and the overall direction of social work practice. When infused with decolonization and anti-oppressive and anti-racist principles, supervision and leadership can become transformative processes that not only support social workers, but also drive systemic change.

Decolonization in Clinical Supervision and Leadership

Decolonization in social work practice must involve a profound re-evaluation of existing power dynamics, epistemologies, and methodologies. Traditional models of clinical supervision and leadership often reflect Eurocentric perspectives that may inadvertently perpetuate colonial mindsets. Decolonizing these practices requires an intentional shift toward inclusivity, recognition of diverse ways of knowing, and the dismantling of hierarchical structures that marginalize non-Western voices and perspectives. Tuck and Yang (2012) note that "when we write about decolonization, we are not offering it as a metaphor; it is not an approximation of other experiences of oppression. Decolonization is not a swappable term for other things we want to do to improve our societies and schools. Decolonization doesn't have a synonym."

In clinical supervision, decolonization can be practiced by creating spaces that value and integrate the cultural knowledge and lived experiences of both supervisors and supervisees. This involves moving away from a "one-size-fits-all" approach and toward a more personalized, contextually relevant method of supervision. Supervisors must be trained to recognize and challenge their own biases, engage in ongoing cultural competency development, and adopt a stance of cultural humility. This shift allows for a more reciprocal and egalitarian supervisory relationship, where the knowledge and experiences of all participants are valued equally.

Leadership within social work organizations must also embrace decolonization by promoting policies and practices that elevate marginalized voices and challenge systemic inequities. This can be achieved by implementing participatory decision-making processes, fostering diverse leadership pipelines, and ensuring that organizational values align with principles of social justice and equity. Decolonized leadership is not merely about inclusion – it is also about transforming the very structures that have historically excluded certain groups.

Anti-Oppressive Practice in Clinical Supervision and Leadership

Anti-oppressive practice is a critical component of social work that emphasizes the importance of challenging oppression in all its forms. In the context of clinical supervision and leadership, AOP involves a proactive stance against practices and policies that reinforce inequality and discrimination. This requires a thorough understanding of the various dimensions of oppression, including, but not limited to racism, sexism, classism, ableism, and heteronormativity.

Clinical supervision, when viewed through an anti-oppressive lens, becomes a process of critical reflection and action. Supervisors are tasked with not only supporting the professional development of their supervisees, but also fostering an awareness of social justice issues. This involves creating a supervisory environment where power imbalances are acknowledged and addressed, and where supervisees are encouraged to critically examine their own practice and the broader systems in which they operate. Anti-oppressive supervision promotes a culture of accountability, where both supervisors and supervisees are committed to ongoing learning and advocacy.

Leadership that embodies AOP principles is characterized by a commitment to equity, transparency, and justice. Anti-oppressive leaders actively work to identify and dismantle barriers to inclusion within their organizations and the communities they serve. This involves not only addressing overt forms of discrimination, but also challenging more insidious, systemic forms of oppression. Leaders must advocate for policies that promote equity, create opportunities for marginalized groups, and ensure that organizational practices are aligned with anti-oppressive values.

Practice Interventions to Strengthen Clinical Supervision and Leadership

Integrating decolonization and AOP into clinical supervision and leadership requires intentional, targeted interventions. These interventions must be designed to disrupt traditional power dynamics, promote equity, and foster an inclusive and just practice environment.

One such intervention is the implementation of culturally responsive supervision frameworks. These frameworks prioritize the cultural contexts of both supervisees and clients, recognizing that cultural competence is a dynamic and ongoing process. Supervisors can employ reflective practices that encourage supervisees to explore their own cultural identities and biases, as well as the cultural dimensions of their work with clients. This reflective process not only enhances cultural competence, but also strengthens the supervisory relationship by fostering mutual respect and understanding.

Another critical intervention is the development of leadership training programs that focus on decolonization and AOP. These programs should provide current and emerging leaders with the tools and knowledge necessary to recognize and challenge oppressive structures within their organizations. Training should include modules on power dynamics, systemic inequality, and strategies for promoting equity and inclusion. By equipping leaders with these skills, organizations can ensure that their leadership is aligned with their commitment to social justice.

Additionally, organizations can adopt participatory decision-making processes that democratize leadership and supervision. This involves creating structures that allow for the voices of all staff members, particularly those from marginalized groups, to be heard and valued in decision-making processes. Participatory decision-making not only promotes equity, but also enhances organizational effectiveness by ensuring that decisions are informed by a diverse range of perspectives and experiences.

The integration of decolonization and AOP into clinical supervision and leadership is not merely an aspirational goal – it is a necessary evolution for the field of social work. By embracing these lenses, social work practitioners and leaders can create environments that not only support the professional growth and ethical practice of social workers, but also drive systemic change toward a more just and equitable society.

Dr. Nathaniel Currie's book serves as a guide and a call to action for those committed to transforming social work practice through the principles of decolonization and AOP, ensuring that social work becomes a more authentic and reliable force for positive change in the world.

REFERENCES

Fanon, F. (1963). *The wretched of the earth*. Penguin.

Freire, Paulo. (2000 [1970]). *Pedagogy of the oppressed*, 30th ed. New York: Continuum.

Tuck, E., & Yang, K. Y. (2012). Decolonization is not a metaphor. *Decolonization: Indigeneity, Education, & Society*, 1(1), 1–40.

PART I

Content Knowledge and Application

CHAPTER I

Decolonizing Social Work Practice and Clinical Supervision
Beginning the Process

Nathaniel L. Currie

Introduction to Supervision, Decolonization, Liberation Movement

Decolonization Lens

There are many definitions of decolonization and of the decolonial movement. For this text, we chose to begin with the definition provided by First Nations people and, in this text, add and adapt definitions from the Black Power movement, the Chicana/Chicano movements, the American civil rights movement, and feminist theory. Decolonization is "the meaningful and active resistance to the forces of colonialism that perpetuate the subjugation and/or exploitation of our minds, bodies, and lands" (Waziyatawin & Yellow Bird, 2012, p. 3). Decolonial or decoloniality refers to forms of being and thinking that preceded and started with the colonial project and invasion. It means acknowledging and dismantling the hierarchical systems of hetero-patriarchy, race, gender, and class that still govern thought, knowledge, spirituality, and life. These systems are inextricably linked to and fundamental to Western modernity and global capitalism (Mignolo & Walsh, 2018). The formal definition of decolonial/decoloniality/decolonization, especially as it relates to clinical social work practice and community practice, continues to develop. It is often helpful to engage supervisees, colleagues, and communities in the definition, and process of decolonization, as a living definition and, process an evergreen that continues to develop as it engages more diverse people and backgrounds and as it progresses and is made effective. There is a propensity to utilize decolonial as a metaphor for social justice work. In awareness of this propensity, this text will often combine decolonial and anti-oppressive work to demonstrate the necessity to understand both concepts individually and to attend in tandum, throughly, to their complementary work.

At its core, social work supervision does what it was intended, or not intended, to do. Decolonization of social work supervision requires some big work and innovation. Supervision is the true intersection of clinical practice, social justice, and practitioner education. It is critical that the curriculum in field/practicum education/supervision training has components that address the core tenets of social justice, the liberation movement, and decolonization. According to Asakura and Maurer (2018), "Although social justice is a central professional value of social work articulated in ethics codes, clinical social workers have been long criticized for not clearly incorporating this professed commitment into practice … there has, however been a long-standing debate about whether and how clinical social work practice, with its focus on individual-level problems, can also be social justice seeking" (p. 289). The literature goes on to assert that supervision is an ideal place for clinicians to address issues of social justice, inequity, power dynamics, and further decolonization efforts. Supervision can cover a variety of critical social justice topics such as cultural diversity, power dynamics, how to challenge unjust policies and practices, navigating oppressive systems or environments, and the impact of oppression on clients (Asakura & Maurer, 2018). Understanding the application of social justice needs and concerns to clinical work through supervision is paramount to strengthening the discipline and practice of clinical supervision and the overall practice of social work. This and additional topics are expanded across this text.

Social Work Supervision

Social work supervision is *sine qua non* of social work practice. Wilcox et al. (2022) described clinical supervision as the "'*signature pedagogy*' *of psychotherapy training.*" The necessity of supervision is accepted in social work practice and social work leadership. Although challenged from time to time, it continues to be an integral piece of professional preparation and professional practice (Brashears, 1995). Social work supervision is considered to be a core function in the development of social workers' professional identity and practice, and provides an important vehicle through which its outcomes are mediated and supported.

Key stakeholders in supervision may include people/clients and communities who use services, practitioners and educators, those leading, managing, and implementing services, and organizations providing services (Hafford-Letchfield & Engelbrecht, 2018). Models of supervision vary, and have changed over time to reflect innovative, revisited, or updated theories of intervention, and changing organizational structures, missions, client populations, and funding sources (Brashears, 1995). Going beyond practice skills, social work supervisors must possess advanced clinical insight, teaching and guidance skills, and a propensity to see both structural and systematic contributions to a situation, as well as big-picture or desired outcome understanding. Historically, social work education – and thus social work supervision – has used white-centered and Eurocentric values and ideology as the basis of its praxis. In recent years, the practice of social work has been challenged in this area, and has begun to respond by reexamining and revising many of the mechanisms of both practice and supervision. This is – and will be – the decolonization of the profession of social work and the function of social work supervision.

Supervision as Ceremony

Ceremonies can help to show people they are united, that they have an intricate role, and that they are part of a community. Ceremonies can motivate us, stimulate our emotions, and prompt memories. The positive effects of ceremony are universal across civilizations, and are not specific to age or gender. The tradition of ceremony contributes a sense of comfort and belonging, and can stimulate and perpetuate values, ethics, and connection. In developing your own clinical supervision practice and practice voice, consider how reframing supervision as ceremony honors and empowers the supervisee, the supervision process and practice, advances clinical learning, and innovates the necessity and position of clinical supervision within overall social work practice. Offer this concept to supervisees and practicum students as they engage in clinical supervision practice.

Types of Supervision

Social work practice is unique within the helping professions, as it centers and embeds clinical supervision into its regular, required, necessary, best, and continuous practice. A good rule of thumb for clinical supervision is: if you have any direct or indirect contact with individuals or communities, you should continue participation in supervision. Clinical supervision should have a continuous life across any given social work career, and as a social work career develops and advances, so should the type, frequency, purpose, and utilization of supervision. Most practitioners are familiar with practicum and clinical supervision. However, there are other avenues of supervision that strengthen and support professional social work.

Education/Practicum Supervision

Practicum supervision was formerly referred to as field supervision/field practice. However, in recent years, many schools of social work have eliminated the term "field" in all its forms – such as "fieldwork," "field education," "field experience," "in the social work field," or "going into the field" – as it may hold negative associations and connotations with racism and slavery. In lieu of the term "field," forward-moving, anti-oppressive practices have utilized the term "practicum," where the term "field" once was – as in "practicum experience," "Practicum Office," "practicum seminar," and so on. Practicum is a strong choice, as it is defined as "a course of study that involves the experiential and supervised practical application of previously studied theory, process, or concept, and which requires demonstration of known knowledge and skills." The swapping of the term "field" for "practicum" also furthers the process of removing violent, disparaging, and oppressive language from social work practice.

Practicum supervision is often the first experience of clinical supervision for social work students and other clinical students and learners. The object of practicum education and supervision is to create a learning environment that centers experiential learning through clinical experience – meaning that the organization of the student experience should be entirely focused on establishing and growing their clinical skills, their professionalism, and their practice voice. Too often, practicum sites, knowingly or unknowingly, view and utilize practicum education as a "free" or "volunteer" workforce. In many cases, this exploits student labor to benefit agency needs. It is important for practicum supervisors and their agencies to view practicum education as a unique, additional, strength-building program within their practice – one that requires time, commitment, curriculum, program planning, and administration.

To create a successful, impactful, and empowering practicum education experience for student learners, it will be important to carve out set times for both individual and group supervision, group case consultation, shadowing and observational learning, and direct clinical experience. Managing the diversity of types of learning, and keeping caseloads low (about two to four clients in the foundational year, and four to five in the clinical year), protects the learner from labor exploitation and allows for focused, deep-dive ability with the assigned cases and learning process. Practicum supervision should also begin to prepare student learners for more formal clinical supervision to come post-degree completion, where the focus is more on assessment and diagnosis, intervention, evaluation, empowerment, and treatment management of assigned clients.

Clinical Supervision
Perhaps the most common, and most studied, type of supervision practice is clinical supervision, which has the purpose of (1) teaching and advancing the practice of the clinician; (2) ensuring safe, quality, practical, culturally appropriate client treatment, intervention, and care; (3) evaluating care planning, trajectory, and resource accessibility and maintenance; (4) monitoring, discussing, and resolving ethical and social justice issues related to client care and clinician practice experiences; and (5) promoting overall clinician, client, and community empowerment, which is achieved by (1) creating an open, supportive, and safe and brave environment before, during, and after the supervision session; (2) establishing trust, rapport, expectations, and boundaries within the supervisory relationship; (3) setting an intentional and consistent schedule (or holding space for) regular/ceremonious supervision; (4) providing immediate or timely, verbal and/or written, strengths-based feedback and guidance; and (5) for supervisors, remaining engaged, well trained, and committed to sound, advancing, innovative social work practice. Clinical supervision is not a process with the sole goal of earning hours toward licensure, nor is it a function restricted to early career practitioners. Clinical supervision is a process undertaken for the duration of a clinical career, and though its function, frequency, and type of supervision would/should change over time, the commitment to the process is steadfast and career long.

Administrative Supervision
Administrative supervision, or managerial supervision, is not clinical supervision and holds a very different focus, intent, and purpose. In practice, social workers are charged, often by other helping professionals or executive leaders, with the responsibility of both personnel management and clinical supervision. In this process, the responsibilities and identity of the roles of both a manager and a clinical supervisor are merged and blended. This is not a preferred practice, and when these roles are shared by a singular practitioner, it is advised to dialogue with both senior leadership and with supervisees about the need for – and sanctity of – the separation of these two processes. For example, it is advised that management meetings be held separate from clinical supervision and group supervision.

Tasks discussed in management meetings are held separate from the clinical processing and experiential learning of clinical supervision. It is important to establish clear boundaries between the roles and functions. If supervisors are unable to separate these roles due to agency limitations, practitioners will need to rely on themselves, and peer-to-peer support, to create boundaries between the roles of administrative supervision and clinical supervision – protecting the integrity of both roles.

Supervision for Advanced Clinicians
As a commitment to clinical practice endures, so should the commitment and use of clinical supervision. For advanced clinicians, this may look different in approach than in previous supervision relationships, as advanced clinicians are most likely engaging in supervision practice with a professional peer or colleague. When an advanced practice supervisory relationship is created, it will be important to discuss any power dynamics, process expectations, and supervision needs or wants up front as part of establishing supervisory rapport. Creating a supervisory relationship, or mutual supervisory relationship, with professional peers has many advantages, including the advancing and promotion of clinical knowledge, skill, and application, as well as preparation for career advancement. Advanced supervision is not professional mentorship, as a supervisory relationship goes beyond mentorship in its purpose, function, and practice necessity, and its intention to safeguard clinical practice and ethics. Some individuals and agencies have been successful in creating peer supervision groups for later-career and clinical supervisors to continue the process, benefit, and meet the need for continued supervision through all career stages – sort of like "supervise the supervisor" groups. Often these types of groups meet once or twice a month, and many function as drop-in groups to fit in with often busy leadership and advanced practice schedules.

Supervision for Social Work Educators, Academics, and Researchers
While the purpose of clinical supervision is largely geared toward clinical and community practitioners, we can also recognize the benefits of creating peer group supervision opportunities for scholar-practitioners who engage in either/or clinical or community practice, and social work instruction and social work research. These professional peer-to-peer sessions or groups can create opportunities for scholar-practitioners to work through practice, education, ethical, policy, intervention or modality, and

other issues that require additional practice support. These groups are also a prime environment to offer or introduce practice advancements and promote future practice endeavors. Professional supervisory peer groups also have the added benefit of creating a professional social support space that builds professional relationships, and helps decrease the likelihood of professionals feeling isolated or siloed in their practice.

Group Supervision
In previous sections in this chapter, we have discussed several types of group supervision opportunities and their functions. Group supervision is a powerful, empowering, and strong way to teach and learn social work practice, and further clinical skills. Utilizing formal and peer group supervision has been successful in practicum supervision, clinical supervision, advanced practice, and scholar/research supervision, and even in supervision licensing, where post-graduate learners provide peer-to-peer facilitation, study, discussion, and support toward graduate and/or clinical licensure. When creating group supervision opportunities, it will be important to establish group norms, rules, goals, and direction up front, and with participation of all group members. Groups should be goal-directed and offer some type of dependable process that creates buy-in and function for its members. Both clinical and social justice topics are centered across group sessions.

Supervision and Social Work Licensure
Supervision is a prime environment and process for preparing supervisees – both practicum and clinical supervisees – for licensure. In fact, it is one of the significant functions and motivators for practitioners engaged in supervision. Supervisees should be allotted supervision time to discuss, plan for, and review content for licensure exams within supervision. Reviewing and debriefing rationales of just a couple of licensure questions per supervision session is often impactful for the supervisees. Often, licensure material covering anti-oppressive, antiracist, and social justice issues is left out of supervision and general learning and study materials. Re-centering anti-oppressive work to practice should include the intersection of anti-oppressive and social justice work, and licensure. Take a look at some of the licensure examination practice questions provided in this section – they give examples of how licensure examination questions can prepare supervisees for test-taking while offering opportunity to discuss and debrief key social justice issues in practice. See Box 1.1.

> **Box 1.1 Practice Guidance. Social Work Licensing and Anti-Oppressive Practice**
>
> The following guidance contains some examples of how anti-oppressive practice might be tested in social work licensing examinations. Formal examinations are timed and do not offer real-time answer rationales. Try practicing these questions against a timer set for 60 seconds with supervisees. Then discuss in supervision the rationales for both the correct and incorrect answers. For many early career practitioners, this type of clinical learning and processing is often not offered anywhere else outside of clinical supervision.
>
> 1. When conducting an assessment of the risk factors of child abuse for a child of a different ethnic background, a social worker must FIRST:
>   a. be aware of how personal cultural biases affect the social worker's ability to deal with issues of diversity
>   b. realize that assessment models are not a substitute for clinical judgment or experience
>   c. use a strengths' perspective rather than a deficit model to form a partnership with the child's family
>   d. understand the need for appropriate eye contact, tone of voice, and question techniques during the assessment
>
> 2. During a therapy session, a social worker notices that a colleague often interrupts a client of Asian descent when they try to explain how racial issues affect their mental health, saying things like, *"Let's focus on the real problem, not race."* This behavior could be best described as which of the following?
>   a. an appropriate therapeutic technique to keep sessions focused
>   b. a necessary intervention to avoid uncomfortable topics
>   c. a microaggression manifesting as racial invalidation
>   d. a misunderstanding due to cultural differences
>
> 3. An early career clinical social worker is meeting with a new client for the first time. The client is of a different racial background and gender than the social worker. During the intake assessment, the client makes several vulgar and demeaning comments to the social worker regarding their race, appearance, and gender. Finally, the client, after being redirected by the social worker, blurts out a direct racial epithet and refuses to work with the social worker. What should the social worker do *next* to resolve the situation?
>   a. the social worker should do nothing, it is not their place
>   b. respond to the client by saying, "I'm here to support you and hear you, but I'm going to have to ask that you use different words because I find myself distracted by the words you have chosen to use."
>   c. pause the session to seek supervision from their clinical supervisor
>   d. terminate the session and refer the client to another social worker
>
> Answers: 1:a; 2:c; 3:b

Preparing the Practice Environment for Decolonization and Liberation Work

The beginning of the supervision process starts with readiness of the practice environment conducive to anti-oppressive, decolonial work. This is a readiness process that often starts well before the supervision time is in session. As a primer, the supervisor should be sure that the practice environment has the capacity to take on anti-oppressive, decolonial clinical work. Supervisors can begin by assessing engagement from colleagues and leadership, by reviewing training materials, agency policies, and working to create a conducive environment by determining how tools and materials like land acknowledgment statements, positionality statements, use of pronouns, gender-inclusive signage, building accessibility, preparatory empathy, and other welcoming and empowering initiatives will strengthen the environment. You may decide to welcome supervisees to supervision prior to a scheduled session by describing the nature of anti-oppressive practice, and offering preliminary readings, reflection questions, or preparing them for the first session with an agenda. This might be an opportune time to offer an overview of creating safe and brave spaces.

Readiness work also includes planning initial dialogue that sets the process of anti-oppressive, decolonial practice into gear. These dialogues include work with the overall agency, as well as planned, intentional discussion with the supervisee. Note that dialogue regarding anti-oppressive, decolonial practice environment and practice lens is not a one-and-done task – it is a living, ongoing process that lasts the life of the work. This early process to anti-oppressive, decolonial supervision must be an interactive, open-ended process – well planned within the first two or three sessions of the supervision work.

Creation of Safe and Brave Spaces

"What is a safe space?", *"Is a space ever truly safe?"*, *"What type of meaning does brave space have for you?"* These are examples of important questions to ask supervisees in the process of creating safe and brave spaces in supervision and in any group that attempts to broach social justice and decolonial topics. After the facilitator asks these questions and gains responsible discuss from the group, discuss subjectivity of safety. Often the outcome of this discussion, whether by the offering of the group members, or offered by the facilitator, is the concept of "safe enough" – that in creating safe spaces, workers can expect that no space is truly, completely safe (both

for clinicians and for clients), but we can create and maintain a space that is *safe enough*. A safe space is a place, environment, or situation in which a person, group, or category of people can feel confident that they will not be exposed to discrimination, criticism, harassment, or any emotional or physical harm. The space lends itself to vulnerability, recognizing that both safety and vulnerability must occur for growth processes to ensue. Further in the dialogue, and after establishing an understanding of safe spaces, approach the concept of brave spaces in the same fashion – "*What is a brave space?*", "*How does a brave space differ from a safe space?*" Discuss the necessity of bravery in creating space and how it is conducive to liberation work, offer a brave space definition, and then encourage supervisees to add to the definition until the concept "feels right" and accessible. A brave space cultivates a productive dialogue where participants are encouraged to speak honestly and critically from their own experience, toward the end of mutual learning and liberation. We know that in any safe and brave, or vulnerable space, there is risk of hurt feelings, bruised ego or self-esteem, and a range of emotional reactions. This is something to acknowledge in this initial discussion – while also offering a plan to address and resolve these moments through the life of the supervisory relationship. Racism and oppression are not merely an academic enterprise – they combine knowledge and critical self-awareness, which involves risk taking, vulnerability, broaching comfort zones, openness to constructive feedback, and guidance (Miller & Garran, 2017, p. 10), and a parallel process of learning and unlearning. Anti-oppressive, decolonial practice is a living process that challenges all parts of our professional practice and personal selves.

Another area to discuss in creating safe and brave practice and supervision environments is power and power dynamics. The supervisor's authority and power are limited not only in ideology, reluctance, dismissal of hierarchy, and organizational considerations, but also by the countervailing power of the supervisee (Kadushin & Harness, 2014; Savaya & Spiro, 1997). Power in the social work supervisor and supervisee dynamic should not be based on dependency, and should include a dynamic of shared power and decision making – with an acknowledgment of some type of necessary authority. Power dynamics in supervisory relationships are explored in more depth in Chapters 3 and 6 of this text.

Supervision Goal Planning

An activity that is central to supervision practice is goal planning. As an early activity to the supervision process, it is helpful in individual or group supervision sessions to engage supervisees in active goal planning: (1) What are some of your learning goals for your supervision time? (2) What are some areas you would like to strengthen? How might you accomplish this? (3) What are some ways you see yourself further embedding social justice or anti-oppressive models and awareness to your clinical practice? How can we create a goal that supports that? (4) How do you see supervision contributing to your own practice empowerment? Do not rush this process – allow the group or individual some quiet time to think about their goals. Allow time to share these goals and process their importance. As the goals are shared, assist in language that turns these goals into formal, measurable, and strengths-based goals that will guide subsequent supervision sessions. There is no limit to the number of goals established – but three or four goals at a time is often most feasible. Goal planning is a living process that should be revisited and updated regularly. Supervision goal planning also serves the process of readying or priming the space or environment for antiracist and anti-oppression work and practice.

Authenticity

Authenticity is a key quality in social work practice, and one that helps facilitate trust, rapport building, and the formation of meaningful connections in both direct clinical work and within supervisory work. Authenticity is crucial to anti-oppressive, decolonial supervisory practice. Who would trust an inauthentic person to lead or facilitate such important, often vulnerable, intrusive, and at times difficult work? Authenticity facilitated by the supervisor, and encouraged of the supervisee, secures the anti-oppressive, decolonial supervision process. Creating the opportunity for authenticity in supervision practice is acquired or demonstrated in (1) working in partnership with supervisees and program teams in a way that centers mutual respect; (2) promoting and strengthening both direct client empathy and empathy within topics and issues that are discussed and resolved through supervision; (3) setting an expectation of transparency (which requires trust and genuine action) within the supervision relationship and across the program or agency, which includes supervisees reporting or discussing a mistake or practice issue as soon as it arises, in a supervisor's plans and trajectory for supervision and evaluation, and in an agency's practice and policies – for example, disclosing publicly agency salaries, development plans, and action toward agency goals; (4) creating space for supervisees to further their self-awareness, which recognizes existing polarities and requires unbiased assessment of one's own positive and negative aspects; (5) teaching supervisees to lead with their values, and to protect their and their clients' right to self-determination; and finally, (6) centering truth in all aspects of social work practice (Dore, 2024). Authentic social work practice recognizes that people exist within environments – healing and empowerment is contextual. Creating an authentic supervisory relationship also has the benefit of demonstrating this concept to the supervisee, which may assist them in cultivating authenticity in their direct practice. Authenticity, combined with use of self, serves as a tool to establish the rapport that will support future anti-oppressive, decolonial social work practice – both supervisory and direct practice.

Use of Self

The term "use of self" is sometimes confusing for social work students and for the discipline of social work at large. Social workers believe they know what it means when they hear the term, but they have a hard time defining and describing the term when pressed. Use of self in social work practice is the combining of knowledge, values, and skills gained in social work education with aspects of one's personal self – including personality traits, beliefs systems, life experiences, and cultural heritage (Dewane, 2006). Edwards and Bess (1998) describe use of self as

> the application of what you know as a psychotherapist (that is the accumulation of knowledge and techniques from professional education and training) can only be helpful and effective if you are aware of how who you are as a person in the room with the client (that is the accumulation of your own personality traits, personal belief systems, and psychology in the relational matrix with the client) is influencing the therapy.

It is the use of self that enables social workers to strive for authenticity and genuineness with the clients we serve – while at the same time honoring the values and ethics we so highly value in social work practice, while merging our own identities and experiences into the process of clinical or community professional helping. If the social worker is the 'tool' of practice, then use of self is the sound authentic utilization of this tool.

To integrate the authentic self into the skills required in effective social work practice and clinical social work supervision, it may be helpful to view the use of self as the formal, professional modality it is. In clinical social work, we have a rule that we only share of ourselves that which would benefit the client/supervisee. In contemporary practice, this rule remains – but has been redefined with some ease to some of the historical barriers between clinician and client or supervisor and supervisee, while still maintaining our steadfast ethics.

A good analogy for "use of self" is through comparison with a placenta. A mother or birthing person's placenta lets through what will nourish, while blocking what might be harmful to the fetus – even if it is harmless to the mother. As therapists, we don't have a bodily organ for this function (nor does a mother after the birth). We must decide as we interact what will nourish, what might harm, what is too early to introduce, and so on. This is a major function of a self-observing ego – watching over what we say. From asking a question, to introducing a topic, to self-disclosure – an ongoing awareness must be present. This allows the practitioner to know that what they are saying or sharing is appropriate and necessary for the client or supervisee's benefit. What is disclosed in clinical work, supervision, and social work education is never intended for the benefit of the clinician, supervisor, or instructor. Experienced clinicians, supervisors, and instructors understand that their needs have other venues to be met in – that their time in session, supervision, or in class is fully for the client, supervisee, or student. Which is not to say that the relationships formed between clinicians and clients, and supervisors or instructors and supervisees and students – is the same – as it is not. This will be discussed further in this section and in understanding dual relationships.

Practice Voice
Supervision is a prime environment for assisting supervisees in the development of their *practice voice*. A practitioner's practice voice is developed from a sound use of self, authenticity, confidence in practice skills and modalities, confidence and ongoing curiosity about the practice population and community, and a practitioner's own uniqueness and charisma. Facilitating and encouraging supervisees to develop their practice voice is necessary for the ability to skillfully and confidently embrace anti-oppressive and decolonial clinical and community work.

Critical Self-Reflection

Anti-oppressive and decolonial supervisory work requires supervisors to engage supervisees in a critical self-reflection process, which allows supervisees to evaluate how their own beliefs, values, perspectives, and experiences may or may not contribute to biases, discrimination, or oppression against people from other identity groups, with the goal of developing an awareness of their own intersecting identities and awareness of systemic structures of oppression, discrimination, and racism (connect this here in supervision to the CRT tenet, "racism is ordinary not aberrational," which is discussed in depth in Chapter 4). Supervisors have the responsibility to create opportunities for supervisees to develop an understanding of, and a routine for, critical self-reflection. Supervisors should intentionally plan to discuss the critical self-reflection process and its benefits to developing their practice voice, empowering their practice, and furthering their ability to apply anti-oppressive approaches in their direct practice. Some discussion and learning activities suitable for supervision that aim to build supervisee self-reflection include increasing their particular social location awareness, identifying implications for intersectional identities, connecting use of self to self-awareness, intrapersonal insight, and self-actualization, assisting supervisees through various stages of identity development, continued work on metacognitive processes and self-awareness, and a commitment to learning toward discomfort and resolution. These activities are accomplished through engaging and encouraging the supervisee to (1) challenge their own assumptions; (2) unearth, unpack, and challenge their own biases and negative attitudes about other identities; (3) critically and mindfully reflect on their social location, privilege, and learned racism or discrimination; (4) reflect on their experience with ambiguity; (5) work through situations where they are confronting a different reality from what they are familiar with; (6) prepare for constant exposure, constant questioning, and constant challenging; (7) engage in regular metacognitive and reflection opportunities with different modes of reflecting (e.g. speaking, writing, creating, mindful processing); and (8) reflect on their own history as a means of understanding and interrogating existing structures and systems across practice and society.[1] Like many of the anti-oppressive and decolonial processes offered in this section, this is a living or ongoing process. Supervisors are encouraged to check in often with, or listen for action of, critical self-reflection in the supervisee.

Metacognition

Metacognition goes beyond cognition, or *"what I'm thinking about,"* and persists as in, *"thinking about what I'm thinking about."* Metacognition in clinical anti-oppressive practice asks the worker to regularly engage in self-reflection on oneself as a person, practitioner, thinker, leader, and forever learner. This type of self-reflection is best achieved when the supervisee is encouraged to reflect on their experiences with clinicians and community leaders. Metacognition requires supervisees to become introspective of themselves, themselves in their environment, how they show up with clients or in community, and their relationship dynamics across practice, which often assist with planning, processing, and assessing performance and overall clinical work. Supervisors should introduce this concept in supervision and tie it in with both direct clinical work and the embedding of social justice and anti-oppressive work in practice. Explore the concept of metacognition, which is a critical awareness of self, and which facilitates dialogue about their professional strengths and areas for improvement or further learning, and facilitate discussion on intentional ways to become knowledgeable about and engage in strategies that support their practice learning and advancement. When supervisees become more fully aware, they become more flexible about their environments, the facilitated learning of clinical supervision, sharper and more flexible in their ability to process more rigorous concepts like decolonial and liberative work, and more confident in their clinical skills and their abilities to meet the demands in the practice environment.

Critical Consciousness

At its core, critical consciousness is the process of recognizing, examining, and possibly disrupting assumptive systemic and institutional rules, structured identity, and collective – sometimes unspoken – consequences of these rules.

> These assumptions are embedded in unquestioned norms, habits, rituals, and symbols. Behaviors and attitudes that serve to preserve the oppression-privilege interchange are entranced and hidden in ordinariness of everyday life. (Sloan et al., 2018)

Critical consciousness requires and allows us to recognize how privilege and oppression–privilege exists, reproduce, and are marinated, and how the assumptive normality of privileged group(s) is internalized. For example, cisgenderism – a process that denies, denigrates, or pathologizes self-identified gender identities while endorsing and perpetuating the belief that cisgender identities are more valuable than transgender or nonbinary identities – is normalized in the day-to-day life of social work and community practice, from exclusion of transgender and nonbinary identities on intake, assessment, insurance, and other care forms, to normalization of cisgender identity and the othering of identities outside of that. Critical consciousness allows practitioners to automatically recognize where assumptive systemic and institutional rules and structured identity expectations show up and how to resolve them.

Acknowledging Positionality

Other key components of readiness for anti-oppressive, decolonial work include positionality, social location, intersectionality, and exploration of bias. Each of these concepts work toward the identity and practice development of the supervisee. Positionality describes where one is socially located in relation to power at any given point in time or context. It is a theory that incorporates the impact that overlapping identities have on how people create meaning (Sloan et al., 2018; Kezar, 2002). Positionality demonstrates how people make meaning based on complex overlapping identities and one's position in relationship to systemic structures and institutions that provide or limit access to political, economic, and organizational power (Sloan et al., 2018). Positionality requires the worker to recognize power, power dynamics, and privilege – this is explored in depth in Chapter 3. Social location describes how one's privilege and targeted social identities are situated in a matrix of oppression in relation to others or institutional factors. Social location is an intersectional concept. Intersectionality involves the interactions between different axes of identity and of different types of social privilege or oppression (Miller & Garran, 2017, p. 198). Combined in concept and practice, the supervisee will form a heightened and more thorough sense of awareness and ability to analyze and solve complex practice issues and situations. This process also informs the process of exploring and understanding personal and practice bias. Supervision is also a prime environment to facilitate discussion around bias, implicit bias, and explicit bias. Intentionally set session time aside to introduce the topic with education of its concepts, and plan to revisit the conversation in the next session. The goal of engaging the supervisee in understanding of bias is to work to alleviate any known or unknown bias they might have, or at least keep it out of practice. Failure to recognize personal bias and limited or negative attitudes toward others may result in resistance to owning and working through the possibility that one might be racist, sexist, or heterosexist, and/or perpetuate racist, sexist, or heterosexist ideology (Sloan et al., 2018). This in turn limits the clinician's effectiveness in clinical work and is not aligned with anti-oppressive practice.

Dual Relationships in Clinical Supervision, Instruction, and Practicum Education

A natural and related topic to the *use of self* concept is dual relationships. We clarified the important use of boundaries in clinical and supervision relationships when we covered the *use of self* concept in the "Use of Self" section. Further, however, is the topic of dual relationships, which are deserving of their own clarification and innovation under the guidance of a decolonial and liberative lens. First and foremost, dual relationships continue to be highly discouraged and largely unethical in clinical relationships, as in when one party is the clinician or clinician's supervisor or practice leader and the other party is the client or family receiving clinical services. Dual relationships should also be avoided between supervisor or leader and supervisee in clinical and community practice. These roles and rules are explicitly outlined in professional social work codes of ethics and are similar across the helping professions. Some types of dual relationships in clinical work are unavoidable, and supervisors and supervisees alike should consult their code of ethics and formalize their plan to meet clinical needs with boundaries prior to and during the life of the clinical relationship. This is a great topic to persist across supervision relationships as well.

In social work education, faculty/instructor relationships with students, and clinical supervisor relationships with supervisees, are not the same as a therapist's therapeutic or clinical relationship with clients. Therefore, how we conceptualize and assess conduct and boundaries in supposed or potential dual relationships between students and faculty-instructors and students and clinical supervisors differs. The principal guideline for faculty-instructors who are in the position of a supposed dual relationship is that the relationship does not exploit the student in any way (CSWE, 2008). Dual relationships require work and management to avoid exploitation. Boundaries must persist through the life of the instructional and supportive professional relationship.

Managing supposed or potential dual relationships between faculty/instructors and students, which could be used to guide faculty relationships across academia and include advisement, mentorship, employment/management (work-student, teacher assistantship (TA), and research assistantship), extracurricular leadership, fellowships, clinical supervision, and other types of faculty–student relationships, is best guided by considering the following: (a) acknowledging the power dynamic and responsibility of the faculty role and any dual roles, (b) developing a frame for evaluating faculty–student relationships, and (c) fostering and maintaining a climate that supports ethical relationships with students (Biaggio et al., 1997).

It is not uncommon for faculty/instructors and clinical supervisors to serve in multiple roles across clinical education and community work. These complementary relationships of serving as a faculty/instructor and/or advisor and/or practicum liaison and/or clinical supervisor and so on must include ample and often revisited thorough instruction and opportunity to dialogue with students/supervisees on the concepts of dual relationships, their boundaries, how dual relationships show up, which types can be managed ethically, and which should be terminated ethically, as guided and described in professional codes of ethics and for social work educators in the Council for Social Work Education (CSWE) Educational Policy and Accreditation Standards (EPAS) competencies, and with consideration of peer-reviewed literature.

Some ways to monitor and evaluate these relationships with students are to (a) embed relevant questions into field/practicum learning contracts and semester evaluations and (b) utilize the role of the field/practicum liaison and practicum instructor to discuss/evaluate their professional relationships. Practicum seminars should provide additional opportunities to review or examine professional boundaries between students and clinical (field/practicum) supervisors, students and practicum liaisons, and students and practicum placement colleagues (Raskin et al., 2008). These dialogues and processes also assist in role modeling how students may begin to think about and manage any potential role conflicts or dual relationships if they arise, and begin practice insight for supervision roles of their own. See Box 1.2.

Box 1.2 Practice Reflection. Elevating Community-Based Organizations with Anti-Oppressive Practice: Atlanta's NAESM, Inc.

For over five years now, I have maintained a clinical practice and clinical internship program at NAESM, Inc. in Atlanta, Georgia. NAESM, Inc. (2024) – formerly the National AIDS Education Services for Minorities (NAESM) – is a community-based organization founded in 1990 by Rudolph H. Carn, Madam Edna Brown, and Mae Reed, in order to address the lack of, and substandard, HIV/AIDS services being provided to Black gay men in the late 1980s and early 1990s (Figure I.1). NAESM is one of the first African American community-based nonprofit organizations to emerge from the frontlines in the sociopolitical fight against HIV/AIDS in Atlanta, Georgia, and one of the first of its type in the United States. The organization's founders originally distributed condoms and safer sex messages at Atlanta bars and nightclubs frequented by African American men who have sex with men (MSM), and in other areas where African American MSM were known to congregate – a practice that has grown and continues today. In its early years, the organization was also known for its support groups and social opportunities for Black gay men to engage in a celebratory peer-to-peer support context. Today, the organization has expanded to provide HIV and

Decolonizing Social Work Practice

Figure I.1   Community building through outreach at NAESM, Inc., Atlanta, Georgia.

STI testing, counseling, treatment and prevention, critical housing services for people living with HIV, community outreach, and clinical case management and behavioral health services.

This practice environment, population, and cross-discipline approach to behavioral health services sits well within my social work practice and within my identity as a scholar-practitioner. Creating an internship program at this agency five years ago has furthered and advanced my clinical and leadership practice, has created community practice opportunities for over a dozen graduate social work students, and furthered the empowerment mission of the agency and community members who seek therapeutic services. The agency's behavioral health program is somewhat small and largely serves Black and Brown men, of all orientations, living with HIV, through federal Ryan White funding. This allows clients to receive services at zero cost and, in many cases, also provides transportation to and from appointments through ride-share platforms. The clients who receive behavioral health services at NAESM, Inc. are often some of the most vulnerable clients in the city, often living with medical, mental health, and substance use concerns, as well as environmental concerns such as inadequate or unstable housing, or are being unhoused, and experiencing unemployment and food and utility disparities – to name just some of the realities of clients. A traditional model of therapy is not enough to meet the needs of NAESM, Inc.'s community – neither is the merging of empowerment practice with traditional therapeutic work. To meet the intersecting needs and intersecting experiences of oppression and violence, clients must be empowered through a range of anti-oppressive lenses and strategies, through a multisystem, interdisciplinary approach. Social workers are most prepared to meet these exact needs, utilize a multisystem, embed anti-oppressive practice, and deliver sound therapeutic intervention and services.

Recognizing the uniqueness of this agency as not just a provider and safe space for the community but as a learning opportunity for up-and-coming practitioners, I wondered how I could leverage the program to create more accessibility for the community while teaching and developing future clinicians. Then, at the same time I was conceptualizing what a practicum experience might look like at NAESM, Inc., I was hired to build a doctoral course on decolonized clinical supervision for the Doctor of Social Work (DSW) program at Simmons University School of Social Work. What perfect timing. I had served as a practicum supervisor and clinical supervisor in most of my practice sites since earning my clinical license and had built practicum programs at agencies before – this would have to be different. This would be an opportunity to create a practicum experience that focused on and prepared interns immediately for clinical work and anti-oppressive practice. A program that led with the same values that it taught, and that was equally empowering to the interns engaged in the experiences as to the clients engaged in the therapeutic services. Which is exactly what I came to do.

Each year, the program accepts four to six graduate interns, largely from Clark Atlanta University, but also from Georgia State University, Delaware State University, and other local, regional, and distance MSW programs. Clinical interns are provided two to three hours of supervision a week in both individual and group supervision, biweekly case consultation, scheduled lectures, trainings, and off-site learning opportunities. Students are introduced to the community not just in the agency but through outreach and immersion opportunities. Interns provide strengths-based, person-centered, clinical case management and direct therapy to a small caseload of no more than four clients – which allows them to focus on deep dives into therapeutic work and learning and alleviates potential for labor exploitation, an anti-oppressive practice value. Clinical interns are required to demonstrate both clinical practice knowledge and anti-oppressive and empowerment practice knowledge simultaneously throughout their placement. The practicum program has even found space to embed social work license exam preparation with a focus on process and rationales of exam questions. While the majority of our agency staff, clinical interns, and clients identify as Black or Brown, and about 85 percent of our clients identify as gay, queer, or bisexual, we recognize the great in-group diversity between us. Many of our clinical interns do not identify as gay, queer, or bisexual and are not living with HIV, and few have direct experience working with transgender, gender-nonconforming (GNC), and nonbinary people. However, through this practicum experience clinical interns gain real-time, hands-on experience, working with our community and learning about and from our community – this internship creates, strengthens, and perpetuates allyship, a cornerstone of anti-oppressive and liberative work.

Our practicum placement at NAESM, Inc. is rigorous in its clinical practice, relaxed in its environment, celebratory of its team and community, righteous in its liberative work, and steadfast in its mission to empower all people it touches and people in search of a light. It is proof that you can have a brain full of knowledge, a single idea, and create something that will impact the community and the profession of social work for years to come. That is what we do at NAESM, Inc.

REFERENCE

NAESM, Inc. (2024), Retrieved from www.naesminc.org

Summary

Decolonization and its goal to alleviate oppression in clinical and community spaces, and in clinical process, is by and large a multi-action, multisystem process. This chapter provides a beginning dialogue, and offers beginning concepts, frameworks, theory application, and guidance on conceptualizing, creating, and offering the space and process to the individuals and communities social workers and other helping professionals serve. Creating a supervision environment and supervision relationship through concepts like environmental readiness, use of self, critical self-refection, boundaries, are paramount.

Reflection Questions

1. Reflecting on the content of this chapter, what are some things that might have been missing from your previous supervision practice? How might you see that those areas or process are included in future supervision work?
2. How does creating safe and brave spaces in supervision practice model that work for direct clinical and community practice?
3. Drawing on use of self, intersectionality, authenticity, and other chapter concepts, how do you forge/create/establish a meaningful supervisory relationship with a supervisee you don't care for/don't relate to/have a hard time connecting with? What are some practice ways for you to create engagement, and build a practical professional relationship, that strengthens the supervisee?

Reflection Activity

Sometimes it helps to rehearse your conversations regarding power, power dynamics, and power differentials. Reflecting on what you have read in this chapter on the topic of acknowledging and sharing power, how might you introduce or continue dialogue on the topic? Try practicing in a bedroom or bathroom mirror. Notice your facial expressions, how you move your body, your tone, volume, cadence, and speed when speaking. Tap into your confidence, what do you notice? How do these components shape your communication and engagement with supervisees? How might you strengthen them?

Note

1 Simmons University School of Social Work. (2022). Antiracist Teaching Strategies. [unpublished curriculum].

REFERENCES

Asakura, K., & Maurer, K. (2018). Attending to social justice in clinical social work: Supervision as a pedagogical space. *Clinical Social Work Journal*, *46*(4), 289–297.

Biaggio, M., Paget, T. L., & Chenoweth, M. S. (1997). A model for ethical management of faculty–student dual relationships. *Professional Psychology: Research and Practice*, *28*(2), 184–189.

Brashears, F. (1995). Supervision as social work practice: A reconceptualization. *Social Work*, *40*(5), 692–699.

Council on Social Work Education (2008). *Educational policy and accreditation standards*. Council on Social Work Education.

Dewane, C. J. (2006). Use of self: A primer revisited. *Clinical Social Work Journal*, *34*(4), 543–558.

Dore, I. (2024). Feelings of (in)authenticity in social work – A potential guide for ethical practice? *Ethics and Social Welfare*, *18*(1), 1–14.

Edwards, J. K., & Bess, J. M. (1998). Developing effectiveness in the therapeutic use of self. *Clinical Social Work Journal*, *26*(1), 89–105.

Hafford-Letchfield, T., & Engelbrecht, L. (2018). Contemporary practices in social work supervision: Time for new paradigms? *European Journal of Social Work*, *21*(3), 329–332.

Kadushin, A., & Harkness, D. (2014). *Supervision in social work, 5e*. Columbia University Press.

Kezar, A. (2002). Reconstructing static images of leadership: An application of positionality theory. *Journal of Leadership Studies*, *8*(3), 94–109.

Mignolo, W., & Walsh, C. E. (2018). *On decoloniality: Concepts, analytics, praxis*. Duke University Press.

Miller, J. L., & Garran, A. M. (2017). *Racism in the United States: Implications for the helping professions*. Springer.

Raskin, M. S., Wayne, J., & Bogo, M. (2008). Revisiting field education standards. *Journal of Social Work Education, 44*(2), 173–188.

Savaya, R., & Spiro, S. E. (1997). Reactions of practitioners to the introduction of a standard instrument to monitor clinical outcomes. *Journal of Social Service Research, 22*(4), 39–55.

Sloan, L., Joyner, M., Stakeman, C., & Schmitz, C. (2018). *Critical multiculturalism and intersectionality in a complex world*. Oxford University Press.

Waziyatawin & Michael Yellow Bird (eds.) (2012). *For Indigenous minds only: A decolonization handbook*. School for Advanced Research Press.

Wilcox, M. M., Winkeljohn Black, S., Drinane, J. M., Morales-Ramirez, I., Akef, Z., Tao, K. W., DeBlaere, C., Hook, J. N., Davis, D. E., Watkins Jr., C. E., & Owen, J. (2022). A brief qualitative examination of multicultural orientation in clinical supervision. *Professional Psychology: Research and Practice, 53*(6), 585–595.

CHAPTER 2

Utilizing Anti-Oppressive Lens in Social Work Supervision

Nathaniel L. Currie, Ashley Wolfe, Darrin E. Wright, Jack Burke, Gisela Martinez, Gavin Meade, Jad-Évangelo Nasser, and Aydin Olson-Kennedy

Decolonization Lens Continued

What is a decolonial lens? Why are decolonial and anti-oppressive frameworks and lenses important to social work practice, supervision, and leadership? You will discover in this chapter several of the most important and prominent antiracist and anti-oppressive lenses that strengthen social work practice and leadership and can create decolonized practice environments, models, and interventions useful at all levels of clinical practice. Thorough understanding of these lenses assists in an evolved understanding of practice, leadership, and systems creation and maintenance. When introducing decolonial work in supervision practice, leadership, and with practicum students, it helps to begin by creating and curating a space conducive to the work, as we discussed in Chapter 1. This is an intentional process to prepare the environment for depth, scope, intensity, and welcoming of the work.

Following this, it is often helpful to discuss with supervisees, practitioners, and community how language and insight play an important part in the earning of and application of decolonial work. This furthers the readiness process. Consider how language plays a part in decolonial and liberative work. Invite supervisees, practitioners, and community members to assist in exploring, creating, and agreeing on language, terms, and definitions. Understand that language and definitions are ever evolving and should be revisited regularly. Further, it is important to consider the history of social work language and how the innovation of social justice and liberative language merges into, enhances, and strengthens social work language and thus practice.

Unearthing the Oppressive Roots of Social Work Language

Social workers have long appreciated the importance of language as a tool of the profession. In fact, language is the primary facilitator of the helping process. Social workers use language in all facets of the profession, from deepening relationships to facilitating healing to promoting and advocating social justice. Language has also been used to harm, dehumanize, and oppress (Beckett, 2003; Magner & Pineau, 2018), and social workers are often charged with engaging and processing clients, communities, and supervisees in these experiences. As leaders, clinical supervisors in social work and related helping professions have a responsibility to explore the linguistic roots of the profession and, where needed, engage in efforts to reframe oppressive and harmful language the profession has historically sustained.

Social sciences have leaned heavily on cognitive linguistics to show the role that language use has in influencing perception, cognition, and reality (Lakoff, 2004). Social work leaders can use the linguistic concepts of *framing* and *metaphor* to support the interrogation of how language is used in the contexts of oppression, social justice, power, and service (Beckett, 2003). Existing research asserts that successfully applying the concepts of linguistic framing and metaphor has the potential to shape social work practice (Babits, 2001; Vojak, 2009; Willey-Sthapit et al., 2022). Supervisors and leaders who understand these concepts will be able to unearth the harmful language that, too often, practitioners within the social work profession perpetuate or that clients and communities are exposed to outside of practice. When social workers use the language of the oppressor – even to negate it – it strengthens the cognitive power of that language.

Introduction to Framing and Metaphor

To better conceptualize the ways leaders can advance social work practice through intentional use of language, social workers must understand two critical elements of cognitive linguistics: *framing* and *metaphor*. George Lakoff has authored a plethora of works defining and describing linguistic frames, which he states are *"mental structures that shape the way we see the world"* (Lakoff, 2004, p. xi). To illustrate what a frame is, Lakoff challenges readers to not think of an elephant. As soon as the word "elephant" is read – even when it is negated by saying *not* to think of the word – readers conjure an image of an elephant. Every word evokes a cognitive frame, where, when the word is used, an individual's existing knowledge, informed by their experiences, socialization, environment, and perception, is brought into their consciousness to formulate their understanding (Hart, 2023).

Lakoff (2004) argues that as frames are evoked, the cognitive structures associated with the frame are strengthened, meaning that activating those frames becomes easier. This is an important concept to remember as social workers consider how language can rapidly advance from being part of our conversations in clinical supervision to seeping into public discourse to shaping public policy. Framing can support social workers in understanding why an individual might choose or perceive language in a particular way. Further, framing allows social workers to consider our own language use reflectively – to consider our conceptualization of clients, relationships, and systems in supervision. Framing is also a tool to communicate more precisely by evoking frames and cognitive schemas of others in practice (Hart, 2023).

Defined by Lakoff and Johnson (1980), linguistic metaphor challenges the traditional notion of metaphor as a literary device and instead posits that "*human thought processes are largely metaphorical*" (Lakoff & Johnson, 1980, p. 6). There is a relationship between the concepts of framing and metaphor. In metaphor, abstract ideas like emotions ("target domains") can be mapped to concrete frames ("source domains"). When a person hears or reads a sentence that represents a concrete, physical experience like "I opened a drawer," this sentence is not understood in the brain using metaphor. When the sentence involves an abstract idea like an emotion, metaphorical understanding is triggered (Lakoff, 2006).

Lakoff (2006) most frequently uses the metaphor LOVE IS A JOURNEY – represented using all capital letters to reflect linguistic metaphor naming conventions – to demonstrate what metaphor is: an "ontological mapping across conceptual domains, from the source domain of journeys to the target domain of love" (Lakoff & Johnson, 1980, p. 208). The metaphor LOVE IS A JOURNEY maps the target domain, love, to the source domain, journey, meaning that people will understand the concept of love through words that evoke the frame for the word "journey." For example, when someone says "It has been a long road," "This is a dead-end relationship," or "We finally got here after a long, bumpy journey," people easily understand the meaning. Lakoff and Johnson (1980) argue this understanding comes easily because the metaphor is embedded within humans' conceptual cognitive structures.

It is important to note that cognitive linguistics is deeper than simply choosing different words to shift perceptions (Beckett, 2003). If altering word choice alone were effective, increasing the use of words like "diversity," "equity," and "inclusion" in workplaces and schools would equate to those spaces being experienced as more diverse, equitable, and inclusive. Social workers understand that is not true. Spaces do not shift to being more inclusive until people's perceptions and values in those spaces change. This notion is connected to what is mentioned around repeating frames to strengthen the conceptualization of people hearing the words. This is where cognitive linguistics holds true power. Social workers who are equipped with the language to reframe can choose words that actively target the perceptual understanding of those they interact with and create change.

Reframing as a concept is not something foreign to social work practice. Clinicians often utilize cognitive reframing as a practice approach in empowering clients toward their therapeutic goals by consciously changing the way they view, feel, or think about an experience, environment, people, relationship, and so on – eventually resulting in change in how the client behaves.

Implications for Social Work Supervisors and Leaders

Language is power (Vojak, 2009). Historically, language has been used to "other" and oppress, but social workers can also harness its power to create a more socially just world (Beckett, 2003; Magner & Pineau, 2018). It is arguable that social workers, particularly social work leaders, have an ethical imperative to do so. By using linguistic tools like framing and metaphor, social work leaders can support people within their organizations in using human-centered, socially just language.

Building Linguistic Self-Reflexivity in Clinical Supervision

The process of harnessing the power of language begins with teaching social workers to interrogate their own use of language around clients and systems. Supervisors have a role in supporting social workers to build skills in self-reflexivity to build understanding of how they conceptualize clients, systems, and structures. Arguments have been made that social service organizations were designed to maintain oppression (Gil, 1998), and one of the ways that social workers are complacent in this is through language. How social workers talk about the work is how they think about the work.

Take the metaphor SOCIAL WORK IS WAR – a metaphor often reflected in the language of the social work profession through phrases like "recovery is an uphill battle," "front line workers," or "fighting with myself." The use of this metaphor helps to explain the difficulties faced by social workers and their clients through conceptualizing the profession through the frame for "war." This frame includes several elements within it that the social work supervisor might want to explore, such as violence, an enemy, and a side that wins or loses. A supervisor in the room with an individual using language connected to the SOCIAL WORK IS WAR metaphor might ask questions like those seen in Table 2.1. The supervisor can help the social worker better conceptualize their work by exploring what about the profession feels like war, considering who the enemy is, examining how this language does or does not connect to healing and empowerment, and thinking about other ways that a social worker might conceptualize the profession differently (reframing).

The clinical supervisor's role in supporting linguistic reflection has the potential to create career and lifelong change in emerging social workers' conceptualization of what social work is, who clients are, how systems have historically upheld the marginalization of the communities the profession most often serves, and their role in practicing anti-oppressive social work. Most importantly, care changes when social workers talk and think about those they serve in compassionate, respectful, thoughtful ways. Social workers equipped with this knowledge will challenge moments where language about clients does not reflect social work values, and this ignites the power of language to disrupt systems. Systemic oppression is only maintained when social workers conceptualize and talk about their clients, power, and services in the ways that the oppressor intended.

Advancing Socially Just Practice and Policy

If social workers hope to practice in a truly anti-oppressive system where care is not commodified, social workers must reframe what success looks like in social service organizations. This begins in clinical supervision. In many social service organizations, SUCCESS IS PRODUCTIVITY. This metaphor is a direct byproduct of the commodification of care in social services (and care-based services at large). This translates into practice and language through conversations about productivity in supervision. Many organizations encourage supervisors to include discussions about productivity and barriers to productivity in clinical supervision. Think of how quotas or quota systems, which have histories in the slave economy, infiltrate clinical work in the form of a minimum number of required clients to service in a workweek. What if instead, SUCCESS WAS COMMUNITY? Or RELATIONSHIPS?

Table 2.1 *Questioning metaphors in social work discourse*

Metaphor	Common Phrases That Evoke the Metaphor	Questions for Supervisors to Explore/Support Reframing
SOCIAL WORK IS BATTLE	"Social workers are on the front lines." "This is an uphill battle."	What parts of this work feel like battle or war to you? What parts feel like healing? When you think about this battle, who is the enemy? Is it ever the client, and if so, how does this support the relationship? What are other ways to conceptualize social work?
PROBLEMS ARE ENEMIES	"We'll tackle this problem." "This is beatable."	Is there a difference between beating a problem and solving a problem? What language is most empowering to this client when considering solving problems?
CARE IS A COMMODITY	"Increasing healthcare costs." "Productivity."	How do you conceptualize care within the social work profession? Is care tied to a dollar amount? A feeling? A relationship? What language can you use to reinforce how you conceptualize care? How does the way we conceptualize care relate to access? Equity? Power?
SOCIAL WORK IS A MORAL ENTERPRISE (Vojak, 2009) SOCIAL PROBLEMS ARE THE ELEPHANT IN THE ROOM (Hardy, 2024)	"This person needs our help, but we have to be sure not to create dependency." "We cannot ignore the obvious." "Eat the elephant one bite at a time." "Grand challenges of social work." "Wicked problems."	What is the role of power in how social workers conceptualize themselves in relation to clients? Does this framing of a problem/metaphor align with the way that someone experiencing poverty would describe it? Does this framing/metaphor reflect systemic problems that manifest at the individual level in social work? How can this problem be reframed as a systemic issue?

Note: This table identifies metaphors commonly heard in social work discourse, phrases that evoke each, and questions social work supervisors can ask to support shifting conceptualization.

Or CARE? To achieve this conceptualization of success in social service organizations, social work leaders must speak it into existence. Social work leaders must begin with language.

Changing the fundamental conceptualization of a profession and its corresponding systems will not happen overnight, even with significant shifts in language. The impact on public policy and society is too significant to ignore. At the time of the publication of this text, social justice efforts across the country are being linguistically hijacked and painted as "radical" or "extreme." Terms and names for processes like "Critical Race Theory," "DEI," and "African American History" have become vilified. This characterization has tremendous long-term consequences for efforts to create a more diverse, equitable, and inclusive world. Rather than being used for progress, framing and metaphor have been weaponized to linguistically "other" and dehumanize people (Boeynaems et al., 2017; Gonçalves, 2023). See Box 2.1.

> **Box 2.1 Practice Example. The Criminalization of People Living with HIV**
>
> *By Nathaniel L. Currie*
>
> During the height of the American AIDS crisis, 1983 through 1990, major media companies fomented HIV stigma, exacerbated stereotypes, and marginalized vulnerable social groups by leading with stigmatizing reporting instead of facts and science concerning HIV transmission, care, and safety (Currie, 2020). For example, as early as 1983, it was widely known by scientists that HIV was transmitted through biological fluids such as blood and semen and largely driven by condomless sex. Rather than lead with that fact and focus on harm reduction methods, psychoeducation, and community safety, between 1985 and 1989, publications like the *Los Angeles Times* published polls concerning stigmatizing attitudes toward people living with HIV rather than focusing on educating the public. These polls attempted to measure fear and anxiety about HIV, then translated the poll outcomes into newspaper headlines. The groundwork was laid by *The New York Times* in its first article about AIDS, published on July 3, 1981, with a panic-inducing headline that declared, "Rare Cancer Seen in 41 Homosexuals." The stigmatizing pattern of reporting on HIV continued and eventually was enshrined in the first HIV criminalization laws, which were enacted in 1986 in Florida, Tennessee, and Washington with a focus on criminalizing acts that might expose another person to the virus, even if transmission does not occur or is impossible. For example, a person living with HIV who is aware of their serostatus, having oral sex with a seronegative person or while using a condom (transmission improbable); or a person living with HIV spitting on a seronegative person (transmission not possible).

According to the Centers for Disease Control (CDC) (2023), thirty-four states have laws that criminalize HIV exposure through specific legislation that targets HIV or general criminal statutes. Twenty-one states specifically criminalize HIV through sex without first sharing one's status (if it is known) under the stigmatizing belief that if a person's serostatus is known, a seronegative person will not have sex with them, even if transmission is impossible. HIV criminalization, oppressive, stigmatizing, and stereotyping language has been used across each of these policies and their rationales to alter public opinion, bypass medical science, and create a dehumanizing narrative.

REFLECTION QUESTIONS

1. What are some other practice examples where framing and metaphor have been weaponized to linguistically "other" and dehumanize people and communities?
2. What have we learned from the HIV epidemic about narratives and counter-narratives?

REFERENCE

Centers for Disease Control. (18 December 2023). HIV Criminalization and *Ending the HIV Epidemic in the U.S.* www.cdc.gov/hiv/policies/law/criminalization-ehe.html

Currie, N. (2020, June 23). The History of HIV/AIDS in the U.S. The Body. Retrieved from https://www.thebody.com/health/history-of-hiv-aids.

FURTHER READING

Altman, L. K. (1981). Rare cancer seen in 41 homosexuals. *The New York Times*, 3(07).

Brodie, M., Hamel, E., Brady, L. A., Kates, J., & Altman, D. E. (2004). AIDS at 21: Media coverage of the HIV epidemic 1981–2002. *The Nation*, 49, 68.

Closen, M. L., Bobinski, M. A., Herman, D. H., Hernandez, J. F., Schultz, G. P., & Strader, J. K. (1993). Criminalization of an epidemic: HIV-AIDS and criminal exposure laws. *Arkansas Law Review*, 46, 921–983.

Cohen, C. (1999). The Boundaries of Blackness: AIDS and the Breakdown of Black Politics. University of Chicago Press.

Lehman, J. S., Carr, M. H., Nichol, A. J., Ruisanchez, A., Knight, D. W., Langford, A. E., ... & Mermin, J. H. (2014). Prevalence and public health implications of state laws that criminalize potential HIV exposure in the United States. *AIDS and Behavior*, 18, 997–1006.

These dehumanizing metaphors, outlined in Table 2.2, target historically marginalized communities, such as Black, Indigenous, people of color, women, members of the LGBTQIA+ community, and immigrants. This

Table 2.2 *Harmful metaphors in social discourse and public policy*

Metaphor	Common Phrases That Evoke the Metaphor	Reframe Grounded in Social Work Values
IMMIGRANTS ARE ANIMALS (Magner & Pineau, 2018)	"We should lure and bait them." "Immigrants are endangering and threatening our people."	IMMIGRANTS ARE PART OF THE WHOLE
WOMEN ARE PROPERTY / PROPERTY IS A GRASPED THING	"To have and to hold."	WOMEN ARE WHOLE
DRUG USERS/DEALERS ARE THE ENEMY (Thibodeau & Boroditsky, 2011)	"War on drugs." "Eliminate the enemy who is terrorizing our streets."	DRUG USERS/DEALERS ARE HUMAN
UNHOUSED PEOPLE ARE DIRT	"The filth of our city." "The dirty spot in our community." "Clean up our streets."	UNHOUSED PEOPLE ARE HUMAN
MEMBERS OF THE LGBTQIA+ COMMUNITY ARE PREDATORS	"They are coming for your children." "Trying to infiltrate young minds." "These drag shows are harming your children."	MEMBERS OF THE LGBTQIA+ COMMUNITY ARE PART OF THE HUMAN COMMUNITY

Note: This table identifies metaphors heard in public discourse and policy that are overtly dehumanizing or harmful, phrases that evoke each of the metaphors, and how social work should linguistically reframe each metaphor.

problematic discourse is at a record high (Gonçalves, 2023) in many communities at the time of publication of this text. When these frames and metaphors are repeated time and time again on mainstream media, they begin to saturate social discourse, and consequently, influence public policy. Social work supervisors will be integral in reversing this process and linguistically dismantling these systems of oppression brick by brick. Empowered with social work frames and metaphors grounded in the values of this profession, we must speak a more socially just world into existence.

Because language is constantly evolving, there is an ongoing need to situate discussions in supervision within present-day circumstances. As is seen in Table 2.2, the frames and metaphors that permeate public discourse and policy shift to reflect the systems and social context we exist and practice within. If social workers are challenged to interrogate the context behind the language of social discourse and public policy, they will be better equipped to question the systemic targeting of specific groups through harmful frames and metaphors. Moreover, the skills that social workers develop to critically analyze language can then be extended to reframe oppressive and harmful language through the lens of the social work values.

Using Clinical Supervision to Empower Social Workers to Frame

Language exists in every element of social work. Social work supervisors who teach emerging practitioners to frame will affect social change (Beckett, 2003). Every micro application of these concepts creates change in people's conceptualization of systems and clients. This, in turn, results in them shifting their own linguistic framing and exposes more people to new frames grounded within the values of social work. Supervision is one area where emerging professionals can be pushed to acknowledge the importance of linguistics in addressing social work problems and to empower social service practitioners to frame for meaningful change. Through teaching emerging social workers to metacognitively reflect on their own use of language, to identify harmful and oppressive metaphors within organizations and systemically, and to reframe and generate new frames and metaphors steeped in social work values, social work supervisors can create a movement of linguistic social justice in our profession and beyond.

Reflective Questions

1. As you read about linguistic framing and metaphor, were there metaphors you identified within your own practice, organization, or supervision structure that came to mind? Do these frames necessitate reframing efforts? How might you begin this process?
2. How might you use the concepts of framing and metaphor to explore power, the advancement of diversity, equity, inclusion, and belonging, and anti-oppressive practice with clinical supervision?

Next, let's explore the concepts and uses of anti-oppressive lenses in social work supervision and leadership by exploring each lens, its background, and its application, individually. This will provide a base of knowledge to combine with decolonial and liberative processes in practice. Consider the Afrocentric perspective, Feminism, Critical disabilities studies (DisCrit), Critical Latine studies (LatCrit), Gender studies, Queer studies, empowerment practice, and Diversity, Equity, and Inclusion (DEI).

Afrocentric Perspective and Social Work Supervision

As we have established in Chapter 1, clinical supervision is vital in social work, serving as a cornerstone for professional development, ethical practice, and quality client care. It provides social workers with essential support, guidance, and oversight as they navigate complex cases and challenging ethical dilemmas. At its core, clinical supervision helps ensure competent and effective service delivery. Regular meetings with experienced supervisors allow social workers to discuss cases, explore interventions, and receive feedback on their practice. This process enhances clinical skills, promotes critical thinking, and encourages evidence-based approaches (Falender & Shafranske, 2004, 2017).

Supervision also serves a crucial protective function, safeguarding both clients and practitioners. It provides a space to identify and address potential ethical issues, manage risks, and adhere to professional standards and boundaries. This oversight helps prevent burnout, compassion fatigue, and ethical violations (Reamer, 2009). Furthermore, clinical supervision fosters continuous learning and professional growth. Supervisors can introduce new theories, techniques, and research findings, keeping social workers current in their field. This ongoing education is essential in a profession where best practices and societal needs constantly evolve (Falender & Shafranske, 2004, 2017). It also, again, makes supervision a conducive and practical means for introducing decolonial and anti-oppressive theory, practice, and reflection to supervisees.

The reflective nature of supervision promotes self-awareness and emotional intelligence. Social workers learn to examine their biases, reactions, and decision-making processes, leading to more intentional and culturally competent practice. This self-reflection is critical given social work's complex, emotionally charged nature (Parlakian, 2001). Lastly, clinical supervision contributes to social services' overall quality and accountability. It helps maintain professional standards, ensures compliance with organizational policies, and ultimately leads to better outcomes for clients and communities (Rofuth & Piepenbring, 2020).

The Importance of Applying Afrocentric Principles to Clinical Supervision in Social Work

As discussed in the previous section, clinical supervision in social work is critical in developing practical and empathetic practitioners. Ensuring that social workers can provide the highest standard of care to diverse populations is essential. Incorporating Afrocentric principles into clinical supervision is vital for several reasons, including cultural competence, empowerment, and social justice.

Understanding Afrocentric Principles

Afrocentricity is a social theory of change that centers on the experiences and perspectives of African people and their descendants. It emphasizes the importance of understanding the world through an African cultural lens. Fundamental principles of Afrocentricity include the recognition of the historical and cultural contexts of African people, the value of community and collectivism, the importance of spirituality, and the centrality of the African worldview in understanding social phenomena (Asante, 2003; Schiele, 2010).

Enhancing Cultural Competence

Incorporating Afrocentric principles into clinical supervision helps social workers develop a more profound cultural competence. This is crucial in a multicultural society where social workers encounter clients from diverse backgrounds. Afrocentric principles encourage supervisors to train social workers to understand and respect the cultural contexts of their African American clients. This understanding helps build trust and rapport, which is essential for effective social work practice. By appreciating the unique cultural, historical, and social contexts of African American clients and other marginalized groups, social workers can tailor their interventions to be more relevant and practical.

Promoting Empowerment

Afrocentric principles emphasize empowerment and self-determination. In clinical supervision, this translates to encouraging social workers to empower their African American clients and other marginalized groups. This involves recognizing and addressing the systemic and structural barriers that clients may face. Supervisors can guide social workers in developing interventions that address individual needs and promote community strength and resilience. This approach aligns with the Afrocentric value of collectivism, where the well-being of the community is considered as important as the well-being of the individual (Martin & Martin, 2002).

Advancing Social Justice

Social work is inherently a profession committed to social justice. Afrocentric principles align closely with this commitment by highlighting the need to address racial and social inequities. By integrating these principles into clinical supervision, supervisors can instill a strong sense of social justice in social workers. This involves understanding and challenging the systemic racism and oppression that African American clients and other marginalized groups may experience. It also means advocating for policies and practices that promote equity and inclusion. In this way, Afrocentric principles help ensure social workers are practitioners and advocates for broader social change (Wright, 2022).

Incorporating Spirituality

Spirituality often plays a significant role in the lives of African American individuals and communities. Afrocentric principles recognize and value this aspect of the cultural experience. Thus, spirituality in practice will be considered in clinical supervision that applies Afrocentric ideas of strength, resilience, self-worth, and hope. Supervisors can teach social workers how to comprehend and incorporate their clients' spiritual practices and beliefs into their interventions as a way to empower them to overcome life's obstacles. They can also learn how to explore their clients' perceptions of hope, resilience, and self-worth in the face of uncertainty in order to find solutions from their own perspective. This holistic approach can enhance the therapeutic process and support clients' well-being and hope for a better future (Martin & Martin, 2002; Turner, 2017, p. 266).

Application of Afrocentric Principles in Clinical Supervision as a Praxis in Decoloniality and Anti-Oppressive Supervision

Afrocentric principles are a praxis in decolonization and an anti-oppressive approach when applied in clinical social work supervision (Morgaine & Capous-Desyllas, 2014; Schiele, 2010). As discussed in the previous sections, this approach can enhance cultural competence and improve outcomes when working with African American clients and marginalized communities (Martin & Martin, 2002). An extensive overview of the Afrocentric approach's use in clinical social work supervision is provided.

1. Cultural awareness and sensitivity:
   - Encourage supervisees to recognize and value African American and marginalized groups' cultural strengths, traditions, and experiences.
   - Promote understanding of the historical context of racism, oppression, and resilience in African American communities (David, 2014).
2. Holistic approach:
   - Emphasize the interconnectedness of mind, body, and spirit in African American culture and other marginalized groups.
   - Encourage supervisees to consider the broader family and community context when working with clients (Martin & Martin, 2002).
3. Strengths-based focus:
   - Guide supervisees in identifying and building upon the strengths and resources within African Americans and other marginalized groups as they relate to individuals, families, and communities.
   - Promote empowerment and self-determination as fundamental principles in working with clients (Turner, 2017).
4. Culturally relevant interventions:
   - Support supervisees in developing and implementing interventions that align with African American and other marginalized groups' cultural values and practices.
   - Encourage using culturally specific assessment tools and therapeutic techniques (Cummins & Sevel, 2018).
5. Language and communication:
   - Help supervisees understand and respect African American and other marginalized groups' linguistic patterns and their association with help-seeking behaviors.
   - Promote effective cross-cultural communication skills.
6. Community engagement:
   - Encourage supervisees to engage with and learn from African Americans and other marginalized groups through community leaders, organizations, and institutions.

- Promote collaboration with natural support systems within the community.
7. Critical consciousness:
   - Foster awareness of systemic racism and its impact on African American clients and other marginalized groups and communities.
   - Encourage supervisees to challenge their own biases and assumptions.
8. Spirituality and religion:
   - Recognize the importance of spirituality and religion in many African American communities.
   - Guide supervisees in incorporating spiritual beliefs and practices into their work when appropriate and desired by clients.
9. Collectivist orientation:
   - Emphasize the importance of collective well-being and interdependence in African American culture.
   - Encourage supervisees to consider family and community dynamics in their interventions.
10. Cultural humility:
    - Promote ongoing self-reflection and learning about African American and marginalized groups' cultures and experiences.
    - Encourage supervisees to recognize the limits of their knowledge and seek guidance from cultural experts when needed (Derezotes, 2014).
11. Ethical considerations:
    - Address ethical dilemmas when working with African American clients and other marginalized groups, considering cultural values and norms.
    - Guide supervisees in navigating potential conflicts between professional ethics and cultural practices (Barsky, 2018).
12. Advocacy and social justice:
    - Encourage supervisees to advocate for policies and practices that address systemic inequalities affecting African American communities and other marginalized groups.
    - Promote a commitment to social justice as an integral part of social work practice.

Implications for Social Work Education and Practice

Ensuring that future social workers are adequately trained to be culturally proficient is one of the most notable challenges facing social work education (Colvin, 2013). With an accurate understanding of those being served, interventions will be appropriate. This chapter allows social work educators to further understand and incorporate the principles of the Afrocentric perspective into their curriculums alongside other theories to broaden students' exposure and understanding of anti-oppressive practice as a pedagogical approach that enhances multiple ways of knowing. Simultaneously, the Afrocentric perspective offers social work students an opportunity to better understand the importance of utilizing a holistic approach when applying theory to practice with African Americans and other diverse populations.

Similarly, in research, this discussion of the Afrocentric perspective as an anti-oppressive practice offers opportunities to expand the body of knowledge on the perspective to ensure its continued evolutionary growth in decolonizing social work education by including Indigenous ways of knowing and doing. Further research should include methods that explore more in depth, through personal interviews and focus groups, social work students' attitudes and perceptions toward the utilization of ACP. The information gained from these findings would contribute immensely toward its evolutionary growth and use in social work education.

Clinical supervision is indispensable in social work practice. It enhances professional competence, protects clients and practitioners, promotes ongoing learning, fosters self-awareness, and upholds the quality of social services. As such, it should be prioritized and integrated as a core component of social work practice and organizational culture (Rofuth & Piepenbring, 2020). Finally, clinical supervisors can assist their supervisees in developing culturally responsive and effective practices needed when working with African American clients and communities, as well as other marginalized groups, by including the principles of the Afrocentric perspective in social work supervision. This strategy can result in better service delivery, favorable outcomes, and higher client engagement (Schiele, 2017; Tervalon & Murray-Garcia, 1998).

Reflection questions for consideration:
1. How might you incorporate African-centered values and worldviews into the supervisory relationship?
2. How might we honor collectivist approaches and community wisdom in supervision sessions?
3. How might we integrate cultural strengths and Indigenous healing practices into case conceptualization and treatment planning?

4. What strategies can we use to address power dynamics and promote a more egalitarian supervisory relationship?
5. How can we incorporate storytelling, proverbial saying, and other African oral traditions into our supervisory discussions?

Critical Disability Theory and Application to Clinical Practice

Philosophically speaking, critical theory identifies and combats pervasive and omnipresent societal structures through an empowerment, anti-oppressive, and idealized "utopian" perspective (Burghardt, 2011, p. 2). Through critical theory, inequity and oppression can be realized and combatted – this can occur politically (Agger, 1976, p. 12), in education (Giroux, 2023), and socially.

Critical disability theory, or DisCrit, then, is a methodology that encapsulates broad paradigms, orientations, and practices to identify and challenge how society defines mental and physical impairments and the attitudes toward able bodies and disabled bodies (Hall, 2019). Critical disability theory as an orientation challenges the notions of what disability "looks like" and operates from an empowerment perspective by challenging the heteronormative, racist, and ableist system in which we all live. Identification is not enough – there needs to be a recommitment to social justice work to pursue efficacious and needed change (Hall, 2019). Critical disability theory also aims to combat the predilections of traditional disability studies by examining the societal and institutional frameworks in which these studies are based.

To understand critical disability theory and how it relates to clinical supervision, a supervisor must examine both their own and their practice's attempts to be mindful and limit the effects of ableism. Ableism can take many forms in clinical practice, such as overtly disparaging comments, microaggressions, and the physical layout of a practitioner's office that render it inaccessible, contributing to negative well-being in supervisees (Lindsay et al., 2023). For example, a student once pointed out that the term "fall on deaf ears" in a doctoral case study exercise was ableist and disparaging, prompting a rewording of the teaching exercise. The decolonized supervisor must also understand that disability takes many forms, both visible and invisible; therefore, in supervision, the ethical and respectful discussion of disability status should encapsulate information beyond what is overtly discernible in an environment that is welcoming and inclusive.

To best approach this necessity, a supervisor must understand that there is a long and painful history of associating disability with "disease," which many individuals with disabilities fear may cause social rejection, ostracization, discrimination, and increase their stigmatized status in their workplace (Follmer et al., 2024; Kulkarni, 2022; Lindsay et al., 2023). The supervisor must create a liberating culture where disability status can be freely discussed and incorporated into supervision. To avoid operating from an ableist perspective, the supervisor can make accommodations to their physical environment that prevent physical barriers (such as ramps, elevators, and automated doors) for those with physical disability status and provide a safe physical space where supervisees can emotionally process or reduce sensory input for those with emotional disabilities. Consider how the supervisor might simultaneously create a practice environment that does not perpetuate ableism while holding space for practice dialogue and constructive practice critique that reduces or eliminates ableism from social work practice and leadership.

Latino Critical Perspective and Clinical Supervision

The United States' fastest-growing population is the Latino/a/x/e[1] population. As of July 1, 2023, the United States Census estimates the Latino/a/x/e population to be 65.2 million, constituting 19 percent of the nation's population (US Census, 2023). While the Latino/a/x population is often viewed as a single ethnic group, it comprises individuals from 33 countries in Latin America and the Caribbean. This diversity extends to various racial groups and comprises multiple variations of the Spanish language, Indigenous languages, and Creole (Gutiérrez, M & Lechuga-Peña, 2022). Given this diversity, it is crucial to approach the issues within and overlapping this community from a multidimensional and intersectional perspective.

Latino Critical Perspective, or LatCrit, references a branch of Critical Race Theory, an antiracist analytical framework that expands on the central tenets of CRT and addresses issues of discrimination and oppression unique to the Latina/o/x experience (Solorzano & Delgado Bernal, 2001). CRT asserts that the social construction of race produces invisible hierarchical and social structures delineating power and privilege for whites while intentionally and perpetually excluding and oppressing people of color (Delgado & Stefancic, 2012; Valencia, 2008).

LatCrit extends the analysis of power and privilege beyond the Black–white binary paradigm of race to include the discriminatory and oppressive experiences of the Latine a/o/x/e heterogeneous population (Kiehne, 2016). These may include language, immigration status, race, gender, skin color, phenotype, and nationality (Gutiérrez, M & Lechuga-Peña, 2022; Solorzano & Delgado Bernal, 2001). A central concept within LatCrit is the discrimination Latinas/os/x/e face resulting from their nativity, their birthplace (Kiehne, 2016). Nativism is rooted in nationalism, characterized by extreme patriotism and loyalty to one's country, resulting in anti-foreigner sentiment (Huber et al., 2008).

LatCrit emphasizes nativism, which creates a hierarchy of social dominance and power granted to native-born individuals while reinforcing the inferiority of foreign-born Latinas/os/x/e (Kiehne, 2016). This form of discrimination unique to the Latina/o/x community emphasizes that the discrimination Latinas/os/x/e face originates from their multidimensional and intersectional identities, which results in a greater degree of marginalization (Villalpando, 2004).

Integrating LatCrit into clinical supervision is a significant stride in advancing social work's commitment to antiracism. Like CRT, LatCrit challenges existing norms and underscores the impact of oppressive structural forces on Latinos/as/x/e. Using LatCrit as an analytical tool, clinical supervisors can help social workers identify and comprehend the root causes of many of their Latina/o/x clients' issues, often stemming from oppressive systems across multiple and intersectional dimensions (Kiehne, 2016). This understanding is crucial in providing effective support to the community. Clinical supervision also offers a designated time to *check in* with both Latino/a/x/e clinicians and non-Latine clinicians regarding their personal–professional experiences and those of their clients in Latin identity-based discrimination, oppression, and community issues. Pulling in these unique perspectives strengthens the micro and overall supervision experiences for supervisees.

Gender Studies, and Transgender and Critical Transgender Theory

Gender studies, previously known as women's studies, evolved from second-wave feminism's call to attention to the dearth of women's voices and perspectives in higher education (Pilcher & Whelehan, 2004). Despite the overrepresentation of men's voices, the canon was assumed to be universal and represented the everyday experiences of both men and women (Mack, 1994). Indeed, this androcentric perspective resulted in entire fields of scholarship built with biased suppositions about women (Erol & Cuklanz, 2020) and, by extension, white-bodied, non-disabled, cisgender women.

Although gender studies began to expand the canon to include women's voices, it centered the voices and perspectives of women scholars who were white, non-disabled, cisgender, and upper-class, and failed to account for the intersectional oppression of racialized, economically disadvantaged, disabled, queer, and transgender women (Erol & Cuklanz, 2020; Pilcher & Whelehan, 2004; Swan, 2023). Consequently, foundational feminist theories and texts that informed gender studies reproduced the notion of a single-axis view of oppression centered on white cisgender women (Erol & Cuklanz, 2020). Further, as Payne (2020) and Pilcher and Whelehan (2004) illuminate, "women" cannot be understood as a homogeneous group of people with shared experiences. The reductive universalizing of "women" implies the type of woman that all other women are normed to is white, cisgender, heterosexual, and non-disabled. This excruciatingly narrow definition of women is informed and perpetuated by colonization, white supremacy, cissexism, heterosexism, and ableism.

Addressing issues of intersectional oppression of transgender communities, which include transgender women, transgender men, nonbinary, gender non-conforming, agender, bigender, genderfluid, genderqueer, genderless, polygender, two-spirit, and many more (herein transgender) – has been named a concern for social work education and practice since 2008. However, social work education continues to struggle to adequately prepare social workers to confidently and competently address the intersectional oppression transgender people face (Atteberry-Ash et al., 2019; Austin et al., 2019; Bragg et al., 2019; Byers et al., 2019; Davis & Mirick, 2021; Dentato et al., 2016; Goode et al., 2020; Hoff & Camacho, 2019; Jaekal & Holmes, 2019; Kia et al., 2021, 2023; Kroner, 2020; McCarty-Caplan, 2018, 2022; Shelton et al., 2019).

It is plausible that social work practitioners' and supervisors' education did not adequately prepare them with the knowledge to critically assess the intersectional oppression transgender people face, nor the skills necessary to develop an anti-oppressive practice to serve transgender clients. Thus, by extension, they may not have the knowledge needed to adequately supervise future social workers. Transgender and critical transgender theories can support practitioners and supervisors with a foundation from which to build.

Theory Overview

In its early formation, transgender theory's concepts were simple: trans people had ownership of their identity, which was self-actualized and embodied. Gender could be fluid, and gender identity is not based on biology (Nagoshi & Brzuzy, 2010; Roen, 2001). Informed by five principles that are not conditional on one's outward appearance or perceived gender identity, transgender theory asserted that (1) transgender people are who they say they are; (2) transgender people exist and always have; (3) transgender people are not invisible; (4) transgender people should not be subjected to the emotional labor of educating others; and (5) transgender people are the experts on their own bodies and life experiences (Breaux & Thyer, 2021; Nagoshi & Brzuzy, 2010; Nagoshi et al., 2023; Roen, 2001). Transgender theory rejected the enduring thought that transgender people were deviant, and that transness was a pathological condition – that anyone who felt their gender was out of alignment in any degree was insane. This resulted in the validity of one's transgender identity being contingent on professionals, such as psychologists, psychiatrists, and eventually social workers, who, through a diagnostic lens, were seen to be more reliable and trustworthy (Breaux & Thyer, 2021; Marrow, 2023; Nagoshi & Brzuzy, 2010; Nagoshi et al., 2023).

Transgender people have been negotiating multiple forms of marginalization, oppression, isolation, and violence since the colonization of Indigenous peoples. Documented evidence of the violence enacted against trans and gender non-conforming bodies dates back to the 1500s. A Spanish conquistador documented unleashing his troops' dogs on forty male-assigned Cueva Indians for taking on the roles and attire traditionally associated with women (Beemyn, 2020).

One of the earliest known laws restricting gender identity and expression in the United States was passed in the Massachusetts colony in 1690, outlawing "cross-dressing" (Stryker, 2017). Defined by white settler values, "cross-dressing" was seen as deviant and sinful, asserting that gender non-conforming people were under the influence of the devil and had a social disorder (Beemyn, 2020). However, these laws weren't entirely about gender non-conformity. Some argue that the impetus for many of these laws was colonialism, as in the case with laws that outlawed one from wearing clothing that misrepresented their social rank or profession, and white supremacy specifically outlawing Black people from impersonating whites (Stryker, 2017).

Marrow (2023) points out that trans identities and expressions have been pathologized and viewed as deviant and mentally ill by the medical and mental health communities for decades, exposing them to sanist beliefs about their ability to provide reliable testimony about who they were.

Sanism, which refers to the systematic oppression of individuals who have been diagnosed with mental health conditions, manifests in both subtle and overt acts of discrimination and oppression. Sanism diminishes one's epistemic credibility, which is a form of social power; those seen as having epistemic credibility have control over their social world, and those seen as less credible have a credibility deficit, putting them at high risk of exploitation, oppression, and marginalization (Gosselin, 2022; Marsh, 2011). George (2019) explains that "in addition to their perceived non-conformity with hegemonic constructions of masculinity and femininity [transgender] individuals are seen to be refusing to comply with the gender that has been assigned to them by those in a position of (medical or scientific) authority" (p. 265), thus entrapping gender non-conformity as psychiatric disobedience. This disobedience is presupposed on the premise that transgender identities are abnormal, evidenced by the inclusion of transness, listed as gender identity disorder in the *Diagnostic and Statistical Manual of Mental Disorders* (DSM) (American Psychiatric Association, 1980, 1994, 2013). However, with the intention to depathologize transness and instead focus on the distress that can result from gender incongruence, the diagnosis of "gender identity disorder" was replaced with "gender dysphoria" in the DSM-V. However, much of the criteria remained the same.

In psychiatry, normality is defined by superfluity of descriptions of abnormality; that is to say, the definition of abnormality is inherently dependent on prevailing notions of normality (Tosh, 2017). With the proliferation of psychiatric diagnoses now cataloged within the DSM, the "concept of normality has become so constrained that it represents an idealized form of White, middle-class, heterosexual, cisgender masculinity that is impossible to attain" (Tosh, 2017, p. 263).

Oppressive mechanisms, such as race, class, gender, sanism, heterosexism, and cisgenderism, do not function in isolation but interact within a shifting and intricate network influenced by specific contexts and individuals (Baines & Sharma, 2022). Transgender theory acknowledges that, unlike cisgender women who experience sexism and misogyny, trans women face a unique overlap of cisgenderism, sexism, and misogyny described as transmisogyny.

The sanist framework of cisgender being normal and transgender being abnormal has set up a very limited conduit for people to access gender-affirming care without the intrusion of social workers and other professionals, who, because of their assumed cisness and positional power, are credible to confirm or discredit the legitimacy of trans people. Indeed, trans people who experience multiple forms of oppression are at greater risk of being seen as unreliable, resulting in a credibility deficit and a loss of "epistemic power to control one's social environment" (Gosselin, 2022, p. 295). This diminution in epistemic power hinders transgender individuals from fully participating in the decision-making processes of their lives, creating additional barriers to accessing gender-affirming care.

Transgender theory primarily concentrates on the personal beliefs and biases that cisgender people hold about transgender individuals. While well-intentioned, this theory's micro-level approach to addressing the marginalization of transgender people often lacks a lasting impact on the transgender community as a whole. As Archbishop Desmond Tutu aptly noted, "There comes a point where we need to stop just pulling people out of the river. We need to go upstream and find out why they're falling in." While transgender theory focuses on "pulling people from the river," critical transgender theory recognizes that having a meaningful impact on the lives of trans people requires a broader lens – one that acknowledges the violence and inequities trans people face as inextricably linked to all other forms of systemic and institutionalized oppression, marginalization, discrimination, and violence (Spade, 2015). Whereas transgender theory highlights that transgender women experience oppression at the intersection of cisgenderism, sexism, and misogyny, critical transgender theory reveals that Black trans women experience oppression at the intersection of cisgenderism, cissexism, misogyny, racism, and anti-Blackness, exemplified by the concept of transmisogynoir (Krell, 2017). Critical transgender theory explores how disciplinary power – structural oppressions shaped by social norms specific to a culture and geographic region, dictating what society considers appropriate behavior and acceptable identities (e.g., whiteness, heteronormativity, cisnormativity, sanism, ableism) – and population-management power – the inequitable distribution of opportunities across populations – directly affect transgender individuals (Spade, 2015). Critical transgender theory does not suggest that expanding the lens to expose the larger systems and institutions that oppress transgender people should eclipse the day-to-day lived experiences of oppression and marginalization transgender people face. Critical transgender theory recognizes that transgender people are not a conceptual entity used to bolster a theory; rather, they are real people experiencing real oppression that is causing real harm. Indeed, a core principle of critical transgender theory is flipping the script on the cisgender gaze that focuses on what can be learned about trans people, focusing instead on what trans people can teach us (Evans, 2019).

On its own, critical transgender theory is insufficient in guiding social work practitioners and supervisors to develop an anti-oppressive practice with transgender clients. Transgender people are not homogeneous nor monologic. There are endless ways in which one can experience and express their gender, far beyond what the lexicon of gender is able to fully capture or represent. Indeed, how one experiences and expresses their transgender identity, and how that expression is interpreted by others, profoundly impacts how they see the world and how they are seen in the world, thus marginalizing and oppressing some while protecting and privileging others. Those whose transness can be made invisible will have access to cis-assumed privilege. However, that privilege is only an illusion that hangs precariously within the interpretation of others. Conversely, for those whose transness is visible, that very same privilege will be out of reach. The illusion and precariousness of privilege or oppression is universal. However, the consequences that can befall someone when that illusion shatters disproportionally harms those who find themselves at the intersection of multiple marginalized identities. The existing models used to explore intersectional oppression (see Duckworth, 2020; Free Black Thought, 2022; Morgan, 1996) are limited in their ability to capture the liminal and transitional spaces between and within positions of power and oppression, and how the interpretation of one's social identity matters.

Recognizing these limitations, de Vries (2015) developed an eight-plane multidimensional prism (Figure 2.1), with each plane representing a social category such as gender, race, or body size. Within each plane are additional, often unmarked, investigative classifications, such as perceived gender, physical attributes, or fatness. de Vries' (2015) model is unique in that it is a transparent three-dimensional prism rather than a one-dimensional circle or line. Most notably, de Vries' placement of race at the center of the prism underscores that race is the starting point from which all other forms of oppression or privilege emerge. As Ellison et al. (2017) explain, "Black is a modifier that changes everything ... [the] power of blackness to change all that comes after is part of its close relationship to death" (p. 166). Race is not neutral; the protection of whiteness works through everything, including gender (Swan, 2023). de Vries' (2015) model illustrates that transgender people's social identities are contextual and transient; therefore, models of intersectionality need to be adaptable to respond to the multifarious, complex, and interlocked categories of social identities that are assumed to be static and universal. In other words, "intersectionality ... is about ups and downs, stopping and starting – about how we pass through at one moment while being stopped at another, depending upon who is receiving us and what is being received through us" (Ahmed, 2017, p. 222).

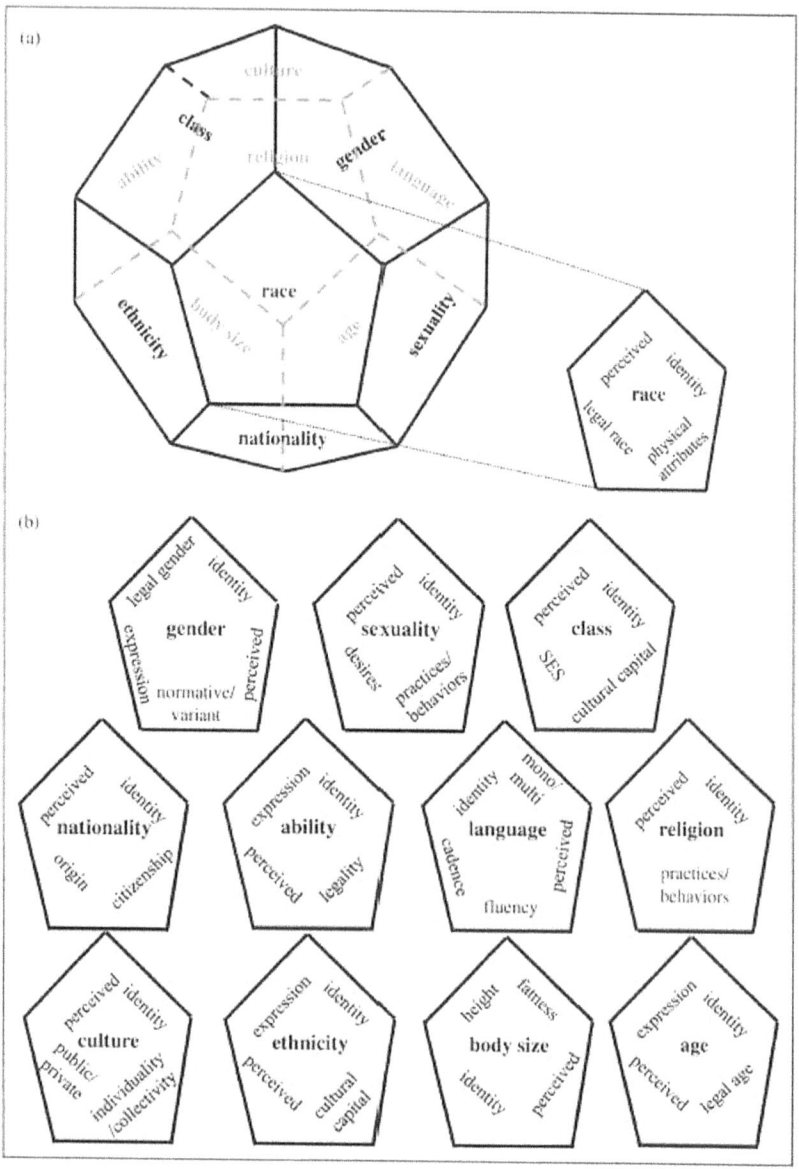

Figure 2.1 Prism of intersectional oppression.

Application to Social Work Practice

Transgender theory can guide social workers to refuse ownership of transgender people's embodied knowledge, rejecting the persistent notion that transgender identities are inherently pathological and refusing to accept the unearned credibility freely given to professionals and cisgender people. Critical transgender theory carves out pathways for transgender people to live in the "skin of theory" (Baldino, 2021); that is to say, transgender people are the sites of knowledge that inform social workers' practice, reorienting practice and theory to adapt to transgender people, rather than demanding transgender people adapt to theory and practice.

While centering a client's worldview in social work practice is often seen as standard, doing so for transgender clients is less common. Given how sanism at both micro and macro levels has systematically invalidated transgender people's embodied self-knowledge – thereby decentering their worldview and making them reliant on cisgender professionals, including social workers, to validate their existence and access to services – critical transgender theory offers valuable guidance to help social workers identify and reject the unearned credibility that sanism confers.

An additional site of intersectional oppression for transgender people involves concerns related to being perceived as visibly transgender versus non-visibly transgender. Those who are perceived to be transgender are at risk of experiencing identity invalidation, therefore increasing their risk of oppression. For example, when a transgender man's transness is perceived as visible, it results in others categorizing him as a woman. Bettcher (2014) describes this phenomenon as "appearance-reality contrast" (p. 392). Conversely, a transgender man whose transness is perceived to be invisible will experience being witnessed, where one's existence, experiences, and emotions are seen and validated, and mirrored, where others reflect back what one sees in themselves. Being witnessed and mirrored are fundamental experiences for all people, but can be especially important for transgender people who experience appearance-reality contrast. Informed by transgender theory, social workers can be witnesses and mirrors for transgender clients, demonstrated by using the correct pronouns and names, which are not conditional on one's outward appearance or perceived gender identity.

How one experiences visibility and invisibility is complex, as perceptions and the resulting consequences of transgender visibility or invisibility are subjective and vary across time, geography, culture, environment, race, gender, age, and other constructs. In most contexts, being perceived as a visible transgender person increases their risk of oppression, discrimination, and even violence, with each of these risks increasing amid each visible marginalized identity they embody, with racialized oppression serving as a central axis through which all other forms of oppression intersect.

By accounting for the additional, often obscured categories within each of the eight planes, social workers can utilize de Vries' (2015) prism to gain deeper insight into the varied experiences of transgender oppression. This understanding reveals the creation of liminal spaces and the transient nature of both privilege and exposure to oppression. With this knowledge, social workers can better identify the complex and overlapping sources of oppression their transgender clients face and respond more effectively to the psychological and emotional needs arising from identity invalidation. Furthermore, this nuanced comprehension of oppression can broaden their understanding of their clients' worldviews and more clearly define actionable steps toward dismantling oppressive systems and structures.

Application to Supervision Practice

> Some forms of violence are dismissed as trivial or not recognized as violence at all, perpetuating their reproduction.
> —Ahmed, Trap Door: Trans cultural production and the politics of Visibility (2017)

As we recall, transgender theory tells us that transgender people are who they say they are irrespective of how their gender is read. de Vries' (2015) prism elucidates that gender-based oppression is multifactorial and can vary depending on how one's gender is read and understood by others – particularly, if their transness is perceived as visible or invisible.

The likelihood of being misgendered is particularly high when one occupies a liminal space of perceived gendered social identities. This misgendering is often manifested through the intentional use of incorrect pronouns (e.g., referring to a transgender woman as *he/him*, a transgender man as *she/her*, or refusing to use *they/them* for a nonbinary person). Ahmed (2017) further explains that intentional misgendering, often dismissed as trivial, is a form of violence against transgender people, positioning them as "not real", and, consequently, as both the source of and responsible for their own exclusion and oppression.

The violence of misgendering is not without consequence. Indeed, challenging and subsequently invalidating someone's gender perpetuates the exclusion of transgender people from gendered public spaces, such as restrooms, locker rooms, and dressing rooms, as well as housing, like college dorms, and social or spiritual groups. It also obstructs transgender people from accessing many gender-segregated social services, such as shelters for unhoused adults, substance use disorder treatment facilities, psychiatric hospitals, and support and therapy groups. In some cases, social services are only offered to one gender group, such as domestic violence shelters. When transgender people point out or challenge their exclusion from these spaces, it can be perceived as threatening to those who are included. This is perhaps most evident in domestic violence services and shelters that typically serve women, where transgender women, whose gender as a woman is called into question, are perceived as a risk to other women. Conversely, and somewhat ironically, transgender men are excluded based on their male gender identity but are not necessarily seen as a threat to women in the same way transgender women are. When transgender people point out their oppression, they are often viewed as the oppressor (Ahmed, 2017).

While the social injustices and oppression of excluding transgender people from all spaces is concerning, their exclusion and oppression from social services is a particularly significant concern for social workers and supervisors.

Cisgenderism exists and operates openly and unapologetically within society. Cisgenderism is ubiquitous in society and found in nearly every environment, such as gendered bathrooms, gendered dressing rooms, and gendered clothing, that is, "women's" clothes. It is common for domestic violence and sexual assault shelters and services to be for "women," and homeless shelters to be "men." Substance use treatment facilities are often sex-segregated, as are inpatient mental health services. It is also common for therapy groups within community health centers to be sex-segregated. Legal identification documents like driver's licenses and insurance cards have sex markers. Sex markers are often used to determine what services one is or is not eligible for. This is of particular relevance for social workers who are often positioned to determine what services clients qualify for, and where they can access those services.

Transgender theory and critical transgender theory can support supervisors and social workers in expanding their perspectives beyond the traditional lenses through which they practice. Rather than denying difference, transgender theory openly acknowledges that the lived experiences of transgender people differ from those of cisgender people (Breaux & Thyer, 2021). It is essential to reject the cisgenderist value system that permeates society, social work education, and practice, and to move beyond a cultural competency framework that often privileges and centers the cisgender perspective. This shift is necessary to equip social workers with the knowledge and skills needed to implement an anti-oppressive social work practice.

Whether supervising post-graduate associates in clinical practice or students in practicum placements and internships, supervisors play a critical role in helping supervisees develop the skills and confidence to address the social injustices their clients experience. Supervisors can utilize transgender theory, critical transgender theory, and de Vries' (2015) prism of intersectional oppression to help supervisees expand their understanding of how the oppression of transgender clients varies based on visibility and invisibility, compounded by intersectional oppression. This approach empowers supervisees to identify pathways for challenging the institutional barriers their clients face, including those within their own agencies and practices. Supporting supervisees to center their trans clients' worldview, depathologize transness, reject sanist views, and model clinical and practice skills where transgender clients live within the skin of the supervisees' theoretical approach to practice.

Modern Queer Theory

It is essential to distinguish between queer as a personal or social identity and queer within the framework of queer theory. For some, queer is used to reject normative taxonomies of sexual and gender identities and expressions, encompassing a wide range of people whose embodied identities and experiences exist outside the cisgender heterosexual paradigm. For others, queer serves as an umbrella term to simplify the lexicon of sexualities and expressions, such as LGBTQ. What makes queer appealing as an identity marker for many is its inherent ambiguity and resistance to clear definition. Although Cohen (2019) and Panfil (2019) argue that "queer" as a social identity is primarily linked to white Western culture, a review of academic and community-driven material shows that "queer" has been relevant to people of color throughout history.

Similar to its use as an identity marker, "queer" in queer theory is not clearly defined. In some factions of queer theory, "queer" refers broadly to anti-normativity, anti-binary, and anti-capitalist structures, exposing how normativity is a tool used to shape and maintain systems of control, with a focus on forms of oppression that seem normal or natural (Erol & Cuklanz, 2020; Grzanka, 2019; Somerville, 2020). In other factions, "queer" refers to how the construction of binary categories of sexuality and gender functions to diminish the complexity of the human experience to serve those in power (Wagaman et al., 2018). Grzanka (2019) contends that the subjective experiences of queer people are the uncontestable root of queer theory. In any case, Ryan (2020) points out that attempting to define queer theory exposes a misunderstanding of its core principles.

Queer theory developed out of the queer activist movement of the 1980s and 1990s, which emerged as a political response to the government's unwillingness to address the AIDS epidemic. Viewed as a disease that primarily affected gay men, the government regarded it as a moral issue, thereby paying little attention to the unfolding crisis. Queer activism challenged and destabilized the distinct categories of heterosexual/homosexual and man/woman, which protected and rewarded heterosexuals while relegating sexual and gender minorities as dispensable, as demonstrated by the government's refusal to acknowledge and take meaningful actions toward preventing the spread of AIDS.

With many of the early queer activists also being students and faculty new in their academic careers, activism began to take shape as a radical theoretical framework within the academy (Brown, 2016) that stressed compulsory heterosexuality was contrived and sustained to "imbue power over the population and the mechanisms of social control [discovering ways] normalcy operate[s] to construct which members of society become desirable or undesirable" (Greensmith, 2022, p. 405).

As queer theory evolved, activists sought to ensure safety and visibility in public for sexual minorities on their terms, while the more mainstream factions of the gay and lesbian community focused on their right to privacy (Brown, 2016). The former was interested in preserving their right to be anti-normative, anti-binary, and anti-capitalist, celebrating difference, whereas the latter focused their efforts on equality, buttressing their argument that gays and lesbians did not choose their sexuality. Coded within the anti-choice narrative was the message that queerness was so undesirable and fundamentally bad that no one would ever choose to be queer. Duggan (2002) described the anti-choice equality movement of assimilation of heteronormative values, customs, and family structures as homonormative. An example of the proliferation of homonormativity, Mulhall (2020) points to the *"It Gets Better"* campaign. The campaign focused on the "freedom, happiness, belonging, love, and ... marriage" that is found in "coming out" (p. 145). Mulhall (2020) described the campaign as a "hopeful, if politically naïve testament of faith in the power of coming out and the coming out narrative" (p. 145). Although the campaign became wildly popular, its homonormative message was shortsighted in that the life circumstances for white, middle-class, non-disabled, cisgender gay youth may get better, but for racialized, transgender and gender-nonconforming, undocumented, socially, politically, and economically disenfranchised youth, coming out was unlikely to make their life circumstances better and more likely to push them further to the margins, therefore further complicating their life (Mulhall, 2020). If early queer activists and theorists principally challenged heteronormativity, this newer wave equally opposed homonormativity in both its practices and rhetoric (Brown, 2016).

Perhaps apropos, there is no consensus on what queer theory is. Green (2002) argued that queer theory is not a theory at all. Rather, queer theory is a loosely bound set of critical standpoints (as cited in Ryan, 2020). Taking a more modern view of queer theory and how it is applied, Ryan (2020) found that queer theory is being used in three distinct ways: as a philosophical issue tied to discourse rooted in sexuality; by purists who seek to return to its historical material roots; and as a methodological approach that extends beyond the realm of sexuality.

Within these three strands, Ryan (2020) describes the first as the least commonly applied and the most recalcitrant, rejecting the criticism that it prioritizes the politics of anti-identity at the expense of material changes that could positively impact communities. Instead, this strand argues that material changes are less important than addressing the "philosophical underpinnings of categorical creation that led to material inequalities in the first place" (Ryan, 2020, p. 88). The second strand, perhaps the most common within the social sciences, upholds queer theory's critique of normativity and binary categories of identity, but unlike the first strand, acknowledges the material consequences of identity (Ryan, 2020). The third strand utilizes queer theory less as a philosophy and more as a methodological approach, focusing on queer theory's emphasis on deconstruction and anti-identity, allowing for application beyond the realm of sexuality and into other areas of scholarship (Ryan, 2020).

Modern queer theory holds that identity is not stagnant and can shift and fluctuate over time and experience, stressing the importance of discouraging the one-directional, linear model of identity (Wagaman et al., 2018). Moreover, modern queer theory emphasizes the importance of praxis. LeFrançois et al. (2022) define praxis as theory in action and the knowledge that it produces, transcending the artificial divide between theory and practice. While theory informs practice and supervision, an anti-oppressive practice emphasizes that theory without action, regardless of the communities served, perpetuates cycles of oppression.

However, despite its anti-binary and anti-normative values, queer theory has become "ironically exclusionary" (Grzanka, 2019, p. 7), often erasing the real-world oppressions of marginalized communities (Ryan, 2020). Now institutionalized and embedded within elite academia, queer theory has lost sight of the radical street activism and politics that once informed it, with much of what is now considered modern queer theory having been generated by elite, white, middle-class academics (Brown, 2016; Grzanka, 2019; Ryan, 2020; Shepard, 2010). With queer theory now rooted in academia rather than from within the community, Shepard (2010) questions how queer theory can claim to be community centered, noting that "it is easier ... to theorize about a problem than solve it" (p. 514). The ascent of queer theory into academia has stripped it from its community-informed and politically engaged roots. Social workers must engage directly with the communities they serve by centering their voices, experiences, and expertise to address issues of social injustice. To do otherwise would be to reenact the oppressive forces social workers aim to dismantle.

Reiterating the aforementioned concerns, some within social work argue that queer theory's academic focus has led to it becoming overly individualized (Webb, 2019) and ill-equipped to address the complex, interwoven challenges social workers face (Webb, 2019). Another concern within social work practice is that queer theory's critique of identity categories detracts from the needs of actual queer and trans communities (Webb, 2019). For example, Benavente and Gill-Peterson (2019) and Chaudhry (2019) point out that within certain strands of queer theory, transgender people are exceptionalized, depicted as figures of potentiality and expansiveness who subvert the binary gender system and are championed as the ultimate representation of queerness.

While queer theory problematizes the social constructs of binary thinking, it tends to oversimplify the complexity of the transgender experience, risking the erasure of transgender people by reducing gender to a performative social construct. This approach can negate the embodied knowledge of one's gender and obscure the perilous realities faced by transgender people at the intersection of multiple oppressions (Chaudhry, 2019; LeMaster & Stephenson, 2021; Nagoshi & Brzuzy, 2010; Stryker, 2004; Wagaman et al., 2018). This issue is perhaps best illustrated by a quote from a transgender person: "You have taken away the identity I worked all my life to build... who am I if you take [my gender] away?" (Kaufmann, 2010, p. 104).

This raises the question: has queer theory taken its critique of identity too far, focusing more on the discursive production of identities rather than on the actual lived experiences of individuals? While understanding the construction of identities is undeniably important, it is equally crucial to consider how individuals experience these realities, particularly those at the intersections of multiple forms of marginalization (Ryan, 2020).

Application to Social Work Practice

Cisnormative binary structures of identity are ubiquitous in society and permeate nearly every environment, such as gendered bathrooms and dressing rooms, and clothing categories, for example, "women's" clothes. Within social work practice, many services and programs are also organized according to cisnormative binary gender categories, such as intimate partner violence and sexual assault services and shelters, and homeless shelters designated for men. Similarly, other services are divided by assigned or assumed genders, such as "men's" and "women's" wings in mental health and substance use disorder treatment facilities. Legal identification documents like driver's licenses and insurance cards include binary sex markers of M or F, which are frequently used to determine eligibility for services, rather than one's gender identity. These cisnormative binary structures are of particular relevance for social workers, who are often responsible for determining which sexed services clients qualify for and where they can access those services.

By applying queer theory's rejection of binary structures and adhering to its roots in activism, social workers can effect change by advocating for policy reforms within their organizations and agencies. Specifically, instead of categorizing and assigning clients to services based on legal sex markers, they can allow clients to self-select services based on their gender identity. However, offering clients this autonomy alone may still result in the exclusion of transgender people. A more impactful change might be for social workers to advocate for the desegregation of services based on binary sex and gender categories entirely. By integrating queer theory with transgender theory, critical transgender theory, and de Vries' (2015) prism of intersectionality, and by being informed by the communities they serve, social workers can critically assess how to create spaces that move beyond cisnormative binary structures, making them more inclusive of queer and transgender communities. In doing so, social workers continue to develop and refine anti-oppressive social work practice and put theory into action. A combined theoretical approach such as this aligns with anti-oppressive social work praxis, recognizing that no single theory can adequately address the complex web of intersectional oppression.

Application to Supervision Practice

Social work has long been recognized for its commitment to serving clients and family systems, with a strong emphasis on research-informed practice. However, it is crucial to acknowledge that the field has faced criticism for perpetuating oppressive practices rooted in white supremacy, colonialism, and neoliberal perspectives (Maylea, 2020). Given that methodology is one of the primary ways queer theory is applied (Ryan, 2020), it is essential to critically examine social work's role in the production of knowledge, particularly in the context of its ongoing efforts to advance anti-oppressive practice.

The importance of research in social work education and practice is clearly articulated in both the Council on Social Work Education (CSWE) standards and the NASW Code of Ethics. Research is fundamental to social work, as it deepens our understanding of social phenomena, explores how clients experience their lives across various settings and circumstances, identifies interventions that best address the oppressive systems they encounter, and evaluates the effectiveness of those interventions. Despite this emphasis on research, social work programs at both the bachelor's and master's degree levels often leave students inadequately prepared to conduct research independently without supervision and mentorship. This highlights the significant role supervisors play not only in practice or clinical contexts, but also in research, where they frequently serve as mentors or lead investigators. Expanding our understanding of who a supervisor is and what a supervisor does benefits the field and practice of social work. In many ways, this broadened perspective can be seen as "queering" supervision.

Traditional variable-driven research methods significantly influence the questions researchers ask, even when attempting to capture the complexities of intersectionality (Ryan, 2020). Variables are inherently one-dimensional, creating fixed categories that are often applied additively. This approach fails to account for the experiences of individuals situated at the intersections of multiple forms of oppression, particularly those whose experiences cannot be neatly categorized (Grzanka, 2019).

Queer theory posits that identities can shift and fluctuate over time, with individuals embodying multiple identities at different times, some more salient than others. Variable-based research, however, tends to place identities and experiences into rigid categories that do not accurately reflect the complex, multidimensional lives of the communities social workers serve. One of the most salient criticisms of queer theory is its insufficient attention to how identity categories impact communities differently based on varying social identities. This critique is particularly relevant to transgender communities, who may feel that queer theory's assertion that gender is socially constructed overlooks the embodied knowledge transgender people have about their own lives.

In Grzanka (2019), queer of color critique theorist Lisa Bowleg provides a practical example of how queer theory can be applied in research. Rather than asking, "How do you experience discrimination as a woman? As a Black person? As a lesbian?" – a variable-driven, additive methodological approach – a queer methodological approach that captures intersectional oppression might ask, "Do you experience discrimination in [a specific environment]? If so, how?" (p. 9).

Supervisors mentoring emerging researchers – whether in master's or doctoral studies, or as junior or early career practitioners – can encourage the exploration of alternative methods to capture data using queer theory or queer methodologies. By moving away from additive, variable-based questions, they help push social work practice further toward an anti-oppressive praxis.

Empowerment Theory and Practice in Supervision

Empowerment theory in social work uses intervention methods to help guide people toward building autonomy and control in their lives. This theory recognizes that oppression primarily contributes to disempowerment experienced across several marginalized groups (Turner, 2017). Empowerment is integral to restorative (Mallon, 1999) and healing practices. Empowerment practice is a practice modality deserving of great understanding in social work and should be coupled with any and all types of interventions, restorative work, and social justice initiatives. Any practitioner holding the role of therapist, case worker, instructor, collaborator, investigator, facilitator, co-activist, ally, leader, and so on, has the positionality to enact and engage empowerment of people (Freire, 1973; Germain & Gitterman, 1995; Lee, 2001). Supervisory relationships must also be enacted and engaged through empowerment. Empowerment of supervisees facilitates empowerment of clients and communities through direct care work, and hopefully beyond. Empowerment practice concepts are widely taught in schools of social work and should be reiterated and reexamined through social work supervision. See Box 2.2.

Box 2.2 Practice Guidance. Dudley Street Neighborhood Initiative Boston

By Nathaniel L. Currie

Teaching community organizing, empowerment practice, and multi-system approach to equity, social justice, and liberation is a responsibility I hold in both my clinical practice with my supervisees – about six or seven each calendar year – and in my Social Work with Diverse Populations course at Clark Atlanta University – about thirty-five students across two sections each year – which is held each fall and is a required course for our two- and three-year program Master of Social Work (MSW) students. Social work is a profession aligned with case study, vignette, and experiential learning. When we cannot put practitioners or students in a real-life teaching scenario, we often depend on this modality to offer direct practice instruction and example.

The Dudley Street Neighborhood Initiative, or DSNI, is a nonprofit, community-run organization based in Roxbury, Massachusetts. It was founded in 1984 by residents of the Dudley Street Neighborhood, along with members of the Riley Foundation, as an effort to rebuild the poverty-stricken community surrounding then-Dudley Square (now Nubian Square). It is known as the first and only community-run grassroots organization to gain "the power of eminent domain" by the Boston Redevelopment Authority. DSNI is a community organizing and community planning group. It is not a developer, not a social service provider; however, the organization has created dozens of brand-new affordable homes for the community, has created and implemented community programming and empowerment initiatives, and demonstration, and solved a myriad of community problems (Holding Ground Productions, 2024).

The DSNI model organizes the entire community – including youth, elders, and all of the many ethnic groups – to be heard, to be active, and to lead. Formal leadership in the form of governance is determined by all community stakeholders. The organization's board is chosen by community vote, with key constituencies represented by allotted seats. In a very real sense, DSNI is an exercise in democracy, giving life to the notion that true power comes from the people (Holding Ground Productions, 2024), an empowerment practice example of *"nothing about us, without us."*

Whether your supervisory practice is direct clinical work, community work, or administration and leadership, it is important for anti-oppressive supervisory practice to lend practice guidance to all levels of social work – the micro, mezzo, and macro. The Dudley Street Neighborhood Initiative (DSNI, 2024) is a strong case study in community-based practice and community organizing that assists in shaping the worldview, sense of possibility, and linkage to all parts of social work practice for the supervisee. The media resource site has several activities and reflection questions to elicit learner participation and practice reflection. How might the Dudley Street Neighborhood Initiative and similar community-based practice examples strengthen your supervisory and leadership practice?

> **Media Resources:**
> Holding Ground Productions. (1996). *Holding ground: The rebirth of Dudley Street.*
> Holding Ground Productions. (2013). *Gaining ground: Building community on Dudley Street.*
>
> REFERENCES
> DSNI (2024). DSNI. Accessed September 1, 2024, www.dsni.org.
> Holding Ground Productions (2024). The DSNI Model. Accessed September 1, 2024, https://holdinggroundproductions.com/viewers-guide/background-dsni-dudley-street-neighborhood/the-dsni-model/.

Building Cultural Humility with Individuals of Different Foreign Experiences

Understanding Cultural Humility

Cultural humility is an essential framework for engaging meaningfully with individuals from diverse backgrounds, particularly those whose experiences are shaped by trauma, colonialism, and marginalization. This concept goes beyond traditional cultural competence, which often focuses on acquiring knowledge about different cultures. Instead, cultural humility emphasizes a lifelong commitment to self-reflection and personal growth, acknowledging that understanding others is an ongoing process that involves recognizing and addressing one's own biases and limitations (Lekas et al., 2019). Think critical self-reflection, critical consciousness, and biases topics covered in Chapters 1 and 2 of the text.

Examining Intersectionality within Cultural Humility

A fundamental step in developing cultural humility is an introspective examination of one's own intersectionality. Intersectionality, as defined by Crenshaw (2017), is the interconnected nature of social categorizations such as race, class, and gender, which create overlapping and interdependent systems of discrimination or disadvantage. Recognizing how these aspects of one's identity interact with systems of power and privilege is crucial. For instance, an individual from a socioeconomically privileged background may find it challenging to fully understand the experiences of those from marginalized communities. This is because their own experiences have been shaped by different socioeconomic factors that afford them certain advantages and access to resources that others may not have (Crenshaw, 2017). Crenshaw (2017) persists that if there is no framework to understand a person's problem, then it will be challenging to even see the problem's existence. Understanding one's own and other people's intersectionality is a foundational step to approach cultural humility in clinical work. You can find more on the concept of intersectionality in the Sloan et al. (2018) text.

Cultivating Empathy and Cultural Curiosity

Developing cultural humility also involves cultivating a sense of empathy and cultural curiosity. Cultural curiosity refers to the genuine interest in learning about and understanding the lived experiences of people from different backgrounds. This involves actively seeking to learn about cultural practices, historical contexts, and social challenges faced by individuals from foreign experiences (Lekas et al., 2019). For example, engaging with individuals from post colonial societies or regions affected by conflict requires an openness to learning about their specific historical and sociopolitical contexts. This understanding helps in appreciating the complex layers of their experiences, which cannot be fully understood through a one-size-fits-all approach or assumed or superficial knowledge (Fischbach, 2020).

Empathy is a key component in this process. It involves not only recognizing the hardships faced by others but also deeply understanding their emotional and psychological impacts. Empathy is enhanced when practitioners take the time to listen actively and engage with individuals' stories without making assumptions or drawing premature conclusions. For example, working with refugees from conflict zones necessitates an empathetic approach that acknowledges their trauma and displacement experiences, which are shaped by a complex interplay of historical and personal factors. This understanding goes beyond merely acknowledging their pain; it involves validating their experiences and providing support that is sensitive to their unique contexts (Perreira & Ornelas, 2013).

Clinical social work supervision practice is a prime location for new and experienced clinicians to explore cultural humility both within their direct practice and within their personal lives. Intentional discussion within the supervisory session on the topic of cultural humility has potential benefits of strengthening the practitioner's overall awareness and mindfulness of diversity and interwoven cultures into practice, as well as the ability to link several of the important concepts described in this text and their overlapping functions, including empathy, critical reflectivity, critical self-reflection, critical consciousness, and empowerment practice.

De-Centering Oneself

Another critical aspect of cultural humility is decentering oneself. This means recognizing that one's perspective is not universal and that there is a need to make space for others to share their experiences. This is a highly important process for social work practice and aligns with multiple clinical modalities. In practice, this involves creating environments where individuals from marginalized backgrounds feel valued and heard – think safe and brave spaces. This can be achieved by adopting practices that prioritize the voices and experiences of those who are often overlooked or marginalized. For instance, in clinical settings, this could mean adjusting treatment approaches to better align with the cultural and personal backgrounds of patients, rather than applying a one-size-fits-all model that may not account for their unique needs (Lekas et al., 2019).

Committing to Ongoing Education

Cultural humility involves a commitment to continuous education and self-improvement. Practitioners should engage in continuous learning about different cultures and the specific challenges faced by various communities. This can be achieved through professional development opportunities, such as workshops, seminars, and courses focused on cultural competence and humility. It also includes staying informed about current events and changes in social and political climates that impact marginalized communities. This commitment to lifelong learning helps practitioners remain responsive to the evolving needs of those they serve and fosters a more inclusive and empathetic practice (Crenshaw, 2017). A commitment to continuing education is also a social work value that should be discussed in social work education and social work supervision. It is grounded in an ethical principle articulated in the *NASW Code of Ethics*: "*Social workers practice within their area of competence and develop and enhance their professional expertise.*" Continuing education, in addition to being in line with the demands of cultural humility practice, also further provides the practitioner with the opportunity to acquire new and necessary information and demonstrate a conscious, self-directed and continuous effort toward personal and professional development (National Association of Social Workers, 2023).

Addressing Power Imbalances

Incorporating cultural humility into practice also requires addressing power imbalances that exist within professional relationships and which have been discussed across the chapters of this text. Recognizing and challenging power dynamics is essential for building equitable and respectful interactions. For example, in therapeutic or clinical settings, practitioners must be aware of how their own positionality might influence their interactions with clients. This awareness helps to ensure that clients from marginalized backgrounds are not further disempowered or invalidated. Instead, practitioners should work toward creating a partnership where clients' perspectives and experiences are respected and integrated into the support they receive (Fischbach, 2020).

Building cultural humility with individuals from diverse backgrounds involves a multifaceted approach that includes self-reflection, empathy, cultural curiosity, and an ongoing commitment to learning. By examining one's own intersectionality, practitioners can better understand how their experiences influence their interactions with others. Cultivating cultural curiosity and empathy allows for a deeper appreciation of the unique experiences of individuals from foreign contexts. De-centering oneself and addressing power imbalances further contribute to creating a more inclusive and respectful practice. Ultimately, cultural humility is about recognizing and valuing the rich diversity of experiences and perspectives that individuals bring to the table, and continuously working toward understanding and supporting them in a meaningful and respectful manner.

Summary

In this chapter, we have discussed multiple anti-oppressive and liberative lenses and their application to clinical social work supervision and leadership practice. This chapter covers the use of language and narrative in AOP, multiple practice theories and areas of study that support or enhance AOP, the use of empowerment and cultural humility approaches, and the highly functional use of clinical supervision as a center for this work. Looking forward, how do frameworks such as DEIPAR and CRT strengthen the areas covered in this chapter?

Reflection Questions

1. How might you begin to challenge yourself with your language in social work practice? What are some of the benefits of strength-based or language neutrality in social work practice and leadership?
2. Is your current practice centered in cultural humility? In what ways might you embed or enhance this area of practice today?

Note

1 The U.S. Census first utilized the term Hispanic to collect data on the population in the US in the 1970s. Hispanic defines a group of people in the US from or descending from colonized Spanish-speaking countries in Latin America, the Caribbean, or Spain. The term Hispanic is used interchangeably with Latina/o/x. However, the term Latina/o/x, introduced in the US Census in 2000, emphasizes the community's origins in Latin America, focusing on culture rather than language. This writer will utilize the term Latina/o/x to describe the community as it acknowledges the Indigenous ancestral roots of North, Central, and South Latin America, the Caribbean, and Africa (Gutiérrez, M and Lechuga-Peña, 2022). Latine: pronounced [luh-teen-ae]. Of or relating to people of Latin American origin or descent, living in the United States. Latine is a gender-inclusive term to define Latine individuals. [See text Glossary.]

REFERENCES

Agger, B. (1976). On happiness and the damaged life. In J. O'Neill (Ed.), *On critical theory* (pp. 12–33). The Seabury Press.
Ahmed, S. (2017). An affinity of hammers. In *Trap Door: Trans cultural production and the politics of visibility* (pp. 221–234). Essay, MIT.
American Psychiatric Association. (1980). *Diagnostic and statistical manual of mental disorders: DSM III*. APA.
 (1994). *Diagnostic and statistical manual of mental disorders: DSM IV*. APA.
 (2013). *Diagnostic and statistical manual of mental disorders: DSM-5*. APA.
 (2022). *Diagnostic and statistical manual of mental disorders: DSM-5-TR*. APA.
Asante, M. K. (2003). *Afrocentricity: The theory of social change* (1st ed.). African American Images.
Austin, A., Craig, S. L., Dentato, M. P., Roseman, S., & McInroy, L. (2019). Elucidating transgender students' experiences of microaggressions in social work programs: Next steps for creating inclusive educational contexts. *Social Work Education*, *38*(7), 908–924. https://doi.org/10.1080/02615479.2019.1575956

Babits, M. (2001). Using therapeutic metaphor to provide a holding environment: The inner edge of possibility. *Clinical Social Work Journal, 29*(1), 21–33.

Baines, D., & Sharma, A. (2022). Anti-oppressive practice theory. In *Critical social work praxis* (pp. 118–127). Essay, Fernwood.

Baldino, N. (2021). Living in the skin of a theory. *TSQ: Transgender Studies Quarterly, 8*(3), 283–297. https://doi.org/10.1215/23289252-9008961

Barsky, A. (2018, September 2). Ethics Alive! Cultural Competence, Awareness, Sensitivity, Humility, and Responsiveness: What's the Difference? *The New Social Worker Magazine*. Retrieved January 17, 2024, from www.socialworker.com/feature-articles/ethics-articles/ethics-alive-cultural-competence-awareness-sensitivity-humility-responsiveness/

Beckett, C. (2003). The language of siege: Military metaphors in the spoken language of social work. *The British Journal of Social Work, 33*(5), 625–639.

Beemyn, G. (2020, December 29). Transgender history in the United States – UMass. A special unabridged version of a book chapter from *Trans Bodies, Trans Selves*, edited by Laura Erickson-Schroth. Retrieved November 5, 2022, from www.umass.edu/stonewall/sites/default/files/Infoforandabout/transpeople/genny_beemyn_transgender_history_in_the_united_states.pdf

Benavente, G., & Gill-Peterson, J. (2019). The promise of trans critique. *GLQ: A Journal of Lesbian and Gay Studies, 25*(1), 23–28. https://doi.org/10.1215/10642684-7275222

Bettcher, T. M. (2014). Trapped in the wrong theory: Rethinking trans oppression and resistance. *Signs: Journal of Women in Culture and Society, 39*(2), 383–406. https://doi.org/10.1086/673088

Boeynaems, A., Burgers, C., Konijn, E. A., & Steen, G. J. (2017). The effects of metaphorical framing on political persuasion: A systematic literature review. *Metaphor & Symbol, 32*(2), 118–134.

Bragg, J. E., Nay, E. D., Miller-Cribbs, J., & Munoz, R. T. (2019). Implementing a graduate social work course concerning practice with sexual and gender minority populations. *Journal of Gay & Lesbian Social Services, 32*(1), 115–131. https://doi.org/10.1080/10538720.2019.1654425

Breaux, H. P., & Thyer, B. A. (2021). Transgender theory for contemporary social work practice: A question of values and ethics. *Journal of Social Work Values and Ethics, 18*(1), 72–89. https://doi.org/10.55521/10-018-109

Brown, G. (2016). Queer movement. In *The Ashgate research companion to lesbian and gay activism* (pp. 73–86). Routledge.

Burghardt, M. (2011). The human bottom of non-human things: On critical theory and its contributions to critical disability studies. *Critical Disability Discourses, 3*. https://doi.org/10.25071/1918-6215.31560

Chaudhry, V. V. (2019). Centering the "evil twin." *GLQ: A Journal of Lesbian and Gay Studies, 25*(1), 45–50. https://doi.org/10.1215/10642684-7275278

Cohen, C. (2019). The radical potential of queer? Twenty years later. *GLQ: A Journal of Lesbian and Gay Studies, 25*(1), 140–144. https://muse.jhu.edu/article/712687

Colvin, A. (2013). Building culturally competent social work field practicum students through the integration of Campinha-Bacote's cultural competence healthcare model. *Field Educator, 3*(1), 1–13.

Crenshaw, K. W. (2017). Race, reform, and retrenchment: Transformation and legitimation in antidiscrimination law. In M. McCann (Ed.) *Law and social movements* (pp. 475–531). Routledge.

Cummins, L. K., & Sevel, J. A. (2018). *Social work skills for beginning direct practice: Text, workbook, and multimedia interactive case studies*. Pearson.

David, E. J. R. (2014). *Internalized oppression: The psychology of marginalized groups*. Springer.

Davis, A., & Mirick, R. G. (2021). Microaggressions in social work education: learning from BSW students' experiences. *Journal of Social Work Education, 58*(3), 431–448. https://doi.org/10.1080/10437797.2021.1885542

Delgado, R., & Stefancic, J. (2012). *Critical race theory: An introduction* (2nd ed.). New York University Press.

Dentato, M. P., Craig, S. L., Lloyd, M. R., Kelly, B. L., Wright, C., & Austin, A. (2016). Homophobia within schools of social work: The critical need for affirming classroom settings and effective preparation for service with the LGBTQ community. *Social Work Education, 35*(6), 672–692. https://doi.org/10.1080/02615479.2016.1150452

Derezotes, D. S. (2014). *Multicultural aspects of counseling and psychotherapy: Transforming historical trauma through dialogue*. Sage.

Duckworth, S. (2020, November 12). *Spin the wheel of power & privilege [marginalization & intersectionality]*. This is How You Can. www.thisishowyoucan.com/post/__wheel_of_power_and_privilege

Duggan, L. (2002). The new homonormativity. In R. Castronovo & D. D. Nelson (Eds.) *Materializing democracy* (pp. 175–194). Duke University Press. https://doi.org/10.1215/9780822383901-007

Ellison, T., Green, K. M., Richardson, M., & Snorton, C. R. (2017). We got issues. *TSQ: Transgender Studies Quarterly, 4*(2), 162–169. https://doi.org/10.1215/23289252-3814949

Erol, A., & Cuklanz, L. (2020). Queer theory and feminist methods: A review. *Investigaciones Feministas, 11*(2), 211–220. https://doi.org/10.5209/infe.66476

Evans, E. (2019). Transforming theory: Innovations in critical trans studies. *Paragraph, 42*(2), 255–268. https://doi.org/10.3366/para.2019.0302

Falender, C. A., & Shafranske, E. P. (2004). *Clinical supervision: A competency-based approach*. American Psychological Association.

(2017). Groundwork and rationale. In C. A. Falender & E. P. Shafranske (Eds.), *Supervision essentials for the practice of competency-based supervision* (pp. 3–16). American Psychological Association.

Fischbach, M. (2020). *Black power and Palestine: Transnational struggles for racial justice*. Cambridge University Press.

Follmer, K. B., Miller, M. J., & Beatty, J. E. (2024). Requesting mental illness workplace accommodations: The roles of perceived need and stigma.

Equality, Diversity and Inclusion: An International Journal, 43(7), 1070–1092.
Free Black Thought. (2022, August 30). Six unsettling features of DEI in K-12. *Journal of Free Black Thought.* https://freeblackthought.substack.com/p/six-unsettling-features-of-dei-in
Freire, P. (1973). By learning they can teach. *Convergence, 6*(1), 78–84.
George, D. (2019). Disabling transgender: Identity-politics navigating mentalism and law. *Journal of Ethics in Mental Health, 10*(VI), 1–8. https://doi.org/ https://www.jemh.ca/issue-vi
Germain, C. B., & Gitterman, A. (1995). *The life model of social work practice: Advances in theory and practice* (1st ed.). Columbia University Press.
Gil, D. (1998). *Confronting injustice and oppression: Concepts and strategies for social workers.* Columbia University Press.
Giroux, H. A. (2023). Critical theory and education practice. In *The critical pedagogy reader* (pp. 50–74).
Gonçalves, I. (2023). Promoting hate speech by dehumanizing metaphors of immigration. *Journalism Practice, 18*(2), 265–282.
Goode, R. W., Cowell, M., McMillan, D., Van Deinse, T., & Cooper-Lewter, C. (2020). Preparing social workers to confront social injustice and oppression: Evaluating the role of social work education. *Social Work, 66*(1), 39–48. https://doi.org/10.1093/sw/swaa018
Gosselin, A. (2022). Responding to Sanist microaggressions with acts of epistemic resistance. *Hypatia, 37*(2), 293–314. https://doi.org/10.1017/hyp.2022.9
Grzanka, P. R. (2019). *Queer theory.* Sage Research Methods Foundations. https://doi.org/http://dx.doi.org/10.4135/9781526421036
Gutiérrez, M., & Lechuga-Peña, S. (2022). Latina/o/x critical race theory (LatCrit) in social work praxis: A tool to dismantle racism and build racial equity. *Advances in Social Work, 22*(2), 605–627.
Hall, M. C. (2019). Critical disability theory. In *The Stanford encyclopedia of philosophy* (Winter 2019 Edition).
Hardy, M. A. (2024). Poverty metaphors: An autoethnography in three parts. *Qualitative Social Work, 23*(1), 145–164. https://doi.org/10.1177/14733250231206801
Hart, C. (2023). Frames, framing and framing effects in cognitive CDA. *Discourse Studies, 25*(2), 247–258.
Hoff, D., & Camacho, E. (2019). Social Work Students' Knowledge of and Attitudes towards Working with Transgender Clients. Electronic Theses, Projects, and Dissertations. 830. https://scholarworks.lib.csusb.edu/etd/830
Huber, L. P., Lopez, C. B., Malagon, M. C., Velez, V., & Solorzano, D. G. (2008). Getting beyond the 'symptom,' acknowledging the 'disease': Theorizing racist nativism. *Contemporary Justice Review: Issues in Criminal, Social, and Restorative Justice, 11*(1), 39–51.
Jaekel, K. S., & Holmes, M. B. (2019, April 18). (Trans)gressing faculty development: empowering faculty to support trans (*) college students through a conceptual model for emancipatory education. *Thresholds in Education,*

42(1), 74–88. https://academyedstudies.files.wordpress.com/2019/11/th42_1jaekelholmesfinal.pdf
Kaufmann, J. (2010). Trans-representation. *Qualitative Inquiry, 16*(2), 104–115. https://doi.org/10.1177/1077800409350699
Kia, H., MacKinnon, K. R., & Coulombe, A. (2021). Where is the "T"? centering trans experiences in social work curricula addressing LGBTQ+ issues. *Journal of Social Work Education, 59*(1), 104–118. https://doi.org/10.1080/10437797.2021.1969302
Kia, H., MacKinnon, K. R., & Göncü, K. (2022). Harnessing the lived experience of transgender and gender diverse people as practice knowledge in social work: A standpoint analysis. *Affilia*, 088610992211420. https://doi.org/10.1177/08861099221142040
Kiehne, E. (2016). Latino critical perspective in social work. *Social Work, 61*(2), 119–126.
Krell, E. C. (2017). Is transmisogyny killing trans women of color? *Transgender Studies Quarterly, 4*(2), 226–242. https://doi.org/10.1215/23289252-3815033
Kulkarni, M. (2022). Hiding but hoping to be found: workplace disclosure dilemmas of individuals with hidden disabilities. *Equality, Diversity and Inclusion: An International Journal, 41*(3), 491–507.
Lakoff, G. (2004). *Don't think of an elephant: Know your values and frame the debate*. Chelsea Green Publishing.
(2006). Conceptual metaphor: The contemporary theory of metaphor. In D. Geeraerts (Ed.), *Cognitive linguistics: Basic readings* (pp. 185–238). De Gruyter.
Lakoff, G., & Johnson, M. (1980). *Metaphors we live by*. University of Chicago Press.
Lee, J. A. (2001). *The empowerment approach to social work practice*. Columbia University Press.
LeFrançois, B. A., Macias, T., & Shaikh, S. S. (2022). Critical social work praxis. An introduction. In *Critical social work praxis* (pp. 1–10). Essay, Fernwood.
Lekas, H.-M., Pahl, K., & Lewis, C. F. (2019). Rethinking cultural competence: Shifting to cultural humility. *Journal of Health Care for the Poor and Underserved, 30*(1), 1–10. https://doi.org/10.1353/hpu.2019.0001
LeMaster, B., & Stephenson, M. (2021). Trans (gender) trouble. *Communication and Critical/Cultural Studies, 18*(2), 190–195. https://doi.org/https://doi.org/10.1080/14791420.2021.1907851
Lindsay, S., Fuentes, K., Ragunathan, S., Lamaj, L., & Dyson, J. (2023). Ableism within health care professions: A systematic review of the experiences and impact of discrimination against health care providers with disabilities. *Disability and Rehabilitation, 45*(17), 2715–2731.
Mack, J. B. (1994). The role of the canon in Western education. *Hitotsubashi Journal of Social Studies, 26*(1), 7–16. www.jstor.org/stable/43294350
Magner, T., & Pineau, M. G. (2018). Highlighting shared humanity and prosperity to advance immigration solutions. *Stanford Social Innovation Review*.

May 15, 2018, https://ssir.org/articles/entry/highlighting_shared_humanity_and_prosperity_to_advance_immigration_solution
Mallon, G. P. (1999). Knowledge for practice with transgendered persons. *Journal of Gay & Lesbian Social Services, 10*(3–4), 1–18.
Martin, Elmer P., & Martin, J. M. *Spirituality and the Black helping tradition in social work.* National Association of Social Workers, 2002.
Marrow, E. (2023). "I hope that as our selection becomes more accurate, the number ... will be very few": The creation of assessment criteria for gender-affirming care, 1960s–1980s. *Psychology of Sexual Orientation and Gender Diversity, 11*(2), 183–201. https://doi.org/10.1037/sgd0000633
Marsh, G. (2011). Trust, testimony, and prejudice in the credibility economy. *Hypatia, 26*(2), 280–293. https://doi.org/10.1111/j.1527-2001.2010.01152.x
Maylea, C. (2020). The end of social work. *British Journal of Social Work, 51*, 772–789. https://doi.org/10.1093/bjsw/bcaa203
McCarty-Caplan, D. (2018). LGBT-competence in social work education: The relationship of school contexts to student sexual minority competence. *Journal of Homosexuality, 65*(1), 19–41. https://doi.org/10.1080/00918369.2017.1310547
(2022). Transgender-competence in social work education: The relationship of school contexts to student affirmation of gender expansive people. *Journal of Homosexuality, 69*(3), 525–543. https://doi.org/10.1080/00918369.2020.1826833
Morgan, K. P. (1996). Describing the emperor's new clothes: Three myths of educational (in)equity. In *The gender question in education: Theory, pedagogy, & politics* (pp. 105–122). Westview Press. Used in AWIS' intersectionality fact sheet at www.awis.org/intersectionality/
Morgaine, K. L., & Capous-Desyllas, M. J. (2014). *Anti-oppressive social work practice: Putting theory into action.* Sage.
Mulhall, A. (2020) Queer narrative. In *The Cambridge companion to queer studies* (pp. 142–155). Essay, Cambridge University Press.
Nagoshi, J. L., & Brzuzy, S. (2010). Transgender theory: Embodying research and practice. *Affilia, 25*(4), 431–443. https://doi.org/10.1177/0886109910384068
Nagoshi, J. L., Nagoshi, C. T., & Pillai, V. K. (2023). Transgender theory revisited: Current applications to transgender issues. *Current Opinion in Psychology, 49*, 101546. https://doi.org/10.1016/j.copsyc.2022.101546
National Association of Social Workers. (2023). NASW code of ethics. Retrieved August 15, 2024, from www.socialworkers.org/About/Ethics/Code-of-Ethics/Code-of-Ethics-English
Panfil, V. R. (2019). "nobody don't really know what that mean": Understandings of "queer among urban LGBTQ young people of color. *Journal of Homosexuality, 67*(12), 1713–1735. https://doi.org/10.1080/00918369.2019.1613855
Parlakian, R. (2001). *Look, listen, and learn: Reflective supervision and relationship-based work.* ZERO TO THREE.

Payne, M. (2020). *Modern social work theory* (5th ed.). Bloomsbury.
Perreira, K. M., & Ornelas, I. J. (2013). Painful passages: Traumatic experiences and post-traumatic stress among immigrant Latino adolescents and their primary caregivers. *Journal of Immigrant and Minority Health*, *15*(2), 275–283. https://doi.org/10.1007/s10903-012-9669-6
Pilcher, J., & Whelehan, I. (2004). *50 key concepts in gender studies*. Sage.
Reamer, F. G. (2009, February). Boundaries in supervision. *Social Work Today*, *9*(1). Retrieved July 23, 2024, from www.socialworktoday.com/archive/EoEJanFeb09.shtml
Roen, K. (2001). Transgender theory and embodiment: The risk of racial marginalisation. *Journal of Gender Studies*, *10*(3), 253–263. https://doi.org/10.1080/09589230120086467
Rofuth, T. W., & Piepenbring, J. M. (2020). *Management and leadership in social work: A competency-based approach*. Springer.
Ryan, J. M. (2020). Queer theory. In *Companion to sexuality studies theoretical and methodological diversity* (1st ed., pp. 79–94). Essay, Wiley-Blackwell.
Schiele, J. H. (2010). *Social welfare policy: Regulation and resistance among people of color*. Sage.
——— (2017). The Afrocentric paradigm in social work: A historical perspective and future outlook. *Journal of Human Behavior in the Social Environment*, *27*(1–2), 15–26.
Shelton, J., Kroehle, K., & Andia, M. M. (2019). The trans person is not the problem: Brave spaces and structural competence as educative tools for trans justice in social work. *The Journal of Sociology and Social Welfare*, *46*(4), 97–123. https://doi.org/10.15453/0191-5096.4356
Shepard, B. (2010). Bridging the divide between queer theory sage and anarchism. *Sexualities*, *13*(4), 511–527. https://doi.org/10.1177/1363460710370656
Sloan, L., Joyner, M., Stakeman, C., & Schmitz, C. (2018). *Critical multiculturalism and intersectionality in a complex world*. Oxford University Press.
Solórzano, D., & Delgado Bernal, D. (2001). Examining transformational resistance through a critical race and LatCrit theory framework. *Urban Education*, *36*(3), 308–342. https://doi.org/10.1177/0042085901363002
Somerville, S. B. (2020). *The Cambridge companion to queer studies*. Cambridge University Press.
Spade, D. (2015). *Normal life: Administrative violence, critical trans politics, and the limits of law* (2nd ed.). Duke University Press.
Stryker, S. (2004). Transgender studies: Queer theory's evil twin. *GLQ: A Journal of Lesbian and Gay Studies*, *10*(2), 212–215. https://doi.org/10.1215/10642684-10-2-212
——— (2017). *Transgender history: The roots of today's revolution* (2nd ed.). Seal Press.
Swan, E. (2023). To be accountable: The whiteness of feminist organisation studies. *Organization*, *30*(6), 1195–1201. https://doi.org/10.1177/13505084231189913

Tervalon, M., & Murray-García, J. (1998). Cultural humility versus cultural competence: A critical distinction in defining physician training outcomes in multicultural education. *Journal of Health Care for the Poor and Underserved, 9*(2), 117–125.

Thibodeau, P. H., & Boroditsky, L. (2011). Metaphors we think with: The role of metaphor in reasoning. *PLoS ONE, 6*(2), e16782.

Tosh, J. (2017). Gender non-conformity or psychiatric non-compliance? How organized non-compliance can offer a future without psychiatry. In *Critical inquiries for social justice in mental health* (pp. 255–282). Essay, University of Toronto Press.

Turner, F. J. (2017). Empowerment approach to social work treatment. In F. J. Turner (Ed.), *Social work treatment: Interlocking theoretical approaches* (6th ed., pp. 142–165). Oxford University Press.

US Census Bureau (2023). QuickFacts. www.census.gov/quickfacts/fact/table/US/RHI725222

Valencia, R. R. (2008). *Chicano students and the courts: The Mexican American legal struggle for educational equality.* New York University Press.

Villalpando, O. (2004). Practical considerations of critical race theory and Latino critical theory for Latino college students. *New Directions for Student Services, 2004*(105), 41–50.

Vojak, C. (2009). Choosing language: Social service framing and social justice. *British Journal of Social Work, 39*(5), 936–949.

de Vries, K. M. (2015). Transgender people of color at the center: Conceptualizing a new intersectional model. *Ethnicities, 15*(1), 3–27. https://doi.org/10.1177/1468796814547058

Wagaman, M. A., Shelton, J., & Carter, R. (2018). Queering the social work classroom: Strategies for increasing the inclusion of LGBTQ persons and experiences. *Journal of Teaching in Social Work, 38*(2), 166–182. https://doi.org/10.1080/08841233.2018.1430093

Webb, S. (2019). *The Routledge handbook of critical social work.* Taylor & Francis. https://bookshelf.vitalsource.com/books/9781351264389 (pp. 424–434).

Willey-Sthapit, C., Jen, S., Storer, H. L., & Benson, O. G. (2022). Discursive decisions: Signposts to guide the use of critical discourse analysis in social work. *Qualitative Social Work, 21*(1), 129–146.

Wright, D. E. (2022). Black males' plight to breathe in America – Black racial injustice. *Reflections: Narratives of Professional Helping, 28*(2), 82–86. Retrieved from https://reflectionsnarrativesofprofessionalhelping.org/index.php/Reflections/article/view/1912

FURTHER READING

Balva, D., Mandas, P., & Sacco-Bene, C. (2023). Re-envisioning multiculturalism: Promoting and applying disability competencies within clinical supervision. In K. Wilson & S. Chao (Eds.), *Facilitating social justice, service delivery, and advocacy through multicultural counseling competencies* (pp. 1–23). IGI Global.

Campbell, Fiona Kumari. (2001). Inciting legal fictions: Disability's date with ontology and the Ableist body of the law. *Griffith Law Review, 10*(1), 42–62.

Gossett, R., Burton, J., & Stanley, E. A. (Eds.). (2017). *Trap door: Trans cultural production and the politics of visibility.* MIT Press.

Hicks, S., & Jeyasingham, D. (2024). Sexuality, LQBTQ issues and critical social work thinking with queer and post-queer theories thinking with queer and post-queer theories. In *The Routledge handbook of international critical social work new perspectives and agendas* (pp. 561–575). Essay, Routledge.

Keegan, C. M. (2020). Against queer theory. *TSQ: Transgender Studies Quarterly, 7*(3), 349–353. https://doi.org/10.1215/23289252-8552978

Martino, W., & Omercajic, K. (2021). A trans pedagogy of refusal: Interrogating cisgenderism, the limits of antinormativity and trans necropolitics. *Pedagogy, Culture and Society, 29*(5), 679–694. https://doi.org/10.1080/14681366.2021.1912155

Namaste, V. (2000). *Invisible lives: The erasure of transsexual and transgendered people.* University of Chicago Press.

Namaste, V. K. (2011). *Sex change, social change: Reflections on identity, institutions, and Imperialism* (2nd ed.). Women's Press.

National Association of Social Work (2021). *2021 Revisions to the NASW Code of Ethics. 2021 Amendments Code of Ethics.* socialworkers.org.

National Association of Social Work and Association of Social Work Boards (2013). *Best practices for social work supervision.* NASW Standards in Social Work Supervision (socialworkers.org).

Noe-Bustamante, L., Mora, L., & Lopez, M. H. (2020). About one-in-four US Hispanics have heard of Latinx, but just 3 percent use it. Pew Research Center, 11, www.pewresearch.org/hispanic/2020/08/11/about-one-in-four-u-s-hispanics-have-heard-of-latinx-but-just-3-use-it/.

[Dr. Gerry L. White]. (2021, June 23). *Afrocentric Perspective Lecture by Drs White and Wright CAUWMYJSSW* [Video]. YouTube. www.youtube.com/watch?v=J4Zp2eIVR8Y

Winship, J. (2002). *Social Work Department.* Infusing Spirituality and Religion into Social Work Practice. www.nacsw.org/AudioConf/042902Handouts.htm

Wright, E. D., Jones, K., White, G., Harper, R., & Alhassan, M. (2018). *School of social work handbook.* Clark Atlanta University.

CHAPTER 3

DEIPAR (dee-per) *Supervision*
Leadership and Power-Sharing

Jacqueline T. Dyer

What Is the DEIPAR Framework?

What is the DEIPAR Framework? The DEIPAR Framework, an acronym created by this author, was developed for the Doctor of Social Work (DSW) program at Simmons University School of Social Work. It is an organizing framework designed to help those wanting to incorporate social justice into their work to do so more effectively. DEIPAR is an acronym for the social justice principles of diversity, equity, inclusion, intersectionality, power analysis, and antiracism, which will be discussed in detail later. These are six principles that help to create a solid social justice foundation for a given context and the people within it, when applied to the assessment and related decisions. Why these principles? Attention to DEI (diversity, equity, and inclusion) has been the lens used to generate corrective social justice efforts for populations negatively impacted by social oppression across academic and other organizations. Attempts to address diversity, equity, and inclusion remain incomplete if they do not also attend to intersectional struggles and power dynamics. The framework will be discussed, after its principles have been defined, in relation to power imbalance and power-sharing in supervision.

Application of the DEIPAR Framework

Within the framework, the order of the letters in the acronym provides a basic order for how to unpack the social justice concerns in a given situation. It is a framework, not a theory, that uses the acronym letters to organize the flow of one's thinking about the social justice concerns in a given situation. Understanding the principles of DEIPAR helps one to analyze the situation being considered. The analysis must account for both the people and the environmental issues in the situation. The analysis is a relatively simple interrogation asking, *"What are the social justice themes that can be identified concerning* ...?" (Dyer & Gushwa, 2024). This question is asked for each of the principles in turn, and in relation to the people and the environment. The acronym DEIPAR represents an organizational framing for what principle to consider next after the first one is interrogated. After the complete assessment has been made of the situation, it will be easier to determine what decisions and actions will be needed to facilitate positive and socially just changes in the situation. Those changes can be implemented progressively and strategically.

The interrogation of the situation does not need to follow precisely the order of the acronym letters. For example, you can begin by asking, what are the social justice themes that can be identified concerning *diversity* for the people and for the environment in this situation? Then you can ask, what are the social justice themes that can be identified concerning *power* for the people and for the environment in this situation? It is possible that the person doing the assessment might not be able to answer the questions for some of the principles until after they have responded to the interrogation for the rest. In other words, the person can assess *diversity* and *power* first, in relation to the people and the environment, and only after assessing using these principles can they begin to identify responses for an interrogation of *intersectionality* and *inclusion*. It is possible that once an interrogation has been completed for all the principles, other social justice themes might also be identified.

A Word about Anti-Blackness

The acronym DEIPAR requires incorporation of an antiracism analysis into the situational assessment as separate from that of diversity. This is because racism and anti-Black racism cannot be absorbed into discussions of diversity. In working to dismantle racism, the special case of anti-Black racism must be considered for those whose diversity, equity, and inclusion are being considered. When racism is not identified, it remains invisible, and "the denial of racism, more so than mere avoidance of race, may be particularly pernicious in perpetuating anti-Blackness" (Yi et al., 2023, p. 13). *Anti-Blackness* has been defined as a nonstop denial of humanity and dismissive contempt for the lives and well-being of Black people (Bledsoe & Wright, 2019; Liu et al., 2023; Moore-Lobban, 2023; Wilcox et al., 2024a). National wealth and power were built through the dehumanizing and savage oppression of enslaved Africans, who were treated as property and who were abused and killed through the forcible extraction of their labor (Rowell-Cunsolo et al., 2022, p. 2).

Anti-Black racism is a manifestation of anti-Blackness. Anti-Blackness is connected to having darker skin color, so it affects Black and Brown people more pointedly (Frank et al., 2010). And though it has been characterized as *racism*, interactional biases that specifically arise in relation to Black and Brown people are representations of anti-Blackness. Examples of this include general perceptions of the emotional expressions of Black people as being angry, or the persistent trope of the "angry" Black woman. The term *anti-Blackness* has been used interchangeably with the term *anti-Black racism* (Moore-Lobban, 2023). However, the dehumanization of the people, *anti-Blackness*, is the disease (Thomas & Bucholzt, 2021) that drives the madness and violence of *anti-Black racism*. The perpetuation of the trauma of anti-Black racism is detrimental to the health and well-being of Black people (Kerney et al., 2024; Liu et al., 2023). The discussion of racism and anti-Black racism will be expanded in the related principle later.

Diversity

The literature of diversity discusses the topic from every aspect of human and social presentation, making research findings difficult to synthesize (Bernstein et al., 2020; Harrison & Klein, 2007; LaRue et al., 2023). Diversity is simply about difference, but this refers to variations among the members of a given community, whether that is organizational or more expansive. The literature about diversity is able to identify the categories for which the term is a descriptor, but notes that the concept itself is not clearly defined (Daya, 2014; Harrison & Klein, 2007; Wood et al., 2023). Not having a clear definition of the concept raises the question for me, the author, about whether that resulted from the term being developed by people of one particular group – dominators (hooks, 2009) – or invaders, as they strove to understand and define those different, and possibly less valued, from themselves.

The Council on Social Work Education identifies categories of diversity to include, but not be limited to, "age, caste, class, color, culture, disability and ability, ethnicity, gender, gender identity and expression, generational status, immigration status, legal status, marital status, political ideology, race, nationality, religion and spirituality, sex, sexual orientation, and tribal sovereign status" (CSWE, 2022, p. 9). However, it is the context that makes any of the differences identified. For example, in the workplace, the difference may be within the previously noted demographics among the personnel, or perhaps variations in the skills they bring to, or functions they serve, in the organization (Behnke et al., 2022). Within any community generally, some differences are visible while others are not (Daya, 2014).

The reasons for pursuit of diversity seem to fall into two groupings: "justice- and performance-based" (Brennan, 2023, p. 434). Justice-based diversity efforts aim to create a balanced and representative distribution of all demographic categories. The performance-based efforts utilize diversity for the beneficial generativity known to emerge from varied contributions (Brennan, 2023; Johnson et al., 2024).

Equity

Equity is generally about fairness but moves a bit more beyond just being fair. This is because it is also necessary to "infuse questions of power, privilege, oppression, and culture into our understanding and expectations … to move toward equity" (Mak & Therriault, 2022, p. 60). Though the term is used by some as interchangeable with the term equality, the two terms refer to different things (Johnson et al., 2024). Equality is about making sure that all parties involved in any given situation are treated exactly the same way. The problem with this is that it can perpetuate inequality (Suarez-Balcazar et al., 2023). For example, if any of the parties in the situation do not have the exact same measures of resources, opportunities, or agency as the others, then when everyone is given additional measures that are equally distributed across the parties, the inequities remain unchanged. However, if those with less are given enough additional measures to create equality with all the other parties, that is equity. Equity is the step beyond equality. It is counterintuitive that to create equity, those with less need to be given more rather than everyone being given the same things equally, but doing so facilitates justice.

Inclusion

Inclusion is literally just that – being welcomed or woven into something, being made a part of something, being made to feel like you belong – and its definition varies within research (Cano, 2020; Daya, 2014). It is a kind of expansion on diversity. Diversity tends to be used as a term that calls attention to difference and, relatedly, to the lack of or the need to increase differences. However, that increase does not necessarily focus on how the differences are incorporated into the whole. Inclusion represents that next step that accounts for the quality of incorporating differences. Inclusion moves the needle of difference from merely being added as represented ingredients, by moving toward the justice of creating the "soup" of authentic integration (Behnke et al., 2022; Bernstein et al., 2020). Inclusive integration is one which helps people to feel supported, "validated, accepted and appreciated" (Cano, 2020; Daya, 2014, p. 296).

Of note in the comparison of diversity and inclusion, it can be considered that inclusion is the step beyond diversity. Diversity is a necessary early step that gathers different people together, along the categories noted in that earlier discussion. However, being present does not guarantee respectful or genuine interactions wherein one does not feel the need to alter their personal presentation to navigate the group dynamics. Inclusion becomes the needed step beyond diversity that takes action and generates strategies to facilitate changes in the environment as well as the interactions, to enable people to feel and know they belong where they have landed.

Intersectionality

The term *intersectionality* was coined by Kimberlé Crenshaw (1989) though the conception of it emerged out of feminist theory within the Black and Chicana communities (Almeida et al, 2019). In the origin of the term, it explicated the relationship between gender and race for Black women. It is a pragmatic and still evolving approach to analyzing an issue, a heuristic, and it is also a way of identifying human presentation through a social justice lens (Carbado et al., 2013).

> It requires the analysis of systemic power, privilege, oppression, and social location to be used in understanding multiple identities. Most importantly it is constantly occupied with how the paradigm of dominance and subjugation is being created through knowledge building and acquisition (Almeida et al., 2019, p. 152).

In considering the ways intersectionality is applied, Moradi & Grzanka (2017) advocate for its "responsible stewardship" because of its increasing popularity. This is an important addition to discourses of intersectionality because, as references to intersectionality continue to increase, the likelihood of its dilution also becomes an increased possibility. Anecdotally, I have heard the term used to represent linear connections not related to its Black feminist, social justice origins. Moradi and Grzanka note that such stewardship respects and stays true to the origins of the concept of intersectionality while expanding its application to new contexts. For example, they note that in an analysis of power systems, it "is critical not only to understanding experiences of oppression and marginalization, but also to making visible experiences of privilege" (p. 501). Also, as the discourses relating to intersectionality continue to evolve, the conversants cannot leave Black women behind in the narratives of intersectionality. Doing so would not be true to its origins and would belie the lived experiences of Black women at a racialized and gendered nexus that is rife with additional layers of stigma, discrimination, and oppression (Carbado et al., 2013; Mattsson, 2014; Moradi & Grzanka, 2017).

Power Analysis

Power, like other social justice terms discussed in this chapter, is a thing for which descriptions can be provided, even while the concept itself remains unclear (Karim, 2023). That being the case, a set of descriptions is provided later. It is helpful, for a power analysis, to begin with a basic definition and understanding of the dynamics of power. Power is simply ability; the ability to influence others whether or not they choose to cooperate (Dyer & Flores-Carter, 2024). It changes from one context to another, wherein an individual may find themselves having more or less power (Dyer & Flores-Carter, 2024). It may be seen through decision-making activities or unseen because of efforts unfolding behind closed doors (Gaventa, 2006; Pansardi & Bindi, 2021). Though power has been conflated with dominance, they are separate concepts (Dunbar & Burgoon, 2005). Power can be dormant or undiscovered, whereas dominance is active and is something exerted (Dunbar & Burgoon, 2005).

These descriptions of power also give an understanding of its dynamics. Power is relational and unfolds interactionally, whether between two people, among members of a group, or between groups. While power is differential between parties in a given context, someone with lesser power in that context may nonetheless not be completely powerless (Dunbar & Burgoon, 2005). Power is also associated with action and responsibility, in that having power leads to action- and responsibility-taking for those who have or increase power (Galinsky et al., 2003). The manifestation of power in colonial contexts is also racialized – referred to as the coloniality of power by Quijano (Udah, 2021). It is shaped by colonizers who create "institutions to control and manage colonized populations" and who utilize "an epistemological perspective that legitimizes this form of power and control" (Udah, 2021, p. 87). These collective perspectives are important for understanding the complexities and nuances that can influence the relationship between supervisors and those they supervise. Additional aspects of power will be discussed later in this chapter.

Power analysis is an assessment of the factors and dynamics of power unfolding in a given context. The analysis includes knowledge of who has power over or with whom, under what circumstances, and the racialized complexities. There will be other issues related to power, as noted earlier, that would also need to be identified. For example, you should explore whether there is evidence to indicate that unseen players are influencing outcomes, and identify who those players might be, as well as how their influences can be shifted as needed. All these factors can facilitate clarification of what kinds of decisions and actions would be most beneficial for creating desired changes.

Antiracism

In this chapter, antiracism is equated with efforts that must also include *anti-Black* antiracism strategies. However, before discussing anti-Black racism and its relationship to racism, I will discuss racism. Racism is the belief that one people-group is superior to another, which is an outgrowth of colonialism, discussed later. It is pervasively practiced systemically, structurally, and institutionally. These levels are somewhat difficult to define because the words are used interchangeably across the related literature and research (Feagin, 2006; Jones, 2002; Lopez-Littleton et al., 2023).

Systemic racism is predicated upon white supremacist perspectives that have been woven into every aspect of society and are designed to disadvantage People of Color (Feagin, 2006; Galvan & Payne, 2024; Jones, 2002). These perspectives shape the detrimental treatment of People of Color in any context. *Structural* racism is the incorporation of these perspectives of dominance and subordination based on skin color that generate inequitable treatment into the design of policies, laws, and all levels of governing bodies. The inequities generated by societal governance and functions make it difficult to pinpoint the sources of injustice (Jones, 2002). *Institutional* racism negatively affects access to almost all domains of the social determinants of health – education, housing, economics/income, healthcare, environment (Jones, 2002; Rodgers, 2024).

Racism is a traumatizing form of oppression that denies access to equal power and well-being to People of Color and negatively affects their physical and mental health (Pieterse et al., 2023). Racism requires *races* against which to discriminate, and *race* is a created social construct. Race is "the outcome of the racialization process . . . associated with practices such as conquest and colonization, enslavement, peonage, indentured servitude, and, more recently, colonial and neocolonial labor immigration" (Bonilla-Silva, 1997, p. 471). Moreover, race as understood in modern times is directly connected to the colonization of what is now called the United States (Quijano, 2000). "As time went by, the colonizers codified the phenotypic trait of the colonized as color, and they assumed it as the emblematic characteristic of racial category" (Quijano, 2000, p. 534).

Within this colonial context, the concepts of domination and subordination in relation to race became normalized (Maldonado-Torres, 2007). Additionally, lighter skin color was closer to being human (Maldonado-Torres, 2007), considering the white-skinned dominator as being definitively human. This made room for dehumanization to enter into the treatment of those with darker skin color – the darker the skin, the worse was the treatment. Under coloniality, the dynamics of war are normalized, and "killability and rapeability" are acceptable for a "dispensable population" (Maldonado-Torres, 2007, p. 255). Within these dynamics of coloniality, the dehumanization of Black people, *anti-Blackness*, and anti-Black racism become solidified. Maldonado-Torres equated colonization with war, noting the acts and attributes of war: rape and murder, being unprotected, and being penalized for assumed acts.

The greed-stained anti-Black brutality that began with the Portuguese in 1444 was spread by England, France, Spain, and the Netherlands (de Sousa, 2021), and eventually took its worst form in the US. Each of these colonizers has done their best to minimize or erase their savagery from history. For instance, the remains of 158 enslaved Africans were found in a mass grave used as a trash dump from the fifteenth to seventeenth century in Lagos, Portugal (Ferreira et al., 2019; de Sousa, 2021). Most were "buried without care," and some were still tied up at the time of death (Ferreira et al., 2019). The reason suggested for the carelessness of their burial was that they died before being baptized (Ferreira et al., 2019), after having been enslaved and bound, and so were not considered human or deserving of a proper burial. The bodies of 158 African humans were treated like trash by their colonizers, and six centuries later, their found remains are still being treated like trash by the inheritors of that colonial past. The remains were relegated to a storage facility, then ignored except as research objects (de Sousa, 2021). African people became identified as Blacks under the auspices of colonization and, almost 600 years later, have remained unceasingly subjected to a state of war.

Within the US, as within other nations with a history of colonization, those with darker skin tend to experience worse outcomes when considering the social determinants of health (Rowell-Cunsolo et al., 2022). Within the US, the crime of anti-Black racism results in over 80,000 annually preventable deaths and a four-times higher rate of Black maternal deaths compared to that for white women (Rowell-Cunsolo et al., 2022). As noted earlier, anti-Black racism is the malevolent result of the dehumanization of anti-Blackness. The importance of addressing anti-Blackness when initiating acts of antiracism, rather than whitewashing it in the nonspecific vastness of diversity, is that anti-Blackness is an emphatically vicious and long-enduring form of racism. All racism is not the same, and within the US, People of Color have differential experiences of racism (Liu et al., 2023). As such, when working to dismantle racism in the US, "contexts must begin with rupturing anti-Black racism if we are to further facilitate liberatory possibilities for Black and nonBlack communities of Color" (Liu et al., 2023, p. 245).

Antiracism, then, requires actively working to end all forms of racism, with a particular understanding of the need to end anti-Black racism. Antiracism work requires building a vocabulary of terms such as those described earlier in this section: systemic racism, structural racism, institutional racism, anti-Black racism, and white supremacy. Lopez-Littleton et al. (2023) advocate, in their ADORE Model for dismantling anti-Black racism, for acknowledging the damage caused by the perniciousness of anti-Black racism, for the normalization of Blackness in all its variations, and for the need for community responsibility in making and implementing the changes required to dismantle anti-Black racism. They state that truth-telling is needed to build community, and that lack of a solid knowledge of anti-Black racism will hinder efforts at community building (Lopez-Littleton et al., 2023). Antiracism efforts are daily activities that require noticing and intentionally counteracting the dynamics and harms of racialization and its attendant "isms."

Supervision and Leadership

Supervision is an ongoing standard interaction between colleagues in the same or related professions, where a colleague of higher rank monitors and assesses the professional development of a colleague of lower rank (Peters & Luke, 2021). The colleague of higher rank is usually termed the supervisor, and the one of lower rank, the supervisee. Supervision helps to shape professional identity and confidence, provides professional support, builds professional skills, and maintains a gatekeeping function (Berger & Quiros, 2014; Peters & Luke, 2021; Wade, 2023).

Supervision is a form of intervention informed by a variety of models, which may include being technique- and theory-based, process-based, or some combination thereof (Peters et al., 2022; Susman-Stillman et al., 2020). Process-based supervision can include helping the supervisee develop awareness, empathy, compassion, and reflective capability (Susman-Stillman et al., 2020). Process-type supervision is flexible, shifts focus as needed, and is able to generate strong relationships in the supervisor/supervisee dyad (Peters et al., 2022; Susman-Stillman et al., 2020). The supervisor may have one supervisee or may provide oversight to a group of colleagues. To help the supervisee grow professionally, the supervisor maintains and models appropriate professional boundaries and a safe learning relationship (Berger & Quiros, 2014).

If power is ability, leadership is the way that ability is used. Leadership is relational. One is identified as a leader in relation to the perception of others (Klasmeier et al., 2022). While previously leadership was identified with management and position, it has increasingly become identified with "the ability to and cultivate change" (Haworth et al., 2018, p. 9). Different models of leadership exist and are associated with the styles of interaction that one who leads tends to utilize. These styles or approaches to leadership are not discrete – like power, there is fluidity in leadership, and the same person may utilize different styles at different times. Leadership and supervision overlap notably regarding oversight of subordinates. Both are relational, both have the power to influence their subordinates' professional development, and are engaged in "setting goals, making plans, and providing feedback" (Klasmeier et al., 2022, p. 411). This influence sometimes impacts the subordinates' personal behaviors, whether the supervisor's oversight is positive or abusive. Interestingly, one of the times that supervision is clearly identified as leadership is in the literature about "destructive leadership" (Emmerling et al., 2023; Gauglitz et al., 2023; Rice et al., 2020). Abusive or destructive leadership is one of the manifestations of a relationally unbalanced use of power.

The fluidity of leadership and power contributes to its complexity. Some leadership styles may be charismatic and distributed or democratic; less so, several forms of leadership are characterized as moral forms: ethical, authentic, servant (Emmerling et al., 2023; Haworth et al., 2018; Keenan et al., 2019). No single model of leadership is encouraged within the profession of social work (Haworth et al., 2018). That noted, social workers do tend to incorporate practices that lean toward a social justice style of leadership, including, "challenging injustices and seeking to change mindsets, [being a] conduit for change, and ... organizing relationships and resources" (Keenan et al., 2019, p. 498–499). Social justice leadership and supervision will be discussed later in this chapter.

Issues of Power in Supervision

Social workers have an ambivalent and unexamined relationship with power. Many state a desire to "empower" their clients and communities without reconciling that ambivalence and without examining the perspective inherent in identifying themselves as those who empower others. Wanting to empower others holds a colonizing rescuer or savior assumption that benefits the service provider more than the service recipient. Power can be used for good or ill, and that can occur by the same person, because there is no true binary of being *all good* or *all bad* within the human context. For example, a social worker who removes a child from a neglectful or abusive home may struggle to reconcile being the cause of any trauma experienced by the child through a sudden removal from a familiar environment. Another example is the internal conflict a social worker experiences after causing an unexpected negative impact on one community area following successful advocacy for a different concern. Good acts, even when implemented well, can also have negative outcomes.

A social work supervisor who does not reconcile any internal ambivalence to power can develop unbalanced ways of using power, especially in a supervisory relationship. Those imbalances can manifest as abusive supervision. "Individual-level abusive supervision refers to the leader's sustained display of hostile verbal or nonverbal behaviors toward a particular team member" (Farh & Chen, 2014, p. 1176). Abusive supervision has been described as a form of aggression (Emmerling et al., 2023). These behaviors toward supervisees include humiliation, anger, hostile verbal and nonverbal interactions, intimidation, disrespect, unethical interactions, yelling, coercion, and other similar behaviors (Klasmeier et al., 2022; Rice et al., 2020; Simard & Parent-Lamarche, 2022). The impact on the supervisee of abusive supervision includes feeling inferior and second-guessing oneself, mental stress, feeling excluded and unworthy, and wanting to quit (Farh & Chen, 2014; Hoogh, 2021; Rice et al., 2020). Another manifestation of power imbalance is failure to attend to issues of culture and ethnic difference and not utilizing cultural humility.

Attention to ethnoracial differences in supervision is often overlooked, and expectations for using and teaching culturally informed supervisory approaches for practitioners and clients are unclear (Imeri & Jones, 2022; Willey & Magee, 2018). The problem when these themes are present is twofold. One set of issues is that the power dynamics become racialized. The other is that the attendant supervisor behavior and power dynamics resemble those of abusive supervisors. Racialized power dynamics can be both subtle and overt. The subtle dynamics can include side-stepping ethnoracial discussions and invalidating ethnoracial or cultural experiences (Imeri & Jones, 2022; Wilcox et al., 2024b). The more overt behaviors include undeniable microaggressions toward supervisees and placing blame for experiences of oppression on ethnoracial clients (Wilcox et al., 2024b). Other behaviors include "hostile, derogatory, or negative racial slights and insults" (Wilcox et al., 2024b, p. 273). These kinds of harmful behaviors can silence supervisees, hinder their professional development, and reflect the dynamics that can occur when the supervisor is white. Explicitly valuing diversity and cultural humility, building critical ethnoracial awareness, and attending to the dynamics evident in the power differentials of the supervisory relationship are the responsibilities of a good supervisor (Borders, 2014; Gaspard-St. Cyr, 2023; Hall, 2018; Wilcox et al., 2024b; Willey and Magee, 2018).

The Special Case of Supervisors of Color

When the supervisor is a person of color and the supervisee is white, ethnoracial differences still play a role that creates a power imbalance. However, that imbalance negatively impacts the supervisor. This reality may be a surprising revelation to some, while merely being a confirmation for others – especially if the supervisor is Black and female. Such supervisors may find themselves on the receiving end of racist remarks, challenges to their competence and authority, and/or sexist dynamics. In a study by Hall (2018), one participant stated that "White supervisees demand that I nurture them before they will accept constructive feedback during supervision" (p. 7). Supervisors found themselves having to be hyper-prepared for their supervisory encounters, yet experienced "murmuring and allegations" when holding their supervisees accountable for their professional role and behavior (p. 11). These same participants learned that their white counterparts did not encounter any similar behaviors. While this information comes from only one study, it reflects the anecdotal experiences of this author and others I know.

Social Justice Supervision

Incorporation of a social justice perspective into supervision can counter power imbalances. There are several supervisory models that incorporate social justice into supervision (Dollarhide et al., 2021; Peters & Luke, 2021; Peters et al., 2022). This kind of incorporation needs to be explicitly specified because social justice is not clearly defined and tends to be identified as encompassing other concepts (Furman, 2012). Dollarhide et al. (2021) consider social justice to be the "awareness of systemic oppression plus commitment to social action" that accounts for equitable resources for clients as well (p. 104). Furman (2012) identifies several variations of social justice, one of which is cultural justice, which seems to be closest to what one can consider encompasses social justice leadership/supervision: "cultural justice means the absence of both cultural domination and 'non-recognition' of cultural groups, and associational justice refers to the full participation of marginalized groups in decisions that affect their lives" (p. 193). Understanding these conceptions of social justice, and beyond, is needed to develop a perspective for social justice supervision.

To be socially just, supervision also needs to account for the stresses and attune to the well-being of the supervisee. This includes restoring a sense of vibrancy when job stress and possible compassion fatigue arise, but also helping them to develop as leaders (Wade, 2023; Wallbank & Woods, 2012). A reflective praxis should be incorporated to facilitate a transformative process. Furman (2012) considers praxis an integral part of social justice leadership. Praxis is an ongoing cycle of action–reflection–revised action, where the revisions improve upon the prior cycle of actions. Praxis enables the supervisor to learn from their own mistakes or to reflect on the outcomes of actions based on new learning, to create sustained socially just behavior. Socially just supervision is action-oriented, as noted earlier, and in that it involves teaching and an accountability process; it must remain interactive and relational; and it deconstructs theory, assumptions, and behavior (Dollarhide et al., 2021; Peters & Luke, 2021; Peters et al., 2022). Notably, a socially just supervisor analyzes the colonial power and superior/subordinate dynamics across the triad of supervisor–supervisee–

client interactions to build critical, liberatory awareness and growth (Liu et al., 2023; Mapara, 2022; Peters et al., 2022).

Supervision and Power-Sharing

A social justice supervisory perspective is foundational to developing a process of power-sharing within the supervisory relationship. By traditional definition, the relationship is hierarchical. In that hierarchy, all the power flows unidirectionally from the supervisor in the superior position to the supervisee in the subordinate position. We do not often consider the embedded coloniality in the terminology of supervision, but let us reflect for a moment on the term *supervisor*. Broken down into its Latin root words: *super* means *above, beyond*, or *over*, and *visor* means *look* or *see* (Etymonline.com). There is, in the unexamined traditions of "the prevailing White, middle-class American paradigms" (Peters et al., 2022, p. 106), a colonial dynamic in the relationship that mimics that of the benevolent overseer. Supervisors may resist challenges from the supervisee that cause them to rethink their perspectives, underlying assumptions, or biases – which is especially true when the supervisee is not a member of the dominator culture: "supervisees of color experienced more culturally unresponsive supervision than their White peers" (Wilcox et al., 2024b). The lofty positions held by supervisors create opportunities for potential damage to their supervisees when they do not examine the hierarchical distance and its inherent power imbalance.

This imbalance can begin to be corrected by analyzing the need for change using the DEIPAR social justice lens. Power-sharing decisions can be implemented as a result of the changes suggested or demanded by that analysis. Begin with identifying the social justice issues that affect the supervisee connected to diversity, and the issues of diversity in the organization. Organizational diversity issues, whether positive or negative, impact the environment in which the supervisee functions and, in turn, affect the supervisee. There needs to be an assessment of the environmental dynamics and also the interpersonal diversity dynamics that seem to be present in the supervisory interactions – for person and environment. Once identified, it is important to make decisions about what changes are needed. The assessment continues with the issues connected to the principles of equity, intersectionality, inclusion, and racism, with a pointed exploration of anti-Black racism, on both the individual and environmental levels.

It is important to note, again, that anti-Black racism is connected to dark skin color. The darker the skin tone, the more likely the person will be impacted by anti-Black racism. While we know that within the US the worst forms of this occur with African Americans, we forget that, regardless of ethnicity, the darker a person's dark skin color, the more they will also be negatively affected by anti-Black racism. Exploring anti-Black racism with someone who has dark skin color but is not African American adds nuances to the discussions of ethnicity and culture in the intersectionality analysis. All the principles need to be part of the full analysis of the dynamics that are affecting the quality of the supervisory relationship, the supervisee's ability to feel included and thrive within the organization, and the supervisee–client interactions.

The issues of power are assessed similarly to the other social justice principles, with one notable difference. None of these areas are assessed without input from the supervisor. The supervisor will need to do the full assessment with the supervisee. They will need to unfold their examination over a series of conversations that enable them to take a deeper collective look at the experiences of the supervisee in the environment, and how those have affected their work. By developing ongoing and open discussions of power in the relationship and facilitating supervisee input, the supervisor is engaging in power-sharing (Cook et al., 2018). The information about the quality of the supervisee's interactions and how the supervisee is affected by issues of diversity, intersectionality, inclusion, equity, and racism must come directly from the supervisee. The discussion about supervisory dynamics needs to include an equitable exchange of experiences with the supervisee. Moreover, the supervisor will need to invite the supervisee to comment on assumptions and biases that have emerged in the supervisory interactions and in theory application and skill development discussions.

Power-sharing is one of the ways that the supervisory team can decolonize the supervisory process. They may also want to decolonize the language of that process, including the language that identifies the roles of each participant in the relationship. The fact that one member of the relationship has more experience than the other or others in the group may create an inherent hierarchy (Cook et al., 2018). However, that hierarchy can be defined more by the qualities of a mentoring relationship than by one based in power and unexamined colonial supremacism. While there needs to be greater equity in the conversations, it is the role of the supervisor to attempt to facilitate this. It is also incumbent upon the supervisor to model power-sharing with the supervisee and help the supervisee learn to do the same with their clients (Hall, 2018). This process is also infused with cultural humility, and the supervisor works to address any internal resistances to bias challenges that the supervisee may bring. The greater responsibility for shifting power imbalances and sharing power in the supervisory relationship lies with the supervisor. However, it is beneficial work – for the nature of the supervisory relationship, the quality of supervisee–client interactions that improve service outcomes for clients, and the future of the profession.

Summary

This chapter has covered the tenets and principles of the DEIPAR framework with an in-depth focus on power analysis and power-sharing, and the importance of understanding these concepts in the application of anti-oppressive clinical supervision, agency, and community leadership. Supervisors and leaders have a special responsibility to embed new and innovative methods of practice and leadership to the greatest of their ability and toward collective liberation. Take some time to reflect on this chapter and strategies to find ways you can utilize and incorporate the knowledge and skills you have gained into your direct practice or social work instruction. See Box 3.1.

Reflective Questions

1. In considering the application of the DEIPAR framework to your supervisory context, what changes would you need to make?
2. What elements of colonialism can you identify in your supervisory process?
3. What ways do the application of the DEIPAR framework facilitate decolonizing your supervisory process, inclusive of language/nomenclature changes?

Box 3.1 Case Vignette. DEIPAR in Community Practice

by Gisela Martinez and Jacqueline T. Dyer

United for Families, UFF, is a small community-based health organization located in a suburban community outside a large metropolis. UFF serves low-income families and provides various services, including outpatient mental health treatment. Over the past eight years, UFF's therapists have observed a change in the demographic of one particular population served: the Latine [1] population. UFF has historically served US-born Mexican Americans, Puerto

Ricans, and a few Central American families, providing services in English and Spanish. Recently, however, Spanish-speaking immigrant families from Central America and South America comprise the largest population seeking services. In addition to the changing population, UFF staff report that families seeking services present a new range of clinical issues, including complex migration trauma histories, family separation, family reunification, legal concerns, and acculturation stressors.

To operate the outpatient mental health program, UFF continuously seeks external funding sources. The funding ensures the program's livelihood and opportunities for staff clinical training. Funders are more likely to support mental health programs that utilize evidence-based modalities. Therefore, UFF is intentional in its efforts to secure funding for staff training on evidence-based trauma modalities. Recently, UFF was awarded a grant to train its staff to use an evidence-based trauma modality. The trainer was a US-born white [2] American, and the trauma modality was not explicitly developed to serve Latine families. However, the UFF mental health administrator believes the training will reflect favorably on the organization and significantly enhance the staff's clinical skills in family trauma treatment.

The UFF mental health team is led by Dianne Gonzalez, who serves as both the clinical supervisor and the mental health administrator. Dianne has worked at UFF for 15 years, first as a clinician for eight years before being promoted to clinical supervisor. As a clinical supervisor, Dianne meets individually with all clinicians, holds weekly staff meetings, and provides as-needed clinical support. As the mental health administrator, Dianne has the additional responsibilities of managing the entire mental health clinic and of securing and managing funding. Dianne is the daughter of Mexican immigrants and is a white-skinned US-born Latine who has acculturated to, and internalized, the dominator culture. Due to her upbringing, she is committed to the Latine community, but she cannot relate to the experiences of recently arrived Latine immigrant families. Although she does not speak Spanish and no longer provides direct care as a clinical supervisor, Dianne believes that, based on her cultural upbringing and professional experience, she understands the needs of the Latine population seeking services. In a concerted effort to support the team's commitment to cultural competence, she prepares talking points, facilitates discussions, and oversees cases needing special attention to issues of cultural diversity.

Dianne's clinical team of eight clinicians comprises diverse social workers who provide individual and family therapy. Six of the team members are bilingual, and two only speak English. Their ages vary from mid twenties to late fifties. Dianne is younger than one of her team members. However, Karin, who has now been with the team for four years, and who was the last added team member, is also the youngest team member. Except for Karin, the eight-person team has been together for a total of eight years. The two English-only speakers are part of the founding team. The ethnic composition of the team members is as follows: a Jamaican immigrant; an Ethiopian American; un Chicano, y una Puertorriqueña; three are Centroamerianos – dos from El Salvador, and uno from Guatemala; and Karin es una inmigrante Colombiana Negra.

As the clinician who is the most recent arrival to the United States, Karin offers a unique and valuable perspective as a Latine immigrant. She has the highest Spanish fluency, mastery of clinical terminology, and prior work experience as a social worker in Colombia. Karin relates to the acculturation issues Latine immigrant families face, as she continues to struggle to understand American cultural norms and social expectations. Due to her knowledge, fluency, and perspective, Karin's value to the clinical team is well known.

After receiving the evidence-based trauma modality training, Karin was uncertain about how applicable the modality was for the young Latine immigrant population she serves. Karin experienced some success in implementing specific interventions but also significant challenges in maintaining fidelity to the model. She believes the modality fails to recognize or address cultural differences in Latine immigrant families, including familial expectations and roles. Karin observed this as a pattern and felt uneasy continuing to utilize the modality without modifications. Her discomfort reached a tipping point when, during a family session, a recently arrived Salvadoran family she had been working with before utilizing the modality became visibly agitated. The family requested a break, during which they stated that they felt she was attacking them and "forcing them to change who they are" to be effective parents. This was a change in their response to her working with them since beginning the modality. Karin validated their feelings and attempted to reengage, but the family refused to continue the session. The following day, she arrived at work and received a message from the family requesting to end services with her. Karin was devastated by the news, frustrated with herself for not following her clinical intuition, and frustrated with UFF and Dianne for pressuring her to use the modality with all families without adjusting it to suit their needs.

Karin contacted Dianne and requested a meeting to discuss the situation. During the meeting, she described how the situation unfolded and addressed her concerns about the modality. Dianne was attentive, validated her feelings, and focused her attention on decreasing Karin's level of personal blame for the session's outcome. Dianne stressed the value of utilizing an evidence-based modality to support families with complex trauma histories and attributed Karin's challenges to her limited experience with the modality. She asked Karin to follow up with the family to attempt re-engagement and to normalize the discomfort they experienced as part of the therapeutic process. She emphasized that Karin should utilize her therapeutic rapport to aid the family to move past the incident. To address the issue further, Dianne asked her to present the case during the next meeting so the clinical team could discuss the matter. Karin leaves the meeting feeling invalidated because she believes Dianne is solely focusing on the need to have fidelity to the modality. As an immigrant, Karin believes the family's concerns are valid. She has observed how the clinical lens utilized throughout the modality reflects the Western, individualistic, goal-oriented, time-specific, content-based, white American (Mullan, 2023), all-or-nothing, either–or culture. As she worked exclusively with Latine families, Karin did not understand how UFF could have endorsed the use of the modality with this population without having explored and provided additional clinical supports addressing the cultural differences of the populations served. Dianne had advocated for this modality and is invested in its use in the program. She is unable to see the harm in the modality's assumptions (hooks, 2009).

Two days later, the clinical team gathered for a staff meeting with Karin's presentation as the most important item on the agenda. Karin shared the specifics of the incident and focused on how invalidated, attacked, and alienated the family felt as a result of the intervention. She concluded that maintaining fidelity to the model was compromising her ability to support the family's right to self-determination and that the model was invalidating to Latine culture family values. As facilitator, Dianne thanked Karin for presenting and validated her experience. Before allowing others to share feedback or reflections, Dianne shared her clinical perspective. While acknowledging that culture could impact how families responded to clinical treatment, Dianne stated dismissively that it was inappropriate and potentially harmful to generalize about the culture of an entire community based on one clinician's experience with a family. To engage the team, Dianne asked clinicians to share examples of how their personal or professional experiences as immigrants demonstrated how not everyone in the same culture has the same experiences. As clinicians shared their experiences, the discussion shifted away from analyzing the shortcomings of the modality's use with Latine families to a discussion about the importance of addressing families based on their expressed needs, not cultural presentation. Dianne concluded the session by stating the challenges faced by the team over the next few months would reflect the "growing pains" of clinical implementation. She stressed that time and practice would be the most important elements in achieving confidence and success with the model. She also informed the team she would follow up with the consultant to seek support around implementation issues with diverse populations.

Following the meeting, Karin felt unsure of herself. She viewed Dianne, her clinical supervisor who was a social worker with over 15 years of experience, as knowledgeable. Moreover, Dianne's message about the modality had been clear: it was credible, appropriate, valid, and valuable. As a less experienced clinician, Karin knew she was still learning and benefited from the experience and clinical wisdom of experienced clinicians. Consequently, she began to doubt how valid her concerns were. She began to contemplate the possibility that she had prematurely attributed her challenges to culture without exploring other factors.

REFLECTIVE QUESTIONS

1. How do Karin's experiences as an immigrant reflect use of self in her approach to implementing the modality?
2. What elements of colonization are present in Dianne's interaction with her team and framing of the modality?
3. How should clinicians integrate a socially just (DEIPAR) cultural approach into ethically appropriate clinical practice?
4. What representations of power imbalance are reflected in this case presentation meeting?
   a. How can the imbalance be shifted toward power-sharing?
   b. What would it look like within the supervisory engagement individually and for the group?
   c. What socially just corrective actions aligning with a DEIPAR framework analysis could the supervisor take to counteract the harm she visited upon Karin?

Note

1 Latine: pronounced [luh-teen-ae] Of or relating to people of Latin American origin or descent living in the United States. Latine is a gender-inclusive term to define Latine individuals. [See text Glossary.]
2 Use of lowercase "w" in white deconstructs conscious and unconscious normative values attributed to white supremacy (Daniszewski, 2020).

REFERENCE

hooks, b. (2009). *Teaching critical thinking: Practical wisdom*. Routledge.
Mullan, J. (2023). *Decolonizing therapy: Oppression, historical trauma, and politicizing your practice*. W. W. Norton & Company.

REFERENCES

Almeida, R. V., Werkmeister Rozas, L. M., Cross-Denny, B., Lee, K. K., & Yamada, A. M. (2019). Coloniality and intersectionality in social work education and practice. *Journal of Progressive Human Services, 30*(2), 148–164.

Behnke, J., Rispens, S., & Demerouti, E. (2022). Does the interplay of diversity and inclusion buffer the impairment of health and well-being in a STEM organization?. *Journal of Personnel Psychology, 22*(2), 66–75.

Berger, R., & Quiros, L. (2014). Supervision for trauma-informed practice. *Traumatology, 20*(4), 296–301.

Bernstein, R. S., Bulger, M., Salipante, P., & Weisinger, J. Y. (2020). From diversity to inclusion to equity: A theory of generative interactions. *Journal of Business Ethics, 167*(3), 395–410.

Bledsoe, A., & Wright, W. J. (2019). The anti-Blackness of global capital. *Environment and Planning D: Society and Space, 37*(1), 8–26.
Bonilla-Silva, E. (1997). Rethinking racism: Toward a structural interpretation. *American Sociological Review, 62*(3), 465–480.
Borders, L. D. (2014). Best practices in clinical supervision: Another step in delineating effective supervision practice. *American Journal of Psychotherapy, 68*(2), 151–162.
Brennan, J. (2023). Diversity for justice vs. diversity for performance: Philosophical and empirical tensions. *Journal of Business Ethics, 187*(3), 433–447.
Carbado, D. W., Crenshaw, K. W., Mays, V. M., & Tomlinson, B. (2013). Intersectionality: Mapping the movements of a theory. *Du Bois Review: Social Science Research on Race, 10*(2), 303–312.
Cook, R. M., McKibben, W. B., & Wind, S. A. (2018). Supervisee perception of power in clinical supervision: The power dynamics in supervision scale. *Training and Education in Professional Psychology, 12*(3), 188.
Council on Social Work Education (2022). *Educational policy and accreditation standards for Baccalaureate and Master's social work programs.* Council on Social Work Education: Washington, DC.
Daniszewski, J. (2020, July 20). *Why we will lowercase white.* The Definite Source. https://blog.ap.org/announcements/why-we-will-lowercase-white?fbclid=IwARPraz29jXptrU8678cZK8guhV7uf9REompX7zJl_lf4MlIvi8jQEIHA5Y#:~:text=AP%20style%20will%20continue%20to,capitalize%20Black%20in%20such%20us
Daya, P. (2014). Diversity and inclusion in an emerging market context. *Equality, Diversity and Inclusion: An International Journal, 33*(3), 293–308.
De Hoogh, A. H., Den Hartog, D. N., & Belschak, F. D. (2021). Showing one's true colors: Leader Machiavellianism, rules and instrumental climate, and abusive supervision. *Journal of Organizational Behavior, 42*(7), 851–866.
Dollarhide, C. T., Hale, S. C., & Stone-Sabali, S. (2021). A new model for social justice supervision. *Journal of Counseling & Development, 99*(1), 104–113.
Dunbar, N. E., & Burgoon, J. K. (2005). Perceptions of power and interactional dominance in interpersonal relationships. *Journal of Social and Personal Relationships, 22*(2), 207–233.
Dyer, J. T., & Flores-Carter, K. (2024). Power analysis demystified. In J. T. Dyer & K. Flores-Carter (Eds.), *Infusing social justice into social science practice* (pp. 21–36). Kendall Hunt Publishing.
Dyer, J. T., & Gushwa, M (2024). DEIPAR deeper: A curricular social justice framework and culturally responsive evaluative tool. In J. T. Dyer & K. Flores-Carter (Eds.), *Infusing social justice into social science practice.* (pp. 53–65). Kendall Hunt Publishing.
Emmerling, F., Peus, C., & Lobbestael, J. (2023). The hot and the cold in destructive leadership: Modeling the role of arousal in explaining leader antecedents and follower consequences of abusive supervision versus exploitative leadership. *Organizational Psychology Review, 13*(3), 237–278.

Farh, C. I., & Chen, Z. (2014). Beyond the individual victim: multilevel consequences of abusive supervision in teams. *Journal of Applied Psychology, 99*(6), 1074–1095.

Feagin, J. R. (2006). *Systemic racism: A theory of oppression.* Routledge.

Ferreira, M. T., Coelho, C., & Wasterlain, S. N. (2019). Discarded in the trash: Burials of African enslaved individuals in Valle da Gafaria, Lagos, Portugal (15th–17th centuries). *International Journal of Osteoarchaeology, 29*(4), 670–680. https://doi-org.ezproxy.simmons.edu/10.1002/oa.2747

Frank, R., Akresh, I. R., & Lu, B. (2010). Latino immigrants and the US racial order: How and where do they fit in? *American Sociological Review, 75*(3), 378–401.

Furman, G. (2012). Social justice leadership as praxis: Developing capacities through preparation programs. *Educational Administration Quarterly, 48*(2), 191–229.

Galinsky, A. D., Gruenfeld, D. H., & Magee, J. C. (2003). From power to action. *Journal of Personality and Social Psychology, 85*(3), 453–466.

Galvan, M. J., & Payne, B. K. (2024). Implicit bias as a cognitive manifestation of systemic racism. *Daedalus, 153*(1), 106–122.

Gaspard-St. Cyr, D. (2023). *From my perspective/opinion: A call for culturally responsive supervision.* Leader Live. https://leader.pubs.asha.org/do/10.1044/leader.fmp.28072023.dei-supervise-slp-aud.10/full

Gauglitz, I. K., Schyns, B., Fehn, T., & Schütz, A. (2023). The dark side of leader narcissism: The relationship between leaders' narcissistic rivalry and abusive supervision. *Journal of Business Ethics, 185*(1), 169–184.

Gaventa, J. (2006). Finding the spaces for change: A power analysis. *IDS Bulletin, 37*(6), 23–33. www.powercube.net/wp-content/uploads/2009/12/finding_spaces_for_change.pdf

Hall, J. C. (2018). Black women talk about stereotypical transference enactments in cross-cultural supervision. *Journal of Human Behavior in the Social Environment, 28*(8), 1019–1032.

Harrison, D. A., & Klein, K. J. (2007). What's the difference? Diversity constructs as separation, variety, or disparity in organizations. *Academy of Management Review, 32*(4), 1199–1228.

Haworth, S., Miller, R., & Schaub, J. (2018). *Leadership in social work.* University of Birmingham.

hooks, b. (2009). *Teaching critical thinking: Practical wisdom.* Routledge.

Imeri, J. P., & Jones, J. D. (2022). Understanding the experience of discussing race and racism during clinical supervision for Black music therapy students. *Music Therapy Perspectives, 40*(2), 174–181.

Johnson, K. R., Washington, S. E., Hoyt, C. R., Banks, T. M., Román-Oyola, R., & Hamed, R. (2024). State of the Science – Establishing diversity, equity, and inclusion priorities for occupational therapy research. *American Journal of Occupational Therapy, 78*, 7801349010. https://doi.org/10.5014/ajot.2024.050601

Jones, C. P. (2002). Confronting institutionalized racism. *Phylon, 50*(1/2), 7–22.

Karim, S. (2023). Power-informed practice in social work. *Journal of Social Work, 23*(6), 1062–1079.

Kerney, M. A., Hargons, C. N., Peterson, R., Cannon, B., Stevens-Watkins, D., Burnett, C., & Higgins-Hord, L. (2024). "The State of Your Psyche": Black conceptualizations of mental health. *The Counseling Psychologist, 52*(4), 522–550.

King Keenan, E., Sandoval, S., & Limone, C. (2019). Realizing the potential for leadership in social work. *Journal of Social Work, 19*(4), 485–503. https://doi-org.ezproxy.simmons.edu/10.1177/1468017318766821

Klasmeier, K. N., Schleu, J. E., Millhoff, C., Poethke, U., & Bormann, K. C. (2022). On the destructiveness of laissez-faire versus abusive supervision: A comparative, multilevel investigation of destructive forms of leadership. *European Journal of Work and Organizational Psychology, 31*(3), 406–420.

LaRue, E. A., Fahey, R. T., Alveshere, B. C., Atkins, J. W., Bhatt, P., Buma, B., ... & Fei, S. (2023). A theoretical framework for the ecological role of three-dimensional structural diversity. *Frontiers in Ecology and the Environment, 21*(1), 4–13.

Liu, W. M., Liu, R. Z., & Shin, R. Q. (2023). Understanding systemic racism: Anti-Blackness, white supremacy, racial capitalism, and the re/creation of white space and time. *Journal of Counseling Psychology, 70*(3), 244.

Lopez-Littleton, V., Sampson, C. J., & Corpening, B. (2023). ADORE: A framework for community building to dismantle anti-Black racism in academia. *Public Integrity, 25*(3), 273–284.

Mak, C., & Therriault, J. (2022). Developing a response to behavior plan: The interplay of social–emotional learning and diversity, equity, and inclusion. *Children & Schools, 44*(1), 59–62.

Maldonado-Torres, N. (2007). On the coloniality of being: Contributions to the development of a concept. *Cultural Studies, 21*(2–3), 240–270.

Mattsson, T. (2014). Intersectionality as a useful tool: Anti-oppressive social work and critical reflection. *Affilia, 29*(1), 8–17.

Moore-Lobban, S. J. (2023). Dismantling anti-Black racism with unapologetic boldness: Redefining our values and living them out loud. *The Counseling Psychologist, 51*(8), 1128–1148.

Moradi, B., & Grzanka, P. R. (2017). Using intersectionality responsibly: Toward critical epistemology, structural analysis, and social justice activism. *Journal of Counseling Psychology, 64*(5), 500–513.

Online Etymology Dictionary. (n.d.). www.etymonline.com/search

Pansardi, P., & Bindi, M. (2021). The new concepts of power? Power-over, power-to and power-with. *Journal of Political Power, 14*(1), 51–71.

Peters, H. C., Bruner, S., Luke, M., Dipre, K., & Goodrich, K. (2022). Integrated supervision framework: A multicultural, social justice, and ecological approach. *Canadian Psychology/Psychologie Canadienne, 63*(4), 511.

Peters, H. C., & Luke, M. (2021). Supervision of leadership model: An integration and extension of the discrimination model and socially just and culturally responsive counseling leadership model. *Journal of Counselor Leadership and Advocacy, 8*(1), 71–86.

Pieterse, A. L., Lewis, J. A., & Miller, M. J. (2023). Dismantling and eradicating anti-Blackness and systemic racism. *Journal of Counseling Psychology, 70*(3), 235.

Quijano, A. (2000). Coloniality of power and Eurocentrism in Latin America. *International Sociology, 15*(2), 215–232.

Rice, D. B., Taylor, R., & Forrester, J. K. (2020). The unwelcoming experience of abusive supervision and the impact of leader characteristics: Turning employees into poor organizational citizens and future quitters. *European Journal of Work and Organizational Psychology, 29*(4), 601–618.

Rodgers, C. (2024). Policy advocacy as practice in the context of the social determinants of health. In J. T. Dyer & K. Flores-Carter (Eds.), *Infusing social justice into social science practice.* (pp. 113–124). Kendall Hunt Publishing.

Rowell-Cunsolo, T. L., Bellerose, M., & Haile, R. (2022). Hazards of anti-Blackness in the United States. *International Journal of Social Welfare, 31*(4), 520–528.

Simard, K., & Parent-Lamarche, A. (2022). Abusive leadership, psychological well-being, and intention to quit during the COVID-19 pandemic: A moderated mediation analysis among Quebec's healthcare system workers. *International Archives of Occupational and Environmental Health, 95*, 437–450.

de Sousa, A. N. (2021). *How Portugal silenced 'centuries of violence and trauma'.* Aljazeera. www.aljazeera.com/features/2021/3/10/how-portugal-silenced-centuries-of-violence-and-trauma

Suarez-Balcazar, Y., Arias, D., & Muñoz, J. P. (2023). The Issue Is – Promoting justice, diversity, equity, and inclusion through caring communities: Why it matters to occupational therapy. *American Journal of Occupational Therapy, 77*, 7706347020. https://doi.org/10.5014/ajot.2023.050416

Susman-Stillman, A., Lim, S., Meuwissen, A., & Watson, C. (2020). Reflective supervision/consultation and early childhood professionals' well-being: A qualitative analysis of supervisors' perspectives. *Early Education and Development, 31*(7), 1151–1168.

Thomas, J. A., & Bucholtz, M. (2021). Personal protective equipment against Anti-Blackness: Communicability and contagion in the academy. *Journal of Linguistic Anthropology, 31*(2), 287–292.

Udah, H. (2021). Coloniality of power and international students' experience: What are the ethical responsibilities of social work and human service educators? *Ethics and Social Welfare, 15*(1), 84–99.

Wade, R. (2023). Embedding the A-EQUIP model of restorative supervision in a critical care unit by professional nurse advocates. *British Journal of Nursing, 32*(15), 744–747.

Wallbank, S., & Woods, G. (2012). A healthier health visiting workforce: findings from the restorative supervision programme. *Community Practitioner, 85*(11), 20–23.

Wilcox, M. M., Farra, A., Winkeljohn Black, S., Pollard, E., Drinane, J. M., Tao, K. W., ... & Owen, J. (2024a). Cultural humility and racial microaggressions in cross-racial clinical supervision: A moderated mediation model. *Journal of Counseling Psychology, 71*(4), 304–314.

Wilcox, M. M., Pérez-Rojas, A. E., Marks, L. R., Reynolds, A. L., Suh, H. N., Flores, L. Y., ... & Miller, M. J. (2024b). Structural competencies: Re-grounding counseling psychology in antiracist and decolonial praxis. *The Counseling Psychologist, 52*(4), 650–691.

Willey, C., & Magee, P. A. (2018). Whiteness as a barrier to becoming a culturally relevant teacher: Clinical experiences and the role of supervision. *Journal of Educational Supervision, 1*(2), 33–51.

Wood, D., Mu, T., Webb, A. M., Reeve, H. W., Lujan, M., & Brown, G. (2023). A unified theory of diversity in ensemble learning. *Journal of Machine Learning Research, 24*(359), 1–49.

Yi, J., Neville, H. A., Todd, N. R., & Mekawi, Y. (2023). Ignoring race and denying racism: A meta-analysis of the associations between colorblind racial ideology, anti-Blackness, and other variables antithetical to racial justice. *Journal of Counseling Psychology, 70*(3), 258.

FURTHER READING

Bhattacharjee, A., & Sarkar, A. (2024). Abusive supervision: A systematic literature review. *Management Review Quarterly, 74*(1), 1–34.

Brantley, M. (2023). Burdens of the what-if: Vicarious anti-Black racism and stress for Black mothers. *Journal of Marriage and Family, 85*(4), 941–961.

Gillborn, D. (2018). Heads I win, tails you lose: Anti-Black racism as fluid, relentless, individual and systemic. *Peabody Journal of Education, 93*(1), 66–77.

Herbst, R., Corley, A. M., & McTate, E. (2023). Clinical framework for dismantling antiblack racism in the clinic room. *Clinical Pediatrics, 62*(10), 1129–1136.

Jones, T. M., Fleming, C., Williford, A., & Research and Evaluation Team. (2020). Racial equity in academic success: The role of school climate and social emotional learning. *Children and Youth Services Review, 119*, 105623.

Krings, A., Fusaro, V., Nicoll, K. L., & Lee, N. Y. (2019). Social work, politics, and social policy education: Applying a multidimensional framework of power. *Journal of Social Work Education, 55*(2), 224–237.

Moin, M. F., & Khan, A. N. (2023). The determinants of abusive supervision. *International Journal of Conflict Management, 36*(2), 257–270.

Pierro, A., Raven, B. H., Amato, C., & Bélanger, J. J. (2013). Bases of social power, leadership styles, and organizational commitment. *International Journal of Psychology, 48*(6), 1122–1134.

Raven, B. H. (2008). The bases of power and the power/interaction model of interpersonal influence. *Analyses of Social Issues and Public Policy, 8*(1), 1–22.

CHAPTER 4

If-Then Antiracism Heuristics
Integration of Critical Race Theory in Clinical Praxis

Adriana Aldana and Michelle Zaragoza

Introduction

Social workers frequently serve individuals, groups, and communities facing challenges rooted in systemic oppression and racial inequalities, and this context requires the implementation of tools to guide efforts in dismantling racist structures and practices. As such, educational accreditation standards have increasingly called for the development of social work competencies that integrate antiracist theoretical perspectives and racial justice approaches to practice (CSWE, 2022; NASW, 2021). Yet, questions remain about how social workers engage in antiracist clinical practice and the role of clinical supervision in facilitating praxis.

The increasing interest in Critical Race Theory (CRT) in social work presents an opportunity to develop knowledge, skills, and cognitive-affective processes that help us meet our professional obligation to engage in antiracism practice. In this chapter, we offer one approach that social workers may adopt to translate CRT insights to antiracist social work clinical practice. To this end, we begin by providing a brief overview of theoretical frameworks that inform antiracist social work practice, with an emphasis on CRT. Then we offer CRT-informed heuristics, or mental shortcuts, that prompt self-reflection and practical decision-making. More specifically, we translate three CRT tenets (social construction of race, racism as ordinary, and intersectionality) into clinical practice recommendations and teaching/learning opportunities. The chapter also presents a case vignette activity offering an opportunity for social workers to practice the application of the proposed CRT-informed heuristics. We conclude with recommendations for the continued integration of critical race praxis in clinical settings.

Theoretical Foundations of Antiracist Practice

Professional standards expect that social workers come to understand theories and apply this theoretical knowledge to facilitate antiracism engagement with clients and constituencies (CSWE, 2022). Accordingly, social work education includes exposure to theories of human behavior and person-in-environment, including theories on race, racism, and antiracism. As an interdisciplinary profession, social work education draws from various theoretical frameworks that explicate the complexities of racism, equipping social workers with a conceptual foundation for recognizing racism and analyzing its impact on the communities we serve. These theories have expanded our understanding of racism. In engaging with these theories, social workers might learn that race is shaped by social, economic, and political forces (Omi & Winant, 1993), daily manifestations of racism are interconnected with settler colonialism (McKay et al., 2020) and other social structures, perpetuating its prevalence (Essed, 1991). These theories have also expanded our awareness of racism as systemic and deeply ingrained in many of our societal institutions (Feagin, 2013). Moreover, antiracism frameworks have also advanced our understanding that to dismantle racism, one must move beyond "not being racist" or take a "neutral" stance on race (Kendi, 2019).

CRT, emerging from legal scholarship in the late 1970s and early 1980s, has also progressively influenced social work. Initially conceived by legal scholars, CRT challenged the neutrality of law and highlighted how race and racism are embedded in societal structures and legal systems to address persistent racial injustices in contemporary society (Crenshaw, 1995; Delgado & Stefancic, 2023). Over time, CRT expanded beyond the law to influence various professions, such as education and public health. In social work, its application involves examining how systemic racism shapes policies, practices, and outcomes, advocating for a deeper understanding of racial dynamics and their implications for equity and justice.

Social work scholars note that CRT-informed practice requires a shift away from cultural competence toward an antiracism approach to better address power dynamics and the root causes of inequities within marginalized communities (Abrams & Moio, 2009; Ortiz & Jani, 2010). Accordingly, social work programs have increasingly integrated CRT into their curriculum to equip students with a critical lens to analyze and address racial disparities in client interactions, organizational policies, and community interventions (Aldana et al., 2022; Aldana et al., 2023; Constance-Huggins, 2012; Murray-Lichtman et al., 2023; Nakaoka et al., 2019). By emphasizing the intersectionality of racism with other structural inequalities, CRT encourages social workers to confront implicit biases, advocate for marginalized communities, and promote trauma-informed responsive practices (Tarshis & Baird, 2021). This integration has been pivotal in fostering a more inclusive and effective approach to social work practice, aligning educational goals with the imperative to advance racial justice. Nevertheless, social work novices, as well as more seasoned practitioners, continue to seek practice-oriented resources to help them integrate CRT in clinical settings.

The If-Then Heuristics of CRT-Informed Clinical Praxis

Antiracist social work practice must go beyond having the awareness that racism exists. Instead, critical race praxis requires active and ongoing antiracism reflection, action, and theory integration to advance racial justice (Aldana, 2024). Yet, with few CRT-informed practice models available, social workers are tasked with the urgent need to translate theory into practical implications that advance antiracist praxis.

In teaching and learning about CRT, we have noted that social work students and early career professionals value how learning CRT's core concepts, or tenets, enables them to name and critique the many facets of structural racism. Yet, often social work learners feel CRT is difficult to apply in practice (Einbinder, 2020). This may be in part because CRT is an analytical tool rather than a practice model. Moreover, critical race scholars often communicate theoretical ideas using technical terms and disciplinary language, making the direct application of CRT insights less accessible to a broad audience (Ray, 2022). Therefore, it is up to social work practitioners to translate theoretical principles into practical actions. Using theoretical heuristics is one approach clinicians and supervisors may adopt to translate CRT tenets into clinical practice.

Heuristics are mental shortcuts or practical rules of thumb that enable people to make quick decisions. We hope that these heuristics help simplify the translation of theoretical assumptions into practice recommendations. In the sections that follow, we offer "if-then" heuristics statements informed by three CRT tenets that provide implications for antiracist clinical practice (see Table 4.1).

Rather than proposing a singular practice model, the practice recommendations presented in the following heuristics stem from our interpretation of CRT tenets and synthesis of antiracism clinical practice literature. In doing so, we aim to make direct connections between CRT insights and the variety of antiracism approaches already in use in clinical settings. We hope these heuristics serve as useful educational and training tools for developing theory-driven antiracism praxis.

Table 4.1 *Antiracism heuristics, corresponding CRT tenets, and practice implications*

Antiracism Heuristic	CRT Tenet	Examples of Clinical Practice Implications
If race is socially constructed, then we can deconstruct race	*Race is a Social Construct:* Race is not a biological attribute but rather a system of human classification that was created and has endured for centuries to establish and support white hegemony. Other social identities are also socially constructed.	• Recognize that society holds collective beliefs about race, and our complicity in them, therefore we can contribute to changing racial societal beliefs, attitudes, and interactions • Consciously unlearn and refute internalized color-evasive ideology • Engage in critical self-reflection about one's racial-ethnic identity and biases and take steps to address corresponding power differentials
If racism is ordinary, then antiracism can be ordinary	*Racism is Ordinary:* Racism in the US permeates or is embedded in all facets of society. It structures societal norms, beliefs, policies, practices, and beliefs that negatively shape the experiences of Black, Indigenous, and other racialized people of color and uphold white supremacy.	• Create and maintain space(s) that recognizes and challenges the pervasiveness of racism and white supremacy • Assess for the impact of racism and white supremacy at all levels (intrapersonal, interpersonal, institutional, structural); create a treatment or advocacy plan when appropriate • Avoid perpetuating racial gaslighting or microaggressions when interacting with clients by affirming client's disclosure of racial bias, systemic violence, or oppression • Develop, refine, and/or expand willingness and capability to discuss racism with others

Table 4.1 (cont.)

Antiracism Heuristic	CRT Tenet	Examples of Clinical Practice Implications
If oppression is intersectional, then healing and liberation are intersectional	*Intersectionality:* Racism and other systems of oppression (e.g., classism, cisheterosexism, ableism, religious-spiritual oppression, and sizeism) are interconnected and reinforce each other to create inequality and discrimination.	• Move beyond naming multiple identities to identify how racism and other forms of oppression cause structural vulnerability • Assess for the impact of structural (intersectional) vulnerability on a client's opportunities for healing and liberation; create treatment plan and referrals to community resources as needed • Evaluate clinical practice and organization to ensure equity and inclusion for diverse clients

Heuristic 1: If Race Is Socially Constructed, Then We Can Deconstruct Race

Race is not a biological reality but rather a classification system (re)created by society that differentiates people based on physical characteristics like skin color, hair texture, and facial or cultural features. These social and political categories have no scientific basis and do not determine human abilities, intelligence, or worth, but rather serve to dispossess people from their land, exploit human labor, and maintain a white supremacist colonial patriarchy (Legha, 2023; Ray, 2022). As such, race is socially constructed through beliefs, social interactions, practices, policies, and dominant cultural narratives (Delgado & Stefancic, 2023). Perhaps more importantly, it also points to the opportunity for us to create social change through the dismantling of dominant racist constructions of the self and others. If race is a social construct, then we can deconstruct race.

While race is "a collective hallucination," it still has a material impact on people's livelihoods (Ray, 2022). Put differently, saying that race is a social construct is not equivalent to saying race is "not real," and therefore, we should stop "seeing" race. This form of racial erasure camouflages the structural causes of inequities. Bonilla-Silva's (2006) research on "color-blind racism" has enhanced our understanding of color-evasive ideology, which suggests that modern racial inequality is maintained through subtle, seemingly nonracial or race-neutral frames, rather than overtly racist beliefs. This ideology is composed of four central frames that help to justify racial disparities and inequality: abstract liberalism, cultural racism, minimization of racism, and naturalization. Abstract liberalism involves using ideas associated with political and economic liberalism, such as "equal opportunity" and "individual choice," to explain racial matters, often ignoring systemic inequalities. Cultural racism attributes disparities to cultural deficiencies within minoritized groups, suggesting their culture is the cause of their social position. Minimization of racism downplays the existence and impact of discrimination, often asserting that racism is no longer a significant barrier for people of color. Naturalization frames racial phenomena as natural occurrences, suggesting, for example, that the underrepresentation of students of color in higher education is just a natural response to high dropout rates rather than a product of school segregation and unequal educational opportunities. Expanding on Bonilla-Silva's research, DisCrit scholars (Annamma et al., 2017) call on us to move beyond ableist discourse on "color-blindness" to expand our awareness of how this racial ideology goes beyond the inability to "see" race. Instead, color-evasive racism involves an active avoidance or refusal to recognize racism.

Because we live in a society dominated by color-evasive ideology, most social work programs do not adequately prepare social workers to engage in antiracism or racial justice (Aldana & Vazquez, 2020), and in turn, supervisors do not have the resources necessary to support their mentees. Accordingly, many social workers are unlikely to question the role of race unless they have extensive lived experiences and/or professional training that prompts them to interrogate racism. Thus, another implication for practice inherent in this heuristic is the rejection of color-evasive ideology along with its corresponding frames and tactics. Instead, we must recognize that racial categories reflect power dynamics and differentials that perpetuate inequality.

In practice, we need to continually examine how race, as a system of human classification that has endured for centuries to maintain white hegemony, impacts our clients' lived experiences. For instance, an understanding of the social construction of race can help us avoid misattributing the cause of mental health disparities to someone's race (a proxy for racialized lived experiences) rather than racism (Mounier & Cortez, 2024). Similarly, the concept of racialization – the sociopolitical process by which certain groups are categorized and differentiated based on perceived racial characteristics (Hochman, 2019) – helps us discern that it is racialization, rather than one's racial identity, that positions an individual as either a benefactor of white privilege, a target of racism, or in a liminal social location within a racialized society. Racialization becomes the mechanism through which race becomes a key factor in structuring social relations and institutional practices, often leading to systemic inequity. Thus, comprehending the connection between color-evasive ideology and the social construction of race is essential for antiracist professional development in social work.

Understanding the social construction tenet can be a liberatory notion in social work practice. In clinical practice and supervision, this understanding helps us recognize that the stereotypes, practices, and inequalities associated with race are socially imposed rather than biologically inherent. Acknowledging that identities are not fixed or static but rather relational, contextual, and malleable grants us the opportunity to seek to change collective beliefs about race that reproduce harm or hinder healing within clinical settings. Accordingly, we are called to examine and address the ways that we may have internalized dominant beliefs about one's and others' race and to recognize our (un)conscious role in reproducing collective beliefs about race.

The recommendation for reflexive practice is common within antiracist scholarship and calls for social workers to engage in a self-reflection process before working with clients (Ashley, 2024; Legha, 2023; Tang Yan et al., 2022). Moreover, according to Abrams and Moio (2009), a self-reflective approach is a cornerstone of integrating CRT into social work. Thus, translating the social construction of race tenet for clinical practice heuristics, we offer the following reflective questions to help practitioners and supervisors examine how we may have internalized dominant beliefs about race.

- How do I identify ethnically, racially, or culturally? What circumstances or experiences have informed my identity?
- How does my racial positionality inform my understanding of race dynamics in the US and/or my clinical practice?
- Have I been exposed to or internalized any color-evasive frames? How can these frames influence my interactions in clinical settings? In what ways do I uphold color-evasive racism in my practice?

Reflecting on the social construction of race can help us unpack biased perceptions of clients, professional norms, policies, and the creation of evidence-based practices that privilege whiteness and perpetuate the marginalization of people of color. For example, when assessing familial risk, practitioners may interrogate standardized assessment tools for "family safety" or "neglect" that hinge on white, middle-class norms and cisheteropatriarchal ideals of the nuclear family (Aldana & Capps, in press). By doing so, social workers can develop more equitable and culturally responsive practices that recognize power dynamics within client–practitioner relationships and value the diverse experiences of all clients.

Self-reflection improves knowledge and critical awareness of historical racial oppression and its impact on contemporary systemic racism (Hattley, 2024; Legha, 2023). Practitioners are also better able to recognize and confront their implicit biases and prejudices, which is crucial for mitigating the influence of these biases on clinical judgment and interactions with clients. Critical self-reflection about race assists practitioners in recognizing their positionality and the power dynamics in their therapeutic interactions, which is essential for ethical and equitable practice (Fook & Gardner, 2007; Schmidt & Tronnier, 2024). Reflective practitioners are also better equipped to create a trusting and supportive therapeutic environment, which is essential for effective rapport-building and intervention (Bussey, 2024a; Taiwo, 2022).

Self-awareness and self-reflection serve as an antiracist clinical tool (Ashley, 2024). Yet, research shows that social workers engaged in direct practice often lack commitment to critically reflecting on oppressive discourses affecting their interactions with clients (Taiwo, 2022). The three main obstacles to integrating self-reflection in practice include (1) lack of time for reflection, (2) fear of engaging in reflection, and (3) the possibility of over-reflection. Despite these barriers, clinical practice settings still hold the potential to create space for reflection individually, with colleagues, or with supervisors to enhance one's engagement in antiracism.

Antiracism strategies that recognize the role of race in the lives of clients may also help practitioners minimize racial gaslighting in clinical practice. Racial gaslighting involves manipulating someone into questioning their own experiences of racism (Hattley, 2024). Therefore, acknowledging and discussing race and racism with clients in the therapeutic process is crucial. Social workers can facilitate this by creating a therapeutic space that recognizes the pervasiveness of racism, which we will discuss next. See Box 4.1.

> **Box 4.1 Supervision Considerations I**
>
> CRT-informed clinical supervision requires questioning race-neutral or color-evasive training and practice approaches. To effectively integrate the tenet of the *social construction of race* into clinical praxis, clinical supervisors can help foster more racial reflexivity among trainees/colleagues.
>
> Some recommendations include:
>
> - Supervisor models self-reflection and openness to critique one's complicity in upholding color-evasive ideology and white supremacy.
> - Acknowledge and actively address power imbalances between supervisors and supervisees, as well as between clinicians and clients.
> - Creating (or advocating for) time/space in supervision for reflective activities.
> - Routinely reviewing and examining how clients may be socially constructed or racialized within the practice setting.

Heuristic II: If Racism Is Ordinary, Then Antiracism Can Be Ordinary

One of the foundational tenets of CRT is that "racism is ordinary." This means that racism in the US is pervasive and permeates all facets of society (Delgado & Stefancic, 2023; Ray, 2022). Therefore, racism is embedded in dominant societal norms, beliefs, policies, and practices that negatively shape the experiences of Black, Indigenous, and other racialized people of color, upholding white supremacy and settler colonialism. This tenet challenges the notion that racism is only manifested through overt, individual acts of bigotry, highlighting instead its pervasive and systemic nature of white supremacy. Awareness of the insidious and systemic nature of racial oppression can feel overwhelming to challenge. However, in acknowledging the ordinariness of racism, this tenet prompts us to develop ordinary antiracist beliefs, behaviors, and approaches to incorporate into daily practice decisions that disrupt the ordinariness of racial bias, discrimination, and systemic oppression.

In other words, if racism is ordinary, then antiracism can be ordinary. This statement reminds us that antiracist actions can and should be a routine part of social work, integrated into every level of professional engagement, from micro to macro practice. If we accept the notion that white supremacy manifests in racism at the intrapersonal, interpersonal, institutional, and structural/cultural levels (Legha, 2023), then applying this heuristic in practice means that social workers must address racism in a comprehensive and multifaceted manner. Social workers must continuously develop their racial consciousness to engage in antiracist practice. Racial consciousness refers to a critical awareness of the systemic nature of racism and an acknowledgment of the privileges and disadvantages that come with different racial identities. It also encompasses taking action to challenge racism from the intrapersonal to structural levels.

Racism at the intrapersonal level refers to the internalized beliefs, biases, and attitudes that individuals hold about different racial groups, often shaped by societal stereotypes and prejudices. Internalized racism is the internal acceptance and assimilation of the racist attitudes, beliefs, and stereotypes imposed by the dominant society by individuals belonging to marginalized racial groups. Clinically, internalized racism among people of color may manifest as negative self-perception, self-hatred, and the devaluation of one's own racial or ethnic group, which can adversely affect mental health, self-esteem, and social identity, perpetuating cycles of oppression and inequality (David et al., 2019).

Internalized racism profoundly impacts the mental health of people of color by eroding self-esteem and self-worth, often leading to depression, anxiety, and chronic stress. It causes identity confusion and internal conflict, resulting in feelings of alienation and isolation. This psychological distress can impair academic and professional performance, hinder relationships, and increase reliance on unhealthy coping mechanisms. Additionally, the ongoing stress from internalized racism can manifest in physical health issues, further exacerbating the overall well-being of individuals. Understanding the profound impact of internalized racism on mental health is crucial for developing effective therapeutic interventions and support systems to help individuals overcome these challenges and foster resilience, self-acceptance, and well-being.

Internalization of color-evasive ideology may lead to the inability to recognize the function of whiteness as a socio and political privilege regardless of one's racial-ethnic identity (Versey et al., 2019). Research shows that people develop beliefs about the world and their place in it, which causes them to see their economic, social, and political status as fair (Jost et al., 2004). However, when significant events like trauma or job loss challenge these worldviews, individuals experience distress. This stress can lead to a sense of the world being unjust and cause anxiety and other mental health crises. Thus, internalized color-evasive racism may impact all of us, albeit in different ways. For people of color, internalizing color-evasive beliefs may lead to self-blame for "poor life choices" or lack of effort rather than critical recognition of the structural forces that shaped the opportunities or choices available to them. Versey and colleagues (2019) argue that internalized worldviews that reflect internalized color-evasive ideology may also help explain why some white individuals may feel threatened or traumatized by a perceived loss of status in a diverse society, affecting both mental health and broader mental health policy.

Therefore, attending to internalized racism at the intrapersonal level is necessary. Addressing internalized racism with clients involves sensitive, person-centered strategies that can help mitigate its negative impact on their mental health and socioemotional well-being. This may include informally (e.g., observing or noting with supervisees) or formally assessing (using standardized measures of internalized racism for clients) an individual's internalized racist beliefs. Internalized racism assessment measures are not intended as standardized assessment tools but instead should be used to identify additional concerns (for clinical assessment of internalized anti-Black racism see Smith & Woodford, 2024). Practitioners are also encouraged to self-assess for internalized racism (related to Heuristic I) and seek supervision or consultation for addressing internalized racism within therapeutic intervention with clients.

Interpersonally, social workers must strive to create equitable, inclusive, and respectful interactions with colleagues, clients, and supervisees, actively challenging discriminatory behaviors and attitudes. Antiracist clinical practice, informed by the notion that racism is pervasive, recognizes that historical and contemporary racism contributes to racial disparities in health, mental health, and access to American opportunity structures. Examining the impact of racism on Black, Indigenous, Latinx, Asian, and other racialized groups is essential to conducting more comprehensive biopsychosocial assessments (Smith & Woodford, 2024), developing strong relationships with supervisees, and ensuring the integration of a macro-understanding into micro-level practice (Bussey, 2024a). In clinical settings, recognizing that racism is ordinary may better assist practitioners in validating and helping clients address how their experiences with racial microaggressions, discrimination, and intergenerational trauma have affected them. For clinical supervisors, it is equally important to recognize that clinicians of color may also experience racial discrimination and microaggressions that, if unaddressed or minimized, can diminish trust within the supervisory relationship.

In therapeutic treatment, we can integrate antiracist approaches with various clinical modalities to help clients heal from intrapersonal and interpersonal racism (Ashley, 2024; Magee, 2019). Here are several approaches commonly cited in antiracist scholarship:

1. **Create a Safe Environment:** Establish a trusting therapeutic relationship where clients feel safe discussing their experiences with racism. Validate their feelings and experiences, emphasizing that their struggles are not their fault but a result of systemic racism.

2. **Psychoeducation:** Educate clients, when appropriate, about the concept of internalized racism and how it can affect their self-esteem, mental health, and behavior. Help them understand that internalized racism is a learned response to systemic oppression and not a reflection of their true worth or abilities.
3. **Narrative Therapy:** Encourage clients to tell their stories and reframe their narratives to highlight their resilience and resistance to oppression. This can help clients see themselves as active agents rather than passive victims.
4. **Cognitive Restructuring:** Use cognitive-behavioral techniques to help clients identify and challenge negative thoughts and beliefs about themselves that stem from internalized racism. Encourage them to replace these thoughts with more positive, empowering beliefs.
5. **Mindfulness:** Teach mindfulness and self-compassion techniques to help clients manage stress and develop a kinder, more accepting relationship with themselves.
6. **Strength-Based Approaches:** Focus on clients' strengths, resilience, and cultural heritage. Help them reconnect with and take pride in their racial or ethnic identity, which can counteract the damaging effects of internalized racism.

By addressing internalized racism and facilitating healing from reported experiences of discrimination through these strategies, clinicians can help clients improve their mental health and socioemotional well-being, fostering a more positive self-image and healthier coping mechanisms.

This heuristic also requires gaining or refining skills and knowledge to facilitate open discussions about race within group work. Social work with groups offers an opportunity to address the collective impacts of racialized trauma and foster clients' racial consciousness in a therapeutic setting. Facilitating the healing of racialized trauma within group work requires considering the racial-ethnic composition of the group and cognizance of one's positionality within the group. Rather than a singular approach to all groups, group facilitators should decide whether a mixed-identity group or an affinity group, in which all participants share common experiences or identities, would be most appropriate (for more guidance on antiracist group formations see Schmidt & Tronnier, 2024). The application of intergroup dialogic facilitation approaches can assist social workers in incorporating inclusive and culturally responsive facilitation practices that recognize and value the diverse experiences of all members and attend to racialized power dynamics that arise in group practice (Aldana et al., 2016; Mountz et al., 2024).

Focusing solely on the individual impact of racism is not enough to address the pervasiveness of white supremacy. Institutional practices and policies must be scrutinized and reformed to eliminate systemic biases that disadvantage marginalized communities. In clinical practice, practitioners may critique the Eurocentric and colonial perspective embedded in mainstream theoretical frameworks, evidence-based protocols, and assessment tools (e.g., DSM-V, ACEs). Scholars recommend replacing assessments that problematize or otherize clients with strengths-based, collaborative, and intersectional assessments that are informed by Indigenous knowledge and decolonial practices (Paez et al., 2024). Finally, addressing structural racism requires social workers to engage in policy advocacy and participate in social movements aimed at creating broader societal change. To translate these theoretical implications into practical guidelines, social workers should consider questions such as:

- How prepared am I to address race and racism with colleagues and clients? Do I have any concerns? If so, why?
- What knowledge, skills, or capabilities do I need to develop or refine to enhance my racial literacy?
- How can I advocate for racial equity or healing for my client(s)?

By consistently applying these questions to their practice, social workers can ensure that antiracism becomes an ordinary and integral part of their professional responsibilities, effectively addressing racism at every level. See Box 4.2.

Box 4.2 Supervision Considerations II

CRT-informed clinical supervision involves building the ability to recognize, understand, and respond to the complexities of race and racism. To effectively integrate an awareness of the *racism is ordinary* tenet into clinical praxis, clinical supervisors can help develop greeted racial consciousness among trainees/colleagues.

Some recommendations include:

- Provide training or support for the development of the language and confidence to discuss race and racism openly and constructively, addressing both overt and subtle forms of racism
- Dedicate time during supervision for trainees/colleagues to articulate the ways in which race and racism manifest in clinical practice, including personal interactions, institutional policies, and societal structures
- Assist trainee/colleague in processing instances of racial trauma transference or countertransference

Heuristic III: If Oppression Is Intersectional, Then Healing and Liberation Must Be Intersectional

Black women and women-of-color feminist scholars and activists have contributed significantly to the understanding of how hierarchies of power and social systems intersect to create simultaneous, multiple, and interlocking forms of oppression (Anzaldúa, 1987; Collins, 1990; Crenshaw, 1989; Moraga & Anzaldúa, 1983). Within legal critical race scholarship, Kimberlé Crenshaw is credited with coining the term intersectionality to explain how an examination of oppression requires analysis beyond the single-axis framework of one marginalized identity (e.g., race) to a more complex understanding of the way racism conspires with other forms of oppression (cisheterosexism, classism, etc.) to structure the context and circumstances that make particular social groups vulnerable to discrimination, exclusion, and marginalization. Crenshaw has also described intersectional failures as the shortcomings of policies, legal systems, and social movements in recognizing and addressing the interconnected and overlapping nature of systems of oppression (Southbank Centre, 2016). These failures occur when social strategies and frameworks that aim to address discrimination and inequality overlook the unique experiences of those who exist at the intersections of multiple forms of marginalization. Accordingly, if oppression is intersectional, then healing and liberation must be intersectional.

Applying this heuristic in social work practice requires social workers to approach the individuals and communities they work with – and their organizations – from a structural and intersectional lens. This emphasizes the importance of social workers taking into account the interconnected nature of various social systems that contribute to structural vulnerability. Structural vulnerability refers to one's location in a hierarchical social order in the context of diverse, overlapping, and reinforcing power dynamics (Bourgois et al., 2017; Mounier & Cortez, 2024). Despite this call for structural analysis, popular discourse often interprets intersectional theory to mean that people hold multiple social identities, which grant them privileges or mark them as targets of discrimination. While this understanding of intersectionality is partially true, it falls short of intersectional theory's central aim to challenge and transform systems and structures of oppression (Collins, 2019; Grzanka et al., 2020; Tarshis & Baird, 2021). Crenshaw addressed this misconception in the Southbank Centre (2016) conference talk on intersectionality and gender equality, stating:

Particularly those who have not followed demarginalization from its initial iteration often mistakenly think that intersectionality is only about multiple identities .... That's not, at least my articulation of intersectionality. Intersectionality is not primarily about identity. It's about how structures make certain identities the consequence of and the vehicle for vulnerability. So if you want to know how many intersections matter you've got to look at the context. What's happening? What kind of discrimination is going on? What are the policies, what are the institutional structures that play a role in contributing to the exclusion of some people and not others?

Therefore, integrating an intersectional perspective into antiracist praxis goes beyond naming multiple identities and analyzes how racism and other forms of oppression cause structural vulnerability. A person's structural vulnerability will affect the opportunities available to them and the constraints on their livelihood (Mounier & Cortez, 2024). While acknowledging a client's multiple identities can be an initial step in assessing for structural vulnerability, it is not enough. We must take another step to identify the corresponding systems of oppression that work through the privileging or targeting of identities to structure a client's lived experiences.

Addressing structural racism and its intersection with other systems of oppression also requires social workers to develop structural competence – their capacity to identify, analyze, and address racism in systems, institutions, practices, and policies that produce unjust outcomes (Bourgois et al., 2017; Hernández et al., 2024). Integral to a structural competence approach is the focus on the various upstream forces that shape the outcomes and experiences of clients, groups, and communities with which social workers engage. For example, social workers can ask themselves: "How is the individual's physical and emotional health impacted by structures?" and "How can we respond to structural issues impacting our communities, both inside and outside of the service environment?" (Mounier & Cortez, 2024). The structural assessment framework bridges a macro-understanding to micro-level encounters and is a critical step toward antiracist work, requiring clinical reflexivity, critical consciousness, curiosity, and cultural humility (Bussey, 2024a).

In clinical settings, an intersectional and structural framework challenges social workers to move beyond the Eurocentric frame of individual symptom reduction toward an understanding that clients' lives have intersectional nuances that shape their presenting concerns and experiences. For example, suppose the anxiety and suicidal ideation expressed by a 19-year-old African American female college student (she/her) is quickly addressed through the frame of risk to conduct a risk screening and create a safety plan that seeks to increase her participation in activities on campus. Under these circumstances, a social worker might overlook opportunities to fully understand the intersectional nuances of the student's experience. As a result, the student may feel unseen, invalidated, and further marginalized. Structural assessment prompts social workers to consider the impact of history, systemic forces, socioeconomic context, and political context on a client's circumstances. As social workers operate within this framework, they intentionally highlight factors that restrict or promote an individual's healing and liberation and identify efforts for impactful service provision.

If, instead, the same social worker – prioritizing healing and liberation that is intersectional – comes to learn how attending a historically white institution, being the only African American female student in her computer science class, and struggling to feel like she belongs are all layers of marginalization in her current reality that add to her mental health experience. When discussing strategies for intersectional risk management in social work practice, Ashley (2024) recommends that social workers support and honor the client's current reality (including experiences of power, privilege, or lack thereof), acknowledge differences in identity and social location, maintain a position of curiosity rather than expertise, and listen with genuine concern to gain a comprehensive picture of what is happening. When social workers consider the intersectional nuances that shape their clients' current reality, they can address these aspects with intention in their practice, thus expanding the possibilities and potential for their clients' healing and liberation.

Social workers can also draw from psychological frameworks rooted in social justice that prioritize healing and liberation as intersectional, especially when working with people of color and Indigenous communities who face ongoing marginalization in the United States. For example, Radical Healing, proposed by French and colleagues (2020), emphasizes a process of healing positioned within a dialectic of resisting oppression and moving toward freedom. This approach underscores the importance of recognizing the systemic factors contributing to the trauma of racism while nurturing hope for liberation. It shifts the focus from assigning individual blame to acknowledging systemic oppression, necessitating a departure from deficit-based perspectives to critically consider how communities of color strive for wellness within this context. Radical healing involves recognizing oppression, resisting it, and envisioning the potential for liberation and wellness.

To reiterate, integrating an intersectional lens will require assessing the influence of structural (intersectional) vulnerability on a client's potential for healing and liberation, and developing a treatment plan with referrals to community resources as necessary. Equipped with this holistic understanding, social workers can more readily prioritize work that promotes healing and liberation, as it considers all the complex layers that shape an individual's lived experiences and realities.

At both the institutional level and within micro-practice settings, social workers using an intersectional lens can recognize organizational policies, practices, and systems that contribute to their clients' oppression. Thus, it is crucial for social work clinicians and supervisors to evaluate their clinical practice. These evaluations are not mere formalities – they are essential for identifying and making necessary adjustments to provide the most appropriate care and support to clients. However, evaluations often focus solely on individual outcomes, as many clinical practices emphasize individual outcome measures and assessments. This approach also invites social workers to identify barriers that might contribute to unintended harm, disparities, and exclusion. Evaluating practice with an intersectional lens requires examination of equity and inclusion within the service delivery process. Evaluating the service environment may include considering the language accessibility of services, hours of operation, diversity of staff, and other features of the physical space. In antiracist clinical practice, this may also involve finding accessible ways for clients to provide feedback and inform the delivery of services (Mounier & Cortez, 2024). If the evaluation identifies disparities, social workers can consider organizational or institutional changes to ensure equity and inclusion for all clients. Social workers can also contribute to systemic and structural change. Collaborating with external community partners can assist clinical social workers in engaging in antiracism outside therapeutic settings (Mounier & Cortez, 2024).

Tarshis and colleagues (2021) argue that intersectionality theory is essential to informing anti-oppressive social work education, research, supervision, and practice. We agree with this call for intersectional social work and believe that its application, alongside other CRT-informed antiracist heuristics, can enhance our ability to engage in structural praxis that contributes to racial healing and liberation. While we have discussed the CRT heuristics separately, in reality, antiracism praxis often involves the combination of multiple theoretical perspectives and practice modalities. For instance, an intersectional lens underscores the social construction of all identities, not just race, and the ways that racism is reinforced by and magnifies other systems of oppression. Thus, we must reflect on the multidimensionality of our positionality within clinical settings and the intersectional structural vulnerabilities we must account for in our practice. Accordingly, our last set of reflective questions, while inspired by the tenet of intersectionality, are also informed by the other tenets:

- How do my multiple social identities structure my positionality in clinical settings? How does my positionality shape my perception of clients and their subsequent treatment? (intersectionality + social construction of race/identities)
- What steps can I take to foster an inclusive and antiracist environment within my organization? (intersectionality + racism is ordinary)
- Which institutional policies need to be challenged and reformed to promote racial equity or outcome parity across cases within our organization? How can my positionality assist or hinder my efforts to advocate for change? (intersectionality + racism is ordinary + social construction of race) (see Box 4.3)

Summary

This chapter translates three CRT tenets into heuristics for antiracist practice. These heuristics serve as rules of thumb, guiding the integration of these principles into clinical social work.

By recognizing that race is a social construct, social workers are encouraged to engage in self-reflection about internalized ideas of race. Moreover,

---

Box 4.3 Supervision Considerations III

CRT-informed clinical supervision includes a critical examination of the interconnected axes of power and oppression that shape people's lives. To effectively integrate the tenet of the social intersectionality into clinical supervision, the following recommendations can help clinical supervisors foster structural competency among trainees/colleagues.

Some recommendations include:

- Assist trainees or colleagues in naming the systems of oppression that contribute to clients' structural vulnerability.
- When reviewing cases, prompt supervisees to consider how intersecting systems of oppression (racism, cisheterosexism, classism, etc.) affect clients' well-being.
- Guide supervisees in creating treatment plans that take into account client's structural vulnerability.
- Support supervisees in identifying and challenging organizational policies and practices that may perpetuate inequality and oppression.

one must seek to change collective beliefs about race and reject color-evasive ideologies that perpetuate the racialization of minoritized groups and reinforce white supremacy. Understanding that racism is ordinary necessitates routine incorporation of antiracist practices into clinical approaches, such as validating clients' experiences of racism, assessing the impact of structural racism, and advocating for systemic or institutional change within our spheres of influence. Finally, recognizing the intersectionality of oppression compels social workers to avoid essentializing clients to a single identity and to implement intersectional, anti-oppressive assessment and treatment plans that address the root causes of the social determinants of mental health and well-being. The If-Then Case Vignette Activity offers an opportunity to practise the application of these heuristics to a hypothetical clinical case (see Box 4.4).

Social workers must continually evolve by embracing a commitment to critical race praxis. This involves ongoing, honest, and critical self-reflection, active engagement in antiracism efforts, and openness to exploring the applicability of other antiracism frameworks or CRT tenets not discussed in this chapter. For instance, key CRT tenets such as the voices of color/counter-narratives, differential racialization, critique of liberalism, and interest convergence can also inform antiracism praxis.

Box 4.4 Case Vignette and Activity. CRT-Informed Heuristics

By Adriana Aldana and Michelle Zaragoza

Lupe (she/they) is a 24-year-old self-identifying Latine transgender queer woman seeking mental health services after experiencing symptoms related to trauma resulting from domestic violence and sexual assault in a previous romantic relationship. Lupe sought mental health services to address current concerns, including feelings of sadness, hopelessness, hypervigilance, avoidance of reminders of traumatic events and settings, withdrawal from others and self-isolating behaviors, low self-esteem, and negative beliefs about self.

Lupe discloses a history of trauma, including sexual assault, domestic violence, parental divorce, physical abuse as a child, instances of bullying/harassment, community violence, and prior psychiatric hospitalizations. She has a history of suicidal behaviors, including self-harm (e.g., cutting arms and legs with a blade) as recently as two months ago and a suicide attempt at the age of 18, which led to a psychiatric hospitalization. Lupe also disclosed a history of substance and alcohol use that led to a DUI last year. Lupe disclosed marijuana use at least two times a day and noted the benefits of use to "help relax and keep my mind off things."

Lupe shared she has received previous mental health services, including family therapy when she was 13 years old, individual therapy when she was

18 years old, and as recently as one year ago. She shared negative experiences with prior therapists who were not gender- or LGBTQ+-affirming, made insensitive remarks about the community she lives in, and misused her pronouns. In reviewing Lupe's previous case notes, which were initially filed under a different name, her prior therapist documented her attendance and engagement in services, noting Lupe "is always late," "appears unmotivated to search for employment or engage in career skill development," "engages in high-risk sexual behaviors," and "did not follow-through with referral provided to job-search workshop located outside of client community" due to "none located within proximity to the client." Case notes indicated that Lupe lived in a "dangerous" and "low-income community." Upon asking Lupe about her living arrangement, she reports, "I hope to move out soon." She lives with her grandmother, mother, and younger sister in a three-bedroom home in an urban city near Los Angeles. She lives in a detached back unit studio with her boyfriend of one year. Lupe describes a high-conflict and tense relationship with her mother, who was historically unaccepting of her gender identity and expression.

Lupe studied art at a nearby predominantly white college but took a leave of absence last semester, reporting, "I don't think I was cut out for it." She is currently unemployed, yet wants to find a job. She has a strong support network of five close friends, including her boyfriend. She enjoys singing, making music, art, and tarot reading. Lupe stated her reason for seeking treatment is to "feel more like myself again."

CASE VIGNETTE CRT-INFORMED PRAXIS QUESTIONS

Activity Instructions: Imagine that you are Lupe's clinician. Take time to reflect and journal your response to the following reflective questions. If completing this activity as part of clinical supervision, use these questions and your responses to engage in a critical conversation about how you can further develop your capacity to engage in CRT-informed praxis.

If Race Is Socially Constructed, Then We Want to Deconstruct Race

- What are some color-evasive assumptions I may have made without additional details about my client or their circumstances? What questions would I ask to understand their identity and lived experiences better?
- How am I making sense of the shared or differing racial-ethnic identity between my client and me? Am I making assumptions about shared or differing lived experiences due to our identities? Are these assumptions informed by racialized biases?
- What are the power dynamics between my client and me based on our racial-ethnic identities (or positionality)? What steps can I take to prevent power differentials from being replicated in the treatment planning and my clinical work with them?

If Racism Is Ordinary, Then Antiracism Can Be Ordinary

Am I prepared to discuss race and racism with my client? How might I approach my initial sessions with an antiracist lens?

> How might expressions of racism impact my client's experiences? How would I assess for subtle or covert forms of racial oppression and respond to them? How can I mitigate instances of racial gaslighting or racial microaggressions when interacting with my client? What are some ways that I can affirm or validate client's disclosure of racial discrimination or bias?
>
> If Oppression Is Intersectional, Then Healing and Liberation Are Intersectional
>
> What are my clients intersecting identities? How might the lived experience connected to these identities help us identify the interlocking systems of oppression that contribute to their structural vulnerability?
> What are the intersectional structural vulnerabilities that restrict or afford them opportunities for healing and liberation? Is there anything in the sociopolitical and economic landscape – locally and nationally – that might impact my client and their access to services? When considering my client's structural vulnerability, how might I approach linkages and referrals to community resources and other service providers?
> How can I evaluate my practice or organization to determine if policies or service approaches cause unintended harm, disparities, or exclusion?
> If disparities in access to services or outcome measures exist, what steps can I take to address this and foster a more inclusive approach for all clients at my organization?

Practising the application of CRT-informed heuristics in supervision can further develop social workers' capacity to engage in antiracism. To advance antiracist clinical practice and supervision, social workers must actively advocate for inclusive and equitable environments. Research highlights the importance of a strong supervisory foundation centered on race, fostering authentic relationships, and assessing staff's race consciousness for effective antiracist supervision (Bussey, 2024b). Additionally, integrating an intersectional lens in supervision is crucial for addressing oppression and marginalization and understanding the influence of privilege on supervisory dynamics (Tarshis & Baird, 2021). By embracing these strategies, social workers can create a supervisory environment that fosters the skills and knowledge necessary for effective antiracism praxis.

REFERENCES

Abrams, L. S., & Moio, J. A. (2009). Critical race theory and the cultural competence dilemma in social work education. *Journal of Social Work Education*, 45(2), 245–261.

Aldana, A. (2024). Self-Care is resistance: Rest as a pedagogical tool and critical race praxis. In W. Ashley (Ed.) *Merging clinical social work and antiracism positioning: How to be a clinically sound, antiracist social work practitioner* (Chapter 19). Peter Lang.

Aldana, A., & Capps, J. (in press). Critical race praxis: A process-oriented approach to the integration of critical race theory in social work practice. In S. Nakaoka, L. Ortiz, S. Ault, & N. Vazquez (Eds). *Critical race theory in social work*. Cambridge University Press.

Aldana, A., Nakaoka, S., Vazquez, N., & Ortiz, L. (2023). Fifteen years of critical race theory in social work education: What we've learned. In L. S. Abrams, S. Edmonds Crewe, A. J. Dettlaff, & J. H. Williams (Eds.) *Social work, white supremacy, and racial justice: Reckoning with our history, interrogating our present, re-imagining our future* (pp. 335–351). Oxford University Press.

Aldana, A., Richards-Schuster, K., & Checkoway, B. (2016). Dialogic pedagogy for youth participatory action research: Facilitation of an intergroup empowerment program. *Social Work with Groups*, *39*(4), 339–358.

Aldana, A., & Vazquez, N. (2020). From colour-blind racism to critical race theory: The road towards anti-racist social work in the United States. In G. Singh & S. Masocha (Eds.) *Anti-racist social work: International perspectives* (pp. 129–148). Red Globe Press.

Aldana, A., Vazquez, N., Hosea, T. (2022). Centering anti-racism in social work education: Integration of CRT across an MSW curriculum. *Critical Social Work 24*(1), 20–38. https://doi.org/10.22329/csw.v24i1.7853

Annamma, S. A., Jackson, D. D., & Morrison, D. (2017). Conceptualizing color-evasiveness: Using dis/ability critical race theory to expand a color-blind racial ideology in education and society. *Race Ethnicity and Education, 20*(2), 147–162.

Anzaldúa, G. (1987). *Borderlands/La Frontera: The new mestiza*. Aunt Lute Books.

Ashley, W. (2024). *Merging clinical social work practice and antiracist positioning*. Peter Lang.

Bonilla-Silva, E. (2006). Racism without racists: Color-Blind racism and the persistence of racial inequality in the United States. *Science and Society, 70*(3), 431–434.

Bourgois, P., Holmes, S. M., Sue, K., & Quesada, J. (2017). Structural vulnerability: Operationalizing the concept to address health disparities in clinical care. *Academic Medicine: Journal of the Association of American Medical Colleges, 92*(3), 299.

Bussey, S. R. (2024a). Skills to enhance the efficacy of anti-racist supervision. *Journal of Social Work, 24*(3), 397–414.

Bussey, S. (2024b). The use of structural assessment to bring a macro-understanding to micro-level encounters. In W. Ashley (Ed.) *Merging clinical social work practice and antiracist positioning* (Chapter 12). Peter Lang Publishing Inc.

Collins, P. H. (1990). *Black feminist thought: Knowledge, consciousness, and the politics of empowerment*. Routledge.

(2019). The difference that power makes: Intersectionality and participatory democracy. In O. Hankivsky & J. S. Jordan-Zachery (Eds.) *The Palgrave handbook of intersectionality in public policy* (pp. 167–192). Cham: Springer International.

Constance-Huggins, M. (2012). Critical race theory in social work education: A framework for addressing racial disparities. *Critical Social Work*, *13*(2), 1–16.

Crenshaw, K. (1989). *Demarginalizing the intersection of race and sex: A Black feminist critique of antidiscrimination doctrine, feminist theory and antiracist politics*. University of Chicago Legal Forum, pp. 139–167.

——— (1995). Mapping the margins. In K. W. Crenshaw, N. Gotanda, G. Peller, & K. Thomas (Eds.) *Critical race theory: The key writings that formed the movement*, *3*(15) (pp. 357–383). New Press.

CSWE (2022). Educational policies and accreditation standards for baccalaureate and master's social work programs. www.cswe.org/getmedia/bb5d8afe-7680-42dc-a332-a6e6103f4998/2022-EPAS.pdf

David, E. R., Schroeder, T. M., & Fernandez, J. (2019). Internalized racism: A systematic review of the psychological literature on racism's most insidious consequence. *Journal of Social Issues*, *75*(4), 1057–1086.

Delgado, R., & Stefancic, J. (2023). *Critical race theory: An introduction* (3rd Ed.). NYU Press.

Einbinder, S. D. (2020). Reflections on importing critical race theory into social work: The state of social work literature and students' voices. *Journal of Social Work Education*, *56*(2), 327–340.

Essed, P. (1991). *Understanding everyday racism: An interdisciplinary theory* (vol. 2). Sage.

Feagin, J. (2013). *Systemic racism: A theory of oppression*. Routledge.

Fook, J., & Gardner, F. (2007). *Practising critical reflection: A resource handbook*. McGraw-Hill Education.

French, B. H., Lewis, J. A., Mosley, D. V., Adames, H. Y., Chavez-Dueñas, N. Y., Chen, G. A., & Neville, H. A. (2020). Toward a psychological framework of radical healing in communities of color. *The Counseling Psychologist*, *48*(1), 14–46.

Grzanka, P. R., Flores, M. J., VanDaalen, R. A., & Velez, G. (2020). Intersectionality in psychology: Translational science for social justice [Editorial]. *Translational Issues in Psychological Science*, *6*(4), 304–313. https://doi.org/10.1037/tps0000276

Hattley, J. (2024). The impact of racism and racial gaslighting on practice. In W. Ashley (Ed.) *Merging clinical social work and antiracism positioning: How to be a clinically sound, antiracist social work practitioner* (Chapter 4). Peter Lang.

Hernández, N. K., Milliner, M., Garcia, K., & Mounier, C. (2024). Structural competency and antiracist social work practice with youth and families: Part one, individual and family treatment. In W. Ashley (Ed.) *Merging clinical social work practice and antiracist positioning*. Peter Lang.

Hochman, A. (2019). Racialization: A defense of the concept. *Ethnic and Racial Studies*, 42(8), 1245–1262.
Jost, J. T., Banaji, M. R., & Nosek, B. A. (2004). A decade of system justification theory: Accumulated evidence of conscious and unconscious bolstering of the status quo. *Political Psychology*, 25(6), 881–919.
Kendi, I. (2019). *How to be an antiracist*. Bodley Head.
Legha, R. K. (2023). Getting off the racist sidelines: An antiracist approach to mental health supervision and training. *The Clinical Supervisor*, 42(2), 213–236.
Magee, R. V. (2019). *The inner work of racial justice: Healing ourselves and transforming our communities through mindfulness*. Penguin Random House.
McKay, D. L., Vinyeta, K., & Norgaard, K. M. (2020). Theorizing race and settler colonialism within US sociology. *Sociology Compass*, 14(9), e12821.
Moraga, C., & Anzaldúa, G. (1983). *This bridge called my back: Writings by radical women of color* (2nd ed.). Kitchen Table: Women of Color Press. (1st ed., 1981, Suny Press).
Mounier, C., & Cortez, A. (2024). Antiracist social work practice with youth and families: Applying structural competency to practice settings and with community partners. In W. Ashley (Ed.) *Merging clinical social work practice and antiracist positioning* (Chapter 14). Peter Lang.
Mountz, S., Lipscomb, A., & Fowler, M. (2024). Embodying antiracist practice through mindfulness and intergroup dialogue. In W. Ashley (Ed.) *Merging clinical social work practice and antiracist positioning* (Chapter 16). Peter Lang.
Murray-Lichtman, A., Aldana, A., Izaksonas, E., Williams, T., Naseh, M., Deepak, A. C., & Rountree, M. A. (2023). Dual pandemics awaken urgent call to advance anti-racism education in social work: Pedagogical illustrations. In M. Y. Lee, M. Cheung, M. A. Robinson, M. Rountree, M. Spencer, & M. L. Teasley (Eds.) *Dual Pandemics* (pp. 7–18). Routledge.
Nakaoka, S., Ortiz, L., & Garcia, B. (2019). Intentional weaving of critical race theory into an MSW program in a Hispanic-serving institution. *Urban Social Work*, 3(S1), S115–S128.
NASW. (2021). NASW report to the profession on racial justice priorities and action. https://www.socialworkers.org/LinkClick.aspx?fileticket=29AYH9qAdXc%3D&portalid=0
Omi, M., & Winant, H. (1993). On the theoretical status of the concept of race. In C. McCarthy & W. Crichlow (Eds.) *Race, identity and representation in education*, pp. 3–10. Routledge.
Ortiz, L., & Jani, J. (2010). Critical race theory: A transformational model for teaching diversity. *Journal of Social Work Education*, 46(2), 175–193.
Paez, J., Aguila, K., Hernandez, M. Montoya, M, Lermada Del Aguila, L. X., & Rosales, A. (2024). Indigenous knowledge and relational accountability as antidotes to coloniality of social work practice. In W. Ashley (Ed.) *Merging clinical social work and antiracism positioning: How to be a clinically sound, antiracist social work practitioner* (Chapter 19). Peter Lang.

Ray, V. (2022). *On critical race theory: Why it matters & why you should care*. Random House.

Schmidt, C., & Tronnier, C. D. (2024). Conceptualizing and responding to racial trauma: Racials justice considerations for forming and facilitating groups. In W. Ashley (Ed.) *Merging clinical social work and antiracism positioning: How to be a clinically sound, antiracist social work practitioner* (Chapter 23). Peter Lang.

Smith, L., & Wofford, N. (2024). The impact of anti-Black racism: Perspectives on assessment of racial trauma when working with Black-identified populations. In W. Ashley (Ed.) *Merging clinical social work and antiracism positioning: How to be a clinically sound, antiracist social work practitioner* (Chapter 6). Peter Lang.

Southbank Centre (2016, March). Kimberlé Crenshaw: Intersectionality and gender equality [Video]. YouTube. https://youtu.be/DW4HLgYPlA?si=MT74BB2ish4Gxe_x

Taiwo, A. (2022). Social workers' use of critical reflection. *Journal of Social Work*, *22*(2), 384–401.

Tang Yan, C., Orlandimeje, R., Drucker, R., & Lang, A. J. (2022). Unsettling reflexivity and critical race pedagogy in social work education: Narratives from social work students. *Social Work Education*, *41*(8), 1669–1692.

Tarshis, S., & Baird, S. L. (2021). Applying intersectionality in clinical supervision: A scoping review. *The Clinical Supervisor*, *40*(2), 218–240.

Versey, H. S., Cogburn, C. C., Wilkins, C. L., & Joseph, N. (2019). Appropriated racial oppression: Implications for mental health in Whites and Blacks. *Social Science & Medicine*, *230*, 295–302.

FURTHER READING

Gómez, L. E. (2022). *Inventing Latinos: A new story of American racism*. The New Press.

Harro, B. (2000). The cycle of liberation. In M. Adams (Ed.) *Readings for diversity and social justice*, *2* (pp. 52–58). Routledge.

CHAPTER 5

The Process of Decolonizing Supervision and Leadership (It Do Take Nerve)

Ann Marie Garran, Nathaniel L. Currie, Jack Burke, Rebecca "Bex" Lisenbee, Gavin Meade and Adrianna N. Taylor

Decolonization in Social Work Practice

Decolonization in social work practice involves recognizing and addressing the historical and ongoing impacts of colonialism on marginalized communities. It requires practitioners to reflect on their own positionality and biases, ensuring that services are culturally relevant and respectful of Indigenous knowledge and practices. This process emphasizes collaboration with communities and prioritizing their voices and needs in decision-making (Grosfoguel, 2011). Social workers are called to challenge systemic inequalities and advocate for social justice, fostering empowerment and healing. By integrating decolonial perspectives, social work can promote equity, resilience, and a deeper understanding of the cultural contexts in which individuals and families exist.

Decolonized social work leadership and supervision emphasize the importance of integrating Indigenous knowledge, values, and practices into each aspect of social work theory and practice. A decolonized approach challenges and transforms the historically Eurocentric frameworks that have dominated social work education and practice for decades. Decolonization in social work involves recognizing the ever-present power dynamics at play and working to dismantle oppressive structures that marginalize oppressed and Indigenous communities. In so doing, social workers can reflect on their biases (Garran et al., 2021) and engage in meaningful partnerships with marginalized communities, prioritizing their voices and experiences.

With decolonized leadership, practitioners are encouraged to embrace collaborative and participatory approaches that empower clients and communities. This means fostering environments where diverse voices are heard and respected, and where traditional knowledge systems are valued alongside Western methodologies. Leaders in social work must prioritize cultural humility and ongoing self-reflection, understanding their own positionality and the impact it has on their practice.

Ultimately, decolonized social work leadership and supervision aim to create a more equitable and inclusive practice. By challenging colonial legacies and embracing diverse perspectives, social work can better serve all communities and promote social justice in a meaningful way. This transformative approach not only enriches the profession but also contributes to healing and reconciliation efforts within society.

Supervision in a decolonized context also requires a shift in focus. Supervisors should create spaces for dialogue that honors the lived experiences of practitioners from different backgrounds, particularly those from Indigenous communities. This includes providing mentorship that recognizes the social, historical, and cultural contexts of the individuals being supervised (Hall, 2018). By integrating traditional practices and community engagement into supervision, social workers can enhance their effectiveness and build stronger relationships with clients.

Understanding the decolonizing process is critical in social work because professionals regularly interact with individuals and groups shaped by these socialization patterns. To disrupt oppressive systems, Harro (2013) offers The Cycle of Socialization as a framework to explain how individuals are socialized into societal norms, beliefs, and behaviors through various influences from birth to adulthood. It helps to understand how social structures like family, education, media, and culture shape individuals and perpetuate systems of privilege and oppression.

The Cycle of Socialization describes the process through which individuals are taught social norms, values, roles, and behaviors. This framework offers insight into how people are influenced by their environments, families, educational systems, and cultural institutions. In social work, particularly in clinical, supervisory, and leadership roles, understanding this cycle is crucial to effectively address systemic oppression, personal biases, and social justice issues. The cycle influences how our understanding of systemic oppression shapes professional approaches, decision-making, and interactions with diverse populations.

The Cycle of Socialization (2013) consists of two parts: the beginning and the core. The cycle starts with initial socialization from parents, guardians, and early experiences. As people grow, they internalize societal messages, roles, and behaviors from schools, media, and peer groups. These messages are often influenced by privilege, power dynamics, and oppression. The core of the cycle represents feelings of fear, ignorance, confusion, and insecurity, which can perpetuate harmful beliefs and behaviors, either consciously or unconsciously. The Cycle of Socialization, thus, perpetuates systems of oppression (racism, sexism, heteronormativity, etc.) unless interrupted.

Key Components:

- First Socialization: This occurs through family, caregivers, and immediate community members.
- Institutional and Cultural Socialization: Reinforced by media, education, and religious institutions, further embedding societal norms.
- Internalized Messages: These influence personal biases, fears, and insecurities, which can affect how one interacts with others.
- Enforcements and Rewards: Societal rewards or punishments that reinforce adherence to these norms.

Understanding this process is critical in social work because professionals regularly interact with individuals and groups shaped by these socialization patterns. To disrupt oppressive systems, social workers must recognize the cycle's influence on their clients and themselves.

In clinical social work, practitioners provide direct services, often engaging with individuals, families, or groups facing a range of mental health, emotional, and social challenges. The Cycle of Socialization plays a significant role in shaping the client's worldview and internalized beliefs, which can influence their behavior and mental health.

The Cycle of Socialization encourages a client-centered approach to social work treatment. For instance, social workers must recognize how a client's identity (e.g., race, gender, socioeconomic status) has been shaped by their early socialization and reinforced by institutions. A client from a marginalized community may internalize negative societal messages about their worth, which can manifest as low self-esteem, depression, or anxiety.

Practitioners must be aware of their own biases formed by their socialization process. Unexamined biases can affect clinical judgment, leading to misdiagnosis or improper treatment plans. Self-reflection and active participation in anti-oppressive practices are essential (Goodman, 2011). Many clients face intersectional oppression, where race, class, gender, or sexuality intersect to create compounded experiences of trauma. A clinician's understanding of this can shape their therapeutic interventions, ensuring that the therapy is attuned to the client's unique social and cultural context.

Clinicians also have the opportunity to help clients disrupt the Cycle of Socialization by:

- Encouraging critical self-reflection, which allows clients to examine how societal influences have impacted their self-concept and behavior.

- Promoting empowerment, which helps clients recognize their agency in challenging oppressive systems and narratives.
- Supporting identity development, which helps clients build a healthier, more affirming sense of self, especially for those individuals from marginalized populations.
- Recognizing how the Cycle of Socialization affects ethical decision-making in clinical work. It requires practitioners to challenge their biases and engage in continuous learning, as social workers must adhere to ethical standards that prioritize cultural competence and sensitivity (NASW, 2021).

The Cycle of Socialization and Social Work Supervision

In supervisory roles, social workers are responsible for guiding and mentoring other professionals, ensuring ethical practices, and facilitating professional development. The Cycle of Socialization impacts supervision in several ways (Figure 5.1).

1. Power Dynamics and Hierarchies

Role of Power: Supervisors often occupy positions of power, which can mirror societal hierarchies (Hall, 2018). If supervisors are not conscious of how their socialization influences their perspectives, they may unintentionally replicate oppressive behaviors in the workplace.

2. Equitable Supervision: Supervisors must strive to create an equitable environment where supervisees feel respected, regardless of their background or identity. This requires self-awareness, as supervisors need to confront how their socialization affects their leadership style.

Supervisors must also be proactive in identifying and addressing their own biases and those of their supervisees. By fostering an environment of open dialogue, they can encourage staff to reflect on their internalized beliefs and how these influence their interactions with clients. Getting to this point requires both parties to pay careful attention to how the supervisory relationship is unfolding. Because social work is a profession based on relationships, if a supervisor and supervisee are not connected, it will be much more difficult to navigate "stuck" points or have challenging conversations that can come up in supervisory discussions.

To help disrupt the Cycle of Socialization, supervisors must provide training focused on cultural awareness, antiracism, anti-oppression, and bias reduction. Additionally, encouraging supervisees to explore their

Process of Decolonizing Supervision and Leadership

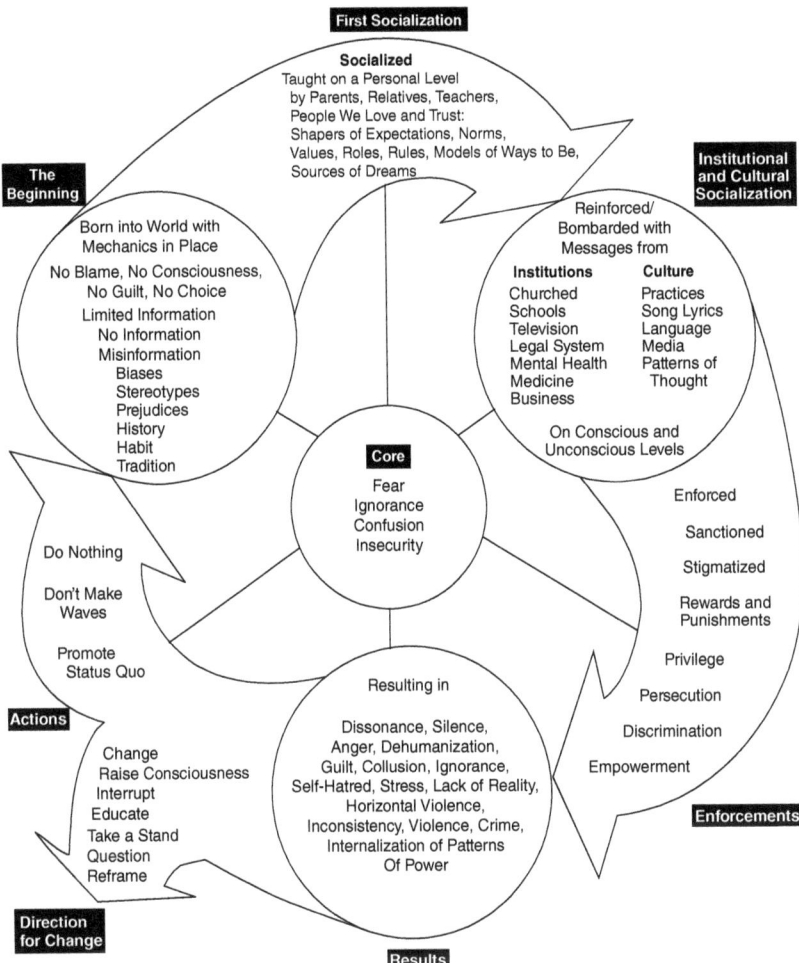

Figure 5.1 The Cycle of Socialization.

socialization experiences fosters growth and promotes ethical practice. Supervisors also play a crucial role in supporting the emotional labor required in social work, particularly for staff from marginalized backgrounds. These workers often experience burnout at higher rates due to the compounded stress of vicarious trauma and systemic oppression. Supervisors should recognize these additional burdens and provide appropriate support, such as reflective supervision and access to mental health resources.

The Cycle of Socialization and Leadership

In leadership positions, social workers shape organizational culture, policies, and practices. The Cycle of Socialization can heavily influence how leaders understand their role in fostering inclusive, equitable, and just workplaces. For instance, leaders have a responsibility to address systemic inequities within their organizations and the communities they serve. To do this, they must first reflect on their own socialization and how it shapes their understanding of power, privilege, and oppression.

Next, leaders must ensure that policies are inclusive and support marginalized groups. This requires understanding how historical and institutional oppression affects different groups and making conscious efforts to disrupt these patterns in the workplace. Thus, social work leaders should be well versed in the ways that systemic inequality occurs at the micro, mezzo, and macro levels and should be able to assess for these inequities at their own agencies and organizations.

Leaders should actively model antiracist and anti-oppressive practices by challenging the status quo and promoting equity. This includes prioritizing diverse perspectives in decision-making processes, dismantling hierarchical structures that perpetuate inequality, and ensuring a culture of accountability. Next, leadership development should emphasize mentorship, particularly for underrepresented groups. Leaders must ensure that social workers from marginalized backgrounds have access to opportunities for advancement and leadership training.

One crucial stumbling block that leaders must also navigate is the ethical challenges that arise from the Cycle of Socialization. Ethical leadership requires transparency, integrity, and a commitment to social justice. Leaders should consistently evaluate their policies and practices to ensure that they are promoting inclusivity and fairness, particularly in hiring, promotion, and staff development.

The Cycle of Socialization has profound impacts on clinical, supervisory, and leadership work in social work. This framework emphasizes how deeply ingrained societal norms are and the importance of conscious effort to challenge and disrupt systems of inequality. By understanding this cycle, social workers can better recognize how systemic oppression and internalized beliefs influence their clients, their colleagues, and themselves. Disrupting the Cycle of Socialization requires conscious efforts in self-reflection, education, and the promotion of equity and justice within both individual practices and institutional structures. Social workers in clinical, supervisory, and leadership roles must continue to challenge their own biases and foster environments that prioritize social justice, diversity, and inclusion in order to break the cycle and create meaningful change.

Decolonizing this cycle involves critically examining and disrupting these processes to challenge colonial narratives and power dynamics. It requires recognizing how colonial histories shape current social norms and identities, particularly for marginalized communities. By fostering awareness of these influences, individuals can reclaim their narratives and identities.

Decolonization encourages the integration of Indigenous knowledge, values, and practices into socialization processes. This shift promotes cultural humility, empowers communities, and fosters an environment where diverse perspectives are respected and valued. Ultimately, decolonizing the cycle of socialization aims to create a more equitable and inclusive society that honors all voices and experiences.

Antiracist and Affirming Supervision and Leadership

Antiracist and affirming supervision and leadership require intentional actions and a commitment to fostering an inclusive and equitable environment. By embracing diversity, promoting open dialogue, and supporting professional growth, leaders can create a workplace culture that values and uplifts every individual. Antiracist and affirming supervision and leadership also involve creating environments where diversity is embraced, and equity is prioritized. Here are some key principles and practices:

1. Commitment to Equity: Prioritize equitable treatment and opportunities for all employees, actively working to eliminate biases and systemic barriers.
2. Transparency and Accountability: Maintain open communication and hold yourself and others accountable for actions and decisions that impact equity and inclusion. Check in with one another regularly to keep the channels of communication open.
3. Inclusive Decision-Making: Involve diverse voices in decision-making processes to ensure a variety of perspectives are considered. This might require active recruitment to engage individuals who represent a range of perspectives and to impress upon them that their perspective is wanted, needed, and valued.
4. Bias Training: Implement regular training sessions to help supervisors recognize and address their own biases. Also, encourage supervisors to provide access to resources and training that support career advancement for all employees, particularly those from marginalized groups.

Difficult and Vulnerable Conversations in Practice

In social work, practitioners often engage in difficult and vulnerable conversations that are essential for supporting clients through challenging circumstances. These conversations may involve topics like trauma, abuse, mental health, addiction, or family conflict. Handling such discussions with sensitivity and professionalism is crucial to building trust and fostering positive outcomes.

One of the key skills in social work is active listening, which involves giving full attention to the client and validating their emotions. Social workers must convey empathy, showing they understand the client's feelings without judgment. This helps clients feel heard and understood, which is critical in conversations about sensitive issues. Active listening also allows social workers to gather necessary information and offer appropriate interventions, making it a vital tool in navigating these difficult conversations.

Navigating Emotional Responses

Difficult conversations often elicit strong emotional reactions, both from clients and social workers. Clients may feel anger, fear, shame, or guilt, while social workers may experience secondary trauma or emotional exhaustion. Managing these emotional responses requires self-awareness and emotional regulation on the part of the social worker. It is essential to remain calm, patient, and nonreactive, even in emotionally charged situations. Social workers must also practice self-care and seek supervision to manage their emotional well-being effectively.

Balancing Professional Boundaries

While empathy and support are vital, maintaining professional boundaries is equally important. Social workers must strike a balance between being compassionate and remaining objective. Boundaries prevent over-identification with the client's struggles, which could compromise the practitioner's ability to provide effective guidance. Clear boundaries also protect both the client and the social worker from becoming enmeshed in unhealthy relational dynamics.

Difficult and vulnerable conversations are integral to social work practice. By employing active listening, managing emotional responses, and maintaining professional boundaries, social workers can navigate these conversations effectively while promoting client well-being and empowerment.

Teaching about Race, Racism, Oppression, and Decolonization

Teaching about race and racism in social work is crucial for preparing practitioners to engage effectively with diverse populations and address systemic inequalities. Social work, rooted in principles of social justice and human rights, must confront the realities of racism that pervade many aspects of society. Educators play a vital role in equipping future social workers with the knowledge, skills, and awareness needed to navigate and dismantle these oppressive structures.

Understanding Race and Racism

Before delving into effective teaching strategies, it is essential to establish a foundational understanding of race and racism. Race is a social construct that categorizes individuals based on perceived physical differences, while racism encompasses both individual prejudice and systemic discrimination that perpetuates inequality. Teaching students about the historical context of these concepts, including colonialism, slavery, and segregation, is vital for understanding their contemporary implications.

Curriculum Development

A comprehensive curriculum should incorporate a variety of perspectives and experiences. This includes exploring the intersectionality of race with other identities such as class, gender, and sexual orientation (Hill Collins & Bilge, 2020). Courses should cover topics like the impact of systemic racism on health disparities, access to resources, and the criminal justice system. Incorporating case studies and real-world examples can help students grasp the complexities of these issues.

Engaging with Diverse Voices

To foster a deeper understanding of race and racism, it is essential to engage with diverse voices. This can be achieved by inviting guest speakers from various racial and ethnic backgrounds, including activists, community leaders, and scholars. Such interactions can provide students with firsthand insights into the lived experiences of marginalized communities, challenging stereotypes and fostering empathy.

Critical Reflection

As we discussed in previous chapters, encouraging critical reflection is a key component of teaching about race and racism. Students should be prompted to examine their own biases, privileges, and positions within the social hierarchy. Assignments that encourage introspection, such as reflective journals or group discussions, can help students process their feelings and thoughts about race. This self-awareness is essential for effective social work practice, as it enables practitioners to recognize and mitigate their biases in client interactions and to grow their critical consciousness (Diemer et al., 2021).

Active Learning Strategies

Active learning strategies can enhance engagement and understanding. Role-playing exercises, simulations, and community-based projects can help students apply theoretical knowledge to practical situations. For example, students might participate in a community service project that addresses a specific racial issue, allowing them to witness the effects of systemic racism firsthand and engage with affected communities.

Addressing Resistance

It is common for students to experience discomfort when discussing race and racism. Educators should create a safe and supportive classroom environment where difficult conversations can take place. Establishing ground rules for respectful dialogue can help mitigate resistance and encourage open exchange. Educators should also be prepared to address defensiveness and challenge students to confront uncomfortable truths about race and privilege.

Teaching about race and racism in social work is not merely an academic endeavor – it is a moral imperative. By equipping future social workers with a comprehensive understanding of these issues, educators can empower them to become advocates for social justice and agents of change. As social work continues to evolve, the integration of race and racism into the curriculum will remain vital for fostering a profession that is responsive to the needs of all communities and committed to dismantling systemic inequalities. Through critical engagement, reflection, and active learning, future social workers can develop the skills necessary to confront racism and promote equity in their practice.

By equipping social work students with the knowledge and skills to address race, racism, oppression, and decolonization, educators can prepare them to be effective advocates for change and champions of social justice. This comprehensive approach ensures that future social workers are ready to engage with diverse communities thoughtfully and ethically, and is crucial for preparing practitioners to advocate for social justice and equity.

Anti-Oppressive Social Work and Supervision

Anti-oppressive social work (AOSW) and supervision are intertwined concepts aimed at addressing and mitigating the various forms of power imbalance, inequality, and discrimination present in both client relationships and professional settings.

Anti-Oppressive Social Work

AOSW seeks to challenge and dismantle systemic oppression that affects marginalized groups. It is rooted in social justice and strives to promote equity and inclusivity. In practice, this approach involves recognizing how power dynamics, privilege, and social structures affect clients' experiences and outcomes (Baines, 2020).

Key principles of AOSW include:

1. Power Awareness: Recognizing the imbalance of power between clients and social workers. Social workers are encouraged to be aware of their own privilege (based on race, gender, class, etc.) and its impact on the therapeutic relationship.
2. Collaboration: Instead of the social worker dictating solutions, AOSW advocates for working collaboratively with clients, recognizing them as experts in their own lives. This empowers clients and creates a more equal partnership.
3. Challenging Oppression: AOSW requires active engagement in identifying and challenging oppressive systems (e.g., racism, sexism, ableism). Social workers not only address these issues on an individual level, but also engage in advocacy and systemic change.
4. Reflective Practice: Social workers must continuously reflect on their practice, acknowledging their own biases and how their actions may reinforce or counteract oppression.
5. Intersectionality: This framework examines how various forms of oppression (based on race, gender, class, sexuality, etc.) intersect and affect individuals differently. Social workers must consider these intersections when assessing and supporting clients.

Anti-Oppressive Supervision

Anti-oppressive supervision (AOS) is the application of anti-oppressive principles within the supervisory relationship. In social work, supervision is a vital process where more experienced professionals (supervisors) guide and support the development of less experienced practitioners (supervisees). AOS recognizes that supervision itself can reinforce or dismantle power imbalances and seeks to create an environment that is equitable, reflective, and supportive of both personal and professional growth.

Key principles of AOS include:

1. Power and Authority Awareness: Supervisors acknowledge the power dynamics inherent in the supervisory relationship and work to mitigate them. This involves creating a safe space for supervisees to express concerns, ask questions, and reflect without fear of judgment or retaliation.
2. Reflective Supervision: Supervisors encourage reflective practice, helping supervisees examine how their identities (race, gender, class) and biases may impact their work with clients. Supervisors also reflect on their own positions of privilege and how these might shape the supervisory relationship.
3. Cultural Awareness and Sensitivity: Supervisors must have a deep understanding of the cultural, social, and historical contexts of their supervisees and clients. They should support supervisees in developing cultural awareness and integrating anti-oppressive approaches into their practice.
4. Collaboration and Empowerment: Similar to client relationships, AOS encourages a collaborative relationship in supervision, where supervisees are encouraged to take an active role in their professional development. Supervisors aim to empower supervisees by acknowledging their knowledge and experiences, promoting a more egalitarian dynamic.
5. Ethical and Social Justice Lens: AOS incorporates an ethical responsibility to challenge social injustices, not only in client work but also in organizational structures. Supervisors guide supervisees in understanding their role in promoting social justice within the profession and beyond.

Intersection of Anti-Oppressive Social Work and Supervision

Anti-oppressive practice in supervision is critical because it ensures that the principles of AOSW are modeled and reinforced throughout professional development. If social workers experience oppressive supervision, they are more likely to reproduce those dynamics in their own practice, potentially harming clients. Therefore, AOS supervision plays a crucial role in promoting ethical, reflective, and socially just social work.

Supervisors are responsible for modeling anti-oppressive values, such as respect, collaboration, and the challenging of systemic injustices, which supervisees can then apply in their client work. Also, supervisors support supervisees in identifying systemic barriers in their work, such as policies that disadvantage certain groups, and work together to find ways to navigate or challenge these barriers. This is an ongoing process through the life of the supervisory relationship.

AOS recognizes the emotional toll that working with oppression and trauma can have on social workers. Supervisors help supervisees manage their well-being, ensuring that they have the resilience to continue practicing ethically and effectively. AOSW and supervision are complementary practices that work together to foster a more just and equitable professional environment. By integrating anti-oppressive principles into both client work and supervision, social workers can better support marginalized communities, challenge oppressive structures, and contribute to systemic change. Creating a *web of resistance* involves building interconnected communities that actively challenge systems of oppression and promote social justice. This concept emphasizes solidarity, collaboration, and the sharing of resources among diverse groups committed to collective action (Garran et al., 2021).

To establish this web, it is essential to identify and connect with various stakeholders, including grassroots organizations, activists, and community members. Hosting workshops, forums, and social events can facilitate dialogue and strengthen relationships, fostering a sense of belonging and mutual support.

Education plays a crucial role in resistance. Providing training on issues like systemic racism, economic inequality, and environmental justice empowers individuals with knowledge and strategies to advocate for change. Utilizing social media platforms can amplify voices, spread awareness, and mobilize grassroots campaigns.

Additionally, creating safe-enough spaces for marginalized communities to share their experiences and strategies encourages resilience and empowerment. It also boosts mental health, as these spaces allow some measure of relaxation. Intersectionality should be prioritized, recognizing that different identities and experiences shape individuals' struggles and strengths.

Through this web of resistance, communities can collectively challenge oppressive systems, promote equity, and cultivate a culture of solidarity. By working together, they can create meaningful change, uplift marginalized voices, and foster a more just society.

Creating a web of resistance to dismantle racism involves weaving together various strategies and efforts to combat systemic oppression and foster inclusivity. This comprehensive approach requires commitment from individuals, communities, and institutions. To effectively dismantle racism, it's crucial to understand its roots and manifestations. Racism is not just individual prejudice – it's a systemic issue embedded in societal structures. It involves power dynamics that privilege certain groups over others based on race.

Creating a web of resistance to dismantle racism is an ongoing process that requires dedication and collaboration. By addressing the issue from multiple angles – education, policy, community engagement, and personal commitment – we can work toward a more equitable and inclusive society. The journey demands resilience, openness, and an unwavering commitment to justice and equality for all.

Maintaining Motivation

Maintaining motivation in the fight to dismantle racism is crucial for sustaining long-term progress. Here are some strategies to keep the momentum going:

Personal Commitment, Community, and Support

1. Engage in ongoing education about racism and its effects. This deepens understanding and reinforces commitment.
2. Practice self-care to prevent burnout. Activism can be exhausting, so it's important to recharge and maintain mental health.
3. Build Support Networks: Connect with like-minded individuals and groups. A supportive community can provide encouragement and new perspectives.
4. Celebrate Milestones: Recognize and celebrate achievements, no matter how small. This helps maintain a positive outlook.

Visible Impact

5. Track Progress: Keep a record of changes and successes in the fight against racism. Seeing tangible results can be highly motivating.
6. Highlight Stories of Change: Share stories of individuals and communities positively impacted by antiracist efforts.

Inspiration and Role Models

7. Learn from Leaders: Study the lives and work of influential antiracist leaders. Their journeys can provide inspiration and guidance.
8. Mentorship: Seek out mentors or become one. Mentorship can offer motivation and a sense of purpose.

Creative Engagement

9. Art and Expression: Use art, music, and writing to express antiracist messages. Creative outlets can inspire and engage others.
10. Innovative Approaches: Experiment with new strategies and ideas to keep the work dynamic and engaging.

Reflection and Growth

11. Regular Reflection: Take time to reflect on personal growth and the impact of efforts. This can reinforce motivation and clarify goals.
12. Adaptability: Stay open to adapting strategies based on what is effective and necessary.

Collective Action

13. Collaborative Projects: Engage in collaborative projects that unite diverse groups. Working together can amplify impact and motivation.
14. Public Engagement: Participate in public demonstrations and campaigns. Collective action can boost morale and visibility.

Maintaining motivation in dismantling racism requires a balanced approach that includes education, community support, visible progress, and personal well-being. By staying connected, celebrating successes, and remaining adaptable, individuals and communities can sustain their commitment to creating a more equitable society.

Allyship

Allyship is another concept that has a living or ever-developing definition, especially as it becomes more widely understood and embedded into both practice and community work. Allyship is the practice of individuals within advantaged/dominant groups providing support to members of underrepresented or marginalized populations in efforts to promote rights, representation, inclusion, and opportunity (Currie et al., 2024; Ayyala & Coley, 2022; Melaku et al., 2021). Allyship is not a one-time action but a lifelong process of growing awareness, developing critical accountability for actions, building trust and relationships with members of the marginalized community, and using power and privilege to advocate for equal and equitable rights (Ayyala & Coley, 2022; Currie et al., 2024). Allyship requires action (Miller & Garran, 2017); it is a process of both learning, unlearning, and evaluating one's privilege and power in a relationship where vulnerability or oppression may occur. Allyship also requires active advocacy for marginalized groups on an individual, systemic, and community level (Gilmore et al., 2024). Allies must be willing to refocus from their needs and then be willing to relinquish power and/or privilege in order to elevate the voices of historically excluded and/or harmed groups. Clinical supervision is an ideal setting to teach and embed this concept into practice, as supervisee are responsible for combining empowerment, relationship building, and social justice into their clinical and community practice.

Allyship in Clinical Work

Clinical work is progressing from a "therapist led" model to a therapeutic partnership with influence from the Liberation Health Theory. With the intent to infuse social justice into clinical work, the Liberation Health Theory has combined popular education, liberation psychology, and radical social work (Martinez & Fleck-Henderson, 2014). Long gone are the days of hubris where the clinician can assume expertise into the lives and experiences of others. Ideally, helping professionals are driven by genuine compassion and a desire to genuinely support and serve. Somewhere along the way, the supremacy embedded into the educational system has hijacked the purest intentions behind this work and replaced them with the misguided values of capitalism and hierarchy. The Liberation Health framework aims to change the current approach and redirect it to one that considers the personal, cultural, and institutional factors that impact an individual and highlights client-centered care that is holistic, critical, empowering, and hopeful (Martinez & Fleck-Henderson, 2014). Through understanding and incorporating frameworks such as Liberation Health, clinicians can transform from "helping professionals" to allies and co-conspirators, which may be a stronger and more effective approach to empowerment-focused clinical work.

Merging Allyship and Leadership

Social work professionals are often employed by schools, hospitals, and military settings, which leads to different types of supervision.

Interdisciplinary social work is important to focus on when discussing supervision because of the unique positionality of social workers within the team. Peer supervision is highlighted in these areas due to the hierarchy of systems and the devaluation of social work practice embedded in other fields. As frustrating as this dynamic can be, it is often the most valuable change agent. Through the building of trusting relationships with other professionals, social workers can work to disarm both superiority and defensiveness by strategically dismantling racism and oppression through peer supervision. Challenging oppression and racism is necessary; however, we must learn to do it with a reduction of shame, as shame can shut people down and create barriers (Miller & Garran, 2017).

Allyship in action is using correct terminology when speaking with nurses, physicians, and other providers, utilizing real-time shame-reducing correction or assisting with the importance of preferred language. Transphobia in healthcare can present as refusal of treatment, misgendering, inappropriate questions, and ridicule (Gilmore et al., 2024; Stonewall, 2015). Using clinical skills in peer interactions is an important part of disrupting the oppression and leading by example for other professionals. One barrier to affirming healthcare for gender minorities is the absence of meaningful education for healthcare professionals (Gilmore et al., 2024). Educating other professionals in non-shaming or blaming ways can be useful and effective in introducing social justice to their professions, where the educational system has intentionally neglected or overlooked them.

Utilizing the situation in the case scenario [referenced in Chapter 6], the social worker was able to develop leadership changes in future policy. The social worker was asked by the NICU (Neonatal Intensive Care Unit) leadership team to partner in the development of a new approach to the birthing process. The social worker utilized this case experience to advocate for parents who identify as nonbinary or caregivers who do not belong to a "mother" or "father" category. Using the term "Parent" or "Caregiver" instead of "mother/father" is one small way to advocate for changes in misgendering the caregivers of patients. The team was receptive to the idea of honoring this language when presented in a nonjudgmental way to emphasize inclusion and with the use of a specific example of when the term could potentially further harm.

Humanity is ever-changing; therefore, the populations served will present with needs that will continually challenge social workers and helping professionals. Not to mention the current political climate that restricts the scope of practice, such as gender-affirming care. One important aspect of allyship is openness to embracing new ideas and delivering care that meets the needs of those who are typically excluded (Gilmore et al., 2024).

Relational Cultural Theory and Supervision

The recognition of oppression in practice settings is a foundational step in an anti-oppressive journey. Supervision offers a responsive space to explore oppression that occurs in everyday practice, and supervisors can cultivate the discussion with curiosity and with a shame-reducing approach utilizing the Relational Cultural Theory (RCT). RCT utilizes an approach grounded in connection, which emphasizes the importance of fostering growth in relationships based on mutual empathy and empowerment (Jordan et al., 2008). This approach can encourage the social work student/candidate to question the current status quo and challenge the norms in the all-too-often stagnation of social work practice in an empathetic and empowered environment. Without connection to their "why," social workers can become apathetic. And apathy can lead to acquiescence (Miller & Garran, 2017).

Complacent helping professionals are often guilty of passive racism and oppression because stagnation often requires conflict in order to elicit change. RCT accounts for the idea that all relationships are challenged by disconnection, misunderstanding, and conflict (Jordan et al., 2008). Ignorance of oppression no longer serves to comply with social work values. Clinicians are rarely taught to question systems, but when systems perpetuate the dominant worldview and social workers remain silent, oppression is reinforced and everyone suffers (Martinez & Fleck-Henderson, 2014). In the words of Audre Lorde, "it is not difference that immobilizes us, but silence."

Cross-Racial/Cross-Gender Clinical Work and Supervision

The undeniable lack of representation among the overall community of clinicians leads to an inevitable dynamic of cross-racial/cross-gender clinical work and supervision. Without this, far too many would go without clinical care or supervision, lending to an even greater lack of access. There is power and privilege inherent to the role of supervisor. This has not often been deconstructed, thus leading to harm, discouragement, and disillusionment on the part of clinicians who hold minoritized identities.

One of the first requirements for serving as a clinician or supervisor is licensure. The recent uncovering of bias and discrimination in the ASWB licensing exam speaks to the ways in which folx with intersectional identities are systemically and systematically prevented from advancing into clinical and leadership roles (Bloxom & Anderson, 2023). Without the abolishing of this system, the keys to this gate-kept distinction will remain disproportionately in the hands of white people. Creating an environment of compassionate responsiveness will encourage vulnerability to be shared and examined. A strong relationship between supervisor and supervisee can create a safe space in which both parties can be vulnerable and create an environment where growth can occur (Bradley et al., 2018).

White clinicians and supervisors underestimate the ways in which their power and privilege can actually benefit the clinical and supervisory relationships. Though powerful and healing, it is arguably nearly guaranteed that an individual will experience some level of being seen and validated by someone with their shared identity or lived experience. What has the potential of holding even more healing power is someone with privileged identities unquestionably holding space, acknowledging, and honoring the experiences of those with minoritized identities, and then moving into service as an active ally and coconspirator joined together against the forces of oppression. Celebrating strengths while recognizing trauma and oppression as being the result of systemic injustices rather than individual deficiencies, and the ability to articulate such phenomena in a way that pierces the consciousness of those with intersectional identities, can deeply enhance the cross-racial/cross-gender clinical relationship. Adopting theoretical frameworks that honor strengths as opposed to pathology is essential to cross-racial/cross-gender clinical work (Miller & Garran, 2017).

Anti-oppression must be infused into formal and informal supervision. A space where cross-racial/cross-gender work is not only properly taught and attended to, but also prioritized, is transformative. This has the ability to expand the hearts, minds, and tangible practices of countless clinicians, extending the impact and the resulting socially just changes beyond one-on-one clinical work to the masses of clinicians and supervisors. The more folx who commit to living and breathing this framework and these practices, the more individuals, families, groups, communities, and institutions have access to culturally relevant and responsive healing resources.

Inclusive Leadership, Authentic Supervision, and Followership

There are many leadership styles and perspectives with their own contextual value. A supervisor who wishes to pursue a decolonized and decapitalized clinical practice will find that incorporating an inclusive leadership style that reflects their mission statement will allow their relationship with supervisees in supervision to flourish, as well as result in an empowered practice. Inclusive leadership works in tandem with cultural humility.

Defined in this work as a form of leadership that "fundamentally addresses individuals' needs for being valued for their uniqueness while feeling part of the group" (Robertson & Perry, 2022, in reference to Shore et al., 2011), inclusive leadership empowers and uplifts the individual perspectives of the employee, while understanding the culture, identity, and background that contributes to their unique perspective. In the context of supervision, this leadership style incorporates the supervisee's group identities and their individual experience of their identity, as well as how both coincide with their clinical practice. This focus also extends to their experience of the organizational culture of their work environment. In this supervisory style, a cooperative relationship between supervisor and supervisee is paramount. It requires openness and a certain degree of professional vulnerability. This cannot be accomplished by approaching supervision via a strictly enforced hierarchical model. Instead, the supervisor must earn the appreciation of the supervisee through trust, rather than expecting respect out of presumed competence due to seniority within a capitalized system and framework.

An inclusive leadership approach incorporates elements of authentic leadership practices into supervision. To decolonize clinical supervision from any approach, a clinical supervisor must first understand that culturally humble supervision has an inarguable impact on their respective organizational culture and supervisory practice; therefore, it is a necessary component to supervision across all leadership perspectives (Upshaw et al., 2020; Wilcox et al., 2022). This is particularly necessary when one considers that supervisors inherently possess a position of power not only with their supervisee, but also in their more heavily weighted influence in the organizational culture of their workplace, particularly if the supervisor is white (Davis et al., 2016; Watkins et al., 2018). To foster a supervisory relationship with a supervisee with authenticity and decolonization in mind, a supervisor should label the identities they feel comfortable sharing in which they experience systemic privilege or marginalization, while engaging in a thorough reflection of their identity and how it impacts their social experience and their clinical work. This can take place as early as the first supervision. This task may elicit feelings of discomfort in the supervisor but, if discussed via the lens of cultural humility and authenticity, it becomes a necessary example of modeling that allows the supervisee to utilize when discussing their identities. It also allows the supervisee to gain confidence that their supervisor is culturally competent and willing to discuss topics relating to their identity. This builds rapport in the supervisory dyad and can be conducive to discussions regarding race, socioeconomic status, or sexual identity status, which have been shown to improve the supervisory working alliance and clinician self-efficacy. The impact of these conversations is especially poignant with white supervisors who are supervising an individual that carries minority identity/ies (Vandament et al., 2022), and are amplified if these conversations are had in greater depth (Phillips et al., 2016).

Pamela Hays' (2022) "ADDRESSING Model" outlines a way for an individual to reflect upon their intersecting identities and how this impacts their clinical practice. As a supervisee myself, I have used this model with supervisors with a great level of success, as it allowed me to have a supervisory relationship wherein we both understood not only each other's intersecting identities, but it also allowed me to feel psychologically safe to discuss these topics in our work environment as my time in supervision progressed. I believe this was a necessary component to demonstrate my supervisor's dedication to operate from a decolonized lens. Additionally, it allowed me to feel more empowered to become an authentic follower.

To first understand how to be an inclusive leader, one must understand the importance of followership, particularly in an empowered and decolonized practice. Followership is an often-unrecognized dimension of a clinical practice and supervision, as a follower is often assumed in Western paradigms to be an individual that is in progress to become a leader, or that becoming a leader is an inevitable and ultimate step of being a follower. Under this misguided purview, the term "follower" becomes almost taboo, as it denotes a "lower" hierarchical precedent of leadership – therefore, in a strict hierarchical system, a "lower" status person. A supervisor must examine this bias and understand that their supervisees and followers often represent the cornerstone of their clinical practice, and that, "It might sound counterintuitive, but followers do not always follow, any more than leaders always lead" (Kellerman, 2019, p. 42). This decolonized and decapitalized viewpoint represents a paradigm shift from the prototypical "naive and subordinate" supervisee to, instead, a form of supervision that allows the supervisee to feel as though they can express their thoughts openly (even when not fully formed) in a public setting without fear of judgment, and both accept and deliver feedback to their supervisor despite inherently being in a position of lower status.

Summary

Through this chapter, frameworks, processes, and guidance have been given to assist clinical supervisors and leaders in the action process of strengthening their supervision and leadership practice toward decolonization and liberation for the clients and communities that benefit from their work, and for the clinicians and colleagues they depend on and engage with in practice. By now you have understood that strengthening clinical supervision and leadership by embedding anti-oppressive practice is a commitment that will develop and evolve over time. In other words, it is not a process that can be undertaken or actioned simply by saying "*we are this now*" or "*we practice like this now.*" It is a mental, emotional, actionable, environmental, and systems commitment and development over a continuum. The process is achieved as results and outcomes are realized and replicated or broadened. In our next chapters, we will provide interdisciplinary focus on this process as well as on leadership and systems process.

Reflective Questions

1. What are some ways you can help build a race equity culture in your agency, organization, or community? What might you need to get started?
2. Where do you still see evidence of coloniality in your community? How have you internalized it? What can you do to move away from a colonial mindset?
3. What is the importance of allyship and "welcoming in" to decolonial process in supervision and leadership practice?

Discussion Questions

1. What does it look like to practice accountability and move toward equity? Where are the opportunities for change? What is already working well? How can you challenge resistance to change?
2. Imagine you were tasked with creating a government agency that would promote positive socialization experiences across the lifecycle. What would you propose to strengthen our society? (See Box 5.1.)

Box 5.1 Case Vignette. Camp Wediko: Clinical Concepts Empowerment Across the Lifespan

By Gavin Meade and Jack Burke

In 1934, Robert A. Young, Ed.D. and his colleagues at Massachusetts General Hospital (MGH) created a summer camp program as an auxiliary facet of their Psychiatric Clinic. The camp was run by Dr. Young, a camp physician, 10 general staff, and two psychologists, all from the MGH Psychiatric Clinic.

The camp, located in southwest New Hampshire, was initially named the Province Lake Camp. The program was designed to have a *"carefully conceived mental health focus rather than the more general benefits of recreational camping"* (Young, 1939). The primary goals of the camp were to provide children that needed a higher level of care a means to receive high-quality psychiatric supports in a wilderness environment away from their families and the hustle and bustle of city life. The camp closed during World War II and was reopened in 1949 by Dr. Young and Dr. Richmond Holder, a psychiatrist on the staff of Massachusetts General Hospital. Located on a new plot of land, the purpose of the camp was "treatment of emotionally disturbed children in a camp setting, training of professional people in the dynamics and therapy of problem children, and research" (Guidance Camps Trust, 1950). This "new" program was named Wediko and was designed to build on the foundation laid by Dr. Young at Province Lake Camp.

Camp Wediko in its conception was guided by four central principles (Figure 5.2). First, the notion that a psychodynamic perspective was key to understanding children's externalizing behaviors, and that the camp staff would interpret problem behaviors through a psychodynamic lens. Second,

Figure 5.2   Camp Wediko, 2024.

Camp Wediko believed that children needed greater freedom for self-expression and a space to exist free of the fear of retaliation or rejection – the sense of unconditional positive regard that is so central to Rogerian theory. This guiding framework of permissiveness leads to the third principle, which highlights the importance of the relationship between campers and staff, as well as the relationships of campers within their specific cabin group. Even from the earliest days of Camp Wediko, campers were sorted into distinct cabin groups. The names have changed over the decades, but a strong identification with cabin group and the focus on peer relationships, conflict, and resolution remains a cornerstone of Camp Wediko. The fourth principle that Camp Wediko was founded on was the idea that each camper would know prior to coming to camp that camp was meant to be fun but also a place to bring immediate and distinct positive change – whether at home, at school, or in the community. Between 1949 and 1954, roughly 35 male-identifying students were seen each summer at Camp Wediko. In 1954, Camp Wediko was moved to its present location in Windsor, New Hampshire, to allow for more students, more staff, female-identifying students, and to provide a more rugged and true "wilderness" experience. Purportedly, *"the purpose of the treatment camp is two-fold: one, to provide a pleasurable group experience for boys who do not obtain much gratification in their daily lives; two, to establish a therapeutic climate that will assist [him] in working out his personal difficulties"* (Wediko, September 1954).

In the ninety years since its beginning much of Camp Wediko has shifted, but the central values on which the program was built remain paramount. However, just as the activities and programs offered within the camp have evolved (the camp no longer teaches behaviorally challenged children to shoot .22 guns), the psychodynamic supremacy of the mid 1950s has given way to a more eclectic, behavioral modality. Campers are positively reinforced throughout the day with coupons they can "spend" weekly, complete a behavioral checklist thrice daily that determines whether they are able to make it to the playground (one of the few times an entire developmental group of students gathers – most other times students are siloed into their specific cabin groups), and receive positive and negative metaphors that are tied to their behaviors. Despite these changes, the guiding ideals and principles of Camp Wediko have remained immutable. The aim of the program is to treat every child with unconditional positive regard, provide a fun and structured therapeutic environment in the woods away from their homes, and empower them to develop more productive and prosocial coping skills for their mental and behavioral health challenges.

This is not to say that the camp is stagnant or unable to change in a way that aims to engender social and cultural change while embodying the ideals of its origin. Rather, the individuals who make up each summer (from the first-year staff to the Director) bring their life experiences and values to help change the program and meet the needs of our population. Put more broadly, and more technically, Camp Wediko operates from an empowerment and anti-oppressive perspective. This work happens daily, both implicitly and explicitly, and can be seen both by general examples as well as specific brief vignettes.

At Camp Wediko, much of the learning for the children in our care comes from the parallel processes of clinical work and empowerment work. While this work looks different for different developmental groups (the youngest students are 8–10 while the oldest are 17–18), the guiding philosophies remain the same. Students from their wake-up in the cabin to their moments immersed in our academic program to meals in the dining hall are constantly in positions where they are learning to change and modify their behavior, reactions, and processes based on the clinical interventions of staff. Through these clinical interventions, empowerment is a guiding constant. In the wake of any kind of serious incident (instance of physical or verbal aggression, self-harm, or general prolonged dysregulation), students process with staff. A common refrain from students is "I had to" or "I needed to because," and much of the work done in processing is combatting these maladaptive coping skills by demonstrating how each individual student has the autonomy and skills to react and act in a more healthy and prosocial manner.

Take, for example, "Jermare." Jermare is a 15-year-old adopted male-identifying Black teenager living with his adoptive parents and their biologic children. Jermare faces behavioral challenges at school that his parents think are racially motivated. Jermare attends a wealthy private school that only has one other student of color in his grade, and struggles to get along with his siblings. At home, Jermare struggles to follow directions (particularly from his adoptive father) and has escalated to the point of throwing things around the house, breaking a television, and stealing his parents' alcohol. At camp, Jermare struggles with authority figures or people that he perceives are challenging him. During group therapy, his clinical supervisor (the clinician attached to his cabin) gently reminded Jermare to try to pay attention to other students and refrain from being distracting with his body. Jermare escalated, engaged in verbal aggression, and ultimately required a physical transport out of the cabin because he was unable to regulate himself. In processing, Jermare was able to identify that he felt like he had no control over his situation and was feeling triggered by the topic being covered in group. He was reminded that at any point, even during group, he can ask for a break to take space. He identified different "choice points" where he could've chosen to do something differently and was able to make a safety plan for the next group therapy session.

Jermare's staff team knew, based on his own report, that Jermare often feels powerless and targeted in social situations. They also knew that he struggled to advocate for himself in those moments of dysregulation. By engaging in processing work and empowering him at different points throughout the process, his staff team demonstrate to Jermare that he can engage differently with his surroundings and develop his autonomy.

During orientation for staff, we teach them "the program is the primary intervention." By this we mean that the mileu-based nature of our program is the primary vehicle for bringing change (rather than one-on-one clinical work, which of course happens but is not the focus of the program). Through programmatic intervention, we are anti-oppressive both for cabin groups and for individuals.

The funding structure of Camp Wediko is both private and public – families pay either out of their own pocket or their tuition is paid by a school district, third-party payer (such as the Department of Children and Families or the Department of Mental Health), or through community organizations funding partial tuition. In any given summer, there is a stark divide socioeconomically between campers that typically – though of course not always – follows racial and ethnic divides. During the 40 days that students are in the same bunk with the same resources and together in a new place, there naturally arise conversations around income inequality, racism, and different family structures. In one summer, a conversation started in group therapy about how it was "unfair" that some campers were getting packages from their families every day or every other day while some campers received none all summer. These packages held notes, which were typically read once and discarded, but also the real treasure: Takis, chips, candy, and the ever-elusive Gatorade powder for water bottles. The supervisor of that group was able to have a conversation about why some campers had packages while others didn't: income inequality. In response, the campers that were getting packages daily decided to pool their snacks into a communal bin that anyone could access. While this example may seem insignificant, it speaks to the power of the relationships and how, for many students, Camp Wediko provides the first place to have authentic and genuine antiracist and anti-oppressive conversations, and create and work through action plans to combat the presence of inequities, even in pooling together candy, snacks, and Gatorade powder packets (resources) for their equitable distribution. There is still, of course, racism and bigotry from students directed toward each other. In processing, however, they are given the chance to work through their vitriol and make a relationship repair with the camper(s) they held a grievance toward.

The anti-oppressive work at Wediko is not just mileu-based but also intentional and individualized. Each summer there are several students who grapple with their gender identity and affectional orientation, and Wediko empowers them to be authentically who they are. This looks like putting them in a cabin group of peers that they feel most comfortable with and referring to them by their correct name and pronouns. At the onset of each summer, during the week of training and orientation to Camp Wediko, staff are engaged in conversations about gender, gender identity, and affectional orientation. Sometimes new staff argue against having these kinds of conversations with children and adolescents and say something to the effect of, "They're just kids! They can't handle it!" They can. While there are many examples of this that stand out, one brief example from a recent past summer stands out. A camper, "Sarah," in a predominantly female-identifying cabin, began the summer with explicit, deeply ingrained anti-transgender prejudices and deeply resented being "forced" to share a cabin with a transgender student. As the summer progressed, Sarah was able to engage in conversations with her staff and show growth. One day she was in an altercation with this specific cabinmate and was incredibly escalated and screaming, "She's such a [long string of expletives], I'm going to beat the [expletive] out of her ... sorry, sorry, he's such a [long string of expletives], I'm going to beat the [expletive] out of him." It would have been incredibly easy for Sarah to misgender the other camper, whether intentionally or by accident, but she did not. Each summer Camp Wediko facilitates these kinds of conversations, and sees positive outcomes. This process also looks like advocating directly to families and care teams on behalf of children who feel unable to access affirming care. Take, for example, "Kevin." Kevin was a recent past camper who was in a predominantly female-identifying cabin and entered the summer using his deadname and she/her pronouns. Over the course of the summer, he disclosed his true name and identity. He struggled in the cabin with his peers and struggled with the summer in general. The following summer, Kevin was placed into a cabin with predominantly male-identifying students and provided affirmations from day one. He had a fantastic summer. This is not to say, of course, that Kevin still did not have challenges (he is, after all, at Wediko for behavioral reasons and not for gender identity reasons), but his summer was hugely improved from one to the next. Part of the difference came from the year that he had – in that year, at the behest of Wediko and after challenging conversations with caregivers and school, he received affirming care at home for the first time.

Since 1934, across different summers, under different names, and with different leadership, Camp Wediko has attempted to provide a life-changing summer for children and adolescents. The work done at Wediko is, at its core, centered around empowerment and anti-oppressive attitudes and fulfills its mission to celebrate and strengthen every camper, counselor, and staff member in unity.

REFLECTION QUESTIONS

1. The environment of inpatient work is unique. A 40-day program where staff and students cohabit 24 hours a day, seven days a week, is even more unique. How can the attitudes of empowerment and anti-oppressive practices that are so easily fostered at Wediko be translated to less relationally focused environments?
2. Camp Wediko has changed greatly since its conception. If you were a senior leader of Camp Wediko, what would you do to continue the mission of training new staff to engender social and cultural change?
3. What does empowerment look like in your own work? Are there similarities to Camp Wediko?

REFERENCES

Baines, D. (ed.). (2020). *Doing anti-oppressive practice: Social justice social work*. Fernwood.

Bloxom, Q., & Anderson, B. (2023). Deconstructing social work exam bias: Advocacy practice guidelines to close the gap. *Journal of Evidence-Based Social Work, 21*(2), 236–264.

Bradley, N., Stargell, N., Craigen, L., Whisenhunt, J., Campbell, E., & Kress, V. (2018). Creative approaches for promoting vulnerability in supervision: A relational-cultural approach. *Journal of Creativity in Mental Health, 14*(3), 391–404.

Collins, P. H., & Bilge, S. (2020). *Intersectionality*. John Wiley & Sons.

Currie, N., Simmons-Horton, S., Burke, J., Farley, R., & Olson-Kennedy, A. (2024). Gender and orientation diversity in the family courts: A guide to terms and present issues. *Family Court Review, 62*(3), 615–634.

Davis, D. E., Hook, J. N., DeBlaere, C., & Placeres, V. (2016). Humility at work. In L. G. Oades, M. F. Steger, A. D. Fave & J. Passmore (Eds.) *The Wiley Blackwell handbook of the psychology of positivity and strengths-based approaches at work* (pp. 191–209). John Wiley & Sons.

Diemer, M. A., Pinedo, A., Banales, J., Mathews, C. J., Frisby, M. B., Harris, E. M., & McAlister, S. (2021). Recentering action in critical consciousness. *Child Development Perspectives, 15*(1), 12–17.

Garran, A. M., Miller, J. L., Rozas, L. W., & Kang, H. K. (2021). *Racism in the United States: Implications for the helping professions*. Springer.

Gilmore, J. P., Dainton, M., & Halpin, N. (2024). Authentic allyship for gender minorities. *Journal of Nursing Scholarship, 56*(1), 5–8.

Goodman, D. J. (2011). *Promoting diversity and social justice: Educating people from privileged groups*. Routledge.

Grosfoguel, R. (2011). Decolonizing post-colonial studies and paradigms of political-economy: Transmodernity, decolonial thinking, and global coloniality. *Transmodernity: Journal of Peripheral Cultural Production of the Luso-Hispanic World, 1*(1), 1–38.

Guidance Camps Trust. (1950, June). *Report to the Trustees of Guidance Camps Trust on the treatment camp* [Unpublished report]. Camp Wediko Archives, Windsor, NH.

Harro, Bobbie. (2013). The cycle of socialization. In M. Adams, W. Blumenfeld, R. Castañeda, H. Hackman, M. Peters & X. Zúñiga (Eds.) *Readings for diversity and social justice*, 3rd ed. (pp. 45–52). Routledge.

Hays, P. A. (2022). *Addressing cultural complexities in psychotherapy and clinical practice: An intersectional approach*, 4th ed. American Psychological Association.

Jordan, J. V., Hartling, L. M., & Baker, J. (2008). The development of relational-cultural theory. Retrieved April 20, 2008.

Kellerman, B. (2019). The future of followership. *Strategy & Leadership, 47*(5), 42–46.

Martinez, D. B., & Fleck-Henderson, A. (2014). *Social justice in clinical practice: A liberation health framework for social work.* Routledge.
Miller, J., & Garran, A. M. (2017). *Racism in the United States: Implications for the helping professions.* Springer.
National Association of Social Workers (NASW). (2017). "Code of Ethics." NASW.
National Association of Social Workers. (2021). Code of Ethics.
Oades, L. G., Steger, M. F., Fave, A. D., & Passmore, J. (2016). The psychology of positivity and strengths-based approaches at work. In L. G. Oades, M. F. Steger, A. D. Fave, & J. Passmore (Eds.) *The Wiley Blackwell handbook of the psychology of positivity and strengths-based approaches at work* (pp. 1–8). John Wiley & Sons.
Phillips, J. C., Parent, M. C., Dozier, V. C., & Jackson, P. L. (2016). Depth of discussion of multicultural identities in supervision and supervisory outcomes. *Counselling Psychology Quarterly, 30*(2), 188–210. https://doi.org/10.1080/09515070.2016.1169995
Roberson, Q., & Perry, J. L. (2022). Inclusive leadership in thought and action: A thematic analysis. *Group & Organization Management, 47*(4), 755–778
Shore, L. M., Randel, A. E., Chung, B. G., Dean, M. A., Holcombe Ehrhart, K., & Singh, G. (2011). Inclusion and diversity in work groups: A review and model for future research. *Journal of Management, 37*(4), 1262–1289.
Stonewall. (2015). *Unhealthy Attitudes.* Stonewall.
Upshaw, N. C., Lewis Jr., D. E., & Nelson, A. L. (2020). Cultural humility in action: Reflective and process-oriented supervision with Black trainees. *Training and Education in Professional Psychology, 14*(4), 277.
Vandament, M. L., Duan, C., & Li, S. (2022). Relationships among supervisee perceived supervisor cultural humility, working alliance, and supervisee self-efficacy among white supervisor and supervisee of color dyads. *Training and Education in Professional Psychology, 16*(3), 244.
Watkins, C. E., Hook, J. N., Mosher, D. K., & Callahan, J. L. (2018). Humility in clinical supervision: Fundamental, foundational, and transformational. *The Clinical Supervisor, 38*(1), 58–78. https://doi.org/10.1080/07325223.2018.1487355
Wediko. (1954, September). *Camp Wediko Research Program: Report of progress* [Unpublished internal report]. Camp Wediko Archives, Windsor, NH.
Wilcox, M. M., Drinane, J. M., Black, S. W., Cabrera, L., DeBlaere, C., Tao, K. W., ... & Owen, J. (2022). Layered cultural processes: The relationship between multicultural orientation and satisfaction with supervision. *Training and Education in Professional Psychology, 16*(3), 235.
Young, R. A. (1939). *Province Lake Camp psychiatric summer program: Program description* [Unpublished report]. Camp Wediko Archives, Windsor, NH.

FURTHER READING

Dipre, K. A., & Luke, M. (2020). Relational cultural theory-informed advising in counselor education. *Professional Counselor*, *10*(4), 517–531.

Ertl, M. M., Ellis, M. V., & Peterson, L. P. (2023). Supervisor cultural humility and supervisee nondisclosure: The supervisory working alliance matters. *The Counseling Psychologist*, *51*(4), 590–620. https://doi.org/10.1177/00110000231159316

Garran, A. M., & Rasmussen, B. M. (2014). Safety in the classroom: Reconsidered. *Journal of Teaching in Social Work*, *34*(4), 401–412.

Harro, Bobbie. (2000). The cycle of socialization. In M. Adams, W. Blumenfeld, R. Castañeda, H. Hackman, M. Peters & X. Zúñiga (Eds.) *Readings for diversity and social justice: An anthology on racism.* (pp. 15–21). Routledge.

Rozas, L. W., & Miller, J. (2009). Discourses for social justice education: The web of racism and the web of resistance. *Journal of Ethnic & Cultural Diversity in Social Work*, *18*(1–2), 24–39.

Schein, E. H. (1990). Organizational culture. *American Psychologist*, *45*(2), 109–119.

Sloan, L., Joyner, M., Stakeman, C., & Schmitz, C. (2018). *Critical multiculturalism and intersectionality in a complex world.* Oxford University Press.

CHAPTER 6

Transforming Leadership and Supervision through the Integration of Anti-Oppressive Practices
Christina Crow Cruz

Introduction: The Importance of Incorporating an Anti-Oppressive Lens

The integration of an anti-oppressive lens in leadership and supervision practice is increasingly recognized as imperative, particularly within the context of a society influenced by multiple forms of oppression. Historically, the supervisor/supervisee dyad has operated within a framework shaped by and reflecting social power dynamics and systemic inequities, which often manifest in interpersonal relationships (Altaha et al., 2023). This can limit meaningful access to opportunities and dehumanize individuals and groups based on identity factors. Consequently, it is essential to explore the contextual factors that shape and influence the supervisory relationship (Pieterse, 2018) and approaches to leadership.

Anti-oppressive practice (AOP) is a conceptual framework that emphasizes a social justice orientation to identify root causes and contributing factors of trauma and disparities and actively challenges inequities. The methodology focuses on process and outcomes, requiring an equity-focused approach to structuring relationships to empower while mitigating the adverse effects of hierarchies (Goitom et al., 2021). Clinical supervision, a cornerstone of professional development, is considered to enhance therapeutic skills and outcomes (Pieterse, 2018), aiming to address three functional areas, including administration, support, and education (Asakura & Maurer, 2018). Integrating AOP into clinical supervision and leadership is more than a theoretical stance; it's a proactive commitment to addressing the underlying causes of inequities and injustice. It encourages supervisors to interrogate their positionalities and biases while empowering supervisees to critically engage with the systemic forces that impact their practice. By embracing AOP, supervisors can cultivate a supervision environment that supports equity, social justice, and transformational, bi-directional learning.

Understanding Anti-Oppressive Practice

Defining Anti-Oppressive Practice

We have defined anti-oppressive practice at length and in nuance throughout this text. Another version of this definition, which is helpful in practicum, supervision, and in leadership spaces where the material is newer for colleagues, includes this definition: Anti-oppression is defined as a "framework and practice that address the process and outcome of challenging and combating oppressive and inequitable forces, structures, and systems while simultaneously supporting the empowerment and liberation of those within the margins from the distorted, unjust, and hegemonic foundation of society" (Wathen & Vargas, 2023, p. 174). The fundamental principles of AOP are identifying and acknowledging power imbalances, taking action to challenge and change them, and promoting the sharing of power (Goitom et al., 2021). This process requires authentic relationships, engagement in reflective practices to discover and address prejudice and oppression (Bussey, 2024; Goitom et al., 2021), accountability to understanding how positionality and social location impact the empowerment of the supervisee(s) and their supervision experience, and actively centering social justice principles for systemic change (Okech et al., 2023). This approach enriches the learning environment for supervisees and facilitates a deeper understanding of the complex societal issues that influence therapeutic outcomes.

Foundational Principles

Integrating an anti-oppressive lens into leadership and supervision involves identifying and addressing oppression within relationships, normalizing discussions about racism and other forms of oppression (Bussey, 2024), and carrying out structural assessments that take into consideration the broader sociopolitical contexts that influence lived experiences (Bussey et al., 2022; Bussey, 2024). An anti-oppressive lens can help bridge the gap between systemic and individual inequities. Foundational leadership skills, such as clear communication, are also crucial for effective AOP, as without them, supervisors may fail to support the supervisee in the navigation of complex issues associated with power dynamics, inadvertently perpetuating oppressive practices (Bussey, 2024). Peters and Luke (2022) outline ten principles of antiracist practice:

1. *Developing Critical Consciousness through Critical Reflexivity*: Encouraging critical reflection on one's own biases and assumptions.

2. *Overcoming Comfort and Fragility through Unlearning Privilege and Domination*: Challenging privilege and power dynamics that perpetuate oppression.
3. *Centering the Margins through Empowerment and Liberation*: Prioritizing the voices and experiences of historically marginalized individuals and communities.
4. *Wellness and Self-care through Acts of Compassion and Vigilance*: Promoting self-care and compassion as essential components of resisting oppression.
5. *Co-Constructing a Brave Space through Relationships and Community*: Fostering supportive relationships and community engagement to create brave spaces for dialogue and growth.
6. *Developing Goals and Assessing Outcomes through Stakeholder Investment*: Engaging stakeholders in setting goals and evaluating the impact of interventions.
7. *Challenging and Disrupting Oppression through Broaching and Accountability*: Addressing oppressive behaviors and holding individuals and systems accountable for their actions.
8. *Identifying and Addressing Barriers through Resistance and Opposition*: Advocating to disrupt barriers that hinder access and equality.
9. *Socioecological Advocacy and Activism through Collective Action*: Engaging in advocacy and activism to challenge systemic injustices.
10. *Redistributing Social, Cultural, and Political Capital through Access and Opportunity*: Promoting equitable distribution of resources and opportunities across diverse communities.

Adopting an anti-oppressive framework in supervision and leadership involves understanding these principles, implementing practical strategies that challenge systemic oppression and promote equity and justice, advocating for structural change, continuously engaging in critical reflection, and empowering supervisees to become change agents within their practice.

Intersectionality and Its Role in Leadership and Supervision

AOP emphasizes the intersectionality of oppression, recognizing how multiple identity factors such as race, class, gender, disability, and sexual orientation intersect to shape individuals' experiences and access to opportunities (Goitom et al., 2021). Leadership and supervision inherently involve a structural power dynamic that influences the interactions within the supervisory relationship and shapes broader ideas, values, and beliefs (Berger et al., 2018). Within supervision and leadership, intersectionality can be used as a tool to analyze these power dynamics (Berzoff, 2023); to prompt the supervisor to critically evaluate how dimensions of diversity affect the dynamics between the supervisor, supervisee, and client; and to address the power differentials (Tarshis & Baird, 2021).

Incorporating intersectionality into supervision and leadership can improve the understanding of power dynamics and mitigate their replication within relationships (Berger et al., 2018). To do this, leaders and supervisors should engage in reflexive practices that recognize and challenge biases, stereotypes, and assumptions, and initiate discussions to explore how diversity factors impact their relationship with the supervisee and the therapeutic process (Tarshis & Baird, 2021). Additionally, supervisors should develop relationships with the supervisee(s), embracing their complex identities and experiences and viewing them as a whole person (Bussey, 2024), being mindful not to reduce the individual to a singular aspect of their identity. This approach can promote authenticity and inclusion, cultivate environments that empower supervisees, challenge inequities, and promote inclusive practices. Embracing intersectionality in AOP also supports the profession's ethical obligation to address and dismantle oppressive structures in practice settings.

Recognizing Power Dynamics in Supervisor Relationships

Recognizing and navigating power dynamics in supervisory relationships is vital to ethical and effective AOP in supervision and leadership. Power may involve coercive influences such as economic incentives or threats, or operate through the establishment of hierarchies and norms. Within leadership and supervision, the use of power may be seen in decisions on career advancement, or manifest through the influence over the professional development and therapeutic decision-making of supervisees (Berger et al., 2018). Leaders should recognize, acknowledge, and mitigate power disparities to create collaborative environments where supervisees are empowered within the relationship.

To cultivate AOP in leadership and supervision, supervisors should critically reflect on how power dynamics, particularly those related to racism and privilege or oppression, impact their relationship and interactions with supervisees (Lipscomb & Ashley, 2017). Critical consciousness, a concept rooted in Freirean principles, emphasizes self-reflection and awareness of intersecting identities and power dynamics, and fosters discussions that challenge norms of oppression within practice and supervision (O'Neil & del Mar Fariña, 2018). This also requires moving beyond tokenism to authentically address differences in identity, power, and privilege within the supervisory relationship (Bussey, 2024). Embracing an AOP lens involves continuous reflection, critical dialogue, and action to promote equity and justice and to support the growth and well-being of supervisees within the supervisory process.

Integrating Anti-Oppressive Principles into Supervisory Practices

Cultural Competence and Humility

In social work and mental health professions, cultural competency is more than a desirable skill – it is an ethical responsibility (NASW, 2024). Cultural competency and humility are critical components of effective anti-oppressive leadership and supervision. While cultural competence emphasizes understanding and respecting cultural differences, critical cultural competence also addresses power dynamics and systemic injustices embedded within cross-cultural interactions (Lusk et al., 2017). Supervisors must examine their own bias and privilege; facilitate discussion on systemic inequities impacting the relationship between the supervisor, supervisee, and client (Lipscomb & Ashley, 2017); engage in critical reflection and dialogue, create space for supervisees to explore their cultural assumptions (Asakura & Maurer, 2018); and navigate power dynamics and diverse identities within the supervisory relationship to foster equitable and inclusive professional development (Lusk et al., 2017). Research suggests that culturally competent supervision increases supervisees' knowledge, self-awareness, and empathy toward individuals from diverse backgrounds (King et al., 2020). Cultural competence and humility in supervision support supervisees in developing more nuanced conceptualizations of cases and culturally responsive interventions (King et al., 2020), enhancing their understanding of cultural context, identities, and values. Through an AOP lens, this is also foundational to recognizing and actively challenging oppression (Lusk et al., 2017).

Strategies for Creating Inclusive Supervisory Environments

Integrating anti-oppressive principles into leadership and supervisory practices, including intentionality, humility, and active engagement regarding issues of oppression, is important for fostering an inclusive supervisory environment. An intentional approach utilizing AOP involves recognizing inherent power differentials that may create barriers to open communication and dialogue. Modeling humility and critical self-reflection encourages supervisees to participate in parallel practices, as space is created where supervisees feel able to express concerns and ideas (Okech et al., 2023). An example of an inclusive approach to supervision that helps mitigate power imbalance is taking an active role in the professional development of supervisees by involving them in a collaborative approach to goal setting. Supervisors should be attentive to those who hesitate to share their voice, particularly those with historically marginalized identities, and create "brave spaces" where inclusion and mutual respect are valued (Okech et al., 2023). Supervisors can adopt these strategies to foster inclusive environments benefiting the supervisee(s)' growth and strengthening the organizational culture through culturally responsive practices.

Addressing Implicit Bias and Microaggressions in Supervision

Leaders and supervisors in social work have the ethical responsibility to address diversity within the supervisory relationship, which includes implicit bias and microaggressions (ACA, 2014). Implicit bias can manifest in supervisory interactions and influence the development and well-being of supervisees. Microaggressions have been recognized within the context of traumatic stress, and in situations with inherent power differentials – such as clinical supervision – microaggressions have the potential to exacerbate trauma among supervisees (Pieterse, 2018). Tokenism may also lead to feelings of invalidation and a reduced sense of safety (Lipscomb & Ashley, 2017). Supervisors should remain mindful of these dynamics within the supervisory dyad, as the expression of implicit bias can significantly impact the supervisee, the relationship, and the environment.

Social work leaders play an important role in initiating dialogue around personal bias and promoting critical and reflexive thinking among supervisees. Reflexivity encourages leaders to engage in ongoing self-reflection, questioning both what they teach as well as how their own experiences influence supervisees' learning and development (Rogerson et al., 2022). To effectively address implicit bias and microaggressions, leaders must model accountability (Okech et al., 2023), lean into unfamiliar roles and responsibilities, and acknowledge and apologize for microaggressions when they occur – whether directed toward supervisees or observed in interactions with clients and colleagues. Demonstrating humility and self-awareness promotes a culture of growth within the supervisory context

(Lipscomb & Ashley, 2017). Effectively managing implicit bias and microaggressions in supervision requires continuous self-reflection, awareness, humility, and proactive efforts to cultivate a supportive environment that fosters the professional growth and well-being of supervisees.

Promoting Equity and Social Justice in Supervisory Roles

Promoting equity and social justice within supervisory roles and practice environments is fundamental to inclusion and empowerment. Asakura and Maurer (2018) identified key concepts in social justice–oriented practice, highlighting power analysis and critical reflection on privilege and oppression, transparent application of ethics, utilizing practices that consider the sociopolitical and cultural impact on clients, and advocacy for systemic change. Social justice is a goal and a process, and its relational aspect should be grounded in empowerment and respect (Asakura & Maurer, 2018).

Modeling Anti-Oppressive Behaviors and Culturally Affirming Leadership

Fostering an environment where supervisees feel empowered to challenge assumptions and address power dynamics is crucial for anti-oppressive and culturally affirming leadership. By actively engaging in critical self-reflection and demonstrating respect for diverse perspectives, supervisors can model anti-oppressive behaviors (Asakura & Maurer, 2018). Culturally affirming supervision involves actively promoting diversity, equity, and inclusion within teams. This includes modeling accountability for social justice, providing culturally responsive feedback, and advocating for inclusive policies and innovative approaches to practice within the supervisory context that may resonate with broader and more diverse identities (Okech et al., 2023). Supervisors who focus on examining how diverse identities and experiences influence dynamics are more likely to demonstrate culturally responsive leadership. This approach helps to disrupt the impacts of oppressive experiences. Supervisors can utilize AOPs, demonstrating how to engage in actions and behaviors that identify, acknowledge, and challenge various forms of oppression, and model responsibility for and address harm (Okech et al., 2023).

Advocating for Structural Changes within Organizations

Anti-oppressive supervision and leadership involve a conscious effort to incorporate ethical awareness, critical consciousness, and organizational and structural change into practice. Leaders should advocate for structural changes within their organizations to dismantle systemic oppression and promote equitable and just practices (Lusk et al., 2017; Rogerson et al., 2022). Some approaches include identifying and addressing institutional biases, integrating cultural competency into organizational structures, and advocating for anti-oppressive policies and procedures.

Clinical supervision is multifaceted, involving administrative oversight, clinical guidance, and educational support, and is inherently hierarchical, influenced by organizational policies and regulatory requirements (Kadushin & Harkness, 2014). Within institutional contexts, these functions overlap with power and structural oppression (Lipscomb & Ashley, 2017) and may inadvertently perpetuate inequities. O'Neil and del Mar (2018) propose the utilization of critical conversations in supervision, encouraging engagement in dialogue regarding bias, intersectionality, positionality, social location, relational intersections, power structures, and the promotion of AOPs. This model facilitates a deeper understanding of how institutionalized oppression manifests within organizational and supervisory contexts. Einbinder (2020) also emphasizes the importance of praxis – the integration of critical theory with practice – to discover shared power and a collective understanding of institutional factors perpetuating oppressive forces and to refocus work to disrupt these systems.

Effective leadership utilizing an anti-oppressive lens requires a commitment to challenging and dismantling structural barriers – from administrative policies to clinical interventions and practices. The integration of cultural competence and critical consciousness into leadership and supervision is imperative to address systemic oppression and promote social justice (Rogerson et al., 2022), and critical culturally competent leadership necessitates organizational participation across all levels (Lusk et al., 2017). A more expansive approach to cultural competence should be employed to extend beyond the acknowledgment of differences to actively confront systems of oppression (Lusk et al., 2017). This approach aims to create environments where the impacts of systemic oppression are mitigated within organizations.

Ethical Considerations in Anti-Oppressive Leadership and Supervision

Leaders and supervisors face ethical dilemmas that require an anti-oppressive approach, such as confronting institutional discrimination (Einbinder, 2020), issues of confidentiality and intersectionality, and other power dynamics within interpersonal and organizational contexts. They should engage in critical reflection for themselves and with the supervisees, support the supervisees in navigating these dilemmas through advocacy for ethical practice, understand approaches to challenge systemic injustices within their roles, and display a commitment to social justice.

Confidentiality and Intersectionality

Current research has assessed supervisors' effectiveness and the quality of their supervisory relationships through several critical lenses. Lipscomb and Ashley (2017) note that qualities impacting the perceived safety of a supervisor are grounded in their capability to adopt an intersectionality-informed perspective, use inclusive language, and demonstrate readiness to engage in dialogue that involves critiques of dominant cultural narratives. It has also been posited that differing social affiliations of the supervisor and supervisee, such as race, culture, class, and sexual orientation, may impact authenticity in supervisory relationships (Berger et al., 2018). Additionally, Egan et al. (2017) emphasize the importance of trust, confidentiality, role tensions, relationships, reflective practice, and safety in supervision. They found that a supportive supervisory relationship that utilizes critical reflection and discussions through an anti-oppressive lens, addressing both macro perspectives and clinical details, enhances the effectiveness of supervision. This underscores the complex interplay of intersectional identities, effective communication, and relational dynamics in shaping the supervisory process and the importance of utilizing AOP.

Navigating Power Dynamics Ethically

Leaders have an ethical responsibility to prepare supervisees with the skills to effectively address issues of racism, structural violence, and oppression (Tarshis & Baird, 2021). This ethical imperative highlights the importance of integrating anti-oppressive and social justice principles into supervision. In a thematic review of the literature, Asakura and Maurer (2018) delineate three core elements of integrating social justice into clinical supervision: addressing power dynamics in supervisory relationships, fostering reflective practices, and cultivating advocacy skills. Integral to effective supervision is the recognition and ethical navigation of power dynamics, particularly with the intersection of race and racism, paying attention to the supervisory relationship and the impacts on the supervisee's experience. Supervisors should initiate intentional dialogues about racism and other forms of oppression with supervisees to acknowledge and discuss power differentials inherent in the supervisory relationship. This proactive approach is essential, as supervisees may not feel safe initiating such discussions themselves given the power dynamics (Pieterse, 2018). It is also important to acknowledge that leaders and supervisors from marginalized racial backgrounds and/or with other stigmatized social identities may themselves experience racial trauma and other forms of oppression within supervisory contexts. This can manifest through direct racial hostility from supervisees, institutional invalidation, and lack of organizational support, which undermines their competence and efficacy (Pieterse, 2018) and impacts the well-being and safety of the supervisor. Supervisors of color encounter unique challenges that add to the complexity of their supervisory roles. They may face skepticism about their leadership competency; racially and culturally responsive interventions may be dismissed by supervisees; and a higher expectation of multicultural competence is placed on them compared to their white counterparts (Pieterse, 2018). These challenges highlight the ethical responsibility to acknowledge individual and group experiences of oppression – of both the supervisor and supervisee – and to address power dynamics for improved institutional support.

Self-Reflection and Professional Development

Cultivating Cultural Self-Awareness

Continuous self-reflection, reflexive practices, and professional development are foundational for effective anti-oppressive supervision and leadership. Within that, cultivating cultural self-awareness is valuable, and involves critical self-examination of one's history, personal identities, and their relationships and intersections with systems of oppression (Bussey et al., 2022). Engagement in critical self-reflection facilitates the management of personal biases and awareness of positionality, power, and oppression, thus supporting more ethical and equitable practices by bringing to light the hidden nature of oppression and uncovering opportunities to challenge the status quo (Lusk et al., 2017). Learning about deep cultural aspects, such as world views, values, and communication styles, beyond surface-level characteristics, such as holidays, food, and flags, helps leaders understand the realities of their supervisees and clients (Lusk et al., 2017). Authentic leadership is also a component of culturally competent leadership, which requires emotional labor and the demonstration of compassionate use of self (Lusk et al., 2017).

Engaging in Critical Self-Reflection and Supervision

Engaging in critical self-reflection within the context of supervision is essential for supervisees to develop AOPs. Supervisors can use reflexive practice assignments, create "brave spaces" for supervision, and provide transformative learning opportunities. These approaches foster environments that encourage introspection, challenge assumptions, and promote ethical awareness, social justice, and advocacy.

Critical self-reflection in supervision involves sharing and receiving feedback in a trustworthy environment and helps manage personal bias, increase self-awareness, and improve self-regulation. Rogerson et al. (2022) assert that discussing thoughts and feelings within supervision allows for deeper insights into one's own biases and values and provides the opportunity to receive feedback from others. This facilitates personal growth by engaging in uncomfortable conversations, gaining different perspectives, and navigating complex social issues (Rogerson et al., 2022).

An effective method to foster critical self-reflection is through reflexive practice assignments. Journaling, for example, encourages introspection and self-reflection, uncovering internalized biases that may impact perceptions of self and others. Reflective practice assignments create spaces for supervisees to critically examine their assumptions and biases, developing a deeper understanding of their own identities. Arao and Clemens (2013) advocate for creating "brave spaces" where supervisees feel empowered to explore uncomfortable issues, including personal biases, privilege, power, and oppression. This approach challenges supervisees to move past superficial understanding of complex issues and engage in meaningful dialogue that promotes critical self-reflection (Arao & Clemens, 2013).

Transformative learning opportunities, such as high-fidelity simulations, allow supervisees to confront ethical dilemmas, expand their perspectives, challenge schemas, move outside of their comfort zone, and promote self-examination and integration of new knowledge and skills into their practices (Rogerson et al., 2022). Transformative learning experiences empower supervisors to navigate complex institutional dynamics and simultaneously increase supervisees' ability to critically self-reflect.

Implementing Anti-Oppressive and Supervisory Practices

Implementing anti-oppressive supervisory and leadership practices within organizations requires a deliberate approach that includes policy development and ongoing evaluation. This section explores some of these practices.

Developing Anti-Oppressive Policies and Procedures

Organizations should adopt a structural competency lens that identifies how institutional structures contribute to and perpetuate inequities as a necessary component to effectively changing practice utilizing an anti-oppressive approach (Bussey, 2024). This approach enables interventions at the micro, mezzo, and macro levels, including advocacy for reforms in policies and procedures impacting staff, clients, and communities served (Simon et al., 2022). By identifying and understanding oppressive policies, organizations can also review or create policies that promote equity and inclusion versus maintaining the status quo. Additionally, providing opportunities for supervisees to learn more about multiple systems of oppression, how they are enacted through policies and procedures, and perpetuated within institutions and organizations is essential (Simon et al., 2022) to equip them with the awareness and tools to effectively challenge and change those systems.

Evaluating and Monitoring Progress toward Equity and Inclusion

Developing a plan to evaluate and monitor progress toward equity and inclusion goals is essential. Leaders and supervisors can support the establishment of baselines, benchmarks, and measurable goals with supervisees. Sue et al. (2019), recommend the implementation of an incremental "scaffolding" process with targets, building an infrastructure of knowledge, and developing a goal-oriented process. This involves systematically building supervisees' knowledge of oppression and bias, moving beyond solely case-specific discussions (Sue et al., 2019). Supervisors can offer learning assignments specific to racism and other forms of oppression and utilize nontraditional supervision techniques (Bussey, 2024) aimed at increasing critical cultural competence. This approach is also analogous to a social justice pedagogical strategy recommended by Goodyear (2014), in which supervisors can integrate self-directed learning approaches into their supervision practices (Bussey, 2024).

Engaging in Continuous Improvement and Adaptation

Anti-oppressive supervisory and leadership practices require dedication to continuous learning, unlearning, and adjustment. Within organizations, AOP leaders should advocate for and regularly review policies, guidelines, procedures, and practices to align them with anti-oppressive principles and address emerging challenges. This approach requires responsiveness to the evolving needs of communities, populations, clients, supervisees, and staff. Implementing anti-oppressive supervisory practices is a dynamic, ongoing commitment, and by integrating AOP strategies, organizations can create environments that actively challenge oppressive systems and promote social justice.

Challenges and Opportunities in Anti-Oppressive Social Work Supervision and Leadership

Anti-oppressive supervision and leadership present significant challenges and opportunities for growth. This section explores strategies for approaching challenges and identifies growth opportunities.

Barriers to Implementing Anti-Oppressive Practice

Multiple barriers exist to implementing AOP in leadership and supervision, including intrapersonal, interpersonal, and systemic issues. Challenging the barriers requires the ability to engage in critical conversations about experiences of oppression at the micro, mezzo, and macro levels. Common challenges to these discussions include emotional triggers, fear of judgment and/or invalidation, and skepticism about the potential for meaningful change (Goitom et al., 2021). Barriers such as implicit bias and defensiveness, and ideas based in liberalism, such as colorblindness and meritocracy, further complicate discussions around oppression and privilege, hindering progress toward implementing AOPs (Simon et al., 2022). The persistence of deficit-based views of minoritized individuals and unexamined privilege among leaders is also a challenge to effectively implementing AOP (Lusk et al., 2017). The ability to identify these challenges requires ongoing education, self-reflection, and a commitment to AOP and social justice.

Addressing Resistance and Pushback

AOP as a framework differs from diversity and inclusion efforts in that it focuses on addressing systemic change rather than on differences and ways to increase feelings of inclusion within a group. This demands reflexivity and critical reflection on one's personal and professional identity and on one's role in perpetuating or challenging complex structures within the environment and in relation to others. Resistance to AOPs often stems from discomfort with confronting personal biases and privilege. One of the first steps for meaningful engagement in this process with AOP principles is establishing comfort within discomfort (Goitom et al., 2021). This process can evoke feelings of guilt and shame as individuals confront their complicity in oppressive systems. Effective leadership and supervisory skills required to navigate and address these challenges include fostering open dialogue, bi-directional transfer of ideas, active listening, and reflexivity (Adams et al., 2018). AOP can provide leaders with needed tools to guide them through challenging moments by aiding them in active listening and reflecting on the consequences of their errors (Goitom et al., 2021). This also requires modeling vigilance in one's practices, critical focus on one's positionality and social location (Goitom et al., 2021), and humility, as well as providing opportunities for systemic change.

Seizing Opportunities for Growth and Innovation

Despite challenges, there are many opportunities for growth and innovation in anti-oppressive supervision. Effective strategies "are those that empower supervisees, attend to relational components in supervisory interactions, create a feeling of emotional and physical safety and support, address parallel process, emphasize knowledge, and advocate self-care. Such strategies are self-exploration, an ongoing open dialogue, flattening the power pyramid, creating relational safety, and sharing contemporary trauma knowledge" (Berger et al., 2018, p.128). Supervisors can enhance supervision effectiveness by exploring their positionality, intersecting social identities, social locations, power analysis, and their implications on relationships with their supervisees. To reduce the impacts of structural power within the supervisory relationship, supervisees should be provided with maximum autonomy (while being mindful of external requirements). Transparency and negotiation are also skills that can be applied in leadership and supervision for a more collaborative approach to developing clinical knowledge and enhancing professional skills that empower supervisees and foster a more egalitarian supervisory environment (Berger et al., 2018). By embracing these opportunities for growth and innovation, supervisors and leaders can create environments that challenge administrative and structural oppression and support meaningful knowledge development among supervisees and within their organizations.

Summary (and Call to Action)

Anti-oppressive leadership and supervision is a critical framework for meaningfully changing systems and empowering individuals. We have explored foundational principles, central tenets, implementation strategies, challenges, and opportunities inherent in anti-oppressive supervision and leadership. AOP underscores the need to understand how systemic inequities manifest uniquely for individuals based on their intersectional identity factors, historical oppression, and sociocultural context. Leaders must commit to continuous learning and application of anti-oppressive principles, which include reflexive practice, critical examination of power dynamics, and awareness of evolving social justice issues in organizational settings.

A proactive stance in promoting anti-oppressive supervision involves intentionally identifying and actively challenging oppressive systems within practice settings. This includes awareness of positionality and social location, addressing power dynamics in the supervision dyad as well as within mezzo and macro systems, advocating for culturally responsive interventions, centering and elevating historically marginalized voices, using truth and reconciliation, and advocating for systemic changes that consider and give priority to oppressed populations rather than perpetuating the status quo (Havig & Byers, 2019). Promoting anti-oppressive leadership and supervision is not just a professional responsibility but an ethical imperative. Let us heed the call to action to advance anti-oppressive leadership and supervision, ensuring that our practices reflect our commitment to social justice and the dignity and worth of all people.

Reflective Questions for Individual or Group Discussion

1. As a leader or supervisor, how do I integrate anti-oppressive principles into my ethical decision-making process? How can I ensure that my decisions prioritize the well-being of those who have been historically marginalized?
2. How do I respond when faced with ethical dilemmas involving interpersonal issues of oppression in supervision? And systemic issues of oppression? How can I support my supervisees in navigating these complex ethical challenges?
3. What feedback mechanisms can I establish to ensure that I am accountable for my commitment to AOPs? How can I model transparency and humility to supervisees in this process?
4. What are some steps I can take to advocate for organizational changes that promote anti-oppressive principles in supervision and leadership? How can I influence policy and practice within my organization to align with AOP and social justice goals?

5. What metrics can I use to monitor and evaluate progress toward anti-oppression, equity, and inclusion in practice? How can I support supervisees in developing their own measurable goals? (See Box 6.1.)

Box 6.1 Practice Activity. Holding the Supervisee Accountable to Anti-Oppressive Practice

By Christina Crow Cruz

You are a clinical supervisor at a mental health clinic. One of your supervisees identifies as Black and nonbinary. During one of your supervision sessions, the supervisee discloses feeling challenged by one of their clients, who has made statements invalidating their gender identity and questioning their competence. The supervisee reports feeling distraught and is seeking guidance on how to address these issues with the client while also maintaining a therapeutic relationship.

Example Application of AOP

1. *Acknowledge and validate* the supervisee's experience, recognizing the emotional impact of the microaggressions and bias present in the interpersonal relationship.
2. *Complete a power analysis* of dynamics present in the supervisee–client relationship as well as within mezzo (organizational) and macro (broader social) contexts and explore how systems of oppression can impact the therapeutic process. Reflect on intersectionality.
3. Utilize *reflective practice* and empowerment with the supervisee to examine personal emotional responses to the situation, the impact on their therapeutic approach, and strategies to navigate those challenges.
4. *Develop strategies for advocacy* together with the supervisee to address the client's harmful behavior in a manner that promotes respect and understanding.
5. *Broach organizational support and accountability* such as inclusive policies, staff training on AOP, and approaches to creating inclusive environments.
6. *Commit to ongoing support* to monitor progress and challenges, and support wellness and professional self-care practices.

REFLECTION QUESTIONS

1. What possible power dynamics are present in this case? As a supervisor, how would you approach a discussion about power dynamics with the supervisee?
2. What types of assignments can be provided to encourage reflexive practice? How might you, as a supervisor, also benefit from engaging in reflexive practice in this scenario?
3. What suggestions do you have to establish and monitor the progress of AOP goals in this scenario?

REFERENCES

Adams, Maurianne, Blumenfeld, Warren J., Catalano, D. Chase J., Dejong, Keri, Hackman, Heather W., Hopkins, Larissa E., Love, Barbara, Peters, Madeline L., Shlasko, Davey, & Zuniga, Ximena. (2018). *Readings for diversity and social justice*, 4th ed. Routledge.

Altaha, N., Amoafo-Yeboah, A. K., Cogburn, C. D., Corriders, S. R., Dillard, S., Graham, A., Jayakar, E., Lenard, I., Riedel, M., Sharpe, M., Shugrue dos Santos, C., Stewart, A., Williams, O. F., & Witte, S. S. (2023). Narratives of uprooting anti-Black racism in higher education: Developing a power, race, oppression, and privilege framework in social work. *Smith College Studies in Social Work*, 93(2–4), 106–129. https://doi-org.ezproxy.simmons.edu/10.1080/00377317.2023.2266026

American Counseling Association. (2014). 2014 ACA code of ethics. www.counseling.org/resources/aca-code-of-ethics.pdf

Arao, B., & Clemens, K. (2013). From safe spaces to brave spaces: A new way to frame dialogue around diversity and social justice. In L. M. Landreman (ed.), *The art of effective facilitation: Reflections from social justice educators* (pp. 135–150). Stylus.

Asakura, K., & Maurer, K. (2018). Attending to social justice in clinical social work: Supervision as a pedagogical space. *Clinical Social Work Journal*, 46(4), 289–297. https://doi-org.ezproxy.simmons.edu/10.1007/s10615-018-0667-4

Berger, R., Quiros, L., & Benavidez-Hatzis, J. R. (2018). The intersection of identities in supervision for trauma-informed practice: Challenges and strategies. *Clinical Supervisor*, 37(1), 122–141. https://doi-org.ezproxy.simmons.edu/10.1080/07325223.2017.1376299

Berzoff, J. (2023). Intersectionality: Power differentials, impasses and enactments in clinical practice and in supervision. *Psychoanalytic Social Work*, 30(1), 64–76. https://doi-org.ezproxy.simmons.edu/10.1080/15228878.2022.2073457

Bussey, S. R. (2024). Skills to enhance the efficacy of anti-racist supervision. *Journal of Social Work*, 24(3), 397–414. https://doi-org.ezproxy.simmons.edu/10.1177/14680173231225124

Bussey, S. R., Thompson, M. X., & Poliandro, E. (2022). Leading the charge in addressing racism and bias: implications for social work training and practice. *Social Work Education*, 41(5), 907–925. https://doi-org.ezproxy.simmons.edu/10.1080/02615479.2021.1903414

Egan, R., Maidment, J., & Connolly, M. (2017). Trust, power and safety in the social work supervisory relationship: Results from Australian research. *Journal of Social Work Practice*, 31(3), 307–321. https://doi-org.ezproxy.simmons.edu/10.1080/02650533.2016.1261279

Einbinder, S. D. (2020). Reflections on importing critical race theory into social work: The state of social work literature and students' voices. *Journal of Social Work Education*, 56(2), 327–340. https://doi-org.ezproxy.simmons.edu/10.1080/10437797.2019.1656574

Goitom, M., Riviere, D., & Ramsay, M. (2021). Anti-oppressive practice and early-career systems leaders: How learning and working from an AOP lens supports early-career systems leaders to integrate equity-focused leadership for social innovation. *Organizational Cultures, 22*(1), 39–57.

Goodyear, R. K. (2014). Supervision as pedagogy: Attending to its essential instructional and learning processes. *The Clinical Supervisor, 33*(1), 82–99. https://doi.org/10.1080/07325223.2014.918914

Havig, K., & Byers, L. (2019). Truth, reconciliation, and social work: A critical pathway to social justice and anti-oppressive practice. *Journal of Social Work Values & Ethics, 16*(2), 70–80.

Kadushin, A., & Harkness, D. (2014). *Supervision in social work*, 5th ed. Columbia University Press.

King, K. M., Borders, L. D., & Jones, C. T. (2020). Multicultural orientation in clinical supervision: examining impact through dyadic data. *Clinical Supervisor, 39*(2), 248–271. https://doi-org.ezproxy.simmons.edu/10.1080/07325223.2020.1763223

Lipscomb, A. E., & Ashley, W. (2017). Colorful disclosures: Identifying identity-based differences and enhancing critical consciousness in supervision. *Smith College Studies In Social Work, 87*(2–3), 220–237. https://doi-org.ezproxy.simmons.edu/10.1080/00377317.2017.1324098

Lusk, M., Terrazas, S., & Salcido, R. (2017). Critical cultural competence in social work supervision. *Human Service Organizations: Management, Leadership & Governance, 41*(5), 464–476. https://doi-org.ezproxy.simmons.edu/10.1080/23303131.2017.1313801

NASW (2024, July). *Social Workers' Ethical Responsibilities to Clients.* National Association of Social Workers. www.socialworkers.org/About/Ethics/Code-of-Ethics/Code-of-Ethics-English/Social-Workers-Ethical-Responsibilities-to-Clients

Okech, J. E. A., Rubel, D., Jamaleddine, M., Hutchinson, C., & Redmond, L. (2023). Applying the principles of anti-oppression to group work supervision. *Journal for Specialists in Group Work, 48*(2), 90–108. https://doi-org.ezproxy.simmons.edu/10.1080/01933922.2023.2190775

O'Neil, P., & del Mar Fariña, M. (2018). Constructing critical conversations in social work supervision: Creating change. *Clinical Social Work Journal, 46*(4), 298–309. https://doi-org.ezproxy.simmons.edu/10.1007/s10615-018-0681-6

Peters, H. C., & Luke, M. (2022). Principles of anti-oppression: A critical analytic synthesis. *Counselor Education and Supervision, 61*(4), 335–348.

Pieterse, A. L. (2018). Attending to racial trauma in clinical supervision: Enhancing client and supervisee outcomes. *Clinical Supervisor, 37*(1), 204–220. http://doi-org.ezproxy.simmons.edu/10.1080/07325223.2018.1443304

Rogerson, C. V., Prescott, D. E., & Howard, H. G. (2022). Teaching social work students the influence of explicit and implicit bias: Promoting ethical reflection in practice. *Social Work Education, 41*(5), 1035–1046. https://doi-org.ezproxy.simmons.edu/10.1080/02615479.2021.1910652

Simon, J. D., Boyd, R., & Subica, A. M. (2022). Refocusing intersectionality in social work education: Creating a brave space to discuss oppression and privilege. *Journal of Social Work Education, 58*(1), 34–45. https://doi-org.ezproxy.simmons.edu/10.1080/10437797.2021.1883492

Sue, D. W., Alsaidi, S., Awad, M. N., Glaeser, E., Calle, C. Z., & Mendez, N. (2019). Disarming racial microaggressions: Microintervention strategies for targets, white allies, and bystanders. *American Psychologist, 74*(1), 128–142. https://doi.org/10.1037/amp0000296

Tarshis, S., & Baird, S. L. (2021). Applying intersectionality in clinical supervision: A scoping review. *Clinical Supervisor, 40*(2), 218–240. https://doi-org.ezproxy.simmons.edu/10.1080/07325223.2021.1919949

Wathen, C. C., & Andrade Vargas, E. (2023). Applying the 10 principles of anti-oppression to online psychoeducational groups: Steps to intentional changes in emerging technologies. *Journal for Specialists in Group Work, 48*(2), 172–184. https://doi-org.ezproxy.simmons.edu/10.1080/01933922.2023.2190783

CHAPTER 7

Anti-Oppressive and Intersectional Mental Health Practice in Psycholegal and Other Interdisciplinary Collaborative Settings

Lindsey Sank Davis and Melanie Robinson Findlay

Introduction

Western and Eurocentric understandings of wellness and human behavior have dominated the field of psychology since its inception. Pervasive W.E.I.R.D. (Western, Educated, Industrialized, Rich, and Democratic; Henrich et al., 2010) and white supremacy culture (Jones & Okun, 2001) practices and ideals are part of a broad legacy of colonialism that punishes deviation from the dominant framework.

Individuals with minoritized ethnoracial, sexual, and gender identities have been persistently underrepresented among the mental health workforce serving in systems where these identities are overrepresented. This mismatch results from many complementary social forces that have eased barriers to high-quality education and health care, safe housing, financial security, and economic opportunity for white, upper/middle-class, heterosexual, cisgender, American-born individuals without disabilities, while magnifying these barriers for "others" through the disproportionate impact of both *de jure* and *de facto* practices. These practices include segregation, redlining, mass incarceration, voter suppression, and daily microaggressions in educational, workplace, healthcare, and therapeutic settings (e.g., Alexander, 2010; Nadal, Davidoff, et al., 2015; Rothstein, 2017; Sue et al., 2007). The complexity of these interlocking forms of oppression requires mental health providers to move beyond what Resnicow et al. (1999) referred to as "*surface structure adaptations*" (e.g., identity-based therapist matching), toward a broader "*deep structure sensitivity*" through acknowledgment of oppressive structures, their roles in the daily lives of clients, and the roles clinicians play in oppressive structures (p. 12). This speaks to the need for *all* providers to develop deep structure sensitivity.

Theoretical Foundations for Deep Structure Sensitivity

Intersectionality Theory and intersectional approaches avoid overemphasizing any single aspect of identity, acknowledging that the impact of one identity is modified by another and that all identities affect one's social location (Crenshaw, 1989). For example, a gay white cisgender man may experience privilege by virtue of being white, male, and cisgender but experience oppression due to his sexual orientation; he may navigate some spaces with the privilege of a white man while experiencing homophobic violence in others. Intersectionality has been proposed as an approach to conceptualizing clients using the social determinants of health rather than problematizing them or their narratives (Almeida et al., 2019). Acknowledging that all marginalization has ill effects, and no marginalized person can be truly free, self-proclaimed "Black lesbian" Audre Lorde (1983) discouraged labeling any identity as more marginalized than another, stating that "among those of us who share the goals of liberation and a workable future for our children, there can be no hierarchies of oppression."

Critical Race Theorists have joined in conceptualizing the fight for freedom as a collective fight in which the destinies of all marginalized groups are intertwined. Critical Race Theory (CRT) is an analytical lens through which we can examine laws, policies, and practices that purport to be race-neutral but impose a disproportionate impact on different groups (for example, laws that make no explicit reference to Native and Indigenous Americans but render their land uninhabitable). An emerging field of Critical Race Psychology (CRP; Salter & Adams, 2013) has followed on the tails of CRT, encouraging practitioners and researchers to consider the role of systemic racism and other biases in individual psychology, deconstruct the traditional myth of meritocracy, attend to counternarratives, and utilize other aspects of CRT to improve the ability of research and clinical services to effectively address the concerns of minoritized identity groups. Recent advances in CRP include understanding microaggressions affecting formerly incarcerated men of color from *their* perspective (Crain et al., 2024) and the development of Critical Race Mixed Methodology to examine racialized experiences in education (DeCuir-Gunby, 2020).

A related concept, Minority Stress Theory, was originally posited by a social worker, Dr. Winn Kelly Brooks (née Virginia Brooks, 1977), to capture the disproportionate strain experienced by lesbian women due to the stigma attached to their sexual identities. The concept was further developed and expanded by Meyer (2003) and others (e.g., Hendricks & Testa, 2012), who posited that distal and proximal stressors associated with minoritized sexual and gender identities contribute to unique health risks for LGBTQIA+ individuals. Distal stressors refer to objective events occurring in the outside world, while proximal stressors are the psychic *introjects* of these real or anticipated events, resulting in internalized stigma. Though Meyer's (2003) conceptualization was intended to capture the LGB experience, the model maps well onto the experiences of others facing identity-based marginalization and can help clinicians understand their clients' distress, identity conflicts, and health risks.

Potential Models of Recovery and Empowerment

Feminist approaches to mental health practice emerged to counteract the long history of a male-oriented perspective in psychology and psychiatry, addressing not just sexism but also racism and other oppressive forces through an intersectional lens (e.g., Rosenthal, 2016). Feminist psychology encourages critique of and resistance to social hierarchies that oppress and marginalize.

Queer Theory challenges predominant views of gender and sexuality and intersects with feminism by questioning traditional gender norms and the harm they may cause. Queer theorists (e.g., Sedgwick, 1990) refuse to reinforce the labels and standards of heteronormativity and cisnormativity, highlighting that these ideas are driven by Western cultures and false binaries.

Liberation Psychology interweaves many of these theories and models, connecting the personal and the political, making explicit that one cannot understand an individual's well-being without understanding the well-being of their community, reinforcing a focus on rehabilitating the sociopolitical forces that generate suffering (e.g., Martín-Baró, 1994). Liberation psychology emphasizes the practitioner's development of *critical consciousness* and encourages collaboration with oppressed communities to support social change.

Professional Ethics

The American Psychological Association's Code of Ethics (APA, 2017) calls on psychologists to mitigate their personal biases and avoid participating in or condoning unjust activities. The APA's guiding principles include justice and respect for persons. The National Association of Social

Workers (NASW) takes a stronger position and requires social workers to be *active* participants in reducing the impact of bias in their work. The field of social work is rooted in a commitment to service, integrity, advocating for social justice, and acknowledging and respecting the dignity and worth of persons and relationships (NASW, 2021). Social workers are in-the-trenches professionals who should be trained to conceptualize marginalized individuals and their needs relative to the contexts in which they live (e.g., sociopolitical, economic, and physical environments).

Ladson-Billings (1995) defined *cultural competence* as the capacity to function effectively within one's societal context, and Sue et al. (2009) emphasized that this requires awareness and skills appropriate to work clinically with individuals in that context who may differ in terms of age, race, sexuality, gender, and other identity constructs. The term *cultural humility* has also been introduced and is now preferred in many contexts, acknowledging that there is not just one acceptable set of cultural standards, that culture is constantly evolving, and that maintaining curiosity and willingness to be teachable is preferable to the hubris that self-proclaimed cultural competence may induce (Gottlieb, 2020).

Best Practices, Gold Standards, and Evidence-Based Practices

Prevailing mental health models and methods approved by the dominant culture are often burnished with superlatives like "best practices," "gold standard," or "evidence-based." Their superiority is typically based on empirical research supporting their efficacy; however, little consideration has been given to the diversity of the research samples or the appropriateness of purported indicators of therapeutic success used to reach these conclusions (Aisenberg, 2008; Kirmeyer, 2012). The alleged superiority of these methods is reinforced by the managed healthcare system, in which Western insurance companies have agreed to pay out considerable amounts for some services and providers, while services and providers more closely linked to Indigenous or Eastern practices are often undervalued or not reimbursed at all. This is problematic, as marginalized communities often have limited access to and means to pay for high-quality care, and the care that is most available to them may not comport with their cultural beliefs and practices (e.g., Jimenez et al., 2012).

Research with diverse samples often reveals different conclusions about the effectiveness of practices that have been elevated in the field. For example, Oh and Lee (2016) have discussed the ways that Motivational Interviewing (MI), a commonly used evidence-based practice for the treatment of many conditions, may not work well for individuals from collectivist cultures if practiced to fidelity. The self-determination paradigm that underlies MI and is a core value of social work may conflict with the understandings and preferences of clients who see themselves as inextricable from their families or communities or who value duty and honor highly. If the clinician fails to recognize these factors, they risk common errors that may feel selfish or unnatural to the client because they have been taught to center others' needs.

Borrowing from Ladson-Billings' (2004) critique of the education system post–*Brown v. Board of Education*, we see that many attempts at "equal treatment" in mental health care have been based on the false idea that "equal" means "same," leading to so-called "colorblind" approaches that simultaneously ignore and ironically reinforce pre-existing differences in socioeconomic opportunities amongst identity groups. As a result, any colorblind or culture-blind system inherently caters to the dominant group – middle- to upper-class cisgender heterosexual white Americans. These culture-blind recommendations may be inaccessible, unhelpful, or even harmful to the client.[1] Uncritical fidelity to "evidence-based" models can contribute to misunderstandings in therapy and increase the risk of treatment failure or premature drop-out. In mandated mental health or substance use treatment, this poses an existential threat to the client, who may be perceived as noncompliant and lose their parenting rights, employment, benefits, or freedom.

Collaboration in the Legal System

Collaborations between mental health and legal professionals have the potential to significantly benefit oppressed individuals and groups; however, conflicts may arise from the inherent differences between these systems and their respective goals (Melton et al., 2017). The field of mental health aims to understand, explain, and ameliorate behavioral, cognitive, and emotional difficulties, considering each individual's unique biological, psychological, and social conditions. In contrast, the legal profession seeks to determine the "truth" as it relates to generic laws and must resolve the ambiguities that clinicians learn to adapt to.

Other difficulties for mental health professionals working in the legal system may emerge from demographic discordance. More than 80 percent of attorneys and psychologists in the United States are white and often do not share lived experiences with those whose futures they have the power to shape (American Bar Association, 2024; American Psychological

Association, 2019). Social work has better represented historically oppressed communities, and only 66–71 percent of recent MSW graduates identify as white (Salsberg et al., 2020). This disparate professional representation can be understood as a reflection of the same oppressive structures that push people of color into contact with the legal system.

Additionally, many members of historically oppressed communities distrust attorneys and all representatives of the legal system (Nadal, Quintanilla, et al., 2015), which can cause trepidation about mandated mental health services. Together, these circumstances can put embedded mental health professionals at a distinct disadvantage when attempting to build the rapport necessary to engage clients in assessment and treatment services.

Criminal and Juvenile Justice Systems

The roles of mental health professionals in the criminal and juvenile justice systems include pre-trial, post-trial, pre-release, and post-release positions in evaluating, providing therapy to, and advocating for individuals suspected or convicted of illegal behavior. An evaluator may feel their position is at odds with their role in fighting injustice – by giving their honest assessment of mental illness, parenting capacity, violence risk, or criminal responsibility, a vulnerable individual may lose their access to rights or freedoms. As a therapist, this relationship with the legal system frequently places mental health professionals at the intersection of care and punishment of marginalized individuals. The provision of mandated treatment in the criminal or juvenile justice system poses a potential challenge to social workers' responsibility to "promote the right of clients to self-determination and assist clients in their efforts to identify and clarify their goals" (NASW, 2021) and psychologists' and other counselors' responsibility to respect their clients' autonomy and preferences, as therapeutic goals and timelines may be determined by the Court instead of the clinician–client dyad.

Nonetheless, each clinician can respect their clients' rights to autonomy, even within systems that mandate care. When working with a mandated client, it is critical to understand how they believe they found themselves in their current situation, what their personal history and social context have contributed, what personal beliefs they hold about mental health and therapy, and what personal goals they might have that could be furthered in the process of fulfilling any legal requirements of treatment. The trauma of systemic oppression should be considered while fulfilling mandated treatment objectives, either indirectly – through culturally sensitive and trauma-informed approaches – or directly – through interventions like trauma-focused cognitive behavioral therapy or narrative therapy that target cognitions that have developed from this trauma.

Psychological assessment is another common responsibility of clinicians who work in the legal system. The *Diagnostic and Statistical Manual, 5th Edition* (DSM-5; American Psychiatric Association, 2013) is considered the primary source of diagnostic criteria for psychological disorders in the United States. However, this tome of diagnostic criteria also leans toward the dominant population when defining what is normal or abnormal. A growing number of scholars (e.g., Bryant-Davis & Ocampo, 2005, 2006; McCluney et al., 2017) have argued that the DSM-5 criteria for post-traumatic stress disorder fail to account for trauma symptoms caused by racial discrimination and harassment, as well as anti-Black violence in the media, leading to the development of the Racial Trauma Scale as a new measure for the assessment of racial trauma (Williams et al., 2022).

The application of DSM-5 diagnostic labels has a long history of inequity. Highly stigmatized diagnoses, like conduct disorder and schizophrenia, tend to be overdiagnosed among Black and Latino youth and adults and over-represented in the carceral system (Atkins-Loria et al., 2015). While this may partially reflect the negative psychological effects of minority stress, this cannot explain the *under*diagnosis of depressive and anxiety disorders in these same populations. Similar patterns appear to have emerged among transgender and gender-diverse (TGD) individuals, who are increasingly cast as inherently mentally ill by public figures and are disproportionately diagnosed with psychotic disorders (Barr et al., 2021). These patterns suggest many clinicians fail to integrate historical and social factors affecting TGD and other marginalized identity groups into their intake, conceptualization, and diagnostic processes. As Activist Angela Davis (2013) stated,

> by failing to recognize the material forces of racism that are responsible for offering up such large numbers of [B]lack and Latino youth to the carceral state, the process of criminalization imputes responsibility to the individuals who are its casualties, thus reproducing the very conditions that produce racist patterns in incarceration and its seemingly infinite capacity to expand. (p. 171)

Clinicians must, therefore, develop critical consciousness to avoid becoming a part of this process of criminalization through misdiagnosis of mental illness and violence risk.

One aspect of critical consciousness for evaluators in the legal system is considering the appropriateness of each assessment instrument as it relates to each client's identities. For example, Hastings et al. (2011) found that the Violence Risk Appraisal Guide (VRAG; Quinsey et al., 1998), an actuarial violence prediction measure, was able to predict misconduct and recidivism among male inmates but did not function reliably with female inmates. Nonetheless, many clinicians continue to use the VRAG to predict future violence in female offenders, potentially altering the course of their lives. While there is only preliminary evidence to date (Wood, 2024), the VRAG formula (and its sexual violence equivalent, the SORAG) is also likely to be unreliable when applied to LGBTQ+ individuals.

Best practices for the psychological assessment of TGD individuals in the legal system are also severely lacking, and researchers (Keo-Meier and Fitzgerald, 2017; Webb et al., 2016) have called for advancements in this area but have seen little progress over the past decade. Instruments normed on cisgender heterosexual community members likely lack sensitivity to sexual and gender minorities and their associated challenges in the legal system. Furthermore, there is a critical mismatch between the disproportionately large numbers of LGBTQ+ individuals in the juvenile and adult criminal legal systems and the availability of mental health providers who have been specifically trained to understand their needs (Davis et al., 2024). Though LGBTQ+-identifying providers may be drawn to work in the legal system due to their own experiences, they may also be at higher risk of vicarious trauma and eventual burnout without sufficient supervision and other support, such as community-based care. LGBTQ+ youth and adults of color are at particularly high risk of entry into these systems, demonstrating the need for race, gender, sexuality, and intersectionality to be common mental health competencies rather than areas of specialty.

Family Court Systems

Critical legal scholars (e.g., Schneider, 1992) have noted that some family structures and functions have been recognized and upheld, while others have been unacknowledged or contravened. For example, without "proper" legally recognized relationships between family members, an individual may be denied essential rights – to make medical decisions for a loved one, to access family finances, to visit an incarcerated partner in prison, to pick up a child from school – that others might enjoy in fully recognized families. The US government's refusal to recognize particular forms of family harkens back to the time of enslavement, when these regulations permitted the dominant culture to perpetuate the subjugation of African Americans (Chen & Mulligan, 2025). US laws continue to express and support a particular view of family, based on a white cisgender heterosexual dyad raising their biological children, though modern American families increasingly involve chosen, single, divorced, or queer parents, inconsistent with the traditional conceptions on which the law is based. The desirability of assimilation into mainstream American culture has, therefore, incentivized and imposed on diverse people a nuclear family structure as a benchmark of being a so-called "true American," despite the ways it may not be culturally or logistically appropriate or accessible (Chen & Mulligan, 2025; Schneider, 1992). Mental health professionals should be mindful not to reinforce this hegemonic view of family and can ethically validate and support a variety of family structures.

Child Welfare

Since its inception, America's child welfare system has been motivated by reinforcing Eurocentric values rather than meeting the legitimate need for child protection (Stephens, 2021). The ideology of respecting family values has repeatedly been violated – from Native American children being removed from their families and sent to boarding schools, to African children being sold into slavery, to children being ripped from their mother's bosoms at the Southern border. Since the late 1960s and 1970s, the child welfare system has functioned more effectively as an agency of surveillance and coercive intervention (Raz et al., 2021).

Families of color, specifically Native American and Black families, have disproportionate contact with the child welfare system – 11.5 percent of Black children and 15.4 percent of Native American children will enter the foster care system before the age of 18 (Wildeman & Emanuel, 2014). Black children are more likely than white children to be removed from their homes and are subsequently less likely to be reunified with their families after a period of removal (Raz et al., 2021). Families with lesbian or bisexual parents have also been found to be more than four times as likely to lose custody of their children compared to heterosexual parents (Joslin & Sakimura, 2022). LGBTQ+ youth are estimated to comprise 30 percent of youth in foster care (Baams et al., 2019), and BIPOC LGBTQ+ youth are 1.5 times as likely to experience foster care than white LGBTQ+ youth (Dettlaff & Washburn, 2018). These statistics suggest the child welfare system tends to disproportionately punish deviations from traditional white, heterosexual norms.

Families are frequently judged by the broader society based on the neighborhoods they live in, the schools their children attend, and parental education level, sexual orientation, socioeconomic status, and places of employment. An added layer of judgment lies in the opinion of their children's teachers, doctors, school staff, neighbors, police, and even their therapists, who are not just authorized but *required* to report any knowledge suggestive of child abuse or neglect. When providers and families are from different cultures and have access to different resources, suspicion may arise easily and without appropriate acknowledgment of the potential impact on the parents and children. Research suggests the courts err on the side of removing a child when there appears to be a viable child welfare concern, while overlooking the potential harms to the child caused by the removal itself. Mental health professionals may be able to voice the child's needs by speaking to the court about the psychological impact of being separated from caregivers, siblings, and other family, as well as the disproportionate distribution of these outcomes.

Once in this system, Black children tend to suffer worse consequences than white children, such as remaining in foster care longer and receiving less desirable placements; similarly, LGBTQ+ youth often have a difficult time in the foster system, where they may experience identity-related abuse or be shuffled among multiple placements and ultimately age out into homelessness (Fowler et al., 2017). Youth in foster care – particularly those with unstable placements – are at increased risk of behavioral, social, and mental health problems compared to those with stable foster homes (Baams et al., 2019; Joslin & Sakimura, 2022).

While there are many white youth involved in the child welfare system, their underrepresentation can be understood as the result of white families' behavior being less likely to be recognized, reported, and substantiated as abusive or neglectful; thus, white children are subsequently less likely to be removed from their homes by child welfare agencies (Raz et al., 2021), shielding these children from certain negative developmental pathways associated with removal from the home – but potentially leaving many white children in perilous home situations. If therapists, teachers, and doctors are more vigilant for problems in Black families, attentional and confirmation biases will produce evidence to support their beliefs. If they are not looking at white families with the same watchful eye, however, they are not only less likely to magnify or confabulate a problem, but they are more likely to ignore a real problem that requires attention (Cénat et al., 2021).

Child Custody Matters

As the Guiding Principles and Values of the Association of Family and Conciliation Courts (AFCC) *Guidelines for Parenting Plan Evaluations in*

Family Law Cases (2022) state, "Evaluations are independent, impartial, free of material conflicts of interest, fact-based, methodologically balanced, and culturally informed. . . . Evaluation methods are sensitive to and avoid worsening societal inequities, including, but not limited to, those related to social status, ethnicity, religion, race, language, gender, gender identity, sexual orientation, ability status, age, education, and wealth disparities" (pp. 8–9). Per AFCC, Parenting Plan Evaluators (PPEs; previously known as *child custody evaluators*) should have education and training in "culture and diversity and their significance in the lives of adults, children, and families" and "effects of racism, sexism, poverty, and other socio-cultural issues in the lives of adults, children, and families" (p. 10). PPEs have a responsibility to attend to the identities of family members while sensitively investigating and illuminating critical family issues. Their cultural knowledge must be up to date and relevant to the parties in the cases they accept, and if they must take a case that involves cultures with which they lack familiarity, they should engage the services of a consultant with the requisite knowledge and utilize them throughout the process to understand how to approach the evaluation, how to understand particular pieces of information in their appropriate cultural context, and how to communicate their findings respectfully.

PPEs and other family court professionals must acknowledge that cultural norms and experiences affect what we see as normal or abnormal, and hence what we view as acceptable behavior. For example, research has shown that in custody disputes between different-sex partners, partners who subsequently came out as LGBTQ+ have often lost custody to their cisgender heterosexual co-parent, or even to another family member, because some courts reasoned that simply being raised by an LGBTQ+ parent was harmful to a child (Joslin & Sakimura, 2022). When we have limited exposure to certain communities and their values, we are more apt to pathologize their practices; therefore, we must intentionally expand our cultural awareness in all areas of our lives and commit to seeking out critical feedback on our work to improve on gaps in our awareness.

Intersectional identities exist within a family, and it is common that one parent/caregiver has greater structural power by virtue of their gender, age, ability status, education level, or other factors. PPEs must consider this in their formulations, getting a full understanding of why one parent may be the higher earner or have more contact with the child's providers. As part of a thorough and ethical evaluation process, PPEs reach out to collateral informants outside of the immediate family, which may include other mental health professionals. These professionals should be careful not only to provide facts about diagnoses, treatments, and interactions, but also to contextualize this information within the family, community, religious, and ethnoracial cultures in which the family members operate. Keeping in mind that their recommendations may be written into a court order, the evaluator's recommendations must be physically, linguistically, and financially accessible; reasonably flexible, considering the practical demands on the caregivers; and consistent with the family's cultural practices, to empower the family and support their success.

Interdisciplinary Work in Educational Settings

While an *achievement gap* between white and BIPOC children has been acknowledged for many years, Ladson-Billings (2006) and other scholars have highlighted the root causes of broad disparities in academic achievement, suggesting other terms like the *opportunity gap* might be a better representation of the phenomenon. The opportunity gap has been defined as:

> the unequal and inequitable distribution of resources and experiences on the basis of race, ethnicity, socioeconomic status, English proficiency, disability, immigration status, community wealth, familial situations, geography, or other factors that contribute to or perpetuate inequities in well-being across groups of young children in health, social-emotional development, and education. (National Academies of Sciences, Engineering, and Medicine, 2023, p. xxvii)

Furthermore, Ladson-Billings (2006) has similarly used the term *sociopolitical debt* to emphasize that the roots of these disparities are social, political, and economic – not innate. Mental health professionals have unique and varied opportunities to assist in filling these gaps and repaying these debts by advocating for inclusive education (e.g., Black and LGBTQ+ history, sexual health), connecting with students' parents or caregivers who *themselves* have been marginalized or traumatized by educational systems to engage them in their children's education, and helping classroom teachers to understand the less familiar principles of positive reinforcement that encourage good behavior.

In the 1990s, a proliferation of *zero-tolerance policies* followed the "War on Drugs" and fears of the so-called "superpredator" youth – a new brand of adolescent who allegedly committed violent crimes without remorse. Zero-tolerance policies involve strict rules with harsh punishments, which are applied regardless of the circumstances of a violation or consideration of the young person's abilities or limitations. While zero-tolerance policies are identity-neutral on their face, they account for most of the racial, socioeconomic, and sexual orientation disparities in suspensions and expulsions (Kennedy et al., 2019). These policies have led to another new phenomenon: the school-to-prison pipeline.

The term *school-to-prison pipeline* refers to the increased risk of juvenile and criminal justice contact among youth who are fed into the criminal legal system after experiencing disciplinary issues at school. Research (e.g., Mittleman, 2018; Novak, 2019) has shown that out-of-school suspensions and expulsions are associated with an increased risk of contact with law enforcement. Youth whose personal histories would otherwise indicate a low risk of delinquency are exposed to additional risk during out-of-school punishments, particularly when they live in areas with weak social cohesion and adults are unavailable to supervise (Monahan et al., 2014). This system overwhelmingly affects BIPOC and LGBTQ+ youth, with a particularly elevated risk for LGBTQ+ youth of color (Barnes & Motz, 2018).

Another option available to school systems in many situations is to send these youth to *alternative schools*.[2] These schools serve many functions, including providing a smaller staff-to-student ratio for youth at risk of school failure, educating young people with learning and developmental disorders using more personalized approaches, and supporting students who struggle with emotional and behavioral dysregulation. Often, these schools attempt to educate youth with intellectual disabilities in the same classroom as youth with juvenile offenses and youth with purely emotional disorders, creating a chaotic atmosphere that is not conducive to learning. Districts with the highest percentage of minoritized students send the most students to alternative schools, resulting in a system of alternative schools that is 80 percent Black or Latina/o/x (Kennedy et al., 2019). This overrepresentation of children of color in alternative schools is a parallel and an extension of child welfare system disparities.

Research, Advocacy, and Public Policy

Historically, most mental health research has been conducted using WEIRD principles and nonrepresentative convenience samples. This is due, in part, to the pressures of a pervasive Western-based academic "publish or perish" culture, which parallels white supremacy culture (Jones & Okun, 2001), in which the production of knowledge has become a requirement for job advancement and financial security. Academics are often evaluated based on narrow definitions of scholarly productivity that emphasize the publication of quantitative research in high-impact journals.

As Roberts and colleagues (2020) pointed out in their review of top psychological journals, BIPOC editors, authors, and research participants have been significantly underrepresented, and research that addresses the experiences of marginalized people is often relegated to specialized journals with lower impact factors. Some researchers (e.g., Stroebe, 2024) have gone so far as to explicitly state that the testing of psychological theories does not require diverse research samples.

The potential for decolonizing and queering the development of mental health knowledge and interventions is vast. Community-based participatory research is one starting point for engaging marginalized communities in research on the issues that concern them most but is often set aside in favor of more expeditious research methods. Others have argued that more diverse participant samples are a starting point for research equity – but even when aiming for this, researchers often miss the fact that some of their target population does not have internet access, cannot read or write in English, fears interactions with authorities due to unstable immigration status, or does not have a permanent mailing address or checking account to receive study benefits. Involving the community in research, while sometimes logistically difficult, empowers the community while maximizing the efficiency and impact of the research.

The dissemination of research findings is also an equity issue. Consumers' access to research has been significantly limited by the expenses associated with accessing research databases, the cost of open-access publication, and the slow pace of academic peer reviews due to a lack of reviewers willing to work for free. Alternative forms of dissemination that can reach the communities who most need the results include lay audience presentations and publications, which often do not suffer these same issues. Ideally, "helicopter research" should be avoided; researchers should seek feedback from the communities they research and involve them in the development of future research ideas.

Advocacy at the individual and societal levels is an inherent expectation of social workers, but this role is sometimes questioned in psychology, particularly in academic research. However, working in skewed systems requires mental health workers to advocate for their clients in a variety of systems regularly and to find creative ways to address their unique needs in light of systemic barriers. Professionals can get involved at a larger scale by lobbying for legislative changes to protect and expand patients' rights, particularly those that will most help those with limited access to culturally appropriate services. They can also get involved in the issues affecting the local community they serve, such as public housing initiatives, or the population they serve, such as advocating for Native and Indigenous rights to tribal sovereignty and joining movements for environmental justice. Anti-oppressive practitioners *must* join the fight against the ongoing legislative assaults on diversity, equity, and inclusion practices and education, for the well-being of young people and the future of the helping professions.

Social workers may be particularly interested in getting involved in equity issues in their own field. The *2022 ASWB Exam Pass Rate Analysis* (Association of Social Work Boards [ASWB], 2022) highlighted what many have known for a long time: standardized and high-stakes standardized exams often produce racially disparate outcomes (Au, 2016; Brunn-Bevel & Byrd, 2015; Hursh, 2005). The analysis showed passing rates by race for each state implementing the exam; several showed low passing rates among individuals of color. In response, several states have proposed or passed legislation to eliminate the licensing exam in the name of racial equity. While addressing disparity and fighting for social justice is a tenet of social work, many question whether eliminating the licensing exam is the solution to the problem of racial disparity. A response that would better protect the vulnerable communities served by social workers while increasing the number of BIPOC social workers entering the field might be tightening the standards for graduate social work training and providing better funding to the programs with weak pass rates to ensure students of all demographics possess the core competencies to be ethical providers for vulnerable communities. Social workers and other professionals might advocate for changes field-wide, state-wide, or within their own programs.

Summary

Clinicians working collaboratively in interdisciplinary settings must learn to decenter white supremacist cultural ideals and develop the knowledge and skills to work in a manner that embraces and empowers oppressed and marginalized clients. Many members of historically oppressed communities harbor distrust toward the legal and educational systems due to generations of traumatic experiences, which can obfuscate clinicians' efforts to communicate effectively and build strong rapport. Clinicians must learn to put their worldviews aside so they can see how their clients are affected by the various systems with which they interact daily. These systems have long histories of oppression of BIPOC and LGBTQ+ communities, and working with diverse individuals within these systems requires thoughtfulness about a variety of issues, including when it is appropriate to call child protective services, which psychological assessment tools have adequate research support for use with marginalized populations, and how to adapt evidence-based treatment approaches to match clients' cultural values and practices.

An anti-oppressive approach to practice also involves broader efforts, including research, education, advocacy, and public policy. Providers who identify with anti-oppressive, intersectional, feminist, and liberation ideologies also work to address systemic inequities and barriers to accessing mental health care, such as physical, linguistic, and financial barriers. All mental health workers can advocate for systemic change at the local, state, and national levels and elevate the voices of marginalized people to improve the practice of mental health care and the living conditions of the communities they serve.

Discussion Questions

1. How can supervisors assist clinicians-in-training to effectively address their biases or limitations when working with diverse populations in interdisciplinary settings?
2. How can treatment approaches be matched to a client's culture when no studies have included members of their identity group?
3. What are the potential risks of uncritically applying "best practices" or "evidence-based" models to court-involved clients? How can these risks be mitigated? (See Box 7.1.)

Box 7.1 Case Vignette. Do Children Experience Inequity and Oppression First?

By Lindsey Sank Davis and Melanie Robinson Findlay

An illuminating example comes from the authors' own experiences. A 11-year-old white boy enrolled in a residential program and therapeutic school in Massachusetts repeatedly and brutally assaulted staff and fellow students, often requiring significant medical intervention. He received no consequences for his actions, criminal charges, or threats to his enrollment. In contrast, a 16-year-old Black girl at the same school was discharged immediately with no placement plan in place and charged with assault after engaging in a physical altercation with an 18-year-old peer which resulted in the 18-year-old seeking medical attention for a concussion. When the white clinical supervisor who spearheaded the discharge was asked about this discrepancy, she justified the white student's continued enrollment, stating that his age was a "*protective factor,*" and that the Black student was discharged because the administration needed to ensure the safety of the other students in the program.

Research demonstrates that Black youth are systematically misperceived as older, taller, and more aggressive than they are (Goff et al., 2014; Kennedy et al., 2019). In this case, the decision to discharge the Black student instead of the chronically aggressive white student suggests that decision-makers engaged in the typical dehumanization and adultification that solidifies their placement on the school-to-prison pipeline. The intersectional nature of the students' identities likely contributed to the disparate outcomes of their situations. Physical aggression is more common among boys than among girls (e.g., Archer, 2004) and may be minimized as normative behavior; meanwhile, similar acts of aggression by girls are rarer and may be seen as a violation of gender norms. The Black student's discharge may be due in part to a tendency to view female violence as pathological. These decisions reinforced the privileges of whiteness and masculinity while marginalizing Blackness and femininity, thus setting a precedent within the agency and being observed and iterated by other clinicians and colleagues alike.

REFLECTION QUESTIONS

1. How might the discharge of the 16-year-old Black female resident affect other residents and agency clinicians of all races and genders? How might this discharge create future instances of oppressive practices?
2. How have policies and practices of "safety" and "protective factors" been used to provide for white clients while penalizing, exploiting, or harming Black and Brown clients?

REFERENCES

Archer, J. (2004). Sex differences in aggression in real-world settings: A meta-analytic review. *Review of General Psychology, 8*(4), 291–322. https://doi.org/10.1037/1089-2680.8.4.291

Goff, P. A., Jackson, M. C., Di Leone, B. A., Culotta, C. M., & DiTomasso, N. A. (2014). The essence of innocence: Consequences of dehumanizing Black children. *Journal of Personality and Social Psychology, 106*(4), 526–545.

Notes

1 The authors wish to acknowledge that these terms may have an ableist connotation that casts individuals who are *actually* blind or sight-impaired negatively. The use of "blind" in these terms connotes willful ignorance of the significant roles that race and other identities play in the lives of marginalized people; blind individuals – who are also typically marginalized – are not ignorant of race (Obasogie, 2013).

2 Though many alternative schools offer a specialized curriculum (e.g., performing arts, science) for mainstream students, these are not the schools the authors refer to here. These schools – even specialized public schools like LaGuardia High School in New York City – are often inaccessible to youth of color and youth of low socioeconomic status due to the costs associated with the lessons, supplies, and transportation required to be competitive for admission.

REFERENCES

Aisenberg, E. (2008). Evidence-based practice in mental health care to ethnic minority communities: Has its practice fallen short of its evidence? *Social Work, 53*(4), 297–306.

Alexander, M. (2010). *The new Jim Crow: Mass incarceration in the age of colorblindness*. The New Press.

Almeida, R. V., Werkmeister Rozas, L. M., Cross-Denny, B., Lee, K. K., & Yamada, A. M. (2019). Coloniality and intersectionality in social work education and practice. *Journal of Progressive Human Services, 30*(2), 148–164.

American Bar Association. (2024). *ABA 2023 Profile of Members*. www.abalegalprofile.com/

American Psychiatric Association. (2013). *Diagnostic and statistical manual of mental disorders* (5th ed.). American Psychiatric Publishing.

American Psychological Association. (2017). *Ethical principles of psychologists and code of conduct* (2002, amended effective June 1, 2010, and January 1, 2017). www.apa.org/ethics/code/

  (2019). *Demographics of the U.S. Psychology Workforce*. www.apa.org/workforce/data-tools/demographics

Association of Family and Conciliation Courts. (2022). *Guidelines for Parenting Plan Evaluations in Family Law Cases*. www.afccnet.org/Portals/0/PDF/2022%20Guidelines%20for%20Parenting%20Plan%20Evaluations%20in%20Family%20Law%20Cases1.pdf?ver=u1r1w6hGs2QTJz2Hf_iLoQ%3d%3d

Association of Social Work Boards. (2022). *2022 ASWB Exam Pass Rate Analysis*. www.aswb.org/regulation/research/pass-rates-in-context-an-exam-report-series/

Atkins-Loria, S., Macdonald, H., & Mitterling, C. (2015). Young African American men and the diagnosis of conduct disorder: The neo-colonization of suffering. *Clinical Social Work Journal, 43*(4), 431–441.

Au, W. (2016). Meritocracy 2.0: High-stakes, standardized testing as a racial project of neoliberal multiculturalism. *Educational Policy, 30*(1), 39–62.

Baams, L., Wilson, B. D., & Russell, S. T. (2019). LGBTQ youth in unstable housing and foster care. *Pediatrics, 143*(3), e20174211.

Barr, S. M., Roberts, D., & Thakkar, K. N. (2021). Psychosis in transgender and gender non-conforming individuals: A review of the literature and a call for more research. *Psychiatry Research, 306*, 114272.

Barnes, J. C., & Motz, R. T. (2018). Reducing racial inequalities in adulthood arrest by reducing inequalities in school discipline: Evidence from the school-to-prison pipeline. *Developmental Psychology, 54*(12), 2328–2340.

Brooks, V. R. (1977). *Minority stress and adaptation among lesbian women.* University of California Press.

Brunn-Bevel, R. J., & Byrd, W. C. (2015). The foundation of racial disparities in the standardized testing era: The impact of school segregation and the assault on public education in Virginia. *Humanity & Society, 39*(4), 419–448.

Bryant-Davis, T., & Ocampo, C. (2005). Racist incident-based trauma. *The Counseling Psychologist, 33*(4), 479–500.

(2006). A therapeutic approach to the treatment of racist incident-based trauma. *Journal of Emotional Abuse, 6*(4), 1–22.

Cénat, J. M., McIntee, S. E., Mukunzi, J. N., & Noorishad, P. G. (2021). Overrepresentation of Black children in the child welfare system: A systematic review to understand and better act. *Children and Youth Services Review, 120,* 105714.

Chen, A., & Mulligan, C. (2025). Parafamily. *Boston University Law Review, 105,* 385–442.

Crain, E., Davis, L. S., St. Louis, G., Jensen, H., Robertson, I., Meade, G., Carrasco, S., Overbey, D., & Alves, L. (2024). "Are you supposed to be here?": Formerly incarcerated men of color navigating positions of authority. *Journal of Social Issues, 8*(2), 496–530.

Crenshaw, K. (1989). Centering the margins: Intersectionality and social justice. In E. F. Cole & E. Espin (eds.), *A volume in honor of Sandra Harding* (pp. 123–145). The Feminist Press.

Davis, A. (2013). *The meaning of freedom.* City Lights.

Davis, L. S., Crain, E. E., & Sheridan, M. (2024). LGBTQ+-affirming graduate education: Preparing and supporting future family court clinicians. *Family Court Review, 62*(1), 45–67.

DeCuir-Gunby, J. (2020). Using critical race mixed methodology to explore the experiences of African Americans in education. *Educational Psychologist, 55*(4), 244–255.

Dettlaff, A. J., & Washburn, M. (2018). Lesbian, gay, and bisexual (LGB) youth within in welfare: Prevalence, risk and outcomes. *Child Abuse & Neglect, 80,* 183–193.

Fowler, P. J., Marcal, K. E., Zhang, J., Day, O., & Landsverk, J. (2017). Homelessness and aging out of foster care: A national comparison of child welfare-involved adolescents. *Children and Youth Services Review, 77,* 27–33.

Goff, P. A., Jackson, M. C., Di Leone, B. A., Culotta, C. M., & DiTomasso, N. A. (2014). The essence of innocence: Consequences of dehumanizing Black children. *Journal of Personality and Social Psychology, 106*(4), 526–545.

Gottlieb, M. (2020). The case for a cultural humility framework in social work practice. *Journal of Ethnic & Cultural Diversity in Social Work, 30*(6), 463–481. https://doi.org/10.1080/15313204.2020.1753615

Hastings, M. E., Krishnan, S., Tangney, J. P., & Stuewig, J. (2011). Predictive and incremental validity of the Violence Risk Appraisal Guide scores with male and female jail inmates. *Psychological Assessment, 23*(1), 174–183.

Hendricks, M. L., & Testa, R. J. (2012). A conceptual framework for clinical work with transgender and gender nonconforming clients: An adaptation of the Minority Stress Model. *Professional Psychology: Research and Practice, 43*(5), 460–467. https://doi.org/10.1037/a0029597

Henrich, J., Heine, S. J., & Norenzayan, A. (2010). The weirdest people in the world? *Behavioral and Brain Sciences, 33*(2–3), 61–83.

Hursh, D. (2005). The growth of high-stakes testing in the USA: Accountability, markets and the decline in educational equality. *British Educational Research Journal, 31*(5), 605–622.

Jimenez, D., Bartels, S., Cárdenas, V., Dhaliwal, S., & Alegría, M. (2012). Cultural beliefs and mental health treatment preferences of ethnically diverse older adult consumers in primary care. *The American Journal of Geriatric Psychiatry: Official Journal of the American Association for Geriatric Psychiatry, 20*(6), 533–542.

Jones, K., & Okun, T. (2001). *Dismantling racism: A workbook for social change groups.* ChangeWork.

Joslin, C. G., & Sakimura, C. (2022). Fractured families: LGBTQ people and the family regulation system. *California Law Review Online, 13*, 78–107.

Kennedy, B. L., Acosta, M. M., & Soutullo, O. (2019). Counternarratives of students' experiences returning to comprehensive schools from an involuntary disciplinary alternative school. *Race Ethnicity and Education, 22*(1), 130–149.

Keo-Meier, C. L., & Fitzgerald, K. M. (2017). Affirmative psychological testing and neurocognitive assessment with transgender adults. *Psychiatric Clinics, 40*(1), 51–64.

Kirmeyer, L. (2012). Cultural competence and evidence-based practice in mental health: Epistemic communities and the politics of pluralism. *Social Science & Medicine, 75*(2), 249–256.

Ladson-Billings, G. (1995). Toward a theory of culturally relevant pedagogy. *American Educational Research Journal, 32*(3), 465–491.

(2004). Landing on the wrong note: The price we paid for *Brown. Educational Researcher, 33*(7), 3–13.

(2006). From the achievement gap to the education debt: Understanding achievement in U.S. schools. *Educational Researcher, 35*(7), 3–12.

Lorde, A. (1983). *Homophobia and education.* New York Council on Interracial Books for Children.

Martín-Baró, I. (1994). *Writings for a liberation psychology.* Harvard University Press.

McCluney, C. L., Bryant, C. M., King, D. D., & Ali, A. A. (2017). Calling in Black: A dynamic model of racially traumatic events, resourcing, and safety. *Equality, Diversity and Inclusion, 36*(8), 767–786.

Melton, G. B., Petrila, J., Poythress, N. G., & Slobogin, C. (2017). Law and the mental health professions: An uneasy alliance, in *Psychological evaluations for the courts*, 2nd ed. (pp. 3–25). Guilford.

Meyer, I. H. (2003). Prejudice, social stress, and mental health in lesbian, gay and bisexual populations: Conceptual issues and research evidence. *Psychological Bulletin, 129*(5), 674–697.

Mittleman, J. (2018). A downward spiral? Childhood suspension and the path to juvenile arrest. *Sociology of Education, 91*(3), 183–204.

Monahan, K. C., VanDerhei, S., Bechtold, J., & Cauffman, E. (2014). From the school yard to the squad car: School discipline, truancy, and arrest. *Journal of Youth and Adolescence, 43*(7), 1110–1122.

Nadal, K. L., Davidoff, K. C., Davis, L. S., Wong, Y., Marshall, D., & McKenzie, V. (2015). A qualitative approach to intersectional microaggressions: Understanding influences of race, ethnicity, gender, sexuality, and religion. *Qualitative Psychology, 2*(2), 147–163.

Nadal, K. L., Quintanilla, A., Goswick, A., & Sriken, J. (2015). Lesbian, gay, bisexual, and queer people's perceptions of the criminal justice system: Implications for social services. *Journal of Gay & Lesbian Social Services, 27*(4), 457–481.

National Academies of Sciences, Engineering, and Medicine. (2023). *Closing the opportunity gap for young children* (R. Hutton & L. R. Allen, eds.). National Academies Press.

National Association of Social Workers (NASW). (2021). *Code of ethics of the National Association of Social Workers*. www.socialworkers.org/About/Ethics/Code-of-Ethics/Code-of-Ethics-English

Novak, A. (2019). The school-to-prison pipeline: An examination of the association between suspension and justice system involvement. *Criminal Justice and Behavior, 46*(8), 1165–1180. https://doi.org/10.1177/0093854819846917

Obasogie, O. K. (2013). Can the blind lead the blind? Rethinking equal protection jurisprudence through an empirical examination of blind people's understanding of race. *University of Pennsylvania Law Review, 159*(6), 1403–1467.

Oh, H., & Lee, C. (2016). Culture and motivational interviewing. *Patient Education and Counseling, 99*(11), 1914–1919.

Quinsey, V. L., Harris, G. T., Rice, M. E., & Cormier, C. A. (1998). *Violent offenders: Appraising and managing risk*. American Psychological Association.

Raz, M., Dettlaff, A., & Edwards, F. (2021). The perils of child "protection" for children of color: Lessons from history. *Pediatrics, 148*(1), 1–4.

Resnicow, K., Baranowski, T., Ahluwalia, J. S., & Braithwaite, R. L. (1999). Cultural sensitivity in public health: Defined and demystified. *Ethnicity & Disease, 9*(1), 10–21.

Roberts, S. O., Bareket-Shavit, C., Dollins, F. A., Goldie, P. D., & Mortenson, E. (2020). Racial inequality in psychological research: Trends of the past and

recommendations for the future. *Perspectives on Psychological Science, 15*(6), 1295–1309.
Rosenthal, L. (2016). Incorporating intersectionality into psychology: An opportunity to promote social justice and equity. *American Psychologist, 71*(6), 474–485. https://doi.org/10.1037/a0040323
Rothstein, R. (2017). *The color of law: A forgotten history of how our government segregated America.* Liveright.
Salsberg, E., Quigley, L., Richwine, C., Sliwa, S., Acquaviva, K., & Wyche, K. (2020). *The social work profession: Findings from three years of surveys of new social workers.* Fitzhugh Mullan Institute for Health Workforce Equity, George Washington University. www.cswe.org/CSWE/media/Workforce-Study/The-Social-Work-Profession-Findings-from-Three-Years-of-Surveys-of-New-Social-Workers-Dec-2020.pdf
Salter, P., & Adams, G. (2013). Toward a critical race psychology. *Social and Personality Psychology Compass, 7*(11), 781–793.
Schneider, C. E. (1992). The channeling function in family law. *Hofstra Law Review, 20*(3), 495–532.
Sedgwick, E. K. (1990). *Epistemology of the closet.* Penguin.
Stephens, T. N. (2021). Distinguishing racism, not race, as a risk factor for child welfare involvement: Reclaiming the familial and cultural strengths in the lived experiences of child welfare-affected parents of color. *Genealogy, 5*(1), 11.
Stroebe, W. (2024). The myth of the need for diversity among subjects in theory-testing research: Comments on "Racial inequality in psychological research" by Roberts et al. (2020). *Perspectives on Psychological Science, 19*(3), 576–579.
Sue, D. W., Capodilupo, C. M., Torino, G. C., Bucceri, J. M., Holder, A. M. B., Nadal, K. L., & Esquilin, M. (2007). Racial microaggressions in everyday life: Implications for clinical practice. *American Psychologist, 62*(4), 271–286.
Sue, S., Zane, N., Nagayama Hall, G. C., & Berger, L. K. (2009). The case for cultural competency in psychotherapeutic interventions. *Annual Review of Psychology, 60*, 525–548.
Webb, A., Heyne, G., Holmes, H. E., & Peta, J. L. (2016). *Which box to check: Assessment norms for gender and the implications for transgender and nonbinary populations.* Society for the Psychology of Sexual Orientation and Gender Diversity. www.apadivisions.org/division-44/publications/newsletters/division/2016/04/nonbinary-populations
Wildeman, C., & Emanuel, N. (2014). Cumulative risks of foster care placement by age 18 for US children, 2000–2011. *PLoS ONE, 9*(3), e92785.
Williams, M. T., Osman, M., Gallo, J., Pereira, D. P., Gran-Ruaz, S., Strauss, D., Lester, L., George, J. R., Edelman, J., & Litman, L. (2022). A clinical scale for the assessment of racial trauma. *Practice Innovations, 7*(3), 223–240.
Wood, L. (2024). *Criminal and Recidivism Risk Factors among LGBTQ+ Individuals.* Unpublished doctoral research project. William James College.

PART II

Leadership and Systems Practice

CHAPTER 8

Dismantling Systems That Traumatize and Oppress
A Comprehensive Approach

Ann Marie Garran, Nathaniel L. Currie, and Jad-Évangelo Nasser

**Dismantling Systems That Traumatize and Oppress:
A Comprehensive Approach**

The persistence of systems that both oppress and traumatize individuals and groups is a pressing moral, social, and political issue. Throughout history, hierarchical structures of power – be they rooted in colonialism, racism, patriarchy, capitalism, or other forms of systemic inequality – have caused immense harm. These systems inflict trauma on marginalized populations, leaving deep psychological, social, and economic scars that persist across generations.

At the heart of these oppressive systems is the imbalance of power and the pernicious effects of white supremacy. Whether manifested through unjust laws, exclusionary policies, cultural marginalization, or exploitative labor practices, these structures maintain control by disenfranchising certain groups. Often, the trauma caused is twofold: it is both psychological, in the form of fear, stress, and emotional harm, and material, through deprivation of resources, opportunities, and autonomy.

Dismantling such systems is not just a matter of reform or addressing surface-level symptoms. It requires profound structural change – uprooting the foundations that allow oppression to persist and rethinking our societal, economic, and political institutions. Moreover, it calls for a commitment to healing, repair, and justice for those who have suffered. Only by addressing the root causes of oppression and trauma can we begin to build systems that prioritize equity, dignity, and human well-being.

This chapter will explore the ways that systems in place have long impeded progress in multiple forms for those who live on the margins. It will examine the historical origins of these systems, the psychological and social impact of oppression, and the practical methods by which they can be deconstructed. What are the steps required to dismantle systems of trauma and oppression? Finally, it will argue for the need for an inclusive, intersectional approach that centers the voices of those most affected by systemic harm.

The Historical Roots of Oppression: Colonialism and Imperialism

To understand the complexity of dismantling oppressive systems, it is essential to first acknowledge their historical roots. Oppression, whether based on race, class, gender, or other identity markers, is not a new phenomenon in the United States. Its foundations date back centuries, embedded in colonial expansion, slavery, imperialism, feudalism, and patriarchy.

Colonialism remains one of the most significant origins of modern systems of oppression in the United States. European colonial powers expanded their influence by subjugating Indigenous peoples across Africa, Asia, and the Americas. They imposed foreign rule, extracted infinite resources, and enforced systems of governance that oppressed local populations, often through violence, displacement, and cultural erasure.

Not only did colonialism exploit land and resources, but it also imposed hierarchical racial structures that justified the subjugation of non-European people. The ideology of white supremacy legitimized the enslavement and genocide of millions. Even today, many of the world's political and economic inequalities can be traced back to colonial history, as former colonies struggled with poverty, political instability, and the long-term impacts of racial trauma (Martins, 2022). The economic wealth of nations like the United States and Britain was built on the backs of enslaved Black people, creating long-lasting racial hierarchies that persist in the form of institutional racism today.

Racism, as an ideology, continues to shape social structures, policies, and economic realities, especially in Western nations. Black, Brown, and Indigenous communities disproportionately experience police violence, mass incarceration, health disparities, and economic deprivation – all consequences of a system designed to preserve the supremacy of one race over others. Further, patriarchal systems situate white men in positions of power and authority while subordinating women and gender minorities. Women have historically been denied the right to vote, work, own property, or make decisions about their reproductive health, while enduring systemic violence in the form of domestic abuse, sexual assault, and workplace discrimination. Women of color were deprived of access to most of these rights for decades after they were granted to white women. Misogyny intersects with other forms of oppression, such as racism and homophobia, to create layers of trauma for marginalized groups.

Capitalism, too, is often cited as a significant driver of social inequality and oppression. At its core, capitalism prioritizes profit over people, perpetuating a system where wealth and power are concentrated in the hands of a few while the majority labor in precarious and exploitative conditions. Capitalism also intersects with other systems of oppression. It exploits racial and gender inequalities to maximize profit, such as through the underpayment of women and people of color or the use of prison labor. The trauma caused by poverty, inadequate healthcare, and lack of education is often overlooked but is a direct result of the capitalist model (Martins, 2022). Dismantling capitalism, or at the very least radically reforming it, is crucial to addressing the structural roots of economic and social trauma.

The trauma inflicted by oppressive systems manifests in both psychological and material harm. Oppression is not just an abstract societal issue – it deeply affects the well-being of individuals and communities.

Psychological Impact of Oppression

One of the most insidious effects of oppression is the psychological trauma it inflicts on marginalized individuals. Those who are subjected to systemic racism, sexism, classism, and other forms of discrimination often experience chronic stress, anxiety, depression, and feelings of worthlessness. In addition to myriad physical health concerns (Priest & Williams, 2021), research has shown that experiences of discrimination and social exclusion are linked to long-term mental health issues, such as posttraumatic stress disorder (PTSD), as well as generalized anxiety and mood disorders.

For instance, Black Americans in the United States who have endured generations of racial violence and segregation often carry the psychological weight of this history. The concept of *racial trauma* refers to the mental and emotional damage caused by racism, including the fear of violence, microaggressions, and the daily stress of navigating a hostile world (Hardy, 2023). Similarly, women and LGBTQ+ individuals who face gender-based violence, harassment, and discrimination often suffer from psychological trauma, leading to higher rates of depression and suicidal ideation. These traumas extend far past the individual and have deleterious effects on communities as well.

Oppression and trauma have profound psychological impacts, leading to chronic stress, anxiety, and depression. Constant exposure to oppressive environments can result in PTSD-like symptoms, such as hypervigilance and emotional numbness. Individuals may internalize negative stereotypes, experiencing low self-esteem and identity conflicts, particularly when navigating intersecting marginalized identities.

Socially, oppression can cause isolation and strain relationships due to difficulties in trust and communication. At the community level, oppression results in collective trauma, perpetuating cycles of disadvantage. Despite these challenges, many communities demonstrate resilience and resistance, fostering healing and empowerment (Menakem, 2017).

Culturally competent therapeutic interventions and strong support networks are essential for individuals to process trauma and develop coping strategies. Advocacy and empowerment activities can also help restore a sense of agency and purpose, promoting overall well-being and resilience in the face of adversity.

Racial trauma, a form of race-based stress, stems from experiences of discrimination, systemic racism, and microaggressions. This trauma affects the mental, emotional, and physical well-being of marginalized individuals, leading to long-lasting effects such as depression, anxiety, and low self-esteem. The pervasive impact of racial trauma highlights the urgent need for effective interventions to address both individual and community healing (Mullan, 2023). Tackling racial trauma requires a multifaceted approach, including psychological interventions, community support, education, and policy reform. In this essay, we explore the key strategies and interventions to eradicate racial trauma, focusing on individual-level therapies, community-driven initiatives, educational reform, and systemic change.

Community-Level Trauma

Oppression also creates and sustains trauma at the community level. When entire groups of people are subjected to recurring systemic violence and exploitation, it disrupts the formation and maintenance of social cohesion and trust. Communities that have experienced displacement, colonization, or economic exploitation often face intergenerational trauma, where the effects of past injustices are passed down through generations (Methot, 2019). For example, Indigenous communities in North America continue to suffer the consequences of colonization, including land dispossession, cultural erasure, and forced assimilation – all of which contribute to high rates of suicide, substance abuse, and poverty.

The trauma caused by oppression also manifests in the form of *collective memory*, where communities remember past injustices and are shaped by them. This collective memory can serve as both a source of strength and a burden, as it informs community identity and solidarity but also perpetuates feelings of loss, grief, and injustice.

Economic and Social Harm

The material consequences of oppression are perhaps the most visible. Systemic racism, sexism, and classism are all designed to deprive marginalized groups of economic opportunities, leading to entrenched poverty and inequality. The lack of access to quality education, healthcare, and housing keeps entire communities in cycles of deprivation.

Economic oppression is often coupled with social exclusion, where marginalized groups are denied participation in political and cultural life. This exclusion further compounds the trauma of being marginalized, as individuals feel powerless to change their circumstances or influence the systems that oppress them. Dismantling these barriers requires a concerted effort to redistribute wealth, power, and opportunities in a more equitable way.

Racial trauma can be understood at different levels of society, typically categorized into micro, mezzo, and macro levels which describe the scope and impact of trauma on individual, community, and societal structures within broader systems. What follows is a brief explanation of those levels.

- *Micro Level of Trauma* – This level refers to trauma experienced at the individual or personal level. Examples include feeling isolated in majority-white spaces as a person of color or being followed in a store. People experiencing trauma at the micro level might also internalize racist imagery about their own group after repeated exposure to negative associations. Individuals might experience emotional distress, cognitive dysfunction, physical symptoms, or changes in behavior as a result. What helps? Support, community, personal healing practices, and psychotherapy are all helpful approaches.
- *Mezzo Level of Trauma* – This level of trauma refers to community or small-group level trauma, for instance within a family, school, workplace, or local community. This level explores how individuals within specific racial groups experience and cope with trauma collectively. Troubled family dynamics, group conflicts, and community-based violence are all forms of mezzo-level trauma. This type of trauma affects entire groups, leading to collective stress, decreased cohesion, and emotional difficulties. Additionally, families often become fractured, communities are less safe, and mental health

issues are more common. What helps? Community-based interventions are a powerful tool, as are crisis response teams. Family treatment or conflict resolution can also be useful.
- *Macro Level of Trauma* – This level of trauma affects broader societal systems and structures, including institutional, cultural, or national levels. Historical trauma, systemic oppression, and global crises are all examples of macro-level trauma. This level of trauma often leads to widespread social inequality, intergenerational trauma, chronic stress, and a sense of powerlessness. Redlining and biased lending practices that prevent people of color from building wealth in certain residential areas is an example of macro-level trauma, as entire communities face systemic marginalization and disenfranchisement. What helps? At this level, policy changes that focus on inequality and institutional injustices are critical to addressing this trauma. Advocacy and large-scale mental health initiatives should also be part of interventions at this level.

Of note, trauma at the macro level influences mezzo and micro levels. For instance, systemic racism (macro) can cause trauma in communities (mezzo), which in turn deeply affects individuals (micro). Effective trauma responses often require addressing all three levels to ensure individual, community, and societal healing. This approach is a tall order but a necessary one. Understanding trauma through these three levels helps social workers design interventions that not only support individuals but also work toward healing communities and societal structures that perpetuate trauma. Each level has its unique challenges but also overlaps with the others, requiring multi-level strategies for effective recovery and resilience-building (Hardy, 2023).

Racial trauma at these three levels is interrelated. For instance, individual trauma (micro) is often influenced by broader systemic inequalities (macro), and collective group experiences (mezzo) can reinforce individual feelings of alienation or solidarity. Furthermore, institutional policies (macro) create environments where racial trauma becomes normalized at the community (mezzo) and individual levels (micro). In the end, addressing racial trauma requires interventions at all levels, from personal healing to systemic reforms.

Dismantling Oppressive Systems

Dismantling systems of trauma and oppression requires a multifaceted, intersectional approach that addresses both the structural and cultural roots of inequality (Garran et al., 2022). These systems are complex and deeply entrenched in society. However, several strategies can serve as a roadmap for systemic change. One of the most immediate ways to address systemic oppression is through policy reform. Laws and policies shape our institutions, and by changing them, we can begin to dismantle some of the structures that perpetuate inequality. For example, in the context of racial justice, reforms such as ending discriminatory policing practices, abolishing cash bail, and addressing racial disparities in sentencing are crucial steps in dismantling the carceral state (Alexander, 2012).

Similarly, gender-based oppression can be addressed through policies that guarantee reproductive rights, provide paid parental leave, and ensure equal pay for equal work. On the economic front, reforms such as raising the minimum wage, expanding access to healthcare, and implementing wealth taxes on the ultra-rich can help address the economic inequalities that are at the root of much systemic oppression. However, while policy reform is necessary, it is not sufficient. Laws can be changed, but unless there is cultural and societal buy-in, they may not be enforced or effectively implemented. Legal reform, then, must be accompanied by broader efforts to change societal attitudes and power structures.

Education and Awareness

Education plays a crucial role in dismantling oppressive systems. Many people are unaware of the historical and contemporary realities of oppression because these narratives are often omitted from mainstream education. By educating individuals about the history of racism, colonialism, patriarchy, and capitalism, we can begin to change the way people understand power and privilege.

Educational reforms should focus on creating curricula that are inclusive of diverse perspectives and histories. For example, teaching about the contributions of Black, Indigenous, and other marginalized groups can challenge the dominant narratives that have long erased their experiences. Similarly, comprehensive sex education that addresses gender, consent, and sexual diversity can help to combat sexism and homophobia.

Public awareness campaigns and media representation also play a role in educating society. When marginalized groups see themselves represented in media in a positive and authentic way, it challenges stereotypes and promotes empathy. However, media representation alone is not enough – it must be coupled with structural changes to ensure that marginalized voices are heard and valued in all areas of society (Harro, 2013).

The fight against oppression requires solidarity among marginalized groups, but it also demands inclusivity and intersectionality (Adams et al., 2018). Often, social movements become siloed, focusing on a single issue (e.g., racial justice, gender equality) without recognizing how different forms of oppression intersect. For example, the experiences of a Black woman cannot be fully understood by looking at either race or gender alone – her oppression is shaped by both factors simultaneously.

Building inclusive movements requires centering the voices of those most affected by multiple forms of oppression. It means creating spaces where Black, Indigenous, LGBTQ+, disabled, and other marginalized individuals can lead, rather than being tokenized or sidelined. Intersectional feminism, for example, is a framework that seeks to understand how different forms of oppression intersect and how they can be dismantled together.

Economic inequality is a root cause of much systemic oppression, and addressing it is key to dismantling systems of trauma. Capitalism, as it currently operates, perpetuates inequality by concentrating wealth and power in the hands of a few and exploiting the labor of many. Economic justice requires redistributing wealth and resources in a way that ensures all people have access to basic needs such as housing, healthcare, and education.

Finally, dismantling systems of oppression requires healing – not just for individuals but for communities and nations. The trauma inflicted by oppression is deep, and it will not be undone overnight. Healing involves acknowledging the harm that has been done, offering reparations, and creating spaces for collective grieving and healing (Singh, 2019).

Restorative justice is one approach that seeks to repair harm by focusing on reconciliation and accountability, rather than punishment (Hass-Wisecup & Saxon, 2018). In the context of racial justice, restorative justice might involve creating spaces for truth-telling, where communities can speak openly about the harms they have suffered (Hardy, 2023; Singh, 2019), and where those responsible for perpetuating oppression are held accountable.

Healing also involves addressing intergenerational trauma (Mullan, 2023). For communities that have been oppressed for centuries, such as Indigenous peoples and descendants of enslaved Africans, the trauma of oppression is passed down through generations. Programs that promote cultural preservation, mental health services, and community building are essential for healing this deep-seated trauma. What follows are some interventions that are particularly helpful in the healing process.

1. Trauma-Informed Therapy
    At the individual level, psychological interventions such as trauma-informed therapy are critical in addressing racial trauma. Trauma-informed approaches emphasize safety, trustworthiness, and empowerment, tailoring interventions to the unique experiences of racial trauma victims. Some key therapeutic models include:
    - *Cognitive Behavioral Therapy (CBT)*: CBT is an evidence-based approach that helps individuals reframe negative thoughts and behaviors related to their experiences of racism. For racial trauma victims, CBT can address feelings of helplessness, anger, and fear triggered by racial discrimination.
    - *Mindfulness-Based Stress Reduction (MBSR)*: MBSR techniques, such as meditation and deep breathing, help individuals manage stress and trauma by cultivating awareness and promoting emotional regulation. This can be particularly beneficial for individuals experiencing chronic stress related to racial trauma.

In addition to these techniques, having therapists who are culturally aware and trained in racial trauma is essential. Their understanding of the intersection between mental health and race ensures that clients receive empathetic, relevant care.

2. Community Support: Healing through Collective Action
    Community-driven initiatives offer an essential layer of support in the eradication of racial trauma. These interventions focus on collective healing and foster a sense of belonging, which is crucial for individuals dealing with race-based stress. Some effective community-based approaches include:
    - *Support Groups and Safe Spaces*: Support groups specifically for people of color provide a platform to share experiences of racial trauma and receive validation and empathy. These groups can be organized in person or virtually and help foster resilience by building solidarity among members. Safe spaces within institutions, such as schools or workplaces, also serve as environments where individuals may feel free from judgment and racism, though it is critical to remember that safety is differential depending on identity and context (Garran & Rasmussen, 2014).
    - *Cultural Healing Practices*: For many communities, cultural rituals, storytelling, and ancestral practices offer a powerful means of healing. For example, traditional African healing rituals, Indigenous ceremonies, and spiritual gatherings allow individuals

to connect with their heritage, providing emotional relief and fostering collective healing.
- *Mentorship Programs*: Having strong role models who understand the complexities of racial trauma can be profoundly healing. Mentorship programs offer guidance, support, and inspiration for individuals coping with racial trauma, fostering both individual growth and community resilience.

These community-driven efforts create spaces where individuals can express their pain and frustrations and begin to process them, offering a crucial complement to individual therapy.

3. Educational Interventions: Building Awareness and Empathy
   Education is a powerful tool in the fight against racial trauma. Raising awareness of racism's impact and promoting empathy in schools and workplaces can prevent future trauma and promote healing for those who have experienced it. Some educational interventions include:
   - *Antiracism Education*: Incorporating antiracism curricula in schools and professional training programs helps individuals recognize and challenge systemic racism. By teaching the historical context and modern manifestations of racial discrimination, educational institutions can foster critical thinking and encourage students to become advocates for racial justice.
   - *Trauma-Informed Schools*: Schools play a critical role in either perpetuating or alleviating racial trauma. Trauma-informed schools, where educators are trained to recognize and respond to signs of racial trauma, create supportive environments for students of color. This involves implementing restorative justice practices instead of punitive measures, ensuring that students feel safe and valued.
   - *Antiracism and Anti-Oppression Training*: Training for teachers, employers, and healthcare professionals helps reduce the incidence of microaggressions and unconscious bias. This training equips individuals to engage respectfully with diverse populations and provides them with tools to prevent the perpetuation of racial trauma.

Educational interventions are essential to create environments where racial trauma is understood and addressed, preventing further harm and enabling individuals to thrive.

4. Policy Reform: Addressing Systemic Racism
   - While psychological and community interventions address the effects of racial trauma, systemic change is needed to eliminate the root causes. Public policy plays a critical role in dismantling the structures that perpetuate racial trauma. Key policy interventions include:
   - *Criminal Justice Reform*: The criminal justice system in many countries disproportionately targets communities of color, contributing to racial trauma through over-policing, racial profiling, and unjust sentencing. Reforms such as ending racial profiling, abolishing mandatory minimum sentences for nonviolent offenses, and promoting restorative justice can mitigate the racial disparities that fuel trauma.
   - *Healthcare Equity*: Racism in healthcare leads to significant disparities in access to quality care for marginalized communities. Policies that ensure equitable healthcare access, mandate antiracism training for healthcare professionals, and increase funding for mental health services specifically for communities of color are essential steps in addressing racial trauma.
   - *Housing and Employment Equality*: Discriminatory housing policies and unequal access to employment opportunities have contributed to the economic disenfranchisement of marginalized communities. Affordable housing initiatives, antidiscrimination policies in employment, and equal pay legislation are essential for combating the structural inequalities that lead to racial trauma.

Policy interventions are critical for addressing the systemic roots of racial trauma and ensuring long-term, sustainable change. See Box 8.1.

Box 8.1 Practice Guidance. The United States Military: Hope, Healing, and Harm

By Adrianna N. Taylor

To speak about systems that traumatize and oppress without mentioning the United States military would be a wild and gross oversight. This institution, nearly as old as the alleged founding of the nation itself, represents a dissonance in both historical and contemporary contexts. "We need to make sure that the sacrifices of our forebears are not forgotten, especially those who served in silence." – Major General Charles Bolden

---

Historically, the military has unapologetically excluded anyone but cisgender, heterosexual, white males. This means that the Black males who served and died in every conflict of record, as well as the white women who served as helpers and healers for those who served, received little to no honor or acknowledgment despite their sacrifices (Bristol & Stur, 2017). LGBTQIA + folx are only recently no longer criminalized for their identities (Goodhart & Taylor, 2020). It must have been a deeply personal or moral decision to risk one's life to align with the cause of the service members (SMs), despite both living in a country and entering a system that regarded them as subhuman. To enact criminalization for intersectional identities will perhaps forever be one of the greatest injustices by a system designed to protect the freedoms of all within this country.

Contemporarily, there have been performative changes in the form of legalities, policy, DEI programming, and targeted recruitment (Armstrong, 2024). What often remains out of the conversations include predatory recruitment, racial disparities in promotion and punishment, and the number of minoritized folx who separate prematurely, forfeiting what could have been a lucrative and fulfilling career due to systemically supported oppression. The military possesses a structure that offers the illusion of community, shelter, and security, often an enticing form of hope for those from the most impoverished and neglected circumstances. To be faced with a choice between remaining in such circumstances and signing a contract that commits everything, up to and including one's life, is an impossibly unfair decision. Small and exclusive though it may be, with less than 2 percent of the population ever wearing a uniform, military service may be at least partially responsible for causing or exacerbating the mental and emotional distress experienced by the roughly 16 million American veterans (Miller et al., 2023).

For the masses, the military may represent service and sacrifice. For the socially aware, it may represent a necessary evil. For the past or present SMs, it may represent unspeakable trauma and incomparable oppression, muddled with misplaced pride and patriotism (Huiskamp, 2011; Meade, 2021). Without intentional intervention, any institution is susceptible to becoming a replica of society. Despite setting itself apart as a progressive entity that views only a uniform and pledges to protect, this microcosm of society is no exception with regard to perpetuating harm and oppression.

MILITARY MENTAL HEALTH: A SYSTEM WITHIN A SYSTEM

If the military is such a small portion of the general population, then mental health in the military represents a minimal fraction of a fraction. Even more minuscule in number are leaders and supervisors with historically excluded, intersectional identities, both within and outside of mental health (Boyd, 2023). Lack of representation increases experiences of isolation and discrimination, deterring many from help-seeking (Miller et al., 2023). This makes practicing military social work through an antiracist/anti-oppressive lens an even greater challenge.

Imagine entering into any military medical facility where pictures of the faces of leaders line the hallway. Then imagine not a single face, for decades, reflecting a similar image back to you. It is no secret that leaders within the military are predominantly white men (Boyd, 2023). Such demographics continually place white men in positions of power. Antiracism/anti-oppression in the context of the military requires a commitment and resolve asked only of the select few who choose to remain involved with a system that has the power to create lifelong damage. Further, interdisciplinary teams position social workers at the bottom of the hierarchy of authority and value, thus causing mental health decisions to be dictated by a medical model of practice. And perhaps more importantly, this leaves SMs with nondominant identities without access to care from providers with their lived experiences and without clinicians receiving decolonized supervision.

Due to the mission of the military, leaders and supervisors have access to information civilian leaders and supervisors would never have. These even more limited limits of confidentiality place a burden on clinicians: to provide leadership with the minimum amount of information necessary to make a determination about an SM's fitness for duty, or capacity to carry out the mission. Clinicians must be increasingly discriminating about what information is released and fiercely protect the rest, despite pressure from the system to disclose. Anti-oppression in this context is recognizing that one size does not fit all regarding reported mental health experiences and subsequent interventions, as well as remembering and practicing as though the SM, rather than the system, is the client.

There are still many who remain unaware of the presence of social workers within the military, further perpetuating the stigma of mental health among folx in uniform (Ganz et al., 2021). Social workers in the military hold a number of roles within the military that include and extend beyond psychotherapy. Central to being a military social worker is the expectation of operating as a leader first, and a social worker or helper second. Noble though it may sound, the differences in the core values create the potential for ethical dilemmas, compassion fatigue, burnout, and worst of all: shame. To serve in the military and don a uniform is not simply a job, career, or position – it is a lifestyle, a calling, and a culture of its own.

REFERENCES

Armstrong, M. (2024). Racism despite integration: Diversity for the sake of mission readiness in the U.S. military. *Political Research Quarterly, 77*(1), 270–282.

Boyd, K. (2023). The matrix of domination: The structuralized oppression of Black women in the US army and its affect on leadership development. In *Black women's formal and informal ways of leadership: Actualizing the vision of a more equitable Workplace* (pp. 114-139). IGI Global.

Bristol Jr, D. W., & Stur, H. M. (eds.). (2017). *Integrating the US military: Race, gender, and sexual orientation since World War II*. JHU Press.

Ganz, A., Yamaguchi, C., Parekh, B., Koritzky, G., & Berger, S. (2021). Military culture and its impact on mental health and stigma. *Journal of Community Engagement & Scholarship, 13*(4), 1–13.

Goodhart, A., & Taylor, J. (2020, May 29). LGBT Military Service Policies in the United States. *Oxford Research Encyclopedia of Politics*. Retrieved August 5, 2024.

Huiskamp, G. (2011). "Support the Troops!": The social and political currency of patriotism in the United States. *New Political Science, 33*(3), 285–310.

Meade, V. (2021). Patriotism as a construct for understanding military service among LGBTQ+ veterans: A call for research grounded in institutional oppression. *Journal of Veterans Studies, 7*(3), 38–45.

Miller, M. B., Monk, J. K., Flores, L. Y., Everson, A. T., Martinez, L. D., Massey, K., Blanke, E. M., Dorimé-Williams, M. L., Williams, M. S., McCrae, C. S., & Borsari, B. (2023). Impact of discrimination and coping on Veterans' willingness to seek treatment for physical and mental health problems. *Psychology of Addictive Behaviors, 37*(2), 209–221.

Understanding Country-Specific or Culture-Specific Trauma and Navigating Modern-Day Life

Understanding country-specific or culture-specific trauma is essential for effective clinical and equity practice. Trauma experienced by individuals is deeply embedded in their cultural and historical contexts, which can vary significantly from one region to another. To provide meaningful support, practitioners must go beyond superficial knowledge and develop a nuanced understanding of the historical and sociopolitical factors that shape individuals' experiences. This requires a thorough exploration of the colonial histories, systemic oppression, and current sociopolitical realities of various countries and cultures.

Historical Contexts of Trauma

One of the fundamental aspects of understanding culture-specific trauma is recognizing the impact of colonial histories. Colonialism has left a profound and lasting impact on many regions around the world, shaping the socioeconomic and political landscapes of these countries. For instance, in countries like Congo and Haiti, colonial exploitation and resource extraction have led to enduring economic hardships and social instability. The legacy of Belgian colonial rule in Congo, marked by extreme exploitation and violence, has contributed to ongoing conflict and underdevelopment (Nzongola-Ntalaja, 2002). Similarly, Haiti's history of French colonial exploitation and subsequent political interference has resulted in severe economic and social challenges that continue to affect its population (Fick, 1990). In Palestine, the historical context includes the impact of British Mandate policies and the ongoing genocide inflicted on Palestinians in Gaza and neighboring regions. The displacement and statelessness experienced by Palestinians have resulted in a prolonged humanitarian crisis characterized by restricted access to resources and continual conflict (Khalidi, 1997). Understanding these historical contexts is crucial for clinicians and equity practitioners to appreciate the depth of trauma experienced by individuals from these regions and to provide appropriate support.

The Impact of Modern-Day Oppression and Conflict

In addition to historical factors, modern-day oppression and conflict play a significant role in shaping trauma. For example, the Syrian civil war has led to widespread displacement and loss of life, with millions of Syrians forced to flee their homes and seek refuge in other countries (Mastrorocco et al., 2016). The trauma associated with such conflicts includes not only the immediate impact of violence but also the long-term consequences of displacement, loss, and uncertainty about the future.

Similarly, in Yemen, the ongoing conflict has resulted in a severe humanitarian crisis, with widespread famine, disease, and destruction of infrastructure (Gordon et al., 2016). The trauma experienced by individuals in such contexts is multifaceted, encompassing the direct effects of conflict as well as the secondary impacts on mental health and community cohesion.

In Sudan, the legacy of conflict and marginalization has contributed to ongoing challenges. The Darfur conflict, for instance, has resulted in large-scale displacement and trauma among affected populations. Understanding the specificities of these conflicts and their impact on individuals is crucial for providing culturally and contextually appropriate support (Ali, 2010).

The Nuances of Trauma Responses

Understanding that trauma responses can vary significantly based on cultural and historical contexts is essential for effective practice. Trauma is not a monolithic experience – it is shaped by the individual's personal history, cultural background, and social environment. For example, the way in which trauma manifests and is addressed can differ greatly between individuals from different cultural backgrounds. In some cultures, expressing emotions openly may be discouraged, leading individuals to internalize their trauma and exhibit symptoms in ways that may not align with Western conceptualizations of mental health (Hinton et al., 2006).

Moreover, cultural norms and values can influence how individuals perceive and respond to trauma. For instance, in some communities, there may be a strong emphasis on family and community support, which can play a protective role in coping with trauma. Conversely, in other contexts, individuals may experience additional stigma or discrimination, which can exacerbate the effects of trauma (Wells, 2015). Practitioners must be attuned to these cultural nuances to avoid imposing culturally inappropriate interventions and to support individuals in ways that resonate with their values and beliefs.

The Pitfalls of Cultural Assumptions

A critical issue in addressing culture-specific trauma is the danger of making cultural assumptions based on proximity or superficial similarities. For instance, a clinician might assume that the experiences of a Black American patient and a Sudanese patient are comparable simply because they both face racial marginalization. However, this assumption overlooks the unique historical and sociopolitical contexts that shape each individual's experiences. While both may experience marginalization in the US, their backgrounds and the specific nature of their trauma are distinct and must be understood in their own right (Fischbach, 2020).

The imposition of one's own cultural framework on individuals from different backgrounds can lead to misunderstandings and ineffective interventions. For example, using a one-size-fits-all approach to therapy may not address the specific needs of individuals from different cultural backgrounds. Practitioners must engage in cultural humility, continuously seeking to understand the specific historical and cultural factors that influence each individual's experiences and responses to trauma (Lekas et al., 2019).

Personal Reflections on Trauma and Its Impact

Personal experiences can offer valuable insights into understanding trauma and its impact. Reflecting on my own experiences growing up in Lebanon during the 2006 war, where I witnessed bombings and experienced the resulting fear and uncertainty, highlights the importance of acknowledging how past trauma can continue to affect individuals in different ways. The sounds of bombs and gunfire during that time have left lasting triggers, such as reacting strongly to loud "pop" sounds, whether from fireworks or gunshots. This personal history underscores the need for practitioners to recognize that trauma responses are deeply personal and can be influenced by past experiences (Mastrorocco et al., 2016).

Understanding that trauma responses are shaped by individual histories and cultural contexts helps practitioners to approach individuals with sensitivity and empathy. It also highlights the importance of avoiding assumptions and stereotypes, and instead, engaging in a nuanced exploration of each person's unique experiences and needs.

Practical Implications for Practice

Incorporating an understanding of culture-specific trauma into clinical and equity practice requires several practical considerations. First, practitioners should engage in ongoing education about the historical and sociopolitical contexts of the communities they serve. This includes learning about colonial histories, modern conflicts, and cultural norms that influence trauma and coping mechanisms (Crenshaw, 2017). Second, practitioners should adopt a culturally responsive approach that considers the individual's cultural background and personal experiences. This involves avoiding assumptions and being open to learning from individuals about their specific needs and experiences. Creating a therapeutic environment that respects and integrates cultural values can enhance the effectiveness of interventions and support (Wells, 2015). Finally, practitioners should collaborate with community organizations and cultural experts to gain deeper insights into the specific challenges faced by different communities. Building partnerships with local organizations can provide valuable resources and support, and can help practitioners stay informed about current issues and needs within specific cultural contexts (Ali, 2010).

In conclusion, understanding country-specific and culture-specific trauma is essential for providing effective and empathetic support to individuals from diverse backgrounds. By recognizing the historical and sociopolitical factors that shape trauma, acknowledging the nuances of trauma responses, and avoiding cultural assumptions, practitioners can better support individuals in navigating their experiences and achieving meaningful outcomes.

Individual Pain and Collective Pain: How Cross-Cultural Dynamics Can Build Trauma-Informed Community

Understanding both individual and collective pain is crucial in building a trauma-informed community that acknowledges and addresses diverse experiences of oppression and marginalization. This process involves recognizing the unique personal traumas experienced by individuals, while also acknowledging the shared struggles that can unite various marginalized groups. By examining these dynamics, practitioners can foster solidarity and create spaces that support healing and empowerment across cultural boundaries.

The Interplay of Individual and Collective Pain

Individual pain and collective pain are interconnected yet distinct dimensions of trauma. Individual pain refers to the personal, often internalized experiences of trauma, shaped by one's specific life circumstances and history. Collective pain, on the other hand, emerges from shared experiences of marginalization and oppression within a community or group. This collective dimension can be seen in movements for social justice and liberation, where common experiences of discrimination and struggle create a sense of solidarity and shared purpose (Gilroy, 2004). For instance, the Black American struggle for civil rights and the Palestinian quest for self-determination both stem from distinct historical contexts of oppression. Despite their different origins, these movements share a common thread of resistance against systemic injustice and a desire for dignity and freedom. Recognizing these connections can foster solidarity among different groups, creating a shared understanding of the broader patterns of oppression that affect marginalized communities worldwide (Fischbach, 2020).

The Role of Intersectionality in Understanding Pain

Intersectionality, as introduced by Kimberlé Crenshaw (2017), plays a crucial role in understanding how individual and collective pain intersect. It emphasizes that people's experiences of oppression are shaped by multiple, overlapping identities, including race, gender, class, and sexual orientation. This framework helps to illuminate how different forms of marginalization interact and compound each other, leading to complex, multifaceted experiences of pain. For example, a queer Black individual may face unique challenges that differ from those encountered by a queer person of another racial background or a Black person of a different sexual orientation. Their experiences are shaped by the intersection of racial, sexual, and gender identities, leading to specific forms of discrimination and resilience strategies (Crenshaw, 2017). By applying an intersectional lens, practitioners can better understand the nuanced ways in which individual pain is influenced by broader structural factors and work toward more inclusive and effective support strategies.

Building Solidarity through Shared Struggles

Building solidarity between different marginalized groups requires recognizing both the shared and distinct aspects of their struggles. For instance, Black American and Palestinian liberation movements have found common ground in their resistance against systemic oppression and their pursuit of justice. This solidarity is evident in cross-cultural collaborations and mutual support between these groups, which highlight the ways in which different struggles can intersect and reinforce each other (Fischbach, 2020). However, it is important to approach this solidarity with sensitivity and respect for the unique contexts of each group. While shared experiences of oppression can foster connections, practitioners must be cautious not to homogenize diverse experiences or overlook the specific needs of each community. For example, the particular challenges faced by Palestinians under occupation differ significantly from those experienced by Black Americans in the context of racial discrimination in the US. Acknowledging these differences while also recognizing commonalities can help in creating more effective and respectful partnerships (Gilroy, 2004).

Creating Inclusive Spaces for Healing

Creating inclusive spaces that support healing and empowerment involves more than just acknowledging shared struggles – it requires actively fostering environments where diverse experiences are valued and understood. This includes designing programs and interventions that address the specific needs of different communities while also promoting cross-cultural understanding and solidarity.

For instance, trauma-informed practices should be tailored to the cultural and personal backgrounds of individuals. This means incorporating culturally relevant approaches and avoiding one-size-fits-all solutions. Programs should be designed to respect and integrate the diverse experiences and identities of participants, ensuring that their unique needs and perspectives are considered (Hinton et al., 2006). Additionally, creating spaces that bring together individuals from different backgrounds can facilitate mutual learning and support, helping to build a more cohesive and resilient community.

Empowering Cross-Cultural Practices

Practitioners have a crucial role in advancing cross-cultural practices that empower marginalized communities. This involves not only creating inclusive spaces but also advocating for systemic changes that address the root causes of oppression and inequality. By working collaboratively with community organizations and leaders, practitioners can contribute to initiatives that promote social justice and support the well-being of diverse populations (Wells, 2015). For example, practitioners can support the development of curricula and programs that incorporate diverse cultural perspectives and address the specific needs of different communities. This includes integrating cultural competence and humility into training and professional development, as well as engaging with community members to ensure that their voices and experiences inform program design and implementation (Lekas et al., 2019).

In conclusion, understanding individual and collective pain is essential for building a trauma-informed community that supports healing and empowerment across cultural boundaries. By recognizing the interconnectedness of personal and shared struggles, applying an intersectional lens, and creating inclusive spaces, practitioners can foster solidarity and develop effective support strategies. This approach not only acknowledges the unique experiences of individuals but also promotes cross-cultural understanding and collaboration, contributing to a more equitable and supportive society.

Summary

The eradication of racial trauma requires a multifaceted approach, addressing both the individual and systemic causes of racial harm. Psychological interventions, such as trauma-informed therapy, provide personal healing, while community support systems foster collective resilience. Educational initiatives raise awareness of racial trauma and promote empathy, while systemic policy reforms aim to dismantle the structures that perpetuate racial inequality.

Ultimately, healing from racial trauma is not just an individual process but a societal responsibility. By promoting mental health support, community healing, education, and policy change, we can take meaningful steps toward eradicating racial trauma and creating a more just, equitable society for all. To achieve this goal, sustained effort and collaboration are necessary at every level of society – from individuals to communities to policymakers.

Further, the dismantling of systems that traumatize and oppress is both a moral imperative and a practical necessity. It necessitates an honest confrontation with the history of exploitation and violence – a confrontation that many people are loath to acknowledge or consider. The world we live in today is shaped by centuries of violence, exploitation, and dehumanization, but it is also shaped by resistance, resilience, and hope. While the task of dismantling these systems may seem daunting, it is not impossible.

Imagining a world free of oppression means envisioning a society where all people are treated with dignity and respect, where resources and power are distributed equitably, and where the trauma of past injustices is healed. It means challenging the status quo, questioning the systems that govern our lives, and working together to build new structures that prioritize human well-being over profit, power, and control.

This vision of a just world will not be achieved overnight, but it begins with the work we do today. By addressing the historical roots of oppression, acknowledging the harm it continues to cause, and implementing strategies for systemic change, we can begin the process of dismantling the systems that traumatize and oppress. It is a process that requires courage, commitment, and, above all, solidarity. Only through collective action can we hope to create a world where all people are free from the trauma of oppression and able to live their lives with dignity, agency, and joy.

Reflective Questions:

1. How can people in positions of power work to dismantle the systems that empower them while at the same time disadvantage others? How can they work to transfer that power to others?
2. How does intergenerational trauma intersect with oppression? How can we work to reverse or eradicate intergenerational trauma?

Discussion Questions:

1. Name three forms of oppression that currently exist in the United States. What actions or conditions led to these oppressions?
2. How can we work to redistribute power so that those who have been denied it (often for centuries) will have their fair share? What are some impediments to working toward redistribution?

3. Where have I seen evidence of inequities and systemic and structural racism in my community? What three shifts, changes, or actions, can you take to create a more inclusive and equitable environment in your workplace or home community? (See Box 8.2.)

Box 8.2 Case Vignette. Military Based Social Work

By Adrianna N. Taylor

You are an active duty SM, Licensed Clinical Social Worker (LCSW), and the director of a military mental health clinic that supports active duty personnel. You hold the rank of an officer in charge. This role includes clinical and administrative supervision of roughly 40 clinical staff. You are the only Black clinician, which has led to an unspoken dynamic of all Black SMs being referred to your clinical caseload.

An SM was referred to you for care. This particular SM was an enlisted, cisgender, heterosexual Black male in his mid 20s. He has been in the military for seven years. He works as a flight engineer, which comes with additional requirements due to being a "flyer" or on "flight status" – a position that requires him to operate within a moving aircraft. This, as well as his Top-Secret Security Clearance, requires an additional layer of oversight and provides less space for mental health challenges. He has advanced abnormally quickly through the ranks and continues to receive rave performance reviews from his leadership. He recently underwent medical evaluation due to concerns about heart problems. After being cleared medically, it was suspected that he was experiencing anxiety and panic attacks. He agreed to present to mental health voluntarily, at the recommendation of his leadership.

You met with the SM for an initial assessment. Per his self-report, he has been experiencing anxiety and panic attacks both on the ground and in the air. Specifically, he reported his mind and heart racing, becoming abnormally hot or cold, hands shaking, distractibility, difficulty sleeping, restlessness, fidgeting, shortness of breath, chest pains, ruminating thoughts regarding past experiences, and uncharacteristic feelings of fear. None of this has impacted his ability to perform the mission.

You and the SM discussed the process of "being grounded" or taking away his in-air responsibilities for a period of time while he undergoes treatment and heals. This comes with potential career ramifications. He emphatically stated that being grounded would only increase his distress based upon how much he loves his job and is invested in his team. Given the reliability of his report, you trusted that grounding is not in the best interest of his mental health. He works on a team; therefore, his symptoms were not placing himself, others, or the mission at a safety risk.

As you began to build a therapeutic relationship with the SM and learn a great deal about his past experiences, you learned he joined the military to escape poverty and gang violence, but not before witnessing the violent death of his older brother. He was now the primary financial support for his mom and younger sister, sending most of his military pay back home. The SM was involved in a near-fatal car accident, where he was forced to return to duty on short notice after being sleep deprived, resulting in his best friend breaking his back and being discharged from the military. While these traumas were weighing on him, you had a clinical inkling that something was missing, as they did not appear to be at the root of his symptoms.

After several weekly sessions and anxiety/panic-focused interventions, you offered the SM space to provide feedback on how his care is going and any points of improvement from you, as you want to ensure he is seen and heard entirely. At this point, the therapeutic alliance is strong and the SM states, "[T]here is something I have wanted to tell you that I have never told anyone but I am scared it will ruin my career." Having explained the limits of confidentiality to the SM and knowing it might not be possible, you assure him that you will do your best to maintain his confidence and will be honest with him if unable to do so.

The SM shared that 10 years ago, when in high school, he had a "suicide attempt." He went on to share that he put a rope around his neck and attempted to "hang himself" from the deck in his backyard. The rope did not hold, he fell to his feet unharmed, laughed at the irony, and never mentioned this to anyone. He shared this was his reaction to feeling overwhelmed without an outlet, he never made another attempt, and had no desire to die, past or present. You calmly hold space, thank him for sharing, and assure him of the statistics regarding suicidal and morbid ideation. Additionally, you assess for safety and determine he is at low/no risk. He breathes a deep sigh of relief, voicing the shame and fear that he has carried, and how this has been detrimental to his mental well-being.

SMs who are on flight status require flight medicine, doctors specifically assigned to them, to co-sign all mental health documentation. This provides nonmental health providers access to session notes. Additionally, the military limits of confidentiality include "harm to mission," as well as any violations of the Uniform Code of Military Justice. Unlike in civilian institutions, these limits provide SM's leadership access to mental health information that would otherwise require legal action to be taken before disclosure. The SM's concerns are valid in that he could be at risk for fraudulent enlistment due to not disclosing this incident at the time of his joining the military. Additionally, any safety concerns could result in him losing his flight status and/or security clearance. Essentially, the fear regarding what he identified as a youthful mistake could have lasting ramifications for the SM, his family, his livelihood, and his future should anyone beyond the mental health clinic become aware.

You are deeply conflicted and immediately seek supervision and consultation. You staff this case with both your supervisor (LCSW) and a trusted peer colleague (licensed clinical psychologist) – one BIPOC and one white-bodied. Both agree with your initial thoughts that not documenting this specific information is in the best interest of the SM, instead noting his reason for seeking services as being "performance optimization." You also presented this case in group consultation with civilian colleagues who, despite their limited understanding of the nuances of military mental health, provided the same recommendation. This will protect all parties, though it is agreed and understood that, should there be adverse outcomes, you will accept responsibility and potential career consequences. Flight medicine is made up of all white-bodied clinicians and you do not trust the system to properly support this Black male SM. His leadership is provided with the minimum amount of information necessary to support him continuing in his career field without interruption and continuing mental health treatment.

Several weeks later, a deployment clearance for the SM comes across your desk. As his treating provider, his ability to deploy is left up to your clinical judgment. You and the SM have spoken several times in the past about his excitement around deploying, and your recent session confirms his desire and capacity to do so safely and effectively. SMs cannot deploy with an open mental health chart, so treatment must be terminated prior to clearance. You and the SM have three final sessions before ending the therapeutic relationship. SM is cleared to deploy, and you receive no word on his status.

Fast forward several months, you are shopping in a grocery store near the installation and hear "Hey ma'am!" in a familiar voice. The SM approaches you with a huge smile, shares how positive his deployment experience had been, and thanks you for being a healing beacon in his journey. The next year, an article was posted about this SM being a part of an inaugural all-Black flight crew.

REFLECTION QUESTIONS

1. Discuss your thoughts on Westernized ideas/practices of ethics. How did the clinician's practices align or conflict with these ideals?
2. What decisions might you make if you were in the role of clinical supervisor? Administrative supervisor? How might you guide those you supervise through this scenario in a way that is grounded, aligned, and ethical?
3. Operating in an antiracist/anti-oppressive framework, consider how this scenario may have played out differently if: the SM had been white-bodied? The doctors had been Black-bodied? The clinical supervision team had held different identities?

REFERENCES

Adams, M., Blumenfeld, W., Catalano, D. C. J., DeJong, K. S., Hackman, H. W., Hopkins, L. E., Love, B. J., Peters, M. L., Shlasko, D., & Zúñiga, X. (2018). *Readings for diversity and social justice*, 4th ed. Routledge.

Alexander, M. (2012). *The new Jim Crow: Mass incarceration in the age of colorblindness*. The New Press.

Ali, T. (2010). The Arab Spring: The postcolonial trauma of the past and present. In *The Middle East and the Arab Spring*, A. Malik & K. Hussain (Eds.) (pp. 55–76). Routledge.

Crenshaw, K. (2017). *The urgency of intersectionality* [www.ted.com/talks/kimberle_crenshaw_the_urgency_of_intersectionality?utm_campaign=tedspread&utm_medium=referral&utm_source=tedcomshare]. TED.

Fick, C. (1990). *The making of Haiti: The Saint-Domingue revolution from below*. University of North Carolina Press.

Fischbach, M. (2020). *Black power and Palestine: Transnational struggles for racial justice*. Cambridge University Press.

Garran, A. M., & Rasmussen, B. M. (2014). Safety in the classroom: Reconsidered. *Journal of Teaching in Social Work, 34*(4), 401–412.

Garran, A. M., Werkmeister Rozas, L., Kang, H. K., and Miller, J. (2022). *Racism in the United States: Implications for the helping professions*, 3rd ed. Springer.

Gilroy, P. (2004). *After empire: Melancholia or convivial culture?* Routledge.

Gordon, A. L., McLoughlin, S., & Ahmed, A. (2016). The humanitarian crisis in Yemen. *Journal of Global Health, 6*(2), 020201.

Hardy, K. V. (2023). *Racial trauma: Clinical strategies and techniques for healing invisible wounds*. W. W. Norton & Company.

Harro, Bobbie. (2013). "The Cycle of Socialization." In *Readings for diversity and social justice*, edited by Maurianne Adams et al., 3rd ed. (pp. 45–52). Routledge.

Hass-Wisecup, A. Y., & Saxon, C. E. (2018). *Restorative justice: Integrating theory, research, and practice*. Carolina Academic Press.

Hinton, D. E., Pich, V., Chhean, D., Safren, S. A., & Hofmann, S. G. (2006). Cultural influences on trauma responses: From specific symptoms to broad behavioral patterns. *Culture, Medicine, and Psychiatry, 30*(3), 239–259.

Khalidi, R. (1997). *Palestine and the Palestinians*. Harvard University Press.

Lekas, H.-M., Pahl, K., & Lewis, C. F. (2019). Rethinking cultural competence: Shifting to cultural humility. *Journal of Health Care for the Poor and Underserved, 30*(1), 1–10.

Martins, P.M. (2022). *Critical theory of coloniality*. Routledge.

Mastrorocco, T., et al. (2016). Syrian refugees in the Middle East: Health and humanitarian needs. *Global Health Action, 9*(1), 31310.

Menakem, R. (2017). *My grandmother's hands: Racialized trauma and the pathway to mending our hearts and bodies*. Central Recovery Press.

Methot, S. (2019). *Legacy: Trauma, story, and Indigenous healing*. ECW Press.

Mullan, J. (2023). *Decolonizing therapy: Oppression, historical trauma, and politicizing your practice.* W. W. Norton & Company.

Nzongola-Ntalaja, G. (2002). *The Congo: From Leopold to Kabila: A people's history.* Zed Books.

Priest, N., & Williams, D. R. (2021). Structural racism: A call to action for health and health disparities research. *Ethnicity & Disease, 31*(Suppl 1), 285.

Singh, A. A. (2019). *The racial healing handbook: Practical activities to help you challenge privilege, confront systemic racism, and engage in collective healing.* New Harbinger Publications.

Wells, R. (2015). Cultural responses to trauma: A review of cross-cultural studies. *Traumatology, 21*(1), 10–17.

CHAPTER 9

Conducting Community-Based Participatory Research Using a Lens of Anti-Oppression
Insights into Everyday Application

Natalie D. Crawford

Welcomed In: Community-Based Participatory Research

Community-based participatory research (CBPR) has been an essential framework for conducting research, especially with racially minoritized populations since the 1940s (Holkup et al., 2004; Neill, 1998). CBPR frameworks have established a set of research standards for conducting research with community members that most importantly anchor the community as full and equal leaders of research that is being performed within their communities (Israel et al., 2001, 2005, 2010). The balance of power in the relationship between the community and research enterprise are undergirded as fundamental to CBPR frameworks for a myriad of historical and present-day systems of oppression that have devalued the critical perspectives of the community in the production of knowledge on the causes of their most often disadvantaged health outcomes. Therefore, CBPR frameworks have rightfully created a playbook for performing research with a bi-directional benefit between the research enterprise and the community – who has been historically left out of the research enterprise as a contributor, and even more importantly, a thought-leader. This is not only important because a nonbidirectional approach is rooted in continued oppression that drives racial inequities in health, but also because this oppression has responsibility for tainting the perception of research, even that which is conducted using CBPR frameworks. Specifically, the research enterprise is largely responsible for the distrust between research and the community through dehumanization that has resulted in unwillingness to contribute to/participate in research that takes place by purely refusing or by providing inaccurate or incomplete answers (Bloche, 2013; Thomas, 2013). With this, the research rigor and accuracy are compromised, making it more difficult to implicate true causes of disease and develop solutions to reduce pervasive racial inequities in health outcomes. And while uncovering the root causes of illness and inequities in health are important, as a moral and ethical issue, identifying and practicing methods that are aligned with an anti-oppressive CBPR framework are the first step to performing research with rigor and precision. Herein, we will identify essential, practical, and ideal ways to conduct anti-oppressive CBPR drawing from our extensive CBPR-centered research portfolio. Although non-exhaustive of the many ways anti-oppressive practices can be infused within the practice of research, these tools can and should be applied consistently and faithfully.

Engaging in Anti-Oppressive Community-Based Participatory Research

CBPR as a framework is strong but insufficient to guide research scholars through an anti-oppressive practice. To anchor the research in anti-oppression, choosing a complementary practice or research-based framework that specifically addresses the systems of power that have stratified health across the globe. We often rely on critical race theory (CRT) given its practice-based guidelines that shape who performs the research and the way the research is conducted (Ford & Airhihenbuwa, 2010a, b). Even if CRT is not the framework for anchoring anti-oppression in your research, there are some key principles that we believe are necessary.

First, acknowledgment of the ways that racism has and continues to impact the community are substantive and tangential areas of focus. Before engaging with any community, being clear on the pervasiveness of racism in every aspect of life for racially minoritized populations is essential. This clarity is needed even when the community does not understand or acknowledge racism as a fundamental driver of their social, economic, and health outcomes. Second, centering the community in the research. This does not mean that all the work is simply about this community, although that may be the case as well. This means that before ideating about your own or a funders' interests in this community, you allow the community to guide the work by understanding their priorities and needs. One way to practically do this is by activating them as true partners in the research enterprise. This requires more than a typical consultation relationship but one where the community receives both financial and intellectual property benefits. In other words, they are perceived and treated as producers of the knowledge. In many ways, they have functioned in this capacity as researchers and have had difficulty reaching the community across several essential research functions. One major example is the consistent inability of the research enterprise to adequately recruit research participants without input, let alone substantial involvement and help from community members. Yet, these essential tasks have not received the same level of compensation, monetary or otherwise, unless community members have obtained an affiliation with a research institution, and even in these rare cases exclusion from the benefits of research may persist. This devaluing of the benefits that a community provides to research is steeped in oppression because it maintains that communities are unable to do the research and receive support from research funders, unless of course, they are led by a research institution. This notion is false and needs to be upended which supports the next practice that researchers should engage in when performing CBPR: build capacity.

Capacity building can take many forms in the research process. Some researchers view this as putting the bulk of the research funds back into the community by employing community members and their workplaces, or producing knowledge that can improve the individuals, physical structures, and/or policies in the community. There are also many other examples, but true capacity building is empowering the community to do the work independently. For example, training community members to engage in research and offering real education and training opportunities, writing and supporting grants that are led by the community and not the researcher, writing publications with community members so that when they apply for their own independent funding there is a history of successful research engagement. We acknowledge that some of these practices lend to a structurally racist society that requires racially minoritized community members to acculturate and "give in" to the racist structures that maintain our oppression. However, we also acknowledge that without more of the community at the table as true partners, these racist structures will not be continuously challenged and held accountable when they continue to erode the dignity of our community.

This is a natural stepping-stone to the next practice that researchers should engage in when working with community – be willing to give up on your power to perform the research. While not easy, researchers need to acknowledge and be ready to step aside and back when the research should not be performed by them. There are some surface-level indicators of this that I apply to my own research program which has been in service of reducing racial inequities in HIV. A lot of this work has been performed with communities who use drugs/substances and sexually minoritized men because of the increased HIV prevalence and efficiency of HIV transmission in these populations. One surface-level indicator is to always make sure that someone on the research team is a member of the community we are performing research with. However, although I am a member of a racially minoritized community, there are still myriad key ways that my contribution to the production of knowledge for these specific communities could fall short. And although one could read and learn from these communities, a continuous gut check on whether I am appropriately positioned to make recommendations and requirements to the community on many areas of their everyday lives is needed. For example, in my estimation it would be inappropriate for a set of recommendations on sexual behavioral practices specific to sexually minoritized men to be released by a research institution without a sexually minoritized man in some leadership role in the production of those recommendations. This is not to say that there are no other areas where researchers who are not engrained in this community cannot contribute. But, it is to say that unless research understands the core of the community – their love, their pain, their daily triumphs and struggles – research should focus less on trying to change the community itself and ideate on the systems around the community that disallow them from fully realizing their potential. It is possible and critical to still work with the community to shift these systems while not interjecting a glass ceiling perspective on what the community, that one is not truly a part of, should be doing.

Implications for Future Practice Development and Research

The implications for future practice development and research within the framework of CBPR are profound, particularly as they pertain to addressing and dismantling systems of oppression that have historically marginalized racially minoritized populations. Future practice must prioritize the integration of anti-oppressive methodologies that are explicitly designed to challenge and transform the power dynamics between researchers and communities. This requires adopting complementary frameworks, such as CRT, that directly confront systemic inequalities and center the lived experiences of the community in the research process.

A critical implication for future practice is the necessity of genuine power-sharing between researchers and community members. This goes beyond mere consultation and involves equitably distributing both the intellectual and financial benefits of research. Future research initiatives must ensure that community members are recognized as cocreators of knowledge, with tangible benefits that reflect their contributions. This includes financial compensation, opportunities for capacity building, and coauthorship on research publications.

Furthermore, there is a pressing need for capacity building that empowers communities to conduct their research independently. This can be achieved through targeted education, training, and support in grant writing, enabling communities to secure funding and lead research initiatives autonomously. Such practices not only challenge the traditional hierarchical structures within the research enterprise but also foster long-term sustainability and self-determination within communities.

Future research must also recognize the importance of researcher reflexivity, where scholars continuously evaluate their positionality and potential biases. Researchers should be prepared to step aside when appropriate, allowing those with lived experience to take the lead in knowledge production. This shift is crucial in ensuring that research outcomes are not only accurate but also ethically sound and reflective of the community's true needs and aspirations.

Summary

The future of CBPR must be rooted in anti-oppressive practices that promote equity, power-sharing, and community autonomy, ultimately contributing to the dismantling of systemic racism and the advancement of health equity. Social work leadership and practice must incorporate and support CBPR as a mechanism to strengthen processes, intervention, policy creation, and community strategies.

Reflection Questions

1. How might your practice leverage its clinical work and community engagement to create opportunity for community-based participatory research? What unique benefits do these types of projects provide your practice, clients, and the community served?
2. How might research actively work to conduct more equitable, anti-oppressive, and community-empowering research?
3. How might concepts like critical reflectivity, reflexive self-awareness, and critical consciousness benefit community-based research? (See Box 9.1.)

Box 9.1 Practice Vignette. ITHRIVE 365: A Community-Led Intervention

By Justin C. Smith

Black gay, bisexual, and other men who have sex with men (GBMSM) practice positive health behaviors at rates comparable to their peers of other racial groups, yet they experience greater rates of health inequities, including in rates of HIV acquisition (Millett, 2007). Despite this evidence, there

Figure 9.1 Side portrait of happy young Black man looking at cellphone.

currently exists a dearth of accessible and culturally relevant health promotion interventions designed to address the inequities faced by Black GBMSM. To address this gap in services, THRIVE SS, an Atlanta-based HIV service organization founded and led by Black GBMSM living with HIV, developed iTHRIVE 365. This multicomponent intervention incorporates mobile health (mHealth) with organizationally delivered services to increase access to health information, social connections, and HIV care services specifically for Black GBMSM living with HIV. Recognizing the potential for the scale-up and replication of the iTHRIVE 365 intervention in other settings, the leadership of THRIVE SS sought out an academic research team to rigorously evaluate the intervention (Figure 9.1).

The resulting partnership between THRIVE SS, researchers at Rutgers University, and Atlanta's Positive Impact Health Centers led to two research grants funded by the National Institutes of Health (NIH) to support the development of the iTHRIVE 365 mobile app and to study its impact on HIV-related and psychological health outcomes among Black GBMSM living with HIV. In contrast to most other existing mHealth and mobile app interventions in the HIV prevention and care space, the iTHRIVE 365 intervention was conceived by the leadership of THRIVE SS, a community-based organization (CBO), rather than by academic researchers at a university. This distinction reflects principles of CBPR insofar as this is a *community-driven* research project where the community-based organization is in a leadership role in the execution of the project and owns the intellectual property of the mobile app. THRIVE SS would have developed and implemented the iTHRIVE 365 intervention regardless of the research component; however, the leadership of THRIVE SS saw the potential for the future of the intervention and recognized the importance of rigorous evaluation to making the case to replicate and scale the intervention in the future, and actively sought research partners who could conduct the evaluation in a culturally appropriate manner.

The entire iTHRIVE 365 project team reflects the community being served by the app, with the majority of the project team being Black gay men living with HIV. At each step of the app development process, the people served by THRIVE SS, called members, were invited to provide guidance on the features and design of the mobile app, reflecting principles of human-centered design (HCD). THRIVE SS leadership and members were also involved in the development and design of the research protocol and were included as authors on the scientific manuscripts and as presenters on conference presentations resulting from the study components of the project.

iTHRIVE 365 represents the concept of meaningful involvement of people with HIV in design and conceptualization of the programs designed to serve the needs of their own community. In this case, the project reflects the maxim of *"nothing about us, without us"* and is an example of the idea that the people who are closest to the problem must be actively engaged in and involved in developing solutions to the problem. This is yet another facet of community empowerment practice (English et al., 2023).

REFLECTION QUESTIONS

1. What are some of the additional strengths not described in the vignette that were a result of backing community-driven research?
2. *"Nothing about us, without us"* – what does this maxim mean to you? How might it shape your future ideas of community work, research, and policy?

REFERENCES

English, D., Smith, J. C., Scott-Walker, L., Lopez, F. G., Morris, M., Reid, M., ... & Cunningham, D. J. (2023). iTHRIVE 365: A community-led, multicomponent health promotion intervention for Black same gender loving men. *Annals of LGBTQ Public and Population Health*, 4(4), 363–383.

Millett, G. A., Flores, S. A., Peterson, J. L., & Bakeman, R. (2007). Explaining disparities in HIV infection among Black and white men who have sex with men: A meta-analysis of HIV risk behaviors. *AIDS*, 21(15), 2083–2091.

REFERENCES

Bloche, M. G. (2013). Health care disparities – Science, politics and race. In T. A. Laveist & L. A. Isaac (Eds.) *Race, ethnicity and health – A public health reader* (pp. 41–47). Jossey-Bass.

Ford, C. L., & Airhihenbuwa, C. O. (2010a). Critical race theory, race equity, and public health: Toward antiracism praxis. *American Journal of Public Health*, 100(Suppl 1), S30–S35.

(2010b). The public health critical race methodology: Praxis for antiracism research. *Social Science & Medicine, 71*(8), 1390–1398.

Holkup, P. A., Tripp-Reimer, T., Salois, E. M., & Weinert, C. (2004). Community-based participatory research: An approach to intervention research with a Native American community. *ANS: Advances in Nursing Science, 27*(3), 162–175.

Israel, B. A., Coombe, C. M., Cheezum, R. R., Schulz, A. J., McGranaghan, R. J., Lichtenstein, R., Reyes, A. G., Clement, J., & Burris, A. (2010). Community-based participatory research: A capacity-building approach for policy advocacy aimed at eliminating health disparities. *American Journal of Public Health, 100*(11), 2094–2102.

Israel, B. A., Parker, E. A., Rowe, Z., Salvatore, A., Minkler, M., Lopez, J., Butz, A., Mosley, A., Coates, L., Lambert, G., Potito, P. A., Brenner, B., Rivera, M., Romero, H., Thompson, B., Coronado, G., & Halstead, S. (2005). Community-based participatory research: Lessons learned from the Centers for Children's Environmental Health and Disease Prevention Research. *Environmental Health Perspectives, 113*(10), 1463–1471.

Israel, B. A., Schulz, A. J., Parker, E. A., & Becker, A. B. (2001). Community-based participatory research: Policy recommendations for promoting a partnership approach in health research. *Education for Health, 14*(2), 182–197.

Neill, S. J. (1998). Developing children's nursing through action research. *Journal of Child Health Care, 2*(1), 11–15.

Thomas, S. (2013). The color line: Race matters in the elimination of health disparities. In T. A. Laveist & L. A. Isaac & (Eds.) *Race, ethnicity and health – A public health reader* (pp. 35–40). Jossey-Bass.

CHAPTER 10

Combined Use of Servant Leadership Principles and Afrocentric Perspective Principles as Framework to Decolonize Social Institutions' Commitment to Well-being and Inclusion

Darrin E. Wright

Introduction

It has become more apparent that to decolonize social institutions – such as the political, criminal justice, educational, and economic systems – a more profound commitment to inclusion and well-being will require a reimagining of their future that is based on an antiracist and anti-oppressive paradigm. We continue to witness various social institutions inherited or put in place to meet the needs and aspirations of the formerly colonized in Africa, Asia, the Caribbean, and Latin America (the global South), and internally within the United States, falter under the pressures of structural racism and neo-colonialism, a more subtle form of colonialism which emerged in the global South in the form of structural adjustment programs, outsourcing, privatization of human services, and the rise of non-governmental organizations (NGOs) funded by private investors, often with a policy agenda that is contrary to the given realities or needs of the population or communities in question (Mignolo & Walsh, 2018; Wilson, 1998).

In light of these facts, there is an urgent need for fresh research on the subject of producing a brave and adaptable generation of leaders who understand the value of servant leadership (SL) principles coupled with the principles of the Afrocentric Perspective as a framework to create social policies and engage in leadership practices that are sensitive to the needs of Black, Indigenous, and People of Color (BIPOC) and other oppressed groups in general as a conceptualization of a praxis of decoloniality. This chapter will address how these two approaches could contribute to the reinvigoration of upcoming leaders committed to serving BIPOC populations specifically, and other oppressed and marginalized groups.

Unexpected Consequences of the Decolonization Movement and the Civil Rights Era for BIPOC Populations

The decolonization movements in Asia, Africa, and the Caribbean were closely associated with the civil rights movement, and this influence was reciprocal. Leaders of African, Asian, and Caribbean descent felt that the fight for equality in the US was a component of their own fight for equality and recognition abroad. As such, at the end of the colonial period in Africa, Asia, Latin America, the Caribbean, and the victories gained by African Americans during the Civil Rights era, for a very brief period, there seemed to be a glimmer of hope that BIPOC populations globally would be allowed to develop their systems unfettered from their former international and domestic colonizers. However, this notion was short-lived. Each liberated country or community quickly found itself struggling with neo-colonialism, collective imperialism, and structural racism and its successful attempts at rolling back whatever progressive gains were made by BIPOC populations worldwide (Bell, 2014, pp. 34–44; Nkrumah, 1968). One area in which neo-colonialism and structural racism were hugely successful in co-opting was the educational systems in the various newly independent countries in the global South and among African American communities across the United States.

While the faces changed regarding who delivered the educational curriculum, the content within many curricula remained intact, with some marginal inclusion of formerly oppressed groups. For the most part, the curriculum continued to espouse a Eurocentric outlook in its objectives and outcomes used to subjugate and oppress BIPOC populations in the global South and North America by perpetuating a pedagogy that trained BIPOC countries and communities to value the virtue of over-the-top rugged individualism, excessive materialism, and competitiveness to meet the needs of excessive capitalism branded as globalism to ensure the needs of a few at the expense of the masses (Nkrumah, 1968; Schiele & Day, 2014).

The deconstruction, development, and replacement of colonial pedagogies in favor of pedagogies inclusive of Indigenous ways of knowing, being, and doing, underpinned by humanistic values rooted in truth, justice, balance, and harmony, has been attempted in several countries and communities. Examples of these efforts include Tanzania and the United States, where Black Studies and Ethnic Studies curricula were developed at Howard University and Atlanta University to address the contradictions inherent in all colonial educational systems and pedagogy (Abrams et al., 2023). However, no concrete evidence exists of a sustained, intentional approach or strategy to decolonize inherited pedagogies (Baruti, 2006; Nkrumah, 1970).

Impact on BIPOC Communities

Many BIPOC populations who have chosen to or have adopted neo-colonial social and political systems and institutions have held onto leadership approaches and management practices created by their former colonial powers, which were used to regulate and control BIPOC peoples' aspirations, access to power, and resources by perpetuating a Eurocentric worldview that emphasized the distribution of the most rewards and resources to those who are considered to have contributed the most. These post colonial and structurally racist educational systems provided ready-made incubators (Mignolo & Walsh, 2018) – at the same time, marginalizing and oppressing those who do not conform to the defined status quo. Secondly, a value system built on elitism, stratification, and division between the educated and those deemed less educated within the group was shaped and produced within BIPOC populations as a result of these neo-colonial and fundamentally racist educational systems. Because of this value system, leaders who genuinely believe in being "the people's servant" or who embrace a collectivist spirit are not seen as effective leaders in comparison to leaders who are seen as elites, who are self-serving and have a tendency toward "rugged individualism" over what is best for the welfare of the entire community or country (Asante, 1980).

This mindset is frequently demonstrated in social institutions by leaders who support actions and procedures that are incredibly bureaucratic in their organizational structure and highly mechanical in their approach, placing a heavy emphasis on internal task orientation and accomplishing organizational goals without considering the larger welfare of the community as a whole. Additionally, this style of leadership frequently focuses on external tasks. The primary purpose of the leader's actions is to ensure that the interests of politics and capital are prioritized over those of the general public to achieve organizational goals by obtaining resources and legitimacy from the outside world. This type of leadership typically ignores the human element and is directive, powerful, centralized, and goal-oriented alone (Schmid, 2006). This leadership style regards the human factor as a tool to achieve a goal. Regretfully, BIPOC leaders worldwide have stuck to this Euro-Western model of leadership, which prioritizes whiteness in positions of authority in recent decades (Seyama-Mokhaneli, 2024).

Many BIPOC leaders have adopted a transactional leadership style that has left many members of their respective groups feeling cynical, ambivalent, and pessimistic about these social institutions and their capacity to meet the needs of their constituents in a way that is humanistic and treats them with respect, dignity, and worth as individuals. Because of this contradiction in power differential, many people frequently fail to distinguish between organizations led by BIPOC leadership and those similarly handled by privately financed NGOs in the West or global corporate elites (Wilson, 1998).

Implications of Task-Oriented Leadership

The leadership that counts, in the end, is the kind that touches people differently. Implicit in traditional leadership concepts, as we have seen, is the idea that social institutions cannot be improved from within. The responsibilities of stewardship require that obligations and commitments are met, regardless of obstacles. Leadership takes many forms, and while transactional or command-and-control leadership has its place, if transactional leadership styles are practiced as the only dominant strategies, they can breed dependency and a loss of self-efficacy in employees and cast them in roles as subordinates only and not as stakeholders in a shared vision or governance. Subordinates do what they should but little else (Asante, 1980).

Need for a Paradigm Shift

"The great leader is a servant first" (Greenleaf, 1970). *Servant leadership* is how leaders can get the necessary legitimacy to lead. Successfully providing purpose requires the trust of others; for trust to be forthcoming, those being led must have confidence in the leader's competence and values. Social institutions provide an ideal setting for joining the practice of SL to the goals and mission of social institutions (*The Jossey-Bass Reader on Education Leadership*, 2006).

One way the SL serves others within social institutions is by becoming an advocate on their behalf. Additionally, several principles in SL are necessary to be effective. (1) It is purposeful: SL provides a continuous stream of actions by an organization's formal leadership, which has the effect of inducing clarity, consensus, and commitment regarding the organization's primary purposes; (2) Servant leaders embrace the concept of Empowerment. Servant leaders believe that everyone is free to do what makes sense as long as their decisions embody the values shared by the community. Empowerment cannot be practiced successfully apart from enablement, that is, efforts by social institutions to provide support and remove obstacles to people's dignity, worth, and self-development through a sense of shared meaning; and (3) Servant leaders foster leadership by outrage: The leader's responsibility is to be outraged when empowerment is undermined and purposes are ignored (*The Jossey-Bass Reader on Education Leadership*, 2006).

Power Over versus Power To or With

Another essential concept embedded in SL is the social construct of Power. Power can be understood in two ways, (1) "Power over," which emphasizes controlling what people do when they do it and how they do it, and (2) "Power to or with," which views Power as a source of energy for achieving shared goals and purpose. When Empowerment is successfully practiced, administrators exchange "Power over" for "Power to or with." Moreover, "Power over" is rule-bound, while "Power to or with" is goal-bound (*The Jossey-Bass Reader on Education Leadership*, 2006).

Servant Leadership and Moral Authority

Hence, there is an inherent connection between moral authority and SL. Moral authority depends on an individual's credibility to make morally competent decisions (Merriam-Webster, n.d.). Serving others is a critical component of SL. SL is, therefore, a moral and ethical necessity to support future generations of BIPOC leaders in altering and bringing critical consciousness to their duty as servants of the people. According to SL approaches, the core of an administrator's job is to fulfill stewardship obligations. The concept of stewardship establishes an attractive image of leadership. It embraces all the members of the society as a community and all those served by the community as one's extended family (*The Jossey-Bass Reader on Education Leadership*, 2006).

Having established a rationale for why BIPOC leaders should embrace a leadership style rooted in being a servant leader as the first step toward reimagining antiracist and anti-oppressive institutions, it is equally important to note that future BIPOC leaders must also be centered on self. In short, each new pedagogy needs to consider the psychology developed among some BIPOC individuals. BIPOC groups have achieved tremendous success both individually and collectively in a wide range of life's pursuits.

For example, it is a historical fact that many people of African descent around the world have psychological scars from centuries of traumatic experiences under American and European oppression through physical and cultural imperialism practiced through slavery, colonialism, segregation, and apartheid (DeGruy, 2005). Franz Fanon documented this psychological impact well in his work *Black Skins, White Mask* (1952). Fanon studied the psychology of racism and dehumanization inherent in situations of colonial domination among the Francophone Black and Brown world. He applied psychoanalysis and psychoanalytic theory to explain the feelings of dependency and inadequacy that Black and Brown people experience in a white world.

According to Fanon, a low cultural appreciation for things that are Black or Brown, as well as a Eurocentric outlook on life rather than an ethnic perspective that takes into account what is best for the group as a whole, are common manifestations of this feeling of inadequacy and reliance in BIPOC individuals. Likewise, in the groundbreaking work *Afrocentricity: The Theory of Social Change*, Dr. Molefi Asante further emphasizes these claims, stating that non-centered Africans' psychology is problematic because they lack the racial pride, solidarity, and socio-historical consciousness necessary to effect positive change for Black or African people on and off the continent (Asante, 1980). Because Afrocentricity is a social theory of thought and action that, when applied, can lead to the praxis of decoloniality through progressive social change based on social, cultural, and economic justice for BIPOC, a concentrated effort needs to be made to raise the critical consciousness of young BIPOC people (Asante, 1980; Mignolo & Walsh, 2018, pp. 33–50) .

Afrocentricity's Theory through the Lens of the Afrocentric Perspective in Social Work Practice

The Afrocentric Perspective in social work was derived from the varied and collective historical oppressive and traumatic experiences faced by African Americans and other individuals of African descent throughout the Diaspora as a racial group (Martin & Martin, 2003). Regarding its goals, the Perspective takes a focused and universalistic stance (Schiele, 1997). In this way, the Afrocentric Perspective applies its ethical and humanistic principles and values to address similar concerns for all groups and members of the human family who face various forms of cultural, social, and economic oppression, even though it is primarily concerned with advancing the quest for human rights, social and economic justice, and empowerment for people of African ancestry (Schiele, 1997). Thus, Afrocentric social work lends its principles as a praxis to solve societal concerns faced by all people and trains practitioners to address specific psychological, social, spiritual, and economic problems experienced by persons of African origin (Mignolo & Walsh, 2018; Wright et al., 2018).

Emphasis is given to the ability to understand the importance of the role of culture in determining how people or groups who have experienced historical oppression and trauma view their ability to address Power, position, and resources about the larger society in its efforts to advance and transform the human family toward greater humanistic and moral ends (Martin & Martin, 2003; Mitchel et al., 2000).

Foundational Underpinnings of the Afrocentric Perspective

The Perspective features 10 concepts or principles unique to Afrocentric social work practice. These were developed over time at the Atlanta University School of Social Work, where the school exercised its autonomy to reject Eurocentric frameworks and modes of thinking as the only ones and instead embraced its right to investigate Indigenous ways of knowing, being, and doing (Adams, 1981; Carten, 2021). This development took place at the height of the Black Power Movement and at the end of the Civil Rights Era. It had a tremendous psychological impact on Black consciousness specifically, and the critical consciousness needed to examine the systems and structures that uphold discrimination and oppression generally (Bell, 2014). The concepts or principles have remained ever since as a conceptual practice in decolonization; they are conceptualized in a linear and circular way rather than static (Mignolo & Walsh, 2018). Thus, in addition to other theories and practice models, practitioners should consider these 10 principles as conceptual models, listed in Table 10.1, while aiding groups who are vulnerable to marginalization or other types of oppression (Wright, 2022).

While these 10 concepts are the same regardless of whether the practitioner is working with individuals, families, groups, organizations, or communities, social workers must be prepared with culturally responsive knowledge and skills to apply the Afrocentric Perspective concepts at the micro, mezzo, or macro level.

The Afrocentric Perspective prepares social workers to maintain their humanity in the face of dehumanizing conditions they frequently witness

Table 10.1 *Ten concepts specific to the Afrocentric Perspective*

	Perspective	Concept
1.	Humanistic Values	Values that place priority on eliminating human oppression and enhancing human potential, by valuing humanistic principles that advance equity, fairness, social and economic justice practices, and concerns.
2.	Autonomy	The ability to stand up to, resist, and end all types of racism and other forms of oppression against oneself and others.
3.	Strengths Perspective	Identifying group characteristics that can be conceived favorably as a source of resiliency and human advancement.
4.	Matrix Roles	Efficient application of diverse generalist professional roles, competencies, and intervention techniques in eradicating human subjugation and advancing human potential.
5.	Spiritual Balance	Understanding that social structures and natural phenomena must be harmonious or balanced to bring societal change, healing, and communal cohesion.
6.	Collective View of Self	The extent to which one's identity is never separated from one's corporate identity and responsibility to the group, community, or society.
7.	Universalistic and Particularistic Outlook	The degree to which focus is placed on problems and situations within and without the African American community.
8.	Significance of Self-Knowledge and Personal Experience	The validation of the use of self – that is, one's emotions, lived experiences, and values – as a basis for generating knowledge and affecting positive human transformation.
9.	Validation of Circular and Linear Logic	The extent to which a more comprehensive approach to knowing is validated, and the drawbacks of linear logic are recognized and acknowledged as one of several methods of knowing.
10.	Intuitive	Acknowledging and appreciating emotion's role as a human factor in the critical thinking required for client evaluation and assistance.

Sources: Wright (2013), White (2021), Foster (2011, 2014).

and experience while providing services to marginalized populations through a strengths-based approach. It also creates a space where workers can teach and share humanism with everyone, even in a social environment that is frequently hostile to humanistic values and the advancement of social and economic justice concerns (Asante & Dove, 2021).

Furthermore, the Afrocentric Perspective is rooted in human rights, social justice, and empowerment approaches to practice (CAU, 1987, 1999; Martin & Martin, 2003, pp. 227–248; Mitchel et al., 2000).

Key Features of the Afrocentric Perspective's Use within Social Institutions

The Afrocentric Perspective seeks to understand that human beings are not separate from their lived experiences or cultural worldviews. The Afrocentric Perspective believes that one's heritage and lived experiences form the basis for developing an understanding and appreciation for the diversity and heritage of others. Therefore, being mindful of this fact while attempting to assist the Black community and other communities and groups that face oppression and marginalization is critical for developing policies and services that seek to address sociohistorical oppression, trauma, discrimination, and marginalization among people of African descent specifically, and other groups of people generally (Derezotes, 2014; Mignolo & Walsh, 2018; Wright et al., 2018).

From an Afrocentric Perspective, social work professionals and other individuals in leadership roles within social organizations may find the humanistic ideals and a universalistic – versus particularistic or focused outlook – a helpful framework for policy analysis (Schiele, 2000; Wright, 2022). Policies influence practices, and vice versa. Social workers and other related professionals should use these two guiding principles when crafting policies to ensure that, while considering the needs of all parties involved, they also consider how much the intended policies will benefit or hurt BIPOC and other marginalized groups in particular (Wright, 2022). It is essential to consider whether this approach is humanistic, equitable, and just. Does this policy give BIPOC and other disadvantaged groups the ability to take control of their own lives, instead of restricting or stigmatizing individuals seeking assistance from state and local agencies by enforcing stringent social control measures and regulation tactics to dissuade individuals from utilizing public and private services (Mignolo & Walsh, 2018; Schiele, 2013; Wright et al., 2018)?

Summary

Leaders who apply the principles of SL coupled with the principles of an Afrocentric Perspective as an integrative lens seek to apply the notions of decoloniality as a praxis to decolonize social institutions and demonstrate a more substantial commitment to BIPOC well-being and inclusion in the functionality and effectiveness of social institutions by using leadership practices that support socioeconomic justice, honesty, shared governance, and equality as a foundation for societal change, healing, and community solidarity (Foster, 2011; Mignolo & Walsh, 2018).

Reflection Questions

1. In what ways might colonial mindsets influence your leadership style or assumptions? How could you work to decolonize your approach?
2. How can leaders create space for marginalized voices and perspectives in decision-making processes?
3. In what ways could decolonial leadership foster innovation and new ways of problem-solving?
4. How would you apply the principles of the Afrocentric Perspective to your leadership approach?
5. Which of the 10 principles of the Afrocentric Perspective discussed in the chapter could you use most often and why?

REFERENCES

Abrams, L. S., Crewe, S. E., Dettlaff, A. J., & Williams, J. H. (2023). *Social work, white supremacy, and racial justice: Reckoning with our history, interrogating our present, reimagining our future.* Oxford University Press.

Adams, F. V. (1981). *The reflections of Florence Victoria Adams.* Shannon Press.

Asante, M. (1980). *Afrocentricity: A theory of social change.* African American Images.

Asante, M., & Dove, N. (2021). *Being human being: Transforming the race discourse.* Universal Write.

Baruti, K. B. M (2006). *Notes toward higher ideals in Afrikan intellectual liberation.* Akoben House.

Bell, J. (2014). *The Black power movement and American social work.* Columbia University Press.

Carten, A. J. (2021). *Find a way or make one: A documentary history of Clark Atlanta University Whitney M. Young Jr. School of Social Work (1920–2020).* Offord Press.

Clark Atlanta University School of Social Work. (1987, June 30). *Clark Atlanta University School of Social Work: Self-study.* Clark Atlanta University School of Social Work.

(1999, June 30). *Clark Atlanta University School of Social Work: Self-study.* Clark Atlanta University School of Social Work.

Derezotes, D. S. (2014). *Transforming historical trauma through dialogue.* SAGE.

Fanon, F. (1952). Black Skins White Masks. Grove Press.

Foster, S. (2011, March 11). *African retention patterns in social work.* (Wright, D., Interviewer).
(2014). *Integrating the Afrocentric Perspective into the Social Work Curriculum* [Unpublished manuscript]. Clark Atlanta University.
Greenleaf, R. K. (1970). *The servant as leader.* The Robert K. Greenleaf Center for Servant Leadership.
The Jossey-Bass Reader on Educational Leadership. (2006). (2nd ed.). Jossey-Bass.
Leary, J. DeGruy. (2005). *Post traumatic slave syndrome: America's legacy of enduring injury and healing.* Uptone Press.
Martin, E. P., & Martin, J. M. (2003). *Spirituality and the Black helping tradition in social work.* NASW Press.
Merriam-Webster. (n.d.). Moral authority. In Merriam-Webster.com dictionary. Retrieved July 20, 2024, from www.merriam-webster.com/dictionary/moral%20authority
Mignolo, W., & Walsh, C. E. (2018). *On decoloniality: concepts, analytics, praxis.* Duke University Press.
Mitchell, H., Ward, N., & Waymer, R. (2000, June 30). Afrocentric Perspective. *Atlanta University Bulletin,* 1–3.
Nkrumah, K. (1968). *Handbook of revolutionary warfare.* Panaf Books.
(1970). *Class struggle in Africa.* Panaf Books.
Schmid, H. (2006). *Leadership styles and leadership change in human and community service organizations. Nonprofit management & leadership.* John Wiley & Sons, Inc.
Schiele, J. (1997). The contour and meaning of Afrocentric social work. *Journal of Black Studies,* 27(6), 800–819.
Schiele, J. H. (2000). *Human services and the Afrocentric paradigm.* Routledge.
(2013). *Social work practice within an Afrocentric paradigm* (2nd ed.). Oxford University Press.
Schiele, J. H., & Day, P. J. (2014). *Introduction to human services: Through the eyes of practice settings* (3rd ed.). Cengage Learning.
Seyama-Mokhaneli, S. (2024). Critical conscious leadership for decolonization: A Black consciousness perspective of authentically transforming leadership. *Equality, Diversity and Inclusion: An International Journal,* 43(9), 71–87. https://doi.org/10.1108/EDI-01-2023-0033
[Dr. Gerry L. White]. (2021, June 23). *Afrocentric Perspective Lecture by Drs White and Wright CAUWMYJSSW* [Video]. YouTube. www.youtube.com/watch?v=J4Zp2eIVR8Y
Wilson, A. (1998). *Blueprint for Black Power: A moral and political imperative for the twenty-first century.* Afrikan World InfoSystems.
Wright, D. (2013). Afrocentric Perspective in Social Work: *An integrative lens.* Paper Presentation, 11th Biennial Conference of Caribbean & International Social Work Educators, Curaçao, Netherland Antilles, West Indies.
Wright, D. E. (2022). Black males' plight to breathe in America – Black racial injustice. *Reflections: Narratives of Professional Helping,* 28(2), 82–86. https://

reflectionsnarrativesofprofessionalhelping.org/index.php/Reflections/article/view/191

Wright, E. D., Jones, K., White, G., Harper, R., & Alhassan, M. (2018). *School of Social Work handbook*. Clark Atlanta University.

FURTHER READING

Clarke, C. (2020, September 19). *BIPOC: What does it mean and where does it come from?* CBS News. www.cbsnews.com/news/bipoc-meaning-where-does-it-come-from-2020-04-02/

Fuller, N. (1984). *The united-independent compensatory code/system/concept: A textbook/workbook for thought, speech, and/or action, for victims of racism (white supremacy)* (Revised ed.). [Published by author].

Nkrumah, K. (1965). Neo-colonialism, the last stage of imperialism. Thomas Nelson & Sons.

CHAPTER 11

Liberation as Praxis for Antiracist, Anti-Oppressive Approaches to Higher Education and Social Work Using a BlackCrit Lens

Frederick V. Engram Jr.

Liberation as Praxis

The American social experiment was the brainchild of European (white), cisgender, seemingly heterosexual, wealthy men who enslaved Africans. Although they did not solely orchestrate and benefit from the enslavement of Africans in America, white women benefited too (Jones-Rogers, 2019, p. 57), they were its most public advocates and beneficiaries. White men and their beneficiaries, through legislation, reimagined America in a way that did not include its Native populations or stolen Africans as equal stakeholders. This perspective is perpetuated throughout history and provides a direct throughline to the inequity, anti-Blackness, anti-women, anti-Native, anti-immigrant, and anti-Queer ideologies of today. Whiteness operates as an all-encompassing overextension of unearned privilege, which embeds itself into the framework of every American institution from politics to healthcare, to social work, and higher education.

Whiteness as a system destabilizes the humanity of anyone who was not granted entrance into its deceptive brotherhood. Through the legislation of antimiscegenation, white women could lose their access to whiteness by choosing to marry, have sex with, or procreate with those *othered* in America (Battalora, 2013, p. 10). Those who were *othered* in America were Native and African. Antimiscegenation statutes, although seemingly restrictive, were far less likely to be applied to wealthy European men – now classified as white – when, through rape, they procreated with the enslaved African women. The statutes operated more or less as the stroking of the ego of white men, who through these laws, determined what white women could do with their bodies sexually. The same ideology persists today – the one that decides women do not have a right to choose whether or not they carry a pregnancy to term.

Whiteness, since its creation in 1681 (Battalora, 2013, p. 26), through unearned privilege, continues to be the determinant of all things uniquely respectable and American. From the ideals of the *nuclear family*, a

Eurocentric ideology, to the chase for individual capitalistic endeavors, whiteness destroys everything in its wake, declaring one person or group, and their ideologies, as its winner. It is through whiteness that many Americans determine the humanity of the oppressed and minoritized – conditions that they did not create or choose for themselves, but conditions they were born into, simply because of their unchosen racialized category. Although some white people are born poor, through their racialized privilege, they can change the trajectory of their circumstance. Whiteness grants them an unearned invitation into its ranks so long as they choose to abide by its *de facto* rules.

The Rules of Racial Standing are designated as a set of legal conditions that continue to keep the *othered* fighting for legitimacy. In Derrick Bell's *Faces at the Bottom of the Well: The Permanence of Racism* (1992, pp. 111–116), he outlines five rules:

First Rule

The law grants litigants standing to come into court based on their having significant personal interest and involvement in the issue to justify judicial cognizance. Black people (while they may be able to get into court) are denied such standing legitimacy in the world generally when they discuss their negative experiences with racism or even when they attempt to give a positive evaluation of another Black person or of his or her work. No matter their experience or expertise, Black people's statements involving race are deemed "special pleading" and thus not entitled to serious consideration.

Second Rule

Not only are Black people's complaints discounted, but Black victims of racism are less effective witnesses than are whites, who are members of the oppressor class. This phenomenon reflects a widespread assumption that Black people, unlike whites, cannot be objective on racial issues and will favor their own no matter what. This deep-seated belief fuels a continuing effort – despite all manner of Supreme Court decisions intended to curb the practice – to keep Black people off juries in cases involving race. Black judges hearing racial cases are eyed suspiciously and sometimes asked to recuse themselves in favor of a white judge – without those making the request even being aware of the paradox in their motions.

Third Rule

Few Black people avoid diminishment of racial standing, most of their statements about racial conditions being diluted and their recommendations of other Black people taken with a grain of salt. The usual exception to this rule is the Black person who publicly disparages or criticizes other Black people who are speaking or acting in ways that upset whites. Instantly, such statements are granted "enhanced standing" even when the speaker has no special expertise or experience in the subject he or she is criticizing.

Fourth Rule

When a Black person or group makes a statement or takes an action that the white community or vocal components thereof deem "outrageous," the latter will actively recruit Black people willing to refute the statement or condemn the action. Black people who respond to the call for condemnation will receive superstanding status. Those Black people who refuse to be recruited will be interpreted as endorsing the statements and action and may suffer political or economic reprisals.

Fifth Rule

True awareness requires an understanding of the Rules of Racial Standing. As an individual's understanding of these rules increases, there will be more and more instances where one can discern their workings. Using this knowledge, one gains the gift of prophecy about racism, its essence, its goals, even its remedies. The price of this knowledge is the frustration that follows recognition that no amount of public prophecy, no matter its accuracy, can either repeal the Rules of Racial Standing or prevent their operation.

White people and non-white people are not necessarily provided these rules in written form, but they are certainly socialized into them via their families, the law, and the American educational system. When considering the legal cases of groups like *The Exonerated Five* – a group of Black and Brown teens that comprised Dr. Yusef Saleem, Raymond Santana, Antron McCray, Kevin Richardson, and Korey Wise – who were falsely accused and imprisoned for the sexual assault of Trisha Meili in Central Park, in Manhattan, New York on April 19, 1989, as well as the survivors of the 1921 *Tulsa race massacre*, whose case was recently dismissed by the Oklahoma Supreme Court, citing that the case does not fall within the scope of the state's public nuisance statute. The Tulsa survivors have been fighting for justice and financial amends for a century. Each of the aforementioned survivors of white victimization, although not legally connected, are connected within the social context of America as the *othered*. Denying Black people their just due in any form within the American social experiment is taught to even the youngest of white and non-white children.

Liberation Movements

When thinking about the role of liberation movements, we must always consider that their most crucial objective is to free the oppressed. They are not intended to center whiteness in any capacity and must work actively toward disruption of the status-quo, an act that is inherently antithetical to the operation and success of whiteness. Liberation must also become a standard operating praxis within all of the helping professions (*social work, education, healthcare, and the law*), as each profession operates as the frontline for human contact. Uninterrupting the stronghold that anti-Black racism, whiteness via white supremacy, and oppressive deficit thinking have on each of us in our development and training is crucial and necessary. Movement work inspires us and requires of us to be centered in the cause of liberatory praxis and being intentional about that disruption every day and in every way.

Some of the most impactful liberatory movements in America, although with different goals, each had a common enemy or enemies. Their most common opposition is whiteness, and their secondary enemy is white supremacy – both of which are intentionally separated. Whiteness operates as a system that is both embedded within the framework of America and is upheld by everyone, including the oppressed class. White supremacy is the most violent aspect of whiteness that allows for racialized violence via groups like the KKK; Patriot Front; Three Percenters; The Proud Boys; 4Chan; Oath Keepers; and America First, all of whom were complicit and/or present during the Make America Great Again (MAGA) Insurrection against the United States on January 6, 2021. One of the most crucial pieces to moving toward a praxis of liberation I discuss in my book *Black Liberation through Action and Resistance: MOVE*. In Chapter 2, "Our Inheritance Upsets the Oppressor," I discuss how crucial it is for us to realize our power and that there is nothing wrong with us (Engram, 2023). As children, the first time that most Black children face anti-Blackness is via their teachers – a person who has been hired, trained, and trusted to guide our children into and through their formative years.

Spirit Murdering

This experience is referred to as *spirit murdering*. *Spirit murdering* occurs when Black children's souls are crushed because of a lack of care for their humanity by their (usually) white or non-Black teacher (Engram, 2022, p. 51; Love, 2016, p. 2). Although it is not only white teachers who cause this initial and progressive harm, which has greater implications for how Black children see learning spaces later in life, it is damaging. Black children have the unfortunate experience of not being seen as fully human or worthy of protecting, so they are often thrust into punitive experiences that lead toward the school-to-prison pipeline. White teachers who are not culturally aware make snap judgments about Black children and their ability to learn or be taught (Emdin, 2016). Meanwhile, their white counterparts have parents creating groups like *Moms for Liberty*, who do everything to *protect* their children from learning the truth about America, even if it is to the detriment of their children and non-white children.

Imagine a world where Black children and other children of color were as protected, revered, and loved external to their own communities and with the same intention as white children. That is a libratory praxis – one where students are all given the same intentional love, support, encouragement, and redirection that is not steeped in racialized hierarchy but is rooted in equity and justice. Black children who become Black adults, who have experienced teaching as an act of love and not oppression, turn out to be successful, fully imagined, emotionally attached adults – adults who will eventually enter into the helping professions and replicate that love through their service as a result of their own lived experience. Instead, Black students are *pushed out.*

Black children often experience the worst parts of society from the moment they first leave their mother's laps and enter school – if they are lucky. Others begin experiencing anti-Blackness as soon as they breathe their first breath earthside. This is largely due to the improper healthcare their mother might have received during her pregnancy, labor, and postpartum (Blackstock, 2024, p. 151), or the fact that they reside in food deserts redlined by politicians aimed at keeping Black people from ever actually elevating. Each and every form of oppression experienced by Black people in America is a direct result of the enslavement of Africans and the perceptions of their inhumanity. Regardless of all of the advances in the American social experiment, one thing remains the same – Black people are never to be seen as equal and are to be reminded as often as possible.

Application

Social work and higher education are separate disciplines, but each of them is socially responsible for the shaping of society. Each trained professional is credentialed and provided with the tools to be a contributing member of our disciplines and the helping practice. However, what many of our programs fail to do is to directly attack the embedded nature of whiteness and white supremacy in both disciplines. Most students would need to be fortunate enough to choose the right program, course, and professor at the right time to engage with race discourse at the most remedial level. The most educated of scholars still stumble over race and how important it is to every facet of life, so they ignore it. Their ignoring of the importance of race and racism in the American lexicon virtue-signals to our students how unimportant or forbidden its discussion is.

For some white and non-white students, this intentional neglect is a relief. For others, and students of color, this refusal to engage race and racism within our disciplines creates a severe gap in their learning or leaves them with unanswered questions. The way that we approach training and teaching in our disciplines cannot be with whiteness as the protected and non-critiqued class, while simultaneously teaching students that it is the *othered* who are the cause of their own dysfunction. As stated by hooks (2010, p. 7), thinking is an action. hooks also goes on to say that our thoughts are the laboratory where one goes when we need to pose questions and also to find answers (2010, p. 7.) However, if we do not steer our students toward being critical thinkers through liberatory praxis, we are ill-equipping them to ask critical questions or locate the right answers.

The school-to-prison pipeline is most successful within the American educational system because it does not target wealthy white children. As a result of this intentional effort, most well-off white and non-Black children have no idea of its existence – shielded by their parents. This is not the same experience that Black children and children of color have. From our earliest experiences, many of us who were kids playing in the park knew to run when the cops approached. We did not see cops or policing as a helping profession – we saw and see them as a threat to our freedom. Some will ask why this is the perspective of Black people, and that question alone does two things: *(1) highlights your ignorance regarding the experiences of Black people in America, and (2) further proves that white people have no idea what it means to be oppressed in America.*

From the moment that children enter the American educational system, the indoctrination starts. The indoctrination is not as evident to white children because most of the indoctrinators look like them. However, for Black children and children of color, the aspects of social control and anti-Blackness are immediate. Schools are emboldened to replicate an already unequal social order (Heitzeg, 2016, p. 4) – an order that yet again places whiteness and all who are granted admission at the top and then subsequently orders the *othered.* Black children are over-policed within schools and on college campuses, which leads them to being labeled as or immediately seen as deviant, up to no good.

The labeling of Black people within educational spaces offers *de facto* and *de jure* options for rule-breaking (Heitzeg, 2016, p. 36). The intention is to push Black students and students of color out of the educational space for two very distinctly sinister reasons: *(1) white teachers no longer have to deal with them, and (2) children who are not enrolled in school are most likely to commit crimes and if caught are most likely to recidivate, which is the hope of the pipeline.* Educational institutions must use a liberatory approach like *motherwork* as a means of engaging with Black students, which encourages educators to *center grace* and resist anti-Blackness (Watson & Baxley, 2021, p. 144). The punitive response to Black students for uncontrollable things like the fit of their clothing, being late occassionally, hairstyles, age-appropriate temper tantrums, and music choices only further aims to push them out (Morris-Couvson, 2016, p. 56). This current practice is, beyond a reasonable doubt, anti-Black and oppressive.

Understanding Helping Professions through *BlackCrit*

The American educational system, as well as all of the helping professions that it engages, are at their core anti-Black. Many individuals within these professions would like to argue that they are not racist and do not use the *n-word* – and that last part might be true. However, initiatives that they enforce without questioning, and approaches that they use to engage with Black people, are inherently anti-Black. The theoretical framework *BlackCrit* is a critical theory born from the father of all – Critical Race Theory (CRT). In my expert opinion, CRT operates very similarly to the Civil Rights Act of 1964, meaning that before it, no real meaningful measure for understanding Black experiences existed. After it, other marginalized identities have been able to find their way into the light and mainstream discourse.

BlackCrit was coined by Drs. Michael J. Dumas and kihana miraya ross in 2016. BlackCrit acknowledges its birth from and inclusion into CRT. However, BlackCrit does something uniquely different from CRT. CRT was born from critical legal scholars to help us say the quiet thing out loud. *The quiet thing?* **RACE**! Early critical legal scholars, who were largely white, focused on discrimination, but like many well-intentioned white persons, they refused to address the real issue plaguing Black experiences within the law – race and racism. CRT for the first time offered to legal scholarship an opportunity to stop avoiding the harsh realities of the Black lived experience. In the mid 90s, pivotal critical education scholars Drs. Gloria Ladson-Billings and William F. Tate dared to consider how education also needed this critical reckoning.

Through their application of CRT in education, countless scholars have been able to address how race and racism impact education in all aspects. What CRT did not explicitly focus on is anti-Black racism in education – which is where and why BlackCrit is most useful. Dumas and ross (2016) posit that BlackCrit in education helps us to intentionally and more incisively analyze how the specificity of anti-Blackness matters in explaining how Black personhood becomes disregarded, marginalized, othered, and disdained in schools and other education and community spaces (p. 415). Black people are not often given space to simply breathe without suspicion.

Black people are not allowed – and have never been allowed – to have real reactions to real-world experiences that plague us every day. We are always gaslit into believing that our righteous rage, our justified rage, our long-overdue rage is something that we must bury at the base of our souls. Many of us do, and then it kills us – placing us in vulnerable positions because the weight of anti-Blackness was so heavy that it fractures our minds, bodies, and souls. We look for healthy and unhealthy ways of coping to deal with the stress of our existence and are met with suspicion and disbelief. When we tell our medical providers that we are in pain, they deny us. When we tell our department chairs that we feel othered, they ignore us. When we tell our elected officials that we feel invisible, they tell us to vote anyway. The constant disregard is unfathomable to most – yet expected of us.

Liberation as a praxis is not meant to be cookie-cutter or comfortable. It is intended to make all of us think more deeply about the ways that we engage in community and in our professions. It is intended to encourage us to be intentional about the ways that we engage with the marginalized, the dispossessed, the discontent, and the owed – while also being mindful that we do not apply deficit-framed thinking in our approach within the helping professions. White-centered thinking makes many white and nonwhite persons within these disciplines feel that it is up to them to teach Black people and people of color how to survive and thrive. Those same individuals never take into consideration that perhaps the reason why they believe they know what is best for us is tied to their privileged racial standing and savior complex.

Dumas and ross's work helps us to contextualize the very distinct difference in understanding anti-Blackness, which is – although a part of white supremacy – separate (2016, p. 417). Anti-Blackness is a choice that many communities, our own included, choose to engage in. Anti-

Blackness is the default for most groups because it is easier to hate Blackness than it is to make room for it. Anti-Blackness also allows for other marginalized groups, for once in their life, to not be the othered – or so they think. Within the United States, two realities are always in existence and that is the simultaneous acknowledgment of Black suffering coupled with the denial of structural and foundational anti-Blackness (Vargas-Costa, 2018, p. 1). Cross (2021) states that during the nadir of the Black American experience (1877 to the twentieth century), it was remarkably dangerous for Black folks to present themselves as human (p. 78). So we played small, so as not to upend, upset, or minimize whiteness.

The choice to minimize the boldness and brilliance of our Blackness in the face of whiteness was necessary but detrimental. This decision allows for whiteness and white-centered perspectives to operate as our narrative. Choosing to push back with our own counterstorytelling – a tenet of CRT – allows us to be heard and seen. Helping professionals must resist the urge to assume and boldly proclaim to know our stories, or dare to tell our stories, better than us. Like the prison industrial complex that it feeds, the school-to-prison pipeline is created and maintained by coded appeals like anti-Blackness and pseudo race-based fear (Heitzeg, 2016, p. 36). Cross (2021) emphasizes that the line between freedom and incarceration for most folks is unambiguous and clear (p. 85). However, for Black folks, those lines are often blurred. Walking while Black, being educated while Black, buying coffee while Black, and banking while Black can be – and are often – met with state-sanctioned violence (Cross, 2021, p. 85).

Within the field of education, there are countless examples of the dehumanization of Black personhood (Dumas & Ross, 2016, p. 418). How educators within K–12 and higher education are trained has a profound impact on the way that they choose to engage with Black learners. Anti-Blackness is so rampant in academic spaces that even as a faculty member, I am unprotected when my racist white students decide to target me. We are often thrust into defensive positions to protect ourselves, and it is in these moments where our colleagues should show up – and many do not. We are far too often texted or called afterward and asked, *What should I do to help? How can I make this easier for you? Should I say something?* All while they never actually consider that I cannot protect myself and then walk you through how to protect me too. That is your work!

What the helping professions need more than any other discipline are co-conspirators (Engram, 2023, p. 19) which goes further than allyship. We need white people to actively engage in their own decolonized learning in order to best show up for the most marginalized among us, without expectation for forgiveness. Oftentimes white people's engaging in anti-racist, anti-oppressive work is rewarded – when it should actually be expected. Particularly when you are in the helping professions. Your reward is knowing that your practice is sound and the work that you are doing is the right and ethical thing to do. Too many of our disciplines allow people who should not be engaging our youth access to them. Whether it be those like the teacher fired from Bohls Middle School in Texas for telling Black and Hispanic children that being white is best, or the teacher who called the cops on a six-year-old Black girl to have her arrested in Orlando, Florida – they should not be in our disciplines. Truly, that is the responsibility of white people to oust these individuals from our midst, as indicated by Bell in *The Rules of Racial Standing*. (See Table 11.1.)

Summary

The goal of this section is to teach, nudge, and encourage helping professionals to think more intentionally about the way we each engage or have engaged in anti-Blackness. Our professions are ever-evolving but somehow seem to miss the mark on directly addressing the ways that anti-Black racism and oppressive ideologies have taken hold without apology. This section paints a realistic picture of the Black lived experience when engaged with white people (and people who center and/or perpetuate whiteness) within the helping professions. In being intentional about applying an antiracist, BlackCrit lens, we as professionals in the helping professions can and must endeavor to move our disciplines closer toward antiracism and actual helping.

Discussion Questions

1. What does it mean to apply a liberatory praxis within the helping professions?
2. What is the role of the co-conspirator?
3. Why is it necessary to rid the helping professions of anti-Black racism? How might you begin that process in your own practice environment?

Table 11.1 *Dimensions of anti-Blackness within the helping professions*

Oppressive Experience	Assumptions	Centering Grace & Equity	Oppressive Outcomes	Anti-Oppressive Outcomes
When a Black patient indicates that they are experiencing pain.	Patient is a habitual drug misuser and is pretending to be in pain to obtain access to drugs or is "medication seeking."	Providing a culturally aware advocate who has the ability to communicate with and on behalf of the patient.	Patient does not receive the required assistance needed, which could cause distress, a developed mistrust of care providers, and additional long-term issues.	Patient able to receive the appropriate level of treatment or assistance without the burden of proving that they are not misusing drugs.
A Black faculty member complains to their department chair that they are being harassed by a white student who opposes learning about DEI in a DEI-focused course.	Assuming that the faculty member somehow did not make the course content or class expectations clear, and/or has somehow lacked the ability to engage students in learning.	Providing space for the Black faculty member to talk through what they are experiencing without centering whiteness as a default.	Faculty member is not made to feel supported or protected against anti-Blackness.	The Black faculty member feels supported and that they are not alone in their department when anti-Blackness is present.
A Black person sees a police officer and avoids making eye contact with them.	Assuming that the refusal to make eye contact with the police officer means that the Black person is suspicious, guilty, or "hiding something."	Understand the historical relationship between Black people and policing, which stems from slave patrols and is evident throughout American history.	Assumption of guilt could lead to an uncomfortable confrontation with the police, which could end in injury or death.	Not assuming that Black avoidance of the police equates to criminality and instead providing a measured, culturally appropriate approach when engaging.

Source: Engram (2025).

REFERENCES

Battalora, J. (2013). *Birth of a white nation: The invention of white people and its relevance today.* Strategic Book Publishing and Rights.
Bell, D. (1992). The rules of racial standing. In *Faces at the bottom of the well: The permanence of racism* (pp. 111–116). Basic Books.
Blackstock, U. (2024). *Legacy: A Black physician reckons with racism in medicine.* Viking.
Cross Jr., W. E. (2021). *Black identity viewed from a barber's chair: Nigrescence and eudaimonia.* Temple University Press.
Dumas, M. J., & Ross, K. M. (2016). "Be Real Black for Me" Imagining BlackCrit in education. *Urban Education, 51*(4), 415–442.
Emdin, C. (2016). *For white folks who teach in the hood . . . and the rest of Y'all too: Reality pedagogy and urban education.* Beacon Press.
Engram, F. (2022). Who's all over there? Patriarchy, white manning, and deficit framed thinking aimed at spirit murdering Black children . *International Forum of Teaching and Studies, 18*(1), 49–52.
(2023). *Black liberation through action and resistance: MOVE.* Hamilton Books.
Engram, F. V. (2025). Twice as hard: A black parable for existing in higher education. *Freedom: A Journal of Research in Africana Studies, 2,* 75–92.
Heitzeg, N. (2016). *The school-to-prison pipeline.* Santa Barbara, CA: Praeger.
hooks, b. (2010). *Teaching critical thinking: Practical wisdom.* Routledge.
Jones-Rogers, S. (2019). *They were her property: White women as slave owners in the American South.* Yale University.
Love, B. L. (2016). Anti-Black state violence, classroom edition: The spirit murdering of Black children. *Journal of Curriculum and Pedagogy, 13*(1), 22–25.
Morris-Couvson, M. (2016). *Pushout: The criminalization of Black girls in schools.* The New Press.
Vargas-Costa, J. (2018). *The denial of anti-Blackness: Multiracial redemption & Black suffering.* The University of Minnesota.
Watson, T., & Baxley, G. (2021). Centering "Grace": Challenging anti-Blackness in schooling through motherwork. *Journal of School Leadership, 31*(1–2), 142–157.

CHAPTER 12

Reversing the Curse
Liberatory Models for Black Leaders and Clinical Supervisors in the Family Separation System

Sherri Y. Simmons-Horton, Shawna Marie Aarons-Cooke, and Tanya Rollins

Introduction

The powerful Western image of childhood innocence does not seem to benefit Black children. Black children are born guilty.
—Dorothy Roberts

Anti-Black racism in the child welfare system remains embedded in the fabric of American society. The systemic racism and racist practices within the child welfare system represent an extension of chattel slavery, post-Emancipation. Anti-Black racism in the child welfare system is omnipresent across each level within the system and permeates across other structures that purport to provide a benign service to children, youth, and families. Even in its given brand, the *"child welfare"* system presents itself as an entity of benevolence and care. In reality, the child welfare system – hereafter referenced interchangeably as the family separation system or the family policing system – is informed by the ongoing legacy of white supremacy that characterizes Blackness as the antithesis of humanity, and thus, using its power and its actors working in the system, seeks to police and punish Black children and families. Leaders and clinical supervisors working within or adjacent to the family policing system are key actors who engage in the systemization of racism through the execution of policies and practices that impact the experiences and outcomes of Black system-involved children and their parents.

The reality of persistent anti-Black racism present in laws, policies, and practices not only renders racial disproportionality reform efforts impossible but expands the continued carceral culture through the continued recycling of professionals institutionalized in perpetuating anti-Blackness. Specifically, leaders working in the family policing system (i.e., case management supervisors and program directors) and clinical supervisors of emerging child welfare clinicians are actors within the system's microcosm who have the authority to either perpetuate or dismantle the dominant white supremacist culture that persistently targets Black families and children. Of particular concern is the manifestation of systemic anti-Black racism in the decision-making among Black leaders and clinical supervisors.

National workforce demographics (including race/ethnicity, gender, worker training, and role) of staff in the family separation system are rarely collected (Williams-Mbengue & Barbee, 2023). The last available report from the National Survey of Child and Adolescent Well-Being (NSCAW II), published in 2011, solely provided demographics on frontline caseworkers, where these staff were 58 percent white, 24 percent Black, 15 percent Hispanic/Latino/a/x, and 4 percent were indicated as other. Similarly, states do not commonly track workforce demographics. Instead, states more often track trends in staff turnover and caseload ratios. This includes the state of California, which has consistently maintained the highest number of children in the custody of the state. However, Texas, the state indicated as having the second-largest population of children in custody and with persistent overrepresentation of Black children at each decision point, regularly reports demographic data on their workforce. Among those in supervisory or other leadership positions, the number of Black staff holding these positions is slightly higher than that of white staff and those in other racial/ethnic groups (Texas Department of Family and Protective Services, 2024). Despite the limited empirical evidence on the influence of workforce demographics on experiences and outcomes of Black system-involved children, racial, ethnic, and gender diversity among workforce leaders and supervisors could inform an improved understanding of the needs of Black communities that may prevent or limit system involvement. Still, even Black leaders and clinical supervisors are charged with enforcing racist policies and practices, rendering them as complicit (intentionally or unintentionally) as leaders across other racial groups. However, the nuances of Black leaders and supervisors in the family separation system should be considered in the context of "cultural imperialism," where the normalization of white supremacist culture prevails and justifies the separation of Black children from their families (Cantey et al., 2022). Therefore, through the lens of Black Critical Theory (BlackCrit), this chapter will assume the daunting task of examining racism within the system, and the role of leaders and clinical supervisors within and adjacent to the family policing system in sustaining racist practices.

History of Anti-Black Racism in Family Policing

It is important to operationalize the language of anti-Black racism and what it means in the context of the historical and contemporary family policing system. Kendi (2020) provides a direct and simplistic definition of racism as being a combination of ideas, policies, and practices that normalize racial inequities. He further defines a racist as one who supports inequitable policies, with the antiracist being one who supports antiracist policy. These definitions suggest a plain and uncomplicated understanding of a phenomenon broad in its harmful reach to minoritized Black individuals. But the persistent and insidious reality of anti-Black racism is nuanced and requires insight beyond a surface meaning. An understanding of anti-Black racism must be viewed as a condition – a constant presence – manifesting as both subtle and blatant. Authors have offered definitions of anti-Black racism from a theoretical lens, describing it as being dialectical, speaking to the reality of racial oppression of Black bodies and the resistance to oppression (Clarke et al., 2015).

The unique and vicious racism directed at Black people is rooted in colonialism and slavery, which persists in the form of sanctioned policies in systems of oppression. Anti-Black racism is multilayered and exists structurally, systemically, culturally, and individually, and its definition requires a simultaneous focus on whiteness and white supremacy (Damdar, 2018). It is through an ideology of white supremacy that norms and standards for rightness are produced. Further, whiteness ignites white dominance in social, political, economic, and cultural domains in society (Pon et al., 2017). Pertaining to anti-Black racism in the family policing system, Pon et al. (2017) say this system legitimizes anti-Black racism and the particular subjugation of Black mothers, resulting in a multitude of people and industries benefiting from the commodification of Black children. This definition underscores the capitalist underbelly in the family policing system that directly aligns with colonial slavery.

This history of anti-Black racism in the family policing system dates back centuries ago in 1619, at the start of chattel slavery lasting over two centuries, when Black children were born into slavery. The status of Black chattel slaves as inhuman and regarded as property for economic gain was the justification for the brutal treatment of Black children and their parents. The institution of slavery sanctioned the continued forced separation of Black families and children, with enslaved parents being denied any rights to maintain their family units. This meant that enslaved Black individuals could not marry and had no claim to their children, who could be bought, sold, or traded at the discretion of enslavers.

Under the laws of chattel slavery, Black children were considered the property of their enslavers, as Black youth were considered "wards of the state." Black parents, then and now, held no legal rights to custody or to raise and make decisions for their children. Similarly, Black enslaved families experienced the same forced family separation that Black families continue to experience in the current child welfare system, at the hands of legal actors who are given authority over the lives of Black children and their parents. In the "afterlife of slavery," the "modern" child welfare system emerged in the 1850s, when cities on the East Coast became crowded with Irish and Italian Catholic immigrants not considered white, and the Protestant minister Charles Loring Brace developed orphan trains to forcibly remove children from their parents, considered inferior. Meanwhile, Black children were subject to continued enslavement, indentured servitude, and forcible separation from their families and sale. In fact, while the child welfare system was emerging, Black children were excluded from any "care" that was provided to white immigrant children until the 1960s. While the Emancipation Proclamation officially abolished slavery, what followed was a wave of laws and policies that would preserve and expand the carceral state of white supremacy and reestablish the enslavement of Black children and families. For example, southern states enacted Black Codes, where arbitrary or trivial offenses were treated as criminal felonies and harsh punishment including incarceration was applied. Black Codes further prohibited interracial marriage and voting rights and allowed for the seizure of Black children for harsh labor.

It may be argued that the blatant evil intent of the institution of slavery conflicts with the benign presentation of the child welfare system. However, the ideologies and themes across both of these institutions present a continuum of industry, capitalism, and economic gain through the legally sanctioned dehumanization, surveillance, punishment, and control of Black people.

Decision-making "actors" in or adjacent to the American family policing system include social workers, teachers, law enforcement, and family court and juvenile judges (Johnson et al., 2009).

BlackCrit and the Continuation of Anti-Blackness in the Family Separation System

Race persists because it continues to be politically useful.
—*Dorothy Roberts*

This chapter is situated using the framework of BlackCrit. BlackCrit is appropriate for this chapter discussion as the framework examines and

Liberatory Models for Black Leaders 267

underscores anti-Blackness in the family separation system and the role of whiteness as the standard for humanity and morality. BlackCrit further centers the potential, possibilities, and empowerment of Black leaders and clinical supervisors tasked with navigating systemic anti-Black racism as they work in the family separation system.

BlackCrit is a theoretical framework, an extension of Bell's Critical Race Theory, that specifically centers on the presence of anti-Blackness in systems of oppression. BlackCrit intentionally, radically, and unapologetically unveils the antagonistic relationship existing in society between Blackness and humanity. Dumas and Ross (2016) introduced BlackCrit as a theorization existing within and in response to Critical Race Theory (CRT). With their original focus on applying their adapted framework to the marginalization of Black bodies in the education system, the central feature of BlackCrit specifically analyzes and confronts anti-Blackness embedded in the lived experiences of Black individuals (Dumas & Ross, 2016). In short, BlackCrit serves as an extension of CRT that focuses squarely on the Black experience.

BlackCrit is underscored by two foundational pillars – *anti-Blackness* and the *afterlife of slavery* (Wallace, 2022). The pillar of anti-Blackness determines the meaning of Blackness as the antithesis of humanity (Wallace, 2022), thus aligning humanness with whiteness. Under this pillar, Blackness in society is characterized as animalistic and measured by a digress from whiteness (humanity). The afterlife of slavery is the second pillar of BlackCrit and posits that the operation of Blackness is rooted in an understanding of the underpinnings of Blacks as chattel slaves, fixed in the consciousness of society (Hartman, 1997). Basically, "to be Black is to be a slave, to be a slave is to be an object" – and thus, devalued and even deserving of suffering (Wallace, 2022). Through this understanding, anti-Blackness emerges as a justified manifestation of structural oppression in practices and policies in systems.

In applying BlackCrit to a manifestation of anti-Black racism in the family separation system, particularly among Black leaders and clinical supervisors, we see how racist policies and procedures underscore an alignment with the mechanisms used in chattel slavery. Specifically, the targeting of Black children and families for forced separation and in the promotion of commerce. Thus, we apply BlackCrit as a critical race lens to analyze leadership and supervision in the family policing (child welfare) system. Understanding the role of anti-Blackness present in these micro-level roles among professionals in the family policing system through this lens presents a novel perspective that specifically interrogates Black dehumanization so deeply embedded in how administrators and clinical supervisors view and execute their roles.

Anti-Oppressive Clinical Supervision
By Shawna Marie Aarons-Cooke

Anti-oppressive supervision, utilizing a BlackCrit lens, is an opportunity to deliberately disrupt the status quo of anti-Black racism and bias in the family policing and separation system for the explicit purpose of engaging and transforming the workforce. The ultimate aim of anti-oppressive supervision is to eliminate the need for a child and family policing and separation system for Black children and their families. Imagine the possibilities for Black children and families being cared for, loved, supported, respected, and served. Imagine Black children and families thriving, happy, and free! It is a vision absent of oppressive practices, bias, stereotyping, and anti-Black racism. Surveillance, allegations, referrals, mandates, and removals are replaced with availability of support, services, resources, and respite. Concrete needs linked to the root causes of child neglect and maltreatment are met: food, housing, financial compensation and stability, social connection, and comprehensive medical care. Protective factors are cultivated. Social and emotional support and knowledge in parenting, child development, psycho-social-emotional learning, nutrition, health, and wellness are provided. Black identity, culture, and contributions are commonly acknowledged, appreciated, and integrated into society. Historic, current, systemic, and individual acts of anti-Black bias are acknowledged, addressed, decreased, and eventually eliminated, instead of denied or minimized. See Box 12.1.

Box 12.1 Case Vignette. A Black Caseworker Seeking Anti-Oppressive Supervision

By Shawna Marie Aarons-Cooke

Malika is a 40-years-young able-bodied Black/African American heterosexual cisgender married woman – the mother of three sons, aged 7, 14, and 15. Currently a licensed clinical social worker, she pursued a Master of Social Work degree following a 10-year career in public education, during which she was a middle school teacher and later an assistant principal in a school district located in a suburb near New York City. In public education, Malika was exposed to the family separation and policing system due to being a mandated reporter. In both of those roles, she either independently, with supervision, or through supervising others, reported allegations of child abuse and neglect to the mandated reporter hotline. Malika became increasingly inspired to directly intervene and support the children and families she encountered through supervising others, many of whom had concrete needs, trauma, and difficult life circumstances.

Shifting into a social worker position in a children's services program after completing her MSW and ultimately obtaining her LCSW licensure, Malika felt conflicted about her work and was often concerned about what she believed to be harm caused by the very system that was supposedly designed to help children and families. Inspecting homes, checking the refrigerator, looking through kitchen cabinets, and reviewing a parent's completion of various assigned tasks while imposing home visits and dictating services and tasks with prescribed deadlines felt disrespectful and intrusive. The majority of children and families she encountered were of Black African, Caribbean, Indigenous, and Latin heritage. Malika was often assigned the cases her supervisor Carol and team referred to as "most difficult" – supposedly because she was "better able to handle them," "the families trusted her," and "she used to live in this same community growing up," as her supervisor Carol would say. Now in her third year at this agency, Malika was feeling burned out, disillusioned, and untrusting of her supervisor Carol. According to Malika, Carol was oblivious to the ways that she exhibited bias toward the Black children, cultural norms, staff, and Malika – despite completing the required annual cultural competency training. Carol, a 37-years-young cisgender white woman of Italian heritage, would dismiss or avoid any mention of race. She would often say, "I don't see color," "I treat everyone the same," and "I don't have a racist bone in my body" when Malika or other staff members highlighted decisions and attitudes that seemed biased. During meetings, Carol would awkwardly pepper her communication with Black American urban slang, which Malika believed was Carol's effort at being more relatable to the team of primarily Black and Latin caseworkers and clinicians.

During a recent one-on-one supervision session, Malika presented the case of a 24-years-young Black mother of three children – twin 5-year-old sons and a 3-year-old daughter. The allegation of neglect was founded due to the mother's choice not to administer Attention Deficit Hyperactivity Disorder (ADHD) medications recommended by a local psychiatrist after a school-required evaluation. According to their teacher, the boys were hyperactive, disruptive, oppositional, defiant, and aggressive. The mother was forced to have them evaluated in order for them to return to school, which she did; however, she did not agree with the assessment and dual diagnoses of ADHD and Oppositional Defiant Disorder (ODD), nor the recommendation for medication. The mother alleged that the teacher and psychiatrist were biased in their assessments and were not open to any other solutions or interventions to support the twins. Now that Malika had worked with the family providing in-home therapy and monitoring, she agreed with the mother's assessment of the situation. Malika did not observe ADHD or ODD symptomatology in either of the boys. She did not see a need to medicate the twins and did not agree that the mother needed to complete further monitoring or the required parenting program course. Additionally, the mother's work schedule and obligations to her church did not enable her to complete a required parenting skills program, which both Malika and the mother did not think was necessary. Malika found the mother to be attentive, appropriate, and highly skilled as a parent. She was observed to be attuned to her children responsive, instructive, and encouraging. Philosophically, Malika did not believe the case should have been founded for neglect, and she didn't want to follow Carol's guidance to remind the mother that she risked her kids being removed if she didn't complete the parenting skills program and initiate medication for the twins by the prescribed date. When Malika advocated for flexibility and understanding based on her assessment, Carol resorted to criticizing Malika for making excuses and overidentifying with the mother – likely because of their shared identities as Black working mothers of three children. Carol advised Malika that her blind spot was that she overidentified with the children and families on her caseload. Carol further shared that she believed Malika was "always bringing up race and making excuses for the families." Carol ended supervision with, "*These aren't your kids, Malika! She needs to get the boys on meds and take the parenting class. It's really that simple.*"

Malika had a difficult time for the remainder of the day following this supervision session. She felt strongly that Carol's ignorance about the racial social context in the United States and its impact on each of them – as well as the lives of the children and families in care – contributed to her perpetuation of individual and structural racism via their supervisory relationship. Her Black and Latin coworkers on the team had shared similar sentiments in private conversations. Differently, her white coworkers primarily remained silent, with one suggesting Malika was reading too much into things. This coworker additionally speculated that if a Black supervisor had said the same thing, Malika wouldn't think anything of it. Initially unsure what to do in response to yet another dismissive encounter with her supervisor, compounded by the racially divided responses of her coworkers, Malika chose to confer with another supervisor at her agency who she hopes will take an anti-oppressive approach.

QUESTIONS FOR REFLECTION:

1. Does Carol effectively consider the social context of anti-Black racism and bias that may influence her perspectives as well as the lived experiences of Malika, the mother, and the children?

2. Is it possible that anti-Black bias and racism played a role in the assessments and determinations made by the teacher, psychiatrist, and investigative unit?
3. In what ways does Carol's supervision of Malika reflect oppressive practices that harm Malika, the mother, and the children? Consider the specific behaviors and decision points that undermine the supervisory relationship and the lives of this family.
4. Would you see things similarly or differently if Malika's supervisor were Black and behaved in the exact same manner described earlier? What if her supervisor were a Black male?

Applying Anti-Oppressive Principles and Practices

Individuals seeking to embrace an anti-oppressive approach to supervision in the current family policing and separation system must undertake ongoing personal development grounded in the teachings of Paulo Freire, Frantz Fanon, Carter G. Woodson, bell hooks, and Barbara Soloman. These scholars promote consciousness-raising and empowerment of the oppressed. Fanon, Woodson, hooks, and Soloman were Black scholars whose writings speak specifically to the oppression and empowerment of Black people. Miller and Garran (2022) highlight the importance of lifelong learning regarding race, racialization, racism, capitalism, and oppression in social work supervision. Cultivating a continually expanding critical awareness of the realities of past and present oppression, as well as engaging in critical reflection that motivates action to address the inequitable social conditions of the marginalized and oppressed, is necessary if one intends to disrupt their participation in the ongoing oppression of Black children, families, and workers.

The process of learning to critically read dehumanizing social conditions, engaging in critical reflection, strengthening one's critical motivations, and undertaking critical action all comprise what Freire (1996, 2005, 2021) refers to as critical consciousness (Diemer et al., 2016). The potential power of critical consciousness is the motivation it inspires to change oppressive beliefs, behaviors, and systems. Specifically, in the family policing and separation system, critical consciousness is needed among disempowered and marginalized Black children, families, and the workforce. By developing an understanding of oppressive practices, the larger context of anti-Black racism, bias, and marginalization that create the context of the Black experience inside and beyond the family policing and separation system, one has a basis from which motivation for critical action can ensue.

Dr. Cornell West poignantly asks for self-reflection as to how the collective of individuals who comprise the US American society has become so well-adjusted to injustice (West, 2018). He encourages those considering anti-oppressive approaches to have the courage to break out of a normalization of conformity and collusion to injustice: "It's critical to understand your history and then be true to oneself in such a way that one's connection to the suffering of others is an integral part of understanding yourself" (p. 635). Unlearning the ways of oppression becomes a touchstone as well as a rite of passage into anti-oppressive ways of being and supervising. The movement and evolution of one's efforts are from the status quo of oppressive practices to anti-oppressive empowerment practices.

The following section provides guidance from which one can conceptualize personal development in critical consciousness, informed by Black empowerment, liberation models, and a potential for continuous quality improvement in individual, team, and organizational progress. As you explore each sub-area for reflection, keep in mind the aim of moving from oppressive practices to anti-oppressive practices. Though the social norms and standard for many generations may be dominance, power, control, hierarchy, and competition, anti-oppressive practices are grounded in community, co-creation, collaboration, choice, respect, equity, and dignity of all.

Self-Awareness and Positionality

The first area for reflection is self-awareness and positionality. Supervisors of all ethno-cultural identities will benefit from considering the cultural identities that inform one's lived experience, attentive to sources of privilege, power, marginalization, and subordination. Reflect upon one's experiences with racialization and racial identity development. What are the beliefs that one holds about Black/African people? Pay special attention to exposure and internalization of stereotypes, myths, and falsehoods. Assessment tools that can be helpful include the Antiracist Style Indicator (Plummer, 2020), available at https://asi.dlplummer.com, and the Implicit Bias assessment tests, available at https://implicit.harvard.edu/implicit/takeatest.html. The Antiracist Style Indicator can provide objective information as to how effective one is in addressing racism: functioning, under-functioning, or over-functioning. The authors recommend the Race (Black–White) Implicit Assessment Test and the Skin Tone (Light Skin–Dark Skin) Implicit Assessment Test to assist in uncovering areas of anti-Black bias. The aims for one's assessments and reflections are: (1) Assess initial level of awareness, and (2) Inform the directions one may explore gaining further understanding via self-study and formal learning opportunities.

In the case of Carol, she is able-bodied, white of Italian heritage, cisgender, working, and serving in a supervisory role within an agency. She receives unearned privileges based on her known racial identity as white. Carol benefits from the power she holds by her title and role as a supervisor in the agency, with the ability to make decisions that impact her supervisees and all the children and families with whom they work. She may experience subordination due to her gender as a woman. Completing the Antiracist Style Indicator will greatly benefit her in gaining self-awareness as to the ways she may be under-functioning and provide information as to how she can work toward becoming a functioning antiracist. Completing the Implicit Assessment Tests for Black–White and Light Skin–Dark Skin, will likely be compelling and highly informative.

Child(ren) and Youth

Similar considerations are important points of reflection for each child and youth in care. Suspend the temptation to take shortcuts or make assumptions about the child(ren) for whom you are working. Each is a unique individual, even within the same family. What are the cultural and other identities that inform each child's lived experiences and context? What is their current level of racial awareness? How have they internalized Black identity? What, if any, experiences have they had of subordination and/or marginalization? What and where are their sources of Black empowerment? What are their areas of strength, resilience, and support? Which protective factors are active? Holistically, what needs are currently unmet? How can resources be made available to solve any identified areas of need?

The aims of these assessments and reflections are to: (1) See each child with fresh eyes as a lovable and precious being; (2) to gain awareness of each child's risk of harm by you as supervisor, your decisions, the team processes, protocols, and society overall; and (3) honor each child's individuality, history, social context, and worthiness of liberation. A measurement of success is the removal and placement of a child exclusively if the child is in imminent danger. Additionally, any recommendations for a child must be critically scrutinized, mindful of potential for bias, anti-Black racism, and oppression by individual and/or systemic factors. In the case example, the information provided about the twin boys implies that anti-Black bias may have served as the inspiration behind over-surveillance and exaggerated attributions of misconduct by their teacher, as well as the ease with which they were labeled, diagnosed, and recommended for medication.

Family

Each family is ideally assessed and considered in their unique context, mindful of the cultural identities and positionality of each member as well as for the family as a unit. Do all encounters, practices, and recommendations for the family support the dignity and empowerment of each family member? How can chosen family structures and systems be honored? Take into consideration the likelihood that, as a Black family, the members are survivors of intergenerational trauma related to long-standing anti-Black racism, oppression, subordination, and marginalization. Consider what ongoing stressors may be related to financial instability, concerns about physical and psycho-social-emotional safety, risk of police encounters and legal system involvement, and general ongoing surveillance and policing because of anti-Blackness across every socioeconomic class. What resources can be made available to meet the real identified needs of the family without policing, separation, and mandating or dictating their behaviors serving as an arm of further oppression and subordination?

The aims of these reflection points are to (1) cultivate respect, love, and support of Black families thriving; (2) honor the strength, resilience, hope, and creativity prevalent among Black families; (3) provide resources that meet the needs the family identify; (4) cultivate compassion, care, and service among the workforce; and (5) eliminate separations for neglect. The outcome measure of effective anti-oppressive practices for the family can be the provision of resources, that is, financial contributions, rent payments, food purchases, eviction prevention, supported housing placements, linkage to respite services, and linkages to care and additional supports. In the case example, the noted cause of concern to the family are the collective insertion of mandated psychiatric evaluation and pathologizing diagnoses given to 5-year-old typical children, penalization and surveillance by Child Protective Services, and the imposition of parenting classes and administration of medications that the mother does not feel are necessary.

Community

Strengths-based reflections about the Black community include a thorough understanding of Africultural coping strategies and hope thrust as protective factors (Utsey et al., 2000). According to a group of researchers

Liberatory Models for Black Leaders

(Daly et al., 1995), Black US Americans rely on group-driven strengths such as family, community, and social support networks in addition to spiritual approaches like prayer and meditation. They also learned that forming relationships with other Black or African Americans and rituals are utilized for seeking guidance in times of stress. The research of others (Ani, 1990; Hollaway, 1990; Sutherland, 1993) indicates that many spiritual practices from West and Central Africa have been preserved and are practiced by Black African Americans. An African worldview, values, and beliefs are also present among many Black Americans, such as connection to spirituality, nature, and the collective of humanity. Among Black people there seems to be a tendency to believe that all events have meaning and purpose, and that all things are connected. Although the studies on the topic are dated by 10 or more years, the identified coping behaviors are importantly positioned as sources of strength as opposed to as deficiencies, which is how they are seen in traditional Eurocentric coping paradigms (Utsey et al., 2000).

According to Utsey et al. (2000), Africultural coping strategies cluster into four categories: cognitive and emotional debriefing, spiritual-centered coping, ritual-centered coping, and collective coping.

Cognitive and Emotional Debriefing

- Trying to forget about the situation
- Try to remove oneself from the situation
- Finding other things to keep busy
- Convincing oneself that the situation wasn't that bad
- Spending more time than usual doing group activities
- Hoping that things will get better with time
- Seeking out people who will make one laugh
- Getting dressed up in one's best clothing
- Attending a social event to reduce stress
- Watching comedy shows

Spiritual-Centered Coping

- Praying that things will work themselves out
- Attending church or other spiritual gathering to get help from the group
- Reading a spiritual book or scripture for comfort and guidance
- Reading a passage from a daily meditation book
- Asking someone to pray for you
- Asking for blessings from a spiritual or religious person

- Singing a song to help reduce the stress
- Leaving the matter in God's hands

Ritual-Centered Coping

- Lighting a candle for strength or guidance
- Burning incense
- Use a cross or other object that has special powers
- Paying homage to deities and/or ancestors

Collective Coping

- Gather a group of family or friends to help with the problem
- Seek emotional support from family and friends
- Share feelings with a friend or family member
- Remember what a parent or elder once said about dealing with these kinds of situations
- Thought of all the struggles Black people have had to endure to give oneself strength
- Seek advice from an elder in the family or community
- Ask for suggestions on how to deal with the situation during a meeting of social group
- Help others with their problems (prioritizing group needs over individual needs)

Another important protective factor is survival thrust (Kambon, 1992), which means hoping that things will get better with time. This practice is generally thought to have evolved out of the hundreds of years Black Africans were enslaved and oppressed in the United States. Despite the historical and current burdens Black people endure due to the perpetual trauma and assault of anti-Black racism, marginalization, and oppression, a belief in the collective good and eventual liberation of the community that enables hope as well as survival.

Supervisors ideally cultivate an understanding and admiration of Africultural Coping Strategies, recognizing the protective role these strategies play among Black people. Additional aims for anti-oppressive practice include validating hope and the power of hope thrust among Black families, and embracing community empowerment, liberation and collective good for Black people. Supervisors can measure progress by satisfaction surveys for all families who encounter the system. Survey questions will inquire as to respect, hope, support, helpfulness, and rating of experience, potentially including a Net Promoter Score to determine their willingness to refer others to the system.

In the case example, the mother's mistrust of medical interventions and reliance on her spiritual belief system and community is better understood in the context of historic and current anti-Black racism and the prevalence of misdiagnoses for Black children. In fact, her actions align with Africultural Coping Strategies, reflecting implementation of spiritually centered coping as well as cognitive and emotional debriefing. Recognizing and validating her coping strategies and her advocacy for her sons could have served as an empowering intervention. Instead of judging, dismissing, and penalizing her choices, essentially dominating and subjugating her while wielding the power of the family policing and separation system, Carol could have seen what Malika observed as indicators that an injustice had occurred when the investigation for neglect was founded. Overturning the finding, correcting the record, and releasing the mother from supervised services is exemplary of an anti-oppressive approach that can create children and families empowerment system in place of a policing and separation system of dominance and oppression.

Supervisee

The supervisor's role remains accountable to supporting the evolution and critical consciousness raising of supervisees. Points of reflection and coaching for supervisees include cultivating self-awareness, situational awareness, liberatory approaches, and a reality-based knowledge of current and historical harm of anti-Black racism, oppression, marginalization, as well as the traumas caused by the child and family policing system. Supervisors have an obligation to support and monitor the supervisee's contributions to child, family, and community empowerment. This can look like shared decision-making, strengths-based assessments, and the provision of resources to meet the actual and real needs of the children and family in their care.

The three aims of supervisory efforts include: (1) personal transformation of individuals in every role and level of involvement, (2) cultivating a critically conscious workforce committed to Black children and families thriving, and (3) the creation of an impactful Black children and family empowerment system. The Antiracist Style Indicator, Race (Black–White) Implicit Assessment Test, and Skin Tone (Light Skin–Dark Skin Implicit Assessment Test) can be helpful tools for assessment and monitoring of supervisee evolution to functional antiracist with minimal to no bias over time. Measures of success may include high quality children and family assessments reflective of empowerment and collaborative support plans. Additionally, children and family satisfaction surveys and the types and quantities of supportive services provided can be utilized to demonstrate progress.

In the case example, Malika demonstrated a high level of critical consciousness, self-awareness, situational awareness, liberatory approaches, and reality-based knowledge of race and bias. For her ongoing evolution and continued growth as an antiracist, anti-oppressive, empowerment-based worker co-conspiring for the liberation of Black children and families, the Antiracist Style Indicator and Implicit Assessment Tests will be important. Being that she is also a member of the Black community, she is also subject to oppression, bias, and anti-Black racism; therefore, additional support will be helpful for her to prevent burnout and equip her for the parallel process she may experience along with her caseload. She has intersecting oppressed identities as a Black woman subject to subordination, scrutiny, surveillance, and stressors that exceed and differ from her supervisor. Their relationship will benefit from collaboration in cultivating critical consciousness and creating an antiracist, anti-oppressive child and family's empowerment system.

Systems

In closing, reflection and efforts in critical consciousness, motivation, and action in the aforementioned areas set the stage for systems change. With a comprehensive understanding of the systemic oppression, supervisors must remain mindful of the current and historic practices that contribute to systems that oppress Black children and families. Further reflection in the area includes consideration of opportunities to transform the current policing and separation system into an empowerment system for Black children and families. What are the opportunities for transformation – what must be stopped and what must be started? What mechanisms are in place to reward assimilation to dominant social norms (i.e., elevating whiteness and Eurocentrism while denigrating, undermining or erasing Blackness and African centeredness?) What outcome measures reflect a truly caring and supportive system for empowering Black children and families, without harming them?

The aims for reflection at the systems level include: (1) challenge assumptions; (2) see the whole, the parts, and how they are interrelated; (3) work toward the end of the child and family policing and separation system as we know it, supplanting it with the emergence of Black children and family's empowerment system.

Supervision is broadly considered the mechanism for providing guidance, support, education, and accountability across fields and disciplines (Kadushin & Harkness, 2014). Social work interns and interns within the helping and healthcare professions receive supervision as part of their education and practical training. Once employed, supervision

Liberatory Models for Black Leaders 279

becomes the means by which they continue to receive guidance, support, education, and accountability. Similarly, the workforce and interns in the family policing system and adjacent fields (i.e., daycare, education, healthcare, social services, mental health, and addiction services, police, and courts), all have methods for training, accountability, and management via supervision. Given the global implementation of supervision in the hierarchies both within and adjacent to the family policing system, anti-oppressive supervision is a pivotal point of intervention to address the deplorable disparities in the treatment and outcomes of Black children and families. See Box 12.2.

Box 12.2 Case Vignette. Addressing Racial Disparities in Alternative Response

By Tanya Rollins

Yolanda is a program director of a county-run family policing division. Her division conducts Alternative Response Investigations (ARI). ARI is a new program designed to prevent families from fully entering the family policing system by offering services to families to mitigate safety concerns without determining a child abuse or neglect disposition. Yolanda is aware of the documented racial inequities in the family policing system from her master's level social work program and her agency's training program. Yolanda is adamant that she is providing equitable services to all families and that she is leading her division in a fair manner.

Recently, Yolanda's program administrator has informed her that a cursory look at data indicates that Black families are less likely to be referred to the alternative response program. Her program administrator has charged her with determining the course of action to resolve the issue. Yolanda is aware that previous attempts to address racial inequities in her department have been met with resistance at all levels of the department and among interested parties external to the department. Yolanda is hesitant to accept the charge. Yolanda tells a colleague that she thinks that the agency's focus on race and racism is unwarranted, and it is divisive.

The profession of social work calls us to promote our core values of social justice, integrity, and the importance of human relationships as we strive for an anti-oppressive future (Smith et al., 2022). Anti-oppressive practice (AOP) is concerned with "eradicating social injustice perpetrated by societal structural inequalities" (Dumbrill, 2003, p. 102). AOP typically addresses structural inequities along the lines of race, gender, sexual orientation and identity, ability, age, class, occupation, and service usage (Dumbrill, 2003). AOP, like many social justice frameworks, does not directly address anti-Blackness. In addition to this flaw, Dumbrill (2003) suggests that the family policing system is the nemesis of anti-oppressive practice (AOP) as attempts to dismantle systemic inequities as the origins of child welfare lie in the efforts of the privileged to control those they see as a threat to their dominance.

Akin to anti-oppressive clinical supervision, anti-oppressive leadership serves as an opportunity to deliberately disrupt the status quo of traditional leadership modalities used within family policing. Family policing similar to the social work discipline has traditionally subscribed to hierarchical organizational structures and over-relied on traditional methodologies thus contributing to a systemic resistance to change (Sinha, 2020). Hence, social work and family policing continue to emphasize authority-based models as solution mechanisms (Sinha, 2020). Tham and Strömberg (2020) assert that family policing organizations push managers toward a leadership role based on control and authority, prioritizing processes of quantitative measuring, monitoring, and control. These are all characteristics associated with transactional leadership. Traditional leadership styles such as transactional leadership are "rooted in capitalist and imperialist motivations that have led to practices of gaining authority over people" (Daus-Magbual &Tintiangco-Cubales, 2016, p. 184). This form of leadership is rooted in white, Eurocentric, and patriarchal ideologies and thought to be neutral (Khalifa et al., 2013). Transactional leadership, common in government organizations such as family policing, creates policies in which a dominant group benefits and others do not (Daus-Magbual & Tintiangco-Cubales, 2016). These realizations emphasize the importance of re-thinking leadership approaches in family policing and the impact of leadership practices on the outcomes of children and families impacted by this system and other systems.

Family policing has failed to veer past traditional leadership models and meet the challenges of engaging in anti-oppressive and anti-Black practices. Thus, it is of no surprise that current literature related to anti-oppressive leadership within child welfare is scant despite the large degree of scholarship related to the overrepresentation of Black and Indigenous children and families in foster care. Given the dearth of literature related to anti-oppressive leadership that directly addresses anti-Black racism in family policing, we have chosen to incorporate the following principles and practices to complement the overarching framework for anti-oppressive supervision within child welfare and organizations that interlock with child welfare (*all institutions*).

Applying Anti-Oppressive Principles and Practices – Co-creation

While co-creation appears to be a simplistic concept, institutions often have difficulty operationalizing the concept. This difficulty may be seen in the dehumanization of persons impacted by systems of oppression. In addition, co-creating across systems and truly engaging persons harmed by said systems is a difficult and daunting task. Yet, if leaders look to those most impacted by systems, then one begins to lead with liberation at the center. People of color, those most adversely impacted by child welfare, advocates, judges, internal staff, and organizations must be engaged in feedback processes, planning, and implementation with shared decision-making power and leadership (Schelbe & Geiger, 2022; Conley et al., 2018; NCWWI, 2020). Co-creation with the goal of establishing a system that supports not punishes, often involves asking youth and parents affected by the family policing system to revisit trauma including the trauma of family separation. Organizations do not have to engage in trauma porn to impact change. Engaging in trauma porn demonstrates a failure on the part of systems to recognize institutional harm and the mental strain on persons impacted by said systems. Additionally, Schelbe and Geiger (2022) caution family policing, researchers, and interested parties from engaging in tokenism which prevents true collaboration.

Co-creation involves establishing the "we" to create a sense of belonging and opens the door for collective problem-solving (Manuel, 2020) and co-creation of policies, practices, and legislation. Jurisdictions in Texas and Broward County, Florida have created frameworks to engage with those most impacted by systems – the Texas Community Engagement Model (TCEM) and Authentic Family Engagement and Strengthening Approach (AFES) (Best et al., 2021; Rodriguez et al., 2014). Actively engaging in co-creation processes may mitigate the impacts of invisibility and marginalization of Black mothers impacted by the family policing system by providing a venue for expression.

Co-creation of policy, practices, and legislation will also allow for shared learning and may impact the practices and policies of partnering organizations. For instance, social workers are mandated reporters, persons required by law to report suspected child abuse and neglect, yet they are often unaware of the harms of family policing or even how a case proceeds once a report is made. Most mandated reporters have not been informed that "being Black is not an inherent risk factor for child abuse and neglect" (Berkman et al., 2022, p. 298) yet Black children and families are substantially more likely to be reported to the family policing system with the top reporters being law enforcement, educators, and medical professionals (Kelly et al., 2022; Kim et al., 2017). Mandated reporters are often contacting family policing as a plea for help for children and families, yet the report is treated as an allegation of wrongdoing (Melton, 2005). As a reaction to the realities of mandated reporting, JMAC For Families, an organization led by persons impacted by the family policing system, coined the term *mandated supporting* to describe situations in which mandating reporters provide necessary support and or services to families instead of reporting (Mandated Supporting, 2024). By sharing this information with co-creators as one navigates the creative process, involved social workers, community members, and advocates can rethink their role as mandated reporters. They can imagine a world where they replace surveillance with family support by providing services, resources, and respite.

Race-Explicit Strategy

"Leadership is not neutral" (Shah et al., 2022, p. 2). Anti-oppressive leadership requires that we abandon so-called color-blind and race-neutral strategies. Leaders must name racism, anti-Blackness, and other forms of oppression. Leaders must intentionally examine systems of oppression and white supremacy and how they operate within family policing impacting outcomes for children, families, and staff (Conley et al., 2018; NCWWI, 2020). Specifically, leaders must critique how anti-Blackness and the overrepresentation of Black children in the care of the child welfare system is legitimized by a narrative of child welfare professionals as "heroines/heroes who are saving the racial 'other' from their deficient parents" (Pon et al., 2017, p. 76). *BlackCrit* requires that leaders confront the specificity of anti-Blackness, as it is embodied in the lived experiences of social suffering and resistance (Dumas & Ross, 2016). In confronting the specificity of anti-Blackness, leaders should consider that in "public discourse and cultural politics, Black women then become either invisible, marginalized or without an adequate framework to make sense of and explain everyday experiences of multidimensional oppression" (Dumas & Ross, 2016, pp. 422–423).

Leading with an anti-oppressive framework requires that we make the system and inequities visible (Manuel, 2020). Leaders must identify internal and external politics that impact outcomes and strategically act accordingly (NCWWI, 2020). Leaders in Minnesota demonstrated this in the passage of the Minnesota African American Family Preservation Act. While the introduced bill specifically targeted Black children and families and the signed bill removed this distinction, the collective community action is an example of navigating anti-Blackness in successfully enacting legislation that changes the burden of proof required by the family policing system.

Restorative Justice Oriented

Utilizing restorative justice in leadership requires one to be accountable to Black communities and those most impacted by the system. Essentially, we must develop mutual ownership and responsibility in leading change (Wilder et al., 2019). Accountability requires us to do as Du Bois suggested and acknowledge the structural forces shaping institutional disparities (Wilder et al., 2019). Leaders in the family policy system must confront the reliance on carceral logic and its impact on institutional disparities. Weber (2022) describes carceral logic as:

> There are parents and caregivers (the 'terrible few') harming children, and the state, which is deemed to be best situated to keep children safe, must intervene to protect them. This cultural logic, which is rooted in anti-Black racism, requires that the state punish, surveil, and regulate families in order to promote safety.

Denouncing carceral logic will support leaders engaging in truth and reconciliation. "The truth and reconciliation movement has received little attention in the social work literature in the United States yet holds great value as a pathway to the realization of the social justice goals of the profession" (Havig & Byers, 2019). Rooted in the rituals of Indigenous and African populations (Braithwaite, 2018), restorative justice is the name given to a variety of different practices, including apologies, restitution, and acknowledgments of harm and injury, as well as to other efforts to provide healing and reintegration of offenders into their communities, with or without additional punishment (Menkel-Meadow, 2007). According to Menkel-Meadow (2007), in its most idealized form, the four Rs of restorative justice are repair, restore, reconcile, and reintegrate the offenders and victims to each other and their shared community. Transformation of child welfare "lies in remedies formulated by service users" (Dumbrill, 2003, p. 101). Adopting a restorative justice framework requires leaders to re-examine traditional hierarchical organizational structures and power dynamics. Directly associated with supervision in child welfare, this requires relational power acquisition. Restorative justice has been used in child welfare in the form of family-group decision-making. Restorative justice may also take the form of truth and reconciliation commissions, such as the Maine Wabanaki State Child Welfare Truth and Reconciliation Commission, a collaborative effort between family policing and tribes to promote healing and accountability for the centuries of family separation inflicted on Indigenous children and families (Havig & Byers, 2019).

Systemic Analysis

Leading through an anti-oppressive lens requires us to engage in root-cause analysis of disparities. It is not sufficient for us to simply name racism, sexism, anti-Blackness, heterosexism, etc. as the root cause for the current manifestations of oppression. Root cause analysis (RCA) has been defined as a "collective term used to describe a wide range of approaches, methods, and techniques used to uncover causes of a problem" (Andersen & Fager Haug, 2006, p. 13). This requires that child welfare research, identify, and address data and systemic dynamics in a variety of arrangements while utilizing a variety of techniques for dissemination. This also requires that child welfare leaders look beyond agency-generated data to inform decisions. Partnering with community organizations to collect and analyze data is an effective approach to mitigating organizational biases. *Measure* located in Austin, Texas, is a research and data activism organization founded and operated by Black women and committed to elevating the lived experiences and using data to impact change (Our Story, 2024). Organizations such as this are essential in co-creating accessible data and promoting Black empowerment.

Additionally, it is suggested that program analyses are conducted using principles grounded in abolitionism. Weber (2022) suggests utilizing a methodology that includes the following questions: (1) Does the proposal/policy increase or decrease the power of the state? (2) Does the proposal/policy maintain a carceral logic requiring surveillance, regulation, and punishment of families? and (3) Does the proposal/policy end current harms and prevent future harms to Black children and families?

Critical Consciousness and Sustainability

Cultivating a culture of practice (Conley et al., 2018) requires critical consciousness-raising. As mentioned earlier in the chapter, critical consciousness-raising is a process of cultivating critical awareness and action to address oppressive social conditions. To guard against simplistic interpretations of information from an anti-Black perspective, child welfare professionals must constantly engage in CCR and critical self-reflexion (Pon et al., 2017). Leaders must develop a "deepened consciousness of what racism is and how the child welfare system functions to generate or permeate accumulated advantages and disadvantages based on race" (Best et al., 2021, p. 114). Anti-oppressive supervision and leadership strategies are intrinsically connected and thus leaders must take into consideration the cost of time and trauma related to institutional trauma over the course of a lifespan. This requires working with a trauma-informed lens in a holistic manner.

Beyond critical consciousness engagement, leaders must create sustainable change. This requires the incorporation of anti-oppressive practices into the everyday practices, policies, culture, and functioning of

Liberatory Models for Black Leaders 285

child welfare. Child welfare must abandon the "bright, shiny, blinky" approach to change and move toward creating a system that is based on liberation. It has been noted that true integration of policies remains elusive in family policing (Rodriguez et al., 2014). In addition, child welfare must guard against anti-Black practices and policies that are codified into law. This can be accomplished by leaders looking beyond the organization's policy handbook and actively engaging in the political processes. After all, all social work is political (Abramovitz, 1993).

Conclusion/Call to Action

This interactive chapter intentionally underscores the ongoing presence of anti-Black racism in the family separation and policing system, with a specific focus on its presence among Black leaders and clinical supervisors in this system. Distinct from previous work that examines anti-Black racism in the family separation and policing system, this work goes further to offer practical strategies for Black leaders and supervisors to transform how they engage in their practice roles. To be an antiracist and anti-oppressive practitioner is not only to consciously and boldly call out anti-Black racism, but also to be inspired to liberate self, the workforce, supervisees, and clients. Ultimately, the message here is to empower primarily Black leaders and supervisors through increased self-reflection and examination, to develop a heightened confidence to be allies to Black children and families. In summary, we call leaders and supervisors to ACTIVATE through tasks that include:

- Ongoing and critical self-reflection individually and collectively with colleagues engaged, knowledgeable, and invested in liberatory child welfare practice.
- Nurturing and cultivating spaces for professionals in the child welfare workforce (i.e., supervisees, front-line workers) to learn and embrace skills necessary to be empowered anti-oppressive practitioners.
- Consistent modeling of brave liberatory leadership that also reflects a leader's ability to exude humility and authenticity.

Antiracist and anti-oppressive leadership and supervision are imperative in dismantling systemic discriminatory practices in the family policing and family separation system. It is through these roles and positions that sustainable and transformative change can occur. Thus, Black leaders and supervisors in this system should have the necessary tools and skills that digress from the strategies that are informed by white supremacy and social control. Leaders and supervisors must be supported in their journey to transform into anti-oppressive leaders without the risk of repercussions for challenging the status quo. Ultimately, strategies presented in the chapter help to lay a firm foundation for rebuilding and reimagining supportive processes that preserve families and children.

Discussion Questions

1. Using the information presented on anti-oppressive leadership, what actions should Yolanda take in determining the course of action to address the disparity in ARI?
2. How does the call for action in this chapter integrate and overlap with previous themes in lenses offered throughout this text?

Integrated Model of Supervision and Leadership

The integrated model of supervision and leadership (Figure 12.1) is a process model that encompasses three phases – systemic analysis, ideation, and implementation. The first phase, systemic analysis, is primarily focused on reflection, data gathering, and root cause analysis. The second phase, ideation, allows for synthesizing of information collected in the systemic analysis phase and engaging in solution formation. The third

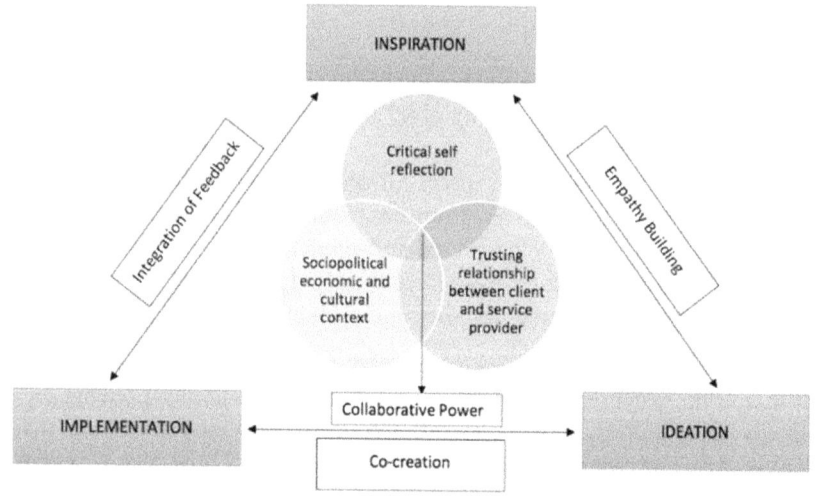

Figure 12.1 Integrated model of supervision and leadership (Sinha, 2020).

phase, implementation, focuses on performance and evaluation. Outcomes are contingent upon co-creation and the centering of impacted persons' voices. There is fluidity and movement through the model which is grounded in critical consciousness, relational power, and liberation. See Box 12.3.

Box 12.3 Case Vignette. Hazel

By Nathaniel L. Currie

Put yourself in the position of the clinical social work supervisor in this case vignette. One of your roles in a community mental health program at a local community health center is to run a practicum clinic and provide group and individual supervision to undergraduate and graduate social work students. A new clinical intern, Hazel, was in her early twenties and, prior to entering practicum, had discussed her history of physical abuse, mentioning she never wanted to have to report abuse or neglect to Child Protective Services, despite understanding that she is a mandated reporter. During this practicum experience, Hazel receives individual supervision from a Licensed Clinical Social Worker (LCSW) who had previously worked in the child welfare system. As Clinical Director, you provided both group supervision and on-site as-needed supervision to the clinic team. Hazel was assigned a client through the clinic and began to provide therapeutic services, which are video recorded. In this instance, the client was a 14-year-old Latina cisgender female who lived with her father and stepmother due to prior neglect by her mother. During treatment, the 14-year-old client disclosed that she smoked marijuana and drank strawberry wine coolers with her mother and minor cousins during a weekend visit, claiming, "*It was awesome*"!

Clinic procedure requires student counselors to obtain immediate supervision if a client makes an allegation of abuse or neglect. Hazel did not come out of the session to report the incident and seek supervision support, and said nothing after the session concluded. Later in the week, during Hazel's one-hour individual supervision session, the supervisor watching the tape realized that the child's statement required a protective services report. Her supervisor walked Hazel through the procedures of writing and filing the report, which Hazel did without resistance. Several days later, with her direct supervisor out of the office, Hazel comes into your office and states, "*I feel like crap, I've ruined her life.*"

Hazel expressed fear that the client would never return for therapy and feared that the client would hate her. She reported imagining all sorts of consequences including that the child's father would no longer allow the child to see her mother and that the child would no longer disclose information if she did return to therapy. She questioned her decision to make an abuse or neglect report and reported feeling angry at her supervisor.

Hazel's reaction was consistent with reactions reported in the literature and did not bode well for future ethical practice. You and Hazel discussed the issue first from a legal standpoint, reminding her that as a mandated reporter she must make the report or risk her future license and possible criminal charges. Then you addressed the issues from an ethical perspective, reviewing the ethical codes including welfare to client, confidentiality, boundaries, and multiple or dual relationships. You challenged Hazel on viewing herself as the child's protector and taking responsibility for her happiness. You linked her reaction to her own personal history and discussed how her countertransference impeded her ability to make ethical decisions. You reviewed potential need for strengthened boundaries and demonstrated how Hazel might create and maintain these boundaries. You asked Hazel to consider any cultural competency issues or concerns.

Finally, you processed her feelings, relating them back to her own history of abuse and focused on how that history brought up pain and fear. While she seemed to express an understanding of her role as a clinical intern and acknowledged how her feelings were impeding her judgment, her difficulty with the situation continued. The next time she met with her client in a recorded session, the client stated, "*Someone called protective services and I had to talk to them*," and Hazel said nothing. She did not admit to making the report and appeared uncomfortable and nervous in the videotaped session. The client made several statements during the session trying to get Hazel to admit her role in the neglect report, but Hazel shut down and said nothing. The client continued by stating that a police officer accompanied the protective service worker, "*a white cop who was rude and probably racist*," and who "*embarrassed and scared the family just being there.*" The client stated further, "*I can't believe somebody would send white cops to our house; we don't need them, we never did.*" Hazel remained silent and abruptly attempted to change the subject. You bring your observations of the session to Hazel in an individual supervision session.

DISCUSSION QUESTIONS

1. What are some key/core issues important to anti-oppressive supervision of the case (worker and client)? List these issues and their importance.
2. Describe your plan and rationale for addressing the key/core issues.
3. From a supervisory/leadership perspective, describe what anti-oppressive lenses and practice might strengthen this program, supervision, and leadership. How might the senior leadership implement these practices in a meaningful and effective way?

FURTHER READING

National Association of Social Workers. (2017). NASW code of ethics. Retrieved March 3, 2021, from www.socialworkers.org/About/Ethics/Code-of-Ethics/Code-of-Ethics-English

Pickover, S., Golomb, S., & Bennett-Garraway, J. (2017). *Case examples in clinical supervision: The challenge of mandated reporting*. The Practitioner Scholar, 6, 108–118.

REFERENCES

Abramovitz, M. (1993). Should all social work students be educated for social change? Pro. *Journal of Social Work Education*, *29*(1), 6–11. https://doi.org/10.1080/10437797.1993.10778794

Andersen, B., & Fagerhaug, T. (2006). *Root cause analysis: Simplified methods and techniques* (2nd ed.). ASQ Quality Press.

Ani, M. (1990). The implications of African-American spirituality. In M. K. Asante & K. W. Asante (Eds.), *African culture: The rhythms of African unity* (pp. 207–231). African World Press

Berkman, E., Brown, E., Scott, M., & Adiele, A. (2022). Racism in child welfare: Ethical considerations of harm. *Bioethics*, *36*(3), 298–304. https://doi.org/10.1111/bioe.12993

Best, C., Cooley, M. E., Colvin, M. L., & Crichlow, V. (2021). Authentic family engagement and strengthening. *Child Welfare*, *99*(5), 97–118.

Braithwaite, J. (2018). Restorative justice and a better future. In J. Braithwaite, *Regulation, crime, freedom* (1st ed., pp. 317–339). Routledge. https://doi.org/10.4324/9781315200361-15

Cantey, N. I., Smith, L. W., Sorrells, S. F., Kelly, D., Jones, C., & Burrus, D. (2022). Navigating racism in the child welfare system. *Child Welfare*, *100*(2), 163–184.

Center for Innovation in Campus Mental Health. What is Anti-Oppressive Practice? (n.d.). https://campusmentalhealth.ca/toolkits/anti-oppressive-practice/what-is-anti-oppressive-practice/

Clarke, J., Pon, G., Benjamin, A., & Bailey, A. (2015). Ethnicity, race, oppression, and social work: The Canadian case. In J. D. Wright (Ed.), *International encyclopedia of the social & behavioral sciences* (2nd ed., vol. 8, pp. 152–156). Elsevier.

Conley, T. L., Sebastian, J., Apollon, D., & Bergman, Y. (2018). *Toolkits*. Retrieved from Race Forward: www.raceforward.org/resources/toolkits

Daly, A., Jennings, J., Beckett, J. O., & Leashore, B. R. (1995). Effective coping strategies of African Americans. *Social Work*, *40*, 240–248.

Damdar, R. N. (2018). *Anti-Black racism in child welfare* (Doctoral dissertation, Toronto Metropolitan University).

Daus-Magbual, A., & Tintiangco-Cubales, A. (2016). The power of ethnic studies: Developing culturally and community responsive leaders. In *"White" washing American education: The new culture wars in ethnic studies* (vol. 1, pp. 181–198). Praeger, an imprint of ABC-CLIO, LLC.

Diemer, M. A., Rapa, L. J., Voight, A. M., & McWhirter, E. H. (2016). Critical consciousness: A developmental approach to addressing marginalization and oppression. *Child development perspectives, 10*(4), 216–221.

Dumas, M. J., & Ross, K. M. (2016). "Be Real Black for Me": Imagining BlackCrit in Education. *Urban Education, 51*(4), 415–442. https://doi.org/10.1177/0042085916628611

Dumbrill, G. C. (2003). Child welfare: AOP's nemesis? In *Emerging perspectives on anti-oppressive practice* (pp. 101–119). Canadian Scholars' Press.

Freire, P. (1996). *Pedagogy of the oppressed (revised)*. New York: Continuum, 356, 357–358.

(2005). *Education for critical consciousness*. Continuum.

(2021).*Pedagogy of hope: Reliving pedagogy of the oppressed*. Bloomsbury.

Hartman, S. V. (1997). *Scenes of subjection: Terror, slavery, and self-making in nineteenth-century America*. Oxford University Press.

Havig, K., & Byers, L. (2019). Truth, reconciliation, and social work: A critical pathway to social justice and anti-oppressive practice. *Journal of Social Work Values and Ethics, 16*(2), 70–80.

Hollaway, J. E. (1990). The origins of African American culture. In J. E. Hollaway (Ed.), *Africanisms in American culture* (pp. 1–18). Indiana University Press.

Johnson, L. M., Antle, B. F., & Barbee, A. P. (2009). Addressing disproportionality and disparity in child welfare: Evaluation of an anti-racism training for community service providers. *Children and Youth Services Review, 31*(6), 688–696. www.sciencedirect.com/science/article/abs/pii/S019074090900019X

Kadushin, A., & Harkness, D. (2014). *Supervision in social work* (5th ed.). Columbia University Press.

Kambon, K. K. K. (1992). *The African personality in America: An African-centered framework*. NUBIAN Nation.

Kendi, I. X. (2020, June 9). Ibram X. Kendi defines what it means to be an antiracist. www.penguin.co.uk/articles/2020/06/ibram-x-kendi-definition-of-antiracist

Kelly, C., Street, C., & Building, M. E. S. (2022). Child Maltreatment 2022. *Child Maltreatment*.

Khalifa, M. A., Dunbar, C., & Douglas, T. R. (2013). Derrick Bell, CRT, and educational leadership 1995–Present. *Race, Ethnicity and Education, 16*(4), 489–513. http://doi.org/10.1080/13613324.2013.817770

Kim, H., Wildeman, C., Jonson-Reid, M., & Drake, B. (2017). Lifetime prevalence of investigating child maltreatment among US children. *American Journal of Public Health, 107*(2), 274–280.

Mandated Supporting. (2024, July 24). Retrieved from JMAC for Families: https://jmacforfamilies.org/mandated-supporting
Manuel, T. (2020). *Strategic case making: The field guide for building public and political will.* The Case Made Press.
Melton, G. B. (2005). Mandated reporting: A policy without reason. *Child Abuse & Neglect, 29*(1), 9–18. https://doi.org/10.1016/j.chiabu.2004.05.005
Menkel-Meadow, C. (2007). Restorative justice: What is it and does it work? *Annual Review of Law and Social Science, 3*(1), 161–187. https://doi.org/10.1146/annurev.lawsocsci.2.081805.110005
Miller, J., & Garran, A. (2022). *Racism in the United States: Implications for the helping professions.* Brooks/Cole.
National Child Welfare Workforce Institute. (2020). Leadership Competency Framework Guide.
Our Story. (2024, July 24). Retrieved from Measure: https://wemeasure.org/about/
Plummer, D. L. (2020). What's your antiracist style? https://asi.dlplummer.com/
Pon, G., Phillips, D., Clarke, J., & Abdillahi, I. (2017). Who's protecting whom? In *doing anti-oppressive practice: Social justice social work.* Fernwood Publishing.
Rodriguez, C., James, J., Runnels, R. C., & Fong, R. (2014). A cross-systems approach to racial disproportionality and disparities. In *Addressing racial disproportionality and disparities in human services: Multisystemic approaches* (pp. 21–38). Columbia University Press.
Schelbe, L., & Geiger, J. M. (2022). Ensuring authentic representation and collaboration along with research to re-design child welfare. *Research on Social Work Practice, 32*(5), 521–526. https://doi.org/10.1177/10497315221074937
Shah, V., Aoudeh, N., Cuglievan-Mindreau, G., & Flessa, J. (2022). Subverting whiteness and amplifying anti-racisms: Mid-level district leadership for racial justice. *Journal of School Leadership, 32*(5), 456–487. https://doi.org/10.1177/10526846221095752
Sinha, A. (2020). Innovating with social justice: Anti-oppressive social work design framework. *Discern: International Journal of Design for Social Change, Sustainable Innovation and Entrepreneurship, 1*(1), 65–77.
Smith, C. F., Aguilar, J. P., Kozu, S., D'Angelo, K. A., Keenan, E. K., & Monroe Tomczak, S. (2022). If anti-racism is the goal, then anti-oppression is how we get there. *Advances in Social Work, 22*(2), 758–778. https://doi.org/10.18060/24646
Sutherland, M. (1993). *Black authenticity: A psychology for liberating people of African descent.* Third World Press.
Tham, P., & Strömberg, A. (2020). The Iron Cage of leadership – The role of first line managers in child welfare. *The British Journal of Social Work, 50*(2), 369–388. https://doi.org/10.1093/bjsw/bcz156
Texas Department of Family and Protective Services. (2024, July 25). Data Book. Retrieved from Texas Department of Family and Protective Services: www

.dfps.texas.gov/About_DFPS/Data_Book/Employee_Statistics/CPS/CPS-Staff_Demographics.asp

Utsey, S. O., Adams, E. P., & Bolden, M. (2000). Development and initial validation of the Africultural Coping Systems Inventory. *Journal of Black Psychology*, *26*(2), 194–215.

Wallace, B. A. (2022). Black critical theory in action: Analyzing the specificity of (anti) blackness. *Journal of African American Studies*, *26*(3), 375–392.

Weber, K. (2022, November 4). Comment: Transforming requires ending the carceral logic of the child welfare system. *Stanford Law and Policy Review Online*, *33*, 34–42.

West, C. (2018). Courage. In M. Adams, W. J. Blumenfeld, D. C. J. Catalano, K. DeJong, H. W. Hackman, L. E. Hopkins, B. J. Love, M. L. Peters, D. Shlasko, & X. Zúñiga (Eds.), *Readings for diversity and social justice* (pp. 635–637). Routledge.

Wilder, J., Amoa, M., Nelson, R., & Bertrand-Jones, T. (2019). Accountability matters: Addressing racial inequity with results-based accountability (RBA). *Race and Justice*, *9*(1), 3–7. https://doi.org/10.1177/2153368718811696

Williams-Mbengue, N. & Barbee, A. (2023). Experiences of professionals of color in the child welfare workforce. Quality Improvement Center for Workforce Development, Children's Bureau. https://qic-wd.org/blog/experiences-professionals-color-child-welfare-workforce

CHAPTER 13

Supervision and Leadership Impact and Overlap on Communities

Nathaniel L. Currie, Jenny Jones, and Larry L. Scott-Walker

Supervision and Leadership

Reaching Communities through Supervision

Social work supervision and agency leadership have the potential and power to reach communities and society through the people, families, and groups that benefit from the services and interventions that social workers provide, as well as through the clinicians and supervisors themselves. Social worker leadership knows well the impact that social workers and their services have on communities. Largely, community impact and empowerment are offered through clinical and human services, advocacy, research, organizing, and social justice. However, social work, especially liberative social work, has the potential to engage communities through other mechanisms, including through media, film, art, storytelling, environmental advocacy and justice, and a myriad of other avenues. Anti-oppressive, decolonial social work practice begs social work leaders to engage across disciplines to both empower and advance social workers and to align with and empower outside people and movements toward liberation.

Social work leaders may consider other nontraditional but effective ways that supervisors and other leaders might engage communities in social justice and liberative work. For instance, community gathering opportunities, celebrations, and the arts have been shown effective in many community practices in strengthening liberative works. In Dr. Bessel van der Kolk's book *The Body Keeps the Score* (2014), he discusses how theater treatment and intervention with teens were used at the Possibility Project in New York City, in Boston public schools, and at the Shakespeare & Company program in Lenox, Massachusetts. These programs, while

Figure 13.1 *Community ii* by Langston Allston.

providing services across various populations served and in programmatic approach, all found great success in the use of the theater arts as a means for trauma treatment, community building, and unity. There have been massive numbers of fine and street art campaigns that communicated community celebration, need, distress, and social commentary. Several major pharmaceutical companies in the United States have used art and theater events as community building and health promotion (and brand promotion) across the country. Many of us are familiar with the Barack Obama "Hope" artwork by Shepard Fairey, which utilized art as social movement, activism, community organizing, and message sending. Some schools of social work have created poetry slams, art installations, and gallery showings to engage students and communities in their teaching and service agendas, like the piece shown here, "Community ii" by Langston Allston, which was shown at the University of Illinois Urbana – Champaign School of Social Work (Figure 13.1). The arts and social justice are deeply intertwined, overlapped, and centered in all successful liberative movement. Consider how your supervision practice, agency leadership, school, or community organizing initiative might strengthen and benefit from an intentional and strategic merger of arts programming or other less traditional creative engagement tactics. See Box 13.1.

Box 13.1 Case Vignette. Art as Social Justice and Liberation Movement

By sarah bricke

The intersection of art and social justice, and the practices of artists, activators, performers, and others who operate in these spaces, has been termed *artivism*. We might think of artivism as a practice in which the originator engages in artmaking in some way (though this does not necessarily have to be in the production of static objects, and often takes other forms, including installation, film and video, or performance), aiming through the work to drive social change. Closely mirroring the broader social justice movement, artivists work toward creating a society that is based on the principles of fairness, equity, and respect for all individuals, emphasizing the importance of ensuring that everyone, regardless of their background, identity, or circumstances, has equitable access to opportunities, resources, and rights. Artivists align their work with liberation movements, using their artwork to spark dialogue, build community networks, encourage participation and collaborative efforts, and reorder or rebuild systems and surroundings. By utilizing these agile methods of *unhiding*, these artworks possess the potential to illuminate realities that would otherwise remain hidden or obscured, reveal ignored or suppressed truths, and counter hegemonic practices that rely on silences to operate.

Activist work is a sustained practice of accountability and transformation. Social justice is often discussed in relation to various social issues, including economic inequality, racial and gender discrimination, environmental justice, and access to education and healthcare. Activists and artivists work toward creating systemic changes that address these and other forms of injustice in society, as do artists. Liberation movements expose tensions, as do artworks.

AFFECT AND EFFECT

Many artists are concerned with *affect*, which in the context of art means the experience by the viewer of the expression of emotion or feelings conveyed by the artist through the artwork. Activist artists, in particular, are often also concerned with *effect* – the result of the viewer's encounter with the art object, action, or event: the impact that this encounter produces. Approaching the affect and effect of activist art by exploring the ways in which the results of such work can be quantified or verified, Stephen Duncombe probed the interrelatedness of activism, effect, art, and affect. He noted: "Good art always contains a surplus of meaning: something we cannot quite describe or put our finger on, but which moves us nonetheless" (Duncombe, 2016, p. 118).

With conceptual artist Steve Lambert, Duncombe cofounded the Center for Artistic Activism, an invaluable resource for artivists. Duncombe has published extensively on this topic, seeking to further understand the relationship between art and activism through ongoing dialogue with collaborators, artists, and curators, as well as social and behavioral researchers and mathematicians. He writes,

> As recent developments in cognitive science suggest, we make sense of our world less through reasoned deliberation of facts and more through stories and symbols that frame the information we receive. And, as any seasoned activist can tell you, people do not soberly decide to change their mind and act accordingly. They are moved to do so by emotionally powerful stimuli.

He goes on to summarize this notion: "Before we act in the world, we must be moved to act. We might think of this as: *Affective Effect* or, if you prefer: *Effective Affect*" (Duncombe, 2016, p. 119).

ENTANGLED: ART AND SOCIAL JUSTICE

Far from merely intersecting, art and social justice are inextricably entangled, especially in the sense that both are involved in complicated circumstances from which it is difficult to escape, but there is the intention to alter these circumstances despite the difficulty of doing so. In the art historical context, there is a long record of art throughout time and place that has been used as a form of protest against injustice. From portraits and monuments to graffiti, political cartoons, performance art, culture and culture jamming, creative expression has been a tool for resisting oppression and advocating for change.

Art has been used to highlight social injustices and bring attention to issues that might otherwise be ignored or marginalized. The struggles and experiences of disempowered, oppressed, and historically excluded identities and communities are depicted *unhidden*, rendered visible (in the case of visual art, literally visible, but also made legible through other art forms). Artworks are able to affect and effect those that encounter them due to their subjective power to invoke what is sometimes otherwise impossible to convey. Art has a unique, nearly impossible to define ability to evoke emotions and create a sense of empathy in viewers or participants. By connecting people emotionally to the experiences of others, art can foster a deeper understanding of social justice issues – and further, can motivate action. Art provides a platform of empowerment through representation: this can empower marginalized groups by giving them a means to express their identity, culture, and experiences in ways that challenge stereotypes and dominant narratives. Art can question and subvert established power structures and norms. By challenging dominant cultural narratives and offering alternative perspectives, artists can disrupt the status quo and provoke critical thinking about social justice issues. The ability of art to challenge power structures is inherent in its power to provoke, inform, and inspire.

Art can play a role in healing communities affected by trauma, violence, or systemic injustice. Community art projects, memorials, and therapeutic art practices can help individuals and communities process pain and imagine resolutions. As an educational tool, art encourages critical thinking and discussion about social justice. Exhibits, performances, and interactive installations engage audiences in dialogue about complex social issues, fostering greater understanding and collective action. The following are examples of artist-activists whose work directly addresses contemporary issues of social justice from perspectives of lived experience, and whose work is illustrative of the power of art to raise awareness and bring about social change.

GREGG BORDOWITZ

Active since the early 1980s, Gregg Bordowitz is perhaps best known for his activism and film work with the group ACT UP (AIDS Coalition to Unleash Power). He self-identifies as a person living with HIV and making work about the experience of living with HIV. Of his early work, Bordowitz writes, "So total was the burden of illness – mine and others – that the only viable response, other than to cease making art entirely, was to adjust to the gravity of the predicament by using the crisis as a lens" (Bordowitz & Meyer, 2004). His early film work documents ACT UP members and other activists engaging in direct action to protest the government's response to the AIDS epidemic, also serving as a means of disseminating information about the disease, safer sex methods, and potential treatments.

As an artist and writer, Bordowitz has been influenced by affect theory:

> Art, as I first understood it, when I started to identify myself as a maker twenty years ago, was a means of expression. This fundamental definition gave way to the various theoretical complications that burdened the whole notion of expression: there is no pure, unmediated communication between sender and receiver; art and its various forms are languages, and as languages they are processes subject to social determinations; the artist's intention is one of several intentions that imbue the work of art with meaning. (Bordowitz, 2001)

His films, among them *Fast Trip, Long Drop* and *Habit*, place him in the role of artist-subject. Intensely personal, the films are powerfully moving in part because of their subjectivity.

PATRISSE CULLORS

Stating that her art practice sustained her in the face of intense criticism and psychological exhaustion, "*My art practice has saved my life, over and over again*" (Noveck, 2023). Patrisse Cullors gives reference to the sustaining and restorative powers of artmaking. Cullors is one of the founders of the Black Lives Matter movement. From its inception in 2013 to her resignation nearly 10 years later, Cullors was actively involved in the organization. During the Covid pandemic, Black Lives Matter became ubiquitous following the murder of George Floyd. She has also cofounded an art collective, the Crenshaw Dairy Mart, with alexandre ali reza dorriz and noé olivas.

TOURMALINE

Working in still images and film, Tourmaline investigates Black and queer histories. Her work centers and elevates transgender activists, including Marsha P. Johnson and Ms. Major, historicizes vanished sites of Black abundance such as Seneca Village, and considers queer communities existing in the margins. While sweeping in historical scope and cultural relevance, Tourmaline's work is also rooted in her lived experience as a Black transgender woman and in her activist work. She has worked at various organizations, including the Sylvia Rivera Law Project and Critical Resistance. Her activist work engages in areas that are overlapping: transgender advocacy, prison abolition, and economic justice.

Tourmaline's films, *Happy Birthday, Marsha!*, (2018) and *Salacia*, (2019) are thematically connected in their function as didactic tools. Committed to an aesthetic that is associated with film at its most lovely, the works can be read as an insistence on affirming the beauty of contested bodies. Tourmaline's work can be seen as embodying her activism; it contains its own history and freedom dreams of a future.

INTERPRETATION

Art and social justice are deeply intertwined, with each influencing and shaping the other in the ongoing struggle for a more just and equitable society. Art as social justice and art as liberation movement can be applied in overlapping ways that mirror art practices. Art can be understood as an encounter (when the viewer encounters the object) and a product (when an artist produces an object). Both ways of experiencing art are valuable and can be done simultaneously or independently.

REFLECTIVE QUESTIONS

1. How have artivists used their activism and their art to challenge societal narratives and promote social justice?
2. In what ways do affect and effect impact art and activism?
3. How can the intersection of art and social justice inspire collective action and create lasting social change within communities?

REFERENCES

Bordowitz, G. (2001). Network society (Making video documentary work about AIDS). *Art Journal (New York. 1960)*, *60*(1), 10–11.

Bordowitz, G., & Meyer, J. S. (2004). *The AIDS crisis is ridiculous and other writings: 1986–2003*. MIT Press.

Duncombe, S. (2016). Does it Work? The Æffect of Activist Art. *Social Research*, *83*(1), 115–134.

Noveck, J. (2023). BLM founder Patrisse Cullors leans into her art. *The Miami Times*, *100*(36).

Facilitative Leadership

So much about social work practice relies on facilitation. Skilled social work leadership is not exempt. According to Breshears and Volker (2012), facilitative leadership *is a process for which a person, acceptable to all members of the group, who is substantively neutral, and who has no decision-making authority intervenes to help a group improve the way it identifies and solves problems and makes decisions to benefit the person/group.* Facilitative leadership is broadly defined, by this text, as a person-to-person or person-to-group process that utilizes trust, rapport, empathy, radical acceptance, and reflection to intervene and solve problems for the benefit of those engaged or affected. Facilitative leadership is unique in its approach in that it, like a therapeutic approach, recognizes that the "social worker is the tool" (p. 2). This is a prime offering for leadership building in supervision – that the social worker *is* the tool. That we use ourselves as mechanisms to heal, intervene, empower, progress, and teach.

Facilitative leadership teaches us that leadership does not have to be hierarchical or top down. Leadership can be inclusive and equitable, a process that includes all group members and highlights their natural leadership qualities, with an identified leader at the helm. It may be helpful to envision leadership as a horizontal line versus a vertical arrow. To access a group as a horizontal line requires acknowledgment and sharing of power. We discussed the use, purpose, and nuances of power within the supervisory relationship in depth in Chapter 3. Building off that text, let's consider the role of power within the role of the facilitative leader when you review Chapter 3.

Transitional Leadership and Succession Planning

"*Movement work is heartbreaking*!" These were the parting words of a social media post from a practitioner who served as an executive director and founder, as she announced her fast-approaching succession from the national nonprofit she had led for most of her adult life – almost 20 years. This practitioner's exclamation is an important and critical reflection of community practice and liberative work. Often, leaders pour their lived experiences, trauma, creativity, and passion into the creation and maintenance of highly needed community spaces, practices, and initiatives – building a movement. It is selfless, forward-thinking, movement work that often receives great attention and intention in early phases but often goes without proper succession planning. Succession planning should begin at the time of induction, or even acceptance, of a leadership position. Leadership is a role that is time sensitive – leadership is not designed, nor should function, in a way that holds long-term appointments. Most social work leaders, higher education leaders, and board directors will describe a five- to seven-year plan in any senior leadership role. Even the presidential office only allows for four to eight years in post. Succession planning is not a common practice among community-based and non-profit organizations, despite support for its effectiveness in supporting leadership development and providing organizational stability during a planned or unplanned transition (Jules, 2021). Transitional leadership is important to community work for several important reasons: (1) it protects the safety, integrity, and stability of the organization (protecting the safe and brave spaces established by the organization through its anti-oppressive, decolonial process); (2) it eliminates the internal and external appearance of administrative and leadership incompetence, which maintains workforce and community support and trust of the agency; (3) it provides opportunity to invite new leadership ideas, practices, insights, and experiences to the culture of the agency; (4) it ensures that the agency does not become comfortable enough to become complacent to innovation, the mission of the agency, and the needs of the community.

A key element of transitional leadership is the need for a strategic plan – not just for meeting agency benchmarks but also for the identified leader/leadership team. All good leaders have an exit or a "pass the torch" strategy – one that is measured and progressed toward with the same care and precision used to secure million-dollar grants, meet programmatic deliverables, and empower the community. This strategic plan might identify potential successors, set a timeline, establish criteria for the type of leader who will be considered, and identify the ways the future leader should instill the values of the organization and continue to expand or strengthen its work.

A crucial element of leadership transition is consistently building the leadership capacity of those within and benefiting from your organization. This can be achieved by training leaders inside and outside the organization on the practices necessary to keep the organization viable and innovative. Focusing on building leadership ensures that the organization isn't fatally harmed when there's a transition of power. Cross-training and mentorship also provide continuity of organizational DNA and ensure that the culture you have established is sustained. It is helpful to see every person in an agency as a leader, and to develop and support them as such.

An additional safeguard that should not be overlooked by the agency or its leadership, coming or going, is the future role of the outgoing leader.

Successful transitions are those in which the new leader has the support of their predecessor. This support may look like the former leader serving in an advisory capacity or as a consultant to ensure the organization continues to operate in ways consistent with the original mission. There is a greater impact to the work, continuity of the agency, and movement when predecessors remain connected – in either formal or informal ways – to the agency or organization. Succession planning allows leaders to decide what their legacy with the organization will be and where they wish to have a major impact during and after their time has commenced.

Preparing Future Leaders

Preparing for agency transition should also include preparing future leaders of both the agency and the community. Who are some of the members of the work who have leadership qualities that could be strengthened for leadership roles? Who are the underdogs with unique and important community experiences that might require mentorship and development to be ready for leadership opportunities? Clinical supervision and other areas of agency leadership are prime locations to begin and further these discussions and personal development. Supervisors have some of the most valuable information and experiences, working directly with agency practitioners and the community at large for considerable stretches of time. Tapping these resources across senior leadership is an invaluable decision.

Preparing future leaders has no specific timeline. In the Dudley Street Neighborhood Initiative (DSNI) case study in Chapter 2, we saw the community organization create youth empowerment programs that supported the neighborhood youth through their childhood and adolescence into young adulthood, and saw several of the youth, as adults who had successfully completed college and other milestones, return to the agency and assume senior leadership roles, where they expanded the youth empowerment programs across the organization. In this example, youth who were empowered by the program became the empowerers of the program.

Agencies and institutions must invest in all workers and community members as if they were the future of the agency, the future of scholarship, and the future of the anti-oppressive movement – because they are. You will notice, even in this text, how many student practitioners and organizers have been contributors. That is by design. There is room for mentorship at every turn and within every project toward liberation. Practitioners do not need to hold the title or role of clinical supervisor or agency leader to mentor and develop future leaders. This is beyond a professional social work value – it is an anti-oppressive practice commitment to grow the movement and develop leaders. Mentorship is pivotal in cultivating future leaders in social work and across communities. Mentorship allows for the instilling of practice values, compassion, empathy, community empowerment, and social justice.

Anti-Oppressive Leadership in Schools of Social Work and Accreditation Programs

The Council on Social Work Education (CSWE) is the accreditation body for all schools of social work in the United States. CSWE, a leadership institution within the profession of social work, is largely responsible for determining the core curriculum of programs offering bachelor's, master's, and doctoral social work degrees. One of the ways this is accomplished is through the Educational Policies and Accreditation Standards (EPAS) guidance – a significantly robust mapping of competencies that social work programs must deliver to ensure a relevant and rigorous social work curriculum.

CSWE's 2022 EPAS defines antiracism as the process of actively identifying and opposing racism and actively changing the policies, behaviors, and beliefs that perpetuate racist ideas and actions. Inclusion is defined as the act of creating environments in which individuals and groups are engaged, respected, valued, supported, and achieved – when all people are welcomed to fully participate. Equity is achieved by promoting justice, impartiality, and fairness within the procedures, processes, and distribution of resources by institutions or systems. The 2022 EPAS articulates a clear commitment of social work education to principles of antiracism, diversity, equity, and inclusion. This commitment is also anchored in NASW's commitment to diversity, which is rooted in the belief that creating a truly diverse, equitable, and inclusive workplace is ethical and requires social workers to acknowledge their position of power vis-à-vis the populations they serve and to practice cultural humility.

EPAS competencies 2 and 3 explicitly address diversity. The enduring commitment is to promote the integration of an anti-oppressive orientation in the learning and mastery of all the competencies. Social work is a public service profession founded on core values of justice, dignity and worth of the person, human relations, integrity, and competence. As a profession, social work is committed to antiracist and anti-oppressive practices in serving diverse groups of people. At its core, social work is charged with dismantling systemic barriers to equality and equity, as defined by accreditation standards required for educational programs in social work. Social work education prepares social workers for this through developing their critical-thinking and problem-solving skills and developing knowledge through research, practice, and scientific inquiry. Accreditation is a systematic and rigorous process of operationalizing this vision of social work and ensuring consumer protection and the public good through quality social work education programs. CSWE-accredited programs are held to higher standards of responsibility for educating students to be respectful and responsible social workers for diverse cultures and communities. Graduates from social work education programs are positioned to advocate for justice, equity, inclusion, and diversity.

CSWE accreditation standards are grounded in these core values and engage competent and qualified educators and community partners to ensure student competency in research, policy, theory, and practice of social work. These standards apply to all social work programs, regardless of whether they are at the undergraduate or graduate level, or whether the course content is offered online or in a classroom. Graduation from a CSWE-accredited social work program provides assurance that the program in which a student enrolls is committed to quality education of students on the social work competencies necessary to enter practice. This offers the opportunity of practice and/or licensure through the completion of a CSWE-accredited degree. It is for these reasons that accreditation bodies have a vital role in assuring that anti-oppressive, decolonial practice is interwoven into broad social work education and clinical licensure.

CSWE's Commission on Accreditation is recognized by the Council on Higher Education Accreditation (CHEA). CHEA recognition assures the public that CSWE's Commission on Accreditation is competent to engage in quality reviews of social work programs based on the CHEA recognition standards, which require accrediting organizations to "demonstrate a commitment to diversity, equity, and inclusion." This could not be more important in our professional practice lives than it is today. At the time of production of this text, several states across the country have advanced legislation that infringes upon freedom in higher education. Florida legislation, as proposed, requires that universities terminate programs which use "pedagogical methodology associated with critical theory," including "critical race studies, critical ethnic studies, radical feminist theory, radical gender theory, queer theory, critical social justice or intersectionality." This is a direct broadside attack on academic freedom. In short, this is oppression. Academic freedom is the underpinning of higher education. Legislation that limits course content and curriculum decisions impinges on academic freedom. Topics that are off-limits are described in terms such as "*divisive*," which is difficult to define and inherently subjective. Educators, not politicians, should make decisions about educational curriculum, pedagogy, and associated research. Decades of research by social work and other scholars document the continuing existence and significant consequences of racism, oppression, and inequality in our country. These words describe a painful and well-documented reality in our society – not an ideology (Council of Social Work Education, 2022). In addition to this attack on academic freedom, the proposed legislation threatens the accreditation status and, in fact, the very existence of social work education programs and social workers serving communities across the nation. Across the United States and its territories, there are more than 125,000 social work students. Without social work education, the resulting depletion of human capital in human services and the health profession workforce will have profound impacts on economic outcomes of state institutions of higher education, health systems, and communities – including the most vulnerable members of society. Social work leaders serve an essential role in the commitment to engage in antiracism, diversity, equity, and inclusion in the preparation of social work students. Therefore, CSWE calls upon social work educators, students, community partners, and allies to protect academic freedom and preserve the capacity of education as a tenet of democracy.

Focused Leadership

Leadership within social work organizations and schools must also embrace decolonization by promoting policies and practices that elevate marginalized voices and challenge systemic inequities. This can be achieved by implementing participatory decision-making processes, fostering diverse leadership pipelines, and ensuring that organizational values align with principles of social justice and equity. Decolonized leadership is not merely about inclusion but is also about transforming the very structures that have historically excluded certain groups. Leadership that embodies anti-oppressive and decolonial principles is characterized by a commitment to equity, transparency, and justice. Anti-oppressive leaders actively work to identify and dismantle barriers to inclusion within their organizations and the communities they serve. This involves not only addressing overt forms of discrimination but also challenging more insidious, systemic forms of oppression. Leaders must advocate for policies that promote equity, create opportunities for marginalized groups, and ensure that organizational practices are aligned with anti-oppressive values.

Social work professional preparation places a strong emphasis on self-awareness at the micro and mezzo levels, challenging us as individuals to closely examine our own biases and experiences and their potential impact on our client relationships and decision-making (Havig & Byers, 2019; Urdang, 2010; Yan & Wong, 2005), and in our participation in supervision and leadership practice. Such self-awareness is frequently associated with concepts such as cultural competence but rarely is it examined as a pathway for critical, antiracist, anti-oppressive practice (Feize & Gonzalez, 2018; Havig & Byers, 2019). Leadership that focuses on anti-oppressive practice and decolonial frameworks and policies must demonstrate awareness of how they are positioned and potentially limited in this decision-making and seek remedy to ensure the presence of all community and practice voices.

Oppression Is Pervasive, but So Is Social Work!

The ultimate goal for anti-oppressive and decolonial social work leadership is to promote social justice and enhance the well-being of all individuals and communities *and* social work practitioners. This is accomplished through the profession's focused and enduring work to acknowledge, address, and ultimately dismantle the systemic oppression within the profession and within society to see these goals achieved. As we have covered throughout this text, intersectionality matters. Social work leaders hold multiple intersecting identities that shape their experiences of oppression and privilege. Social work leaders need to consider how different forms of oppression, such as racism, sexism, ableism, and heterosexism, intersect and compound to create unique experiences of marginalization for their agencies, teams, and colleagues. Self-reflection is critical, as social workers must continuously self-reflect to identify and challenge their biases, assumptions, and privileges. They must be willing to examine how their identities and experiences shape their worldview and how they interact with clients.

Empowerment is key to anti-oppressive social work practice and leadership and aims to empower clients, practitioners, and communities by recognizing and building on their strengths, skills, and knowledge. Goals should be collaborative, and strategies to achieve them should consider sharing power and benefits. Activism is necessary in challenging and changing oppressive structures and practices inside and outside the social work profession. Social workers must engage in activism and advocacy to create social change and promote equity and justice for marginalized communities. Social justice is ubiquitous to the practice of social work, but many social work leaders struggle to center activism in their practice and support it in their teams. Activism must take a centered and intentional role in clinical, supervision, and leadership practices to ensure the process and progress of social justice goals are active and achieved.

Summary

In this chapter, we covered important ways in which social worker leadership requires intentional, thorough, and innovative engagement in communities. Liberative work at its core is about people and communities. Social work and other clinical practices must connect and embed practice work and leadership into local, national, and global communities to become most effective locally and beyond. As leaders accomplish their goals within the agency or community, the utilization of succession planning and transitional approaches makes for a strong and steadfast organization that may continue its mission. Finally, professional accreditation bodies hold responsibility and ownership in furthering the continuation of anti-oppressive education and practices across the helping professions.

Reflection Questions

1. How has your identity as a leader influenced your decision-making? In what ways might your identity need to evolve as you prepare for succession?
2. What are the core values and practices you want to ensure are sustained after your departure from your organization or leadership role? How might you effectively communicate and instill these values or practices with your successor and organization mission?
3. In what ways can you engage your agency or organization team and the community in the overall leadership of the organization in ways that share power and create and maintain equity? (See Box 13.2.)

Box 13.2 Practice Reflection. I THRIVE Because: Starting an Organization to Save My Own Life

By Larry L. Scott-alker

It's June 5, 2007, a day unbeknownst to me at the time with great significance in the HIV movement, as 26 years prior, "AIDS" – the mysterious illness affecting mostly gay men – was uncovered. For me, it was the day I chose to be tested for STIs (sexually transmitted infections) following a difficult breakup. After waiting for what seemed like hours in this sterile Baltimore-based clinic for the HIV tester to return my results, I could tell by her shift in demeanor that the test was positive.

"Do you have an idea of what the result is?" she asked.
"Umm, I don't know!" I answered.
"You tested preliminary positive," she responded almost robotically.
"Did you have suspicions?"
"No! I don't think so," I said, trying to gather myself and the pamphlets she had handed me.
"You seem calm. You aren't going to harm yourself, are you?"

"Not any more than I already have!" I answered, utterly annoyed by this round of questions. I rushed out of the clinic before they could provide me with any additional information, assuring them that I'd call to set up my appointment to be linked to care, which I wouldn't do for six months – at a different clinic, of course. It took half a year for me to process and acquiesce to my new reality. As a Black same-gender-loving man (SGL), born and raised to fear HIV and the stigma that accompanies it, finding the courage took a tremendous amount of soul-searching and a great deal of hand-holding.

May 4, 2015: After nearly a decade working within the Black SGL community, and eight years after getting my test results, I accepted the charge of starting a support network for Black SGL men living with HIV in the Atlanta area. After months of cajoling from a colleague and years of seeing Black men suffer with what was now a pretty manageable condition, I said, "If I do it, it has to be different – celebratory, not sad, like the gay men's discussion groups I hosted in Baltimore!" Holding the awkward exchange with the tester in Baltimore in my mind, and reflecting on the many ways that the HIV institutions I turned to for care and employment chronically failed Black communities, I was eager and anxious. I had just mustered the courage to truly own my HIV status, and still, none of my family members and only a few friends actually knew my secret.

I decided that the group should be virtual, to usurp the stigma and shame of having to go into a building. Online also allowed users to access the information and support in their own space and when they had availability. This virtual venue also allowed me and the other two founders to build the additional confidence needed to facilitate such a space honestly, as none of us had ever publicly disclosed. The virtual safe space was only accessible by invite, either by a group admin or by the referral of friends, lovers, or medical providers, and required extensive vetting. Within weeks, we had over 100 members. As men living with and working in the HIV sector, we knew that the group had to center more than just disease and risk. To fully support our members, we had to cater to what made us feel powerful and connected and defy the desire to trauma-bond endlessly.

Our membership began requesting in-person engagement a little more than a month after establishing the online group, which again presented both a challenge and an opportunity. The online space was bustling with culturally relevant conversation, with public health messaging littered throughout. We didn't have a model for how to translate this into in-person support, yet I had a few must-haves. First, since we were hosting this gathering on a Sunday in Atlanta, it had to feel more like brunch than a support group. As we were personally funding these initial engagements, we weren't bound to the limitations of grants or funders who didn't understand our populations, so we invited the men to bring their favorite spirit to add to the "party" feel.

When the cofounder who begged me to take on the task and I met before what we called our first in-person "BYOB" meet-up, I shared, "I want us to be positively positive. By that, I mean no moping about our statuses. Our facilitation should be strengths- and resilience-based." I told him that I would open and to follow my lead. When nearly 50 men filed into the meeting room at my cofounder's job, I nearly lost my breath and all the nerve I had been mustering. We greeted each man as he entered with a hug and directed them to the food and libations. When everyone had taken their seats, the cofounder began with a welcome after passing out a sign-in sheet. He introduced me to provide additional context and to lead the guys through an icebreaker and discussion. I spoke to the men about the reason we began this support initiative and what they could expect going forward. As a way to allow the brothers to introduce themselves, I asked for everyone to share their name, "Seroversary" (a word I came up with on the fly to refer to their date of diagnosis), and one positive thing that has come from knowing their statuses. The round started with a bit of a challenge as most in attendance, including myself, had never pondered this kind of question, but the men met the challenge head-on.

"My name is Larry, Seroversary is June 5, 2007, and the best thing that has come from knowing my status is this!" I responded, echoing many of the responses that came before me. The conversation that ensued was rich, lively, and cathartic. Men were taking selfies, exchanging numbers, and planning to hang out with brothers they were just meeting. The cofounder and I knew that we had done something that would impact us and the city for years to come.

It's late September, and a member who had just taken up the hobby of photography contacted me to offer his services to shoot a campaign for the group. He wanted me to create the framework and recruit some of the group's members and admins. I knew recruitment wouldn't be hard – I just needed to come up with something meaningful and useful! I felt the campaign should follow the theme and mission of the group, to create normalcy and power for Black SGL men living with HIV, and not just be flat images mostly useful on gay dating apps! After a few days, I thought, "What if we build on the initial icebreaker and center thriving with HIV?" "I THRIVE because..." After scouting an abandoned rail yard, often used for movies, we gathered nine men from various walks of life to shoot what became our first of many "self-love and HIV acceptance campaigns." iTHRIVE was released on World AIDS

Day, December 1, 2015. We told the guys that their photos were theirs to use as conversation starters or reminders of their resilience and urged them to post within the network. To my surprise, one brother used his as a way to disclose, and another followed. Before we knew it, half the campaigns were being shared on social media over and over again.

A month prior to the release of the iTHRIVE campaign, a community partner who worked in pharma, who was also like a mentor and *auntie*, walked up to me at a conference with a check and urged me to incorporate. She proclaimed the power and impact that she foresaw our network having and made me promise to build on this momentum so we could garner greater support and position ourselves to provide the necessary resources to our members. Previously, the two other cofounders and I were united in not wanting to professionalize, as we understood the strings that came along with much of the grant funding and contracts we could receive. On December 4, 2015, the three of us were seated at the dining table of one of our eldest members, deciding the structure and DNA of our new organization, aptly called THRIVE SS (Transforming HIV Resentments Into Victories Everlasting Support Services). What we knew was that we would center our members in every aspect of decision-making, program creation, and service delivery. We would later learn that this is called Meaningful Involvement of People with HIV/AIDS or MIPA – the full inclusion of people living with HIV in all levels of the organization's work. We used our current employers, while largely impactful in their respective realms, as models of what not to do, as we saw clearly their limitations and shortcomings. THRIVE SS would model efforts that were innovative, responsive to the diverse needs of communities, and affirming of all aspects of Black culture, resilience, and life.

We set goals and benchmarks we felt would best serve our communities: increased participation and inclusion of our members in HIV-related advocacy, the creation of materials that supported self-love and acceptance, increased membership, and robust support related and unrelated to a positive HIV status, and of course, ensuring that our membership is able to reduce their viral loads and live healthy lives with HIV. In nine years, we have accomplished those things and more. We have built the largest network for Black SGL men living with HIV in the country. The seven iterations of our engagement survey, which measured where our members fell along the continuum of care, showed that with our support, 9 out of 10 members were in care to treat their HIV, with over 86 percent – at the lowest – being virally suppressed, thus unable to spread the HIV virus. We have helped organizations replicate the Undetectables Support Model to support other demographics of people living with HIV and have incubated several organizations, aiding and supporting them as fiscal sponsors and thought partners. We have supported young queer entrepreneurs and movement makers in funding and fully conceptualizing their initiatives, which are meant to galvanize communities around greater support for people living with HIV. We have presented our models both domestically and globally. Most importantly, we have helped to mitigate the stigmas that so many feel obligated to traverse.

So now, on August 27, 2024, as I reflect on the month after separating from the organization that saved mine and so many others' lives, I'm filled with pride, knowing the amazing things that have come from a commitment to compassionate service. I'm filled with pride knowing that we alleviated so many felt oppressions of our regional community who are Black, queer, and living with HIV. I'm eager to continue the legacy that was born out of a tradition of weaponizing one's shame for the greater good. This journey has shown me the power of community, the importance of resilience, and the profound impact of turning personal trials into collective triumphs. Though my path with THRIVE SS has ended, my dedication to uplifting Black SGL men and advocating for those living with HIV remains unwavering. The work is far from over, and I'm ready to carry forward the torch, knowing that the seeds we planted together will continue to grow and flourish for years to come. So, create and lead that group, organization, movement, or policy that you know will save your life and so many others. See Figure 13.2.

Figure 13.2 *3 Kings* (Kenner, 2017).

REFLECTION QUESTIONS

1. How can grassroots organizations, like THRIVE SS, help combat stigma (s) and promote self-love and acceptance within marginalized communities?
2. In what ways do you think meaningfully involving community members in governance, decision-making, and program creation impacts the success of an organization?
3. What strategies do you believe are key in ensuring the long-term sustainability and growth of grassroots organizations, especially those initially resistant to professionalization?

All of Us
By
Larry Scott-Walker
Liberation is going to take all of us
All of our hands,
All of our fists.
Gonna require that we all don Marsha P. rose halos
And throw each our own respective brick
Fiercely through the windshields of the oppressor
As we take our licks
From Billy clubs to kicks
All of us are bound to get hit
Cause
Freedom is Gonna take all of us
to put our bodies on the line
Be they Black or Brown …
TGNC or Cis
Be them young or experienced
Poor or rich
We all must engage the race
must be prepared for a sprint
And sometimes to ACT Up! by simply dying in place,
completely still … just lying in place
Until they get point or spray what feels like lye in our faces …
And no my baby, I won't lie to your face
"the road to freedom might take us through a cloud of mace …

or worse up the sides mountains of red tape"
But if we're not at the table we're bound to be devoured and die on
  a plate
So we don't have time to waste
Because
Justice is going to take all of us
Our energies and expressions
Our love and life lessons
And sometimes request more than we have to give
That's when tenacity kicks in and asks, "how bad do you want to live?"
And when I offer a resounding "with all of me!"
I'm reminded that I have to give accordingly,
As change requires all of us!

Note

Consultation by Halaevalu Fonongava'inga Ofahengaue Vakalahi (President and Chief Executive Officer, Council for Social Work Education).

REFERENCES

Breshears, E., & Volker, R. (2012). *Facilitative leadership in social work practice*. Springer.
Council on Social Work Education. (2022). 2022–2023 Annual Report. www.cswe.org/getattachment/e0109fb7-3447-4fd5-ad5e-ad89ee07b853/2022-23AnnualReport_Final.pdf?lang=en-US
Feize, L., & Gonzalez, J. (2018). A model of cultural competency in social work as seen through the lens of self-awareness. *Social Work Education*, 37(4), 472–489.
Havig, K., & Byers, L. (2019). Truth, reconciliation, and social work: A critical pathway to social justice and anti-oppressive practice. *Journal of Social Work Values and Ethics*, 16(2), 70–80.
Jules, A. J. (2021). Barriers to succession planning: A case study of Atlanta nonprofit organizations.
Kenner, K. (2017). *3 Kings* [Photograph]. Larry Scott-Walker.
Urdang, E. (2010). Awareness of self – A critical tool. *Social Work Education*, 29(5), 523–538.
van der Kolk, B. A. (2014). *The body keeps the score: Brain, mind, and body in the healing of trauma*. Viking.
Yan, M. C., & Wong, Y. L. R. (2005). Rethinking self-awareness in cultural competence: Toward a dialogic self in cross-cultural social work. *Families in Society*, 86(2), 181–188.

Glossary
Terms and Definitions for Anti-Oppressive Practice

Wisdom begins with the definition of terms.
—Socrates

Ableism	is "a network of beliefs, processes, and practices that produces a particular kind of self and body (the corporeal standard) that is projected as the perfect, species-typical and therefore essential and fully human. Disability, then, is cast as a diminished state of being human" (Campbell, 2001, p. 44).
Afrocentric Perspective	is a culturally grounded social work practice model that acknowledges, codifies, and integrates shared cultural experiences, values, and interpretations among individuals of African origin (Wright et al., 2018). The Perspective considers the interaction of race with other sociocultural characteristics such as gender, ethnicity, social class, ability status, and sexual orientation. Furthermore, the Perspective recognizes African cultural resiliency of family, spirituality, community solidarity, empowerment, cooperation, creativity, and the concept of mutual aid as a foundation to help social work practitioners solve pressing social problems

	that limit human potential and prevent positive social change (Martin & Martin, 2003; Mbiti, 1970; Wright et al., 2018).
Allyship	is the practice of individuals within advantaged/dominant groups providing support to members of underrepresented or marginalized populations in efforts to promote rights, representation, inclusion, and opportunity (Ayyala & Coley, 2022; Currie et al., 2024; Melaku et al., 2021). Allyship is not a one-time action but a lifelong process of growing awareness, developing critical accountability for actions, building trust and relationships with members of the marginalized community, and using power and privilege to advocate for equal and equitable rights (Ayyala & Coley, 2022; Currie et al., 2024).
Anti-Black racism	is a specific and intentional form of prejudice, specifically targeting, explicitly and implicitly, Black identifying individuals, descendants of enslaved Africans, individuals perceived to be Black, and all members of the African diaspora solely for the color of their skin. Anti-Black racism is not solely a product of individual prejudice, but it is systemic and structural. It manifests in the systematic discrimination and marginalization of Black people and communities in all contexts (Comrie et al., 2022). In the child welfare system, anti-Black racism is described as a "pernicious form of racism that is directed at Black people," that is rooted in slavery and colonialism (Pon et al., 2017). In the child welfare system, anti-Black racism and the subjugation of Black mothers is sanctioned for the commodification of Black children (Pon et al., 2017). Given this definition of anti-Black racism, what should be included is

	an understanding that anti-Blackness fundamentally requires a belief in the humanization of whiteness and the dehumanization of Blackness.
Anti-oppressive practice	is an ideology, theoretical lens, and approach with a broad scope in interrupting the marginalization of oppressed groups. Anti-oppressive practice (AOP) directs its focus on how systems and structures create, invest, and protect the unearned privilege and power afforded to some groups while simultaneously upholding inequitable and discriminatory conditions for racialized, gendered, and additional groups who are "*othered*." AOP fundamentally recognizes the existence and persistence of oppression, present on structural, cultural, and personal levels, and it aims to dismantle inequities in any form. It is interdisciplinary and includes models of anti-racism, decolonization theory, feminism, queer theory, and disability justice (Center for Innovation in Campus Mental Health, n.d.). AOP is dynamic, continuous, and evolving, thus requiring ongoing learning, reflection, and engagement. According to the Baylor School of Social Work, AOP for social workers should include five fundamental principles: (1) oppression is pervasive, (2) intersectionality matters, (3) self-reflection is critical, (4) empowerment is key, and (5) activism is necessary (Baylor University Diana R. Garland School of Social Work, 2023). Ultimately, AOP aims to engage social work practitioners in a divestment from learned institutional practices that sanction oppression of targeted marginalized groups.
Anti-oppressive systems	are incorporated plans, strategies, applied theories, actions, and practices that

	challenge systems of oppression in society and beyond; Anti-oppressive systems are strategies, theories, actions, and practices that challenge systems of oppression in society (Amoakohene et al., 2021).
Anti-racism	is fundamentally the opposition of racism, and the identifying and engagement in deliberate actions against it. Anti-racism intentionally and consciously participates in practices and strategies to dismantle individual, community, social, structural, and systemic racism. As with anti-oppressive practice, anti-racism is a dynamic and active process that requires consistent and targeted attention to overt and covert racist actions. While racism exists on systemic, institutional, interpersonal, and individual levels, the broadest level, that of systemic, is typically the primary focus. The goal of anti-racism is to become aware of racism in all its forms and actively change the beliefs, behaviors, and policies that perpetuate racist ideas and actions in individuals, institutions, and systems in order to create an equal society.
Authentic Leadership	is a pattern of leader behavior that draws upon and promotes both positive psychological capacities and a positive ethical climate to foster greater self-awareness, an internalized moral perspective, balanced processing of information, and relational transparency on the part of leaders working with followers, fostering positive self-development (Walumbwa et al., 2008, p. 94).
BIPOC or Black, Indigenous, People of Color	is an acronym/term that acknowledges the distinct histories, cultures, and struggles of Black and Indigenous peoples alongside

other people of color. The term encompasses groups that are not white and, as a result, often are harmed by white supremacy ideology and action. It emphasizes the interconnectedness of these communities in the fight against systemic racism and oppression. By specifically naming Black and Indigenous peoples, BIPOC highlights their often-overlooked experiences within discussions of racial inequality. Further, the term BIPOC is used as a way to reclaim oppressive labels given to racially marginalized groups. Communities often use the term to acknowledge that not all people of color face equal levels of injustice. BIPOC is significant in recognizing that systemic racial injustices severely impact Black and Indigenous people (Watson-Singleton et al., 2023).

Carceral logic is an ideology that is based on views of retribution and control, including imprisonment and violence. Carceral logic is seen as a solution to public safety. It is most commonly applied in the criminal justice realm and has been applied to family policing by abolitionists.

Cisgenderism denies, denigrates, or pathologizes self-identified gender identities while endorsing and perpetuating the belief that cisgender identities are more valuable than transgender or nonbinary identities. It recognizes that the oppression of trans communities is rooted in systemic and structural power.

Cissexism is the belief or assumption that there are (or should be) only two mutually exclusive sexes and two associated, mutually exclusive genders – male/man or female/woman. Cissexism designates individuals

318　　Terms and Definitions for Anti-ppressive Practice

	who identify and/or express their gender differently from their sex assigned at birth as abnormal, leading to both subtle and overt forms of discrimination and dominance that disadvantage gender-diverse people (Clements, 2019).
Co-conspirator	is a person who is a step beyond simple allyship. This individual does not qualify marginalized group members before assisting them. They assist because they believe that any form of oppression is wrong.
Co-creation	as a practice, refers to the collaboration with persons impacted by systems, community, and interested parties to design processes in the development of policy, practices, and research.
Collective Imperialism	refers to a form of economic and political domination exercised by former colonial powers and other developed nations working together to maintain control over newly independent African states and other developing countries. Key aspects of collective imperialism, as described by Nkrumah (1965), include: (1) Cooperation among imperialist powers: Instead of competing for control of former colonies, developed nations collectively collaborated to maintain their influence. (2) Economic domination: Through international financial institutions, trade agreements, and multinational corporations, wealthy nations exert control over the economies of developing countries. (3) Political influence: Imperialist powers interfere in the internal affairs of developing nations, often supporting leaders who are favorable to their interests. (4) Cultural imperialism: The promotion of Western cultural values

Terms and Definitions for Anti-ppressive Practice 319

	and norms to maintain ideological control. (5) Multilateral institutions: Organizations like the World Bank and the International Monetary Fund are seen as tools of collective imperialism, imposing economic policies that benefit developed nations (Nkrumah, 1965) over developing nations.
Colonialism	has been defined as systems and practices that "seek to impose the will of one people on another and to use the imposed people's resources for the imposer's benefit" (Asante, 2006; Schiele, 1994). Colonialism can operate within an environment's political, sociological, and cultural values, and systems, even after an occupation by imposed colonizers has ended. Furthermore, *Colonization* is defined as the act of political, physical, and intellectual occupation of spaces/environments. Often, forceful displacement of Indigenous populations gives rise to settler colonialism, colonial and neo-colonial relations, and coloniality.
Community-based Participatory Research	is a partnership approach to research that equitably involves community members/participants, organizational representatives, and academic researchers in all aspects of the research process, and that centers the voice of the community.
Community-Driven Research	is a collaborative partnership approach to research that involves community members in all aspects of a project. In community-driven research, the community identifies the research priorities and questions, and researchers are then found to partner with the community to address those priorities. "Community-driven research framework provides a process through which researchers

	can engage in a culturally relevant learning process that allows entry to the community, fostering trust, and initiating a mutual collaboration that is embedded within the local context and needs of the community" (Manzo et al., 2023).
Counter-Narratives	are stories and perspectives that challenge the dominant narratives, provide alternative viewpoints, and highlight the experiences of marginalized or oppressed groups. Counter-narratives seek to disrupt the status quo and bring attention to social injustices.
Critical Consciousness	is an ongoing learning process and practice of becoming aware of the realities, causes, correlations, and operationalization of oppression in society for the purpose of inspiring actions to create change – to cultivate collective liberation from all forms of oppression and domination.
Critical Cultural Competence	as discussed by Lusk et al. (2017), builds on the term "cultural competence" by emphasizing the exploration of power and privilege and greater awareness of cultural background, experiences, values, and context.
Critical reflectivity	is the process of becoming aware of "sociohistorical reality which shapes their lives and their capacity to transform that reality" (Freire, 1970). Critical reflection has an "emancipatory element" as it provides people with the "capacity to question and change existing power relations" (Brookfield, 1995; Fook, 1999; Sloan et al., 2018).
Critical self-reflection	refers to the development and process of an awareness of one's own intersecting identities and an increase in one's

	awareness of social, systemic, and systemic social structures and their impact on one's identities and consciousness. Critical self-reflection also incorporates the process of mindfulness, awareness of positionality, reflection, and self-actualization as social and environmental experiences are presented.
Decoloniality	refers to forms of being and thinking that preceded and started with the colonial project and invasion. It means acknowledging and dismantling the hierarchical systems of hetero-patriarchy, race, gender, and class that still govern thought, knowledge, spirituality, and life. These systems are inextricably linked to and fundamental to Western modernity and global capitalism (Mignolo & Walsh, 2018).
Decolonizing the Curriculum	refers to creating courses, lessons, instruction, and other learning that utilize diverse and multicultural course materials. The profession of social work has largely been based on Eurocentric ideas, thinkers, norms, and values. Decolonizing the curriculum may include diversifying the readings and course materials, the centering of BIPOC voices and perspectives on social ills, and removing assumptions and modalities that are based in saviorism. Decolonizing curriculum requires a decentering of whiteness in favor of a more global world view.
Deep structure sensitivity	is a form of critical consciousness that attends to the cultural values and systemic forces affecting members of a marginalized population and incorporates these into all aspects of clinical services.
Dismantling systems of oppression	once oppressive structures are acknowledged and examined; we must

	work in coalition with others to educate people on the harm done to everyone when these systems are maintained. Changing systems, laws, policies, and practices, and helping people to gain a new perspective are some of the ways that we can work together to address these inequalities and change the power dynamics for the better.
Dominant-Narratives	are the widely accepted and culturally reinforced stories, beliefs, and perspectives that uphold and perpetuate the interests of dominant groups in society. These narratives shape societal norms, values, and policies, often marginalizing or silencing alternative viewpoints.
Empowerment theory	in social work uses intervention methods to help guide people toward building autonomy and control in their lives. This theory recognizes that oppression primarily contributes to disempowerment experienced across several marginalized groups (Turner, 2017). Further, empowerment practice is integral to restorative practices (Sloan et al., 2018) and anti-oppressive practices.
Endemic Racism	as in originating where it occurs; particular to area [geographic], system, or culture, the notion that there are distinct human races with inherent differences which determine their abilities, and that based on these supposed abilities that some races are superior and others inferior. Critical Race pedagogy persists that within a American cultural context *racism is permanent, ordinary, and endemic* (Bell, 2005).
Ethnographic interview	is an interactive process learning about the individual within their context (Sloan

Terms and Definitions for Anti-ppressive Practice

	et al., 2018). The process of building rapport and insight offers a window into the individual's personal and world views, perception, environment, and personal and cultural interpretation of events and experiences. Ethnographic interviews and ethnographic research are an important process of anti-oppressive and decolonial practice.
Ethnographic narrative	relating to the qualitative method of research and description that centers narrative, counter narrative, and storytelling of people and cultures within their customs, habits, and mutual differences, as defined by the subjects, and offered from an immersive lens.
Ethnoracial	refers to ethnic differences that account for skin-tone differences as well.
Family separation system and family policy system	describes the more realistic depiction of the "child welfare" system, that is intentionally based on the experiences, realities and outcomes of Black and other marginalized children and families. *Family separation* reflects what is considered the intentional outcome of forcibly separating Black children from their families that align with the historical forced separation of Black children and families during chattel slavery. *Family policing* refers to a process of sanctioned surveillance of Black families taking place through their involvement in other adjacent systems of oppression (welfare system, juvenile system, housing, etc.), and where Black families are "on the radar" and vulnerable to future child welfare involvement.
Femmephobia	refers to the devaluation, degradation, regulation, and resistance of/to femininity

	across all gender and orientations identities and expression, with an emphasis on that of femme-expressive gay/queer men, non-binary people, and transgender/trans-expressive people. Femmephobia is related to misogyny and is rooted in patriarchal ideals, values, and imposed norms (Hoskin, 2019).
Folks/Folx	is a gender-neutral, inclusive way of referring to people. The neutralization of the gender language seeks to undo the implicit and explicit sequestering of expressive language based on masculine and feminine identity, reuniting rather than separating, and is particularly helpful in the inclusion of non-binary identities/expressions. The term folx serves as a linguistic marker of progressive social personae, meaning that it serves the user's identity as much as it serves the identified (Currie et al., 2024).
Framing	refers to the process of using language to evoke cognitive structures that establish meaning for each individual. These structures are tied to an individual's existing knowledge established through their experiences, environment, and perceptions. Linguistic framing is different than the Framing Effect within psychology.
Gender Diversity/Gender-Diverse	are umbrella terms that are used to describe gender identities that demonstrate a diversity of expression within, outside, or beyond the binary framework. Some examples include agender, cisgender, gender-fluid, gender non-conforming, genderqueer, transgender, third-gender, and two-spirit identities (Currie et al., 2024).

Global South	the group of countries that are on the continent of Africa, Latin America, the Caribbean, and the developing parts of Asia (The United Nations Trade and Development UNCTAD) (Di Nicola, 2020).
Hegemonic/Hegemony	*relates to* ruling, leading, supreme; acting as a hegemon; (now esp.) of, relating to, or assuming political or social hegemony, hegemonistic. Further defined as the predominant and pervasive influence of one state, religion, region, class, or group. A hegemonic society functions not just to establish a homogeneous way of thinking, but also to try to make any alternative disappear. One might say hegemony is "the language of conquest" (Kivel, 2013).
Heteronormative	refers to the belief or assumption that heterosexuality is the default or normal mode of sexual orientation. It implies that heterosexual relationships are the standard by which all relationships are judged, and it often involves the expectation that traditional gender roles – such as the idea that men should be masculine, and women should be feminine – are natural and universally applicable.
Heuristic	implies an aid, addition, something complimentary to learning, discovery, or problem-solving, largely by experimental, observational, and especially trial-and-error methods. In anti-oppressive practice this process is important in combining theories, lens, practices, and understandings, to create short cuts to strengthen approaches, methods, and variables.
Homonormative	refers to a set of norms and values that mirror the dominant heteronormative

	standards of society related to gender roles, and relationships. The term critiques the way some aspects of LGBTQ culture may prioritize or normalize behaviors and identities that conform to mainstream, often middle-class, white, cisgender, and monogamous standards.
Intergenerational trauma	refers to the transmission, spoken and unspoken, of adverse events or experiences from one generation to the next. The effects of intergenerational trauma have a profound impact on our emotional well-being. Failure to examine these traumas result in them being passed to another generation.
Intersectionality	a theoretical framework, and also a Critical Race Theory (CRT) tenet, that examines how various forms of oppression, such as racism, cisheterosexism, classism, and sexuality, intersect and overlap, creating complex layers of marginalization and privilege.
Latine,	pronounced [luh-teen-ae] of or relating to people of Latin American origin or descent, living in the United States. Latine is a gender inclusive term to define Latine individuals.
Liberation	is the state of being whole, fully human, autonomous, and free from all forms of oppression whereby individuals, families, and communities of people and living free from injustice, bias, marginalization, stereotype threat, and racism. Taken from Harro's conceptualization of The Cycle of Liberation (2000), liberation is the practice of love; it is finding balance in our individual lives and in the agendas of coalitions; it is the development of

	competence and ability to make something happen consistent with a goal; it is the belief that we can succeed; it is the knowledge that we are not alone; it is the commitment to the effort of critical transformation, to the people in our community, and to the goals of equity and justice, and to love; and it is passion and compassion.
Liberatory Consciousness	is described by Dr. Barbara Love (2018) as an awareness of the dynamics of oppression, each individual's role in maintaining systems of oppression, and the critical need for intentionality for changing systems of oppression, without giving in to despair, hopelessness, or blame. Building on ideas of critical consciousness, Love suggests four elements of liberatory consciousness are awareness, analysis, action, and accountability/allyship.
Liberatory movements	describe movements of liberation that have one sole purpose, and that is to free the marginalized from any aspect of oppression without apology, by any means necessary.
Linguistic metaphor	is the ontological mapping across conceptual domains, from a concrete source domain tied to a linguistic frame to an abstract target domain. Metaphors enhance conceptual understanding by tying an abstract word (such as an emotion) to a concrete frame.
Marginalized Groups	are different groups of people within a given culture, context, and history who are at risk of being subjected to multiple discrimination due to the interplay of different personal characteristics or grounds, such as sex, gender, age,

	ethnicity, religion or belief, health status, disability, sexual orientation, gender identity, education or income, or living in various geographic localities (European Union Agency for Fundamental Rights [FRA] and the Office of the United Nations High Commissioner for Human Rights [UN OHCHR] – Treaty Bodies).
Marginalization	is maybe the most dangerous form of oppression; a whole category of people is expelled from useful participation in social life and potentially subjected to severe material, emotional, and psychological deprivation and even extermination (Young, 2000, p. 41).
Minority stress theory	is a framework that posits that individuals with minoritized identities experience additional identity-related stressors that are both external and internal (e.g., discrimination, bullying, internalized homophobia), which in turn increase the risk of developing mental and physical health problems.
Neo-colonialism	is the state subject to it is, in theory, independent and has all the outward trappings of international sovereignty. In reality, its economic system and, thus, its political policy are directed from outside.
Nomenclature	is the name of something.
Opportunity gap	is similar to the term sociopolitical debt (Ladson-Billings, 2006); a culturally informed term for the disparities among ethnoracial identity groups in terms of academic achievement and success that takes into account the uneven distribution of educational, financial, and other resources.

Organizational culture	is the often-unspoken assumption of values, beliefs, and processes that underlie the goals, work habits, decision-making, conflict resolution, management, and perceived success of any organization. The culture includes both the everyday patterns of work that have developed over time and the deeper hidden assumptions and beliefs that consciously and unconsciously drive that work" (Carlson & Donohoe, 2010, p. 51).
Orientation Diversity/ Orientation-Diverse	are umbrella terms that are used to describe sexual orientation or behavioral patterns that include romantic intimacy, emotional attraction and attachment, and sex behavior (including the lack of these) between people within, outside, or beyond a heteronormative framework. Sexual orientation is a quality distinct from gender identity. For example, a transgender individual may identify as straight, gay, pansexual, etc. (Currie et al., 2024).
POC	is an acronym for People of Color.
Positionality	is the recognition and reflection of one's social location within a matrix of domination, including aspects such as race, gender, class, and other identity markers that grant us privileges or make us targets of oppression. It acknowledges that personal identities and societal structures shape an individual's viewpoint and understanding of the world.
Power analysis	is an interrogation of the manifestations of power, visible and invisible, locations, and its fluidity, between the people in a given situation in order to understand the dynamics that impact the people and shape the events in that situation.

Power differential	is the role difference between two people that results in vulnerability on the part of the less empowered. The perceived power difference may include authority, access to resources, knowledge or information, and self-efficacy.
Praxis	is the practice or application of theory.
Processing	is a means to empower an individual to identify antecedents, triggers, alternative behavior choices, and possible alternative outcomes. In each step of this process, the individual is reminded of their self-efficacy and autonomy.
Race	is a socially constructed social and political category used to classify humans based on cultural and physical characteristics such as skin color, facial features, and hair texture. It is important to note that race is not a biological reality but a concept created to establish and maintain racial hierarchies.
Racialization	is the sociopolitical process by which certain groups of people are categorized, differentiated, and given social significance based on perceived racial characteristics. Racialization assigns social roles and statuses, often leading to unequal treatment and systemic discrimination.
Racism is ordinary	is a principle from CRT that posits that racism is a common and ingrained aspect of society, influencing laws, institutions, and social practices. It underscores the notion that racism is not an aberration but a normalized feature of social interactions and structures.
Reflective self-awareness	is when one examines oneself to realistically assess one's own biases, "knowledge, values, qualities, skills, and

	behaviors" (Henriques, 2016, n.p.; Sloan et al., 2018). Reflection is about looking back on past experiences as a way of understanding one's self and the world (Kondrat, 1999; Sloan et al., 2018).
Reflexive self-awareness	involves the process and ability to notice why things are the way they are, specifically one's part in it.
Restorative justice	is a victim-centered method of peacefully resolving conflict and promoting healing that is rooted in Indigenous culture. Restorative justice is most commonly applied in criminal justice but has been applied to other disciplines such as education and social work.
Sanism	which refers to the systematic oppression of individuals who have been diagnosed with mental health conditions, manifests in both subtle and overt acts of discrimination and oppression.
Scholar-Practitioner	is someone who merges scholarly research with practice application for the purpose of creating practical knowledge, definable skills, and evidence-based tools that positively impact real-world people, problems, and issues. A primary characteristic of scholar-practitioners is that they value knowledge as a means to improve practice and understand that research-based literature has relevance for both program and policy.
School-to-prison pipeline	is a term for the pathway created by punitive systems and policies that push youth with academic and behavioral problems (particularly BIPOC and LGBTQ+ youth) out of schools and into

	the juvenile justice or adult criminal legal system.
Seroversary	is a term used to describe and empower the anniversary of learning one's positive HIV status.
Servant Leadership	is a non-traditional leadership philosophy embedded in behaviors and practices that primarily emphasize the well-being of those served (Greenleaf, 1970).
Social justice	is the action toward and belief that everyone deserves equal rights, opportunities, and treatment regardless of race, economic status, sexuality, or gender identity (Dolan-Reilly, 2013).
Spirituality	is a set of personal beliefs that come from an individual's perception of self and their relationship to both the natural world and some world or reality beyond that which can be seen (Winship, 2002).
Strength Perspective	is a key feature in the Black Helping Tradition, which emphasizes the human capacity for resilience, courage, and ingenuity, and it encourages people and communities to achieve their own goals (Martin & Martin, 2003).
Structural racism	refers to the totality of ways in which societies foster racial discrimination through mutually reinforcing systems of housing, education, employment, earnings, benefits, credit, media, healthcare, and criminal justice. These patterns and practices, in turn, reinforce discriminatory beliefs, values, and distribution of resources (Bailey et al., 2017).
Systemic inequality	refers to historical and current organized patterns of mistreatment and oppression. These oppressive systems are part of the

foundation of the United States, as they are found in laws, policies, and institutions and serve to further reinforce the exploitation of marginalized social groups while elevating those who are dominant.

Transmisia — is the "hatred and systemized discrimination or antagonism directed against transgender, [gender non-conforming], non-binary, genderqueer, and agender persons" (Simmons University Library, 2025). It recognizes that the violence enacted against trans communities is about hatred and supposed fear and, like transphobia, lives in the realm of the personal, but works in tandem with broader systems of oppression and marginalization. Naming the hatred of trans communities as transphobia rather than transmisia fails to recognize how systemic oppression emboldens some to enact violence and harm toward trans communities and continues to alleviate the broader society from addressing trans oppression at a systems level by framing it as a personal fear (Currie et al., 2024).

Transmisogynoir — is oppression at the intersection of cisgenderism, cissexism, misogyny, racism, and anti-Blackness.

Trauma bond — is the process of forming bonds, connections, affinity, likeness, or emotional closeness through the sharing and/or reliving of emotional, experiential, and/or mental trauma exposure.

Trauma porn — is the exploitative practice of continuously highlighting a marginalized group's trauma for the purpose of invoking empathy, consoling, or entertaining non-marginalized groups. This practice often results in marginalized groups reliving traumatic experiences without the

	acknowledgment of re-traumatization. Additionally, it does not provide non-marginalized groups with concrete mechanisms to engage in meaningful change. The term is most commonly associated with media portrayal of communities of color.
Queer/Queering	is a term that originates from the American gay rights activist circles of the 1990s, as a reclaimed and redefined previously derogatory term. Queering refers to playing with both gender and orientation in a sociopolitical sense, often being provocative around gender norms to highlight gender stereotypes of culture. Queer is an identity term, sometimes used as an umbrella term for people who do not identify as straight and cisgender (Currie et al., 2024).
Queer methodology	is informed by queer theory and refers to methods used in research that challenge the use of binary, variable-dependent social identity categories.
Undetectables Support Model	is a model that pairs online, twenty-four-hour, in-person support (inclusive of support groups and other forms of direct service delivery), and "Judy support" (peer-to-peer social activities that are engaging and also raise the health and advocacy literacy of participants). It references the gay/queer colloquial phrase "friend of Judy" and "my Judies," which marks queer/gay friendships and allied trusted individuals ("Judy" as in Judy Garland a friend and ally to queer/gay individuals during her lifetime) for HIV-positive queer/gay/bisexual men.
White supremacy	is a global ideology that is supported by people who identify as white and who are committed to controlling, subjugating,

	and dominating people classified as non-white through systems in all spheres of human activity, such as economics, education, religion, labor, law, politics, entertainment, sex/love, war, and counter-war (Fuller, 1984).
Whiteness and white racialized identity	refer to the way that white people, their customs, culture, and beliefs operate as the standard by which all other groups are compared. Whiteness is also at the core of understanding race in America. Whiteness and the normalization of white racial identity throughout America's history have created a culture where nonwhite persons are seen as inferior or abnormal (www.nmaahc.si.edu, 2024).

REFERENCES

Amoakohene, C., Harris-Mungo, T., & Pankewich, C. (2021, August 12–13). *Anti-Oppressive Practice: An Interactive Conversation* [Virtual]. Collaborations for Change Virtual Conference, Calgary. https://bp-net.ca/news-updates/collaborations-for-change- virtual-conference/

Asante, M. (2006). Forward. In G. J. S. Dei and A. Kempf (Eds.), *Anti-colonialism and education: The politics of resistance* (pp. ix–x). Sense.

Ayyala, R. S., & Coley, B. D. (2022). Promoting gender equity and inclusion through allyship. *Pediatric Radiology, 52*(7), 1202–1206. https://doi.org/10.1007/s00247-022-05345-3.

Bailey, Z. D., Krieger, N., Agénor, M., Graves, J., Linos, N., & Bassett, M. T. (2017). Structural racism and health inequities in the USA: Evidence and interventions. *The Lancet, 389*(10077), 1453–1463.

Baylor University Diana R. Garland School of Social Work. (2023). "5 Things to know about Anti-Oppressive Practice in Social Work." https://gsswstories.baylor.edu/blog/5-things-to- know-about-anti-oppressive-practice-in-social-work.

Bell, D. (2005). *The Derrick Bell reader* (vol. 75). New York University Press.

Brookfield, S. (1995). *Becoming a critically reflective teacher*. Jossey-Bass.

Campbell, Fiona Kumari. (2001). Inciting legal fictions: Disability's date with ontology and the ableist body of the law. *Griffith Law Review, 10*, 42–62.

Carlson, M., & Donohoe, M. (2010). *The executive director's guide to thriving as a nonprofit leader*. John Wiley & Sons.

Centre for Innovation in Campus Mental Health. "Anti-oppressive Practice." https://campusmentalhealth.ca/.

Clements, K. C. (2019). What is cissexism? What does it mean to be cissexist? www.healthline.com/health/ transgender/cissexist

Comrie, J. W., Landor, A. M., Riley, K. T., & Williamson, J. D. (2022, June). *Anti-Blackness/colorism. Moving Toward Antibigotry.* www.bu.edu/antiracism- center/files/2022/06/Anti-Black.pdf

Currie, N., Simmons-Horton, S., Burke, J., Farley, R., & Olson-Kennedy, A. (2024). Gender and orientation diversity in the family courts: A guide to terms and present issues. *Family Court Review, 62*(3), 615–634.

Di Nicola, V. (2020). The Global South: An emergent epistemology for social psychiatry. *World Social Psychiatry, 2*(1), 20–26.

Dolan-Reilly, G. (2013). The definition of social justice. *Social Justice Solutions,* New York, USA, January 15. www.socialjusticesolutions.org/2013/01/15/the-definition-of-social-justice/

Fook, J. (1999). Critical reflectivity in education and practice. In B. Pease & J. Fook (Eds.), *Transforming social work practice: postmodern critical perspectives* (pp. 195–208). Allen & Unwin.

Freire, P. (1970). *Pedagogy of the oppressed.* Herder & Herder.

Fuller, N. (1984). *The united-independent compensatory code/system/concept: A textbook/workbook for thought, speech, and/or action, for victims of racism (white supremacy).* Produce Justice LLC.

Greenleaf, R. K. (1970). The servant as leader. *Greenleaf Center.* www.greenleaf.org.

Harro, B. (2000). The cycle of socialization. In M. Adams, W. J. Blumenfeld, R. Castañeda, H. W. Hackman, M. L. Peters, & X. Zúñiga (Eds.) *Readings for diversity and social justice* (vol. 2, pp. 52–58). Routledge.

Henriques, G. (2016). Self-reflective awareness: A crucial life skill. *Psychology Today, 10,* www.psychologytoday.com/us/blog/theory-of-knowledge/201609/self-reflective-awareness-a-crucial-life-skill.

Hoskin, R. A. (2019) Femmephobia: The role of anti-femininity and gender policing in LGBTQ+ people's experiences of discrimination. *Sex Roles, 81*(11–12), 686–703. https://doi.org/10.1007/s11199-019-01021-3

Kivel, P. (2013). *Living in the shadow of the cross: Understanding and resisting the power and privilege of Christian hegemony.* New Society.

Kondrat, M. E. (1999). Who is the "self" in self-aware: Professional self-awareness from a critical theory perspective. *Social Service Review, 73*(4), 451–477.

Ladson-Billings, G. (2006). From the achievement gap to the education debt: Understanding achievement in U.S. schools. *Educational Researcher, 35*(7), 3–12.

Love, B. J. (2018). Developing a liberatory consciousness. In Adams, M., Blumenfeld, W. J., Catalano, D. C., DeJong, K. S., Hackman, H. W., Hopkins, L. E., Love, B. J., Peters, M. L., Shlasko, D., & Zuniga, X. (eds.), *Readings for diversity and social justice* (4th ed., pp. 610–615). Routledge.

Lusk, M., Terrazas, S., & Salcido, R. (2017). Critical cultural competence in social work supervision. *Human Service Organizations: Management, Leadership & Governance, 41*(5), 464–476.

Manzo, R. D., Yepez, M., Preciado, B., & Merin, L. S. (2023). A community-driven research framework: Integrating promotores as co-researchers. *Progress*

in *Community Health Partnerships: Research, Education, and Action, 17*(4), 689–698.
Martin, Elmer P., & Martin, J. M. (2003). *Spirituality and the Black helping tradition in social work.* National Association of Social Workers.
Mbiti, J. S. (1970). *African religions and philosophy.* Anchor Books.
Melaku, T., Beeman, A., Smith, D. G., & Brad Johnson, W. (2021). Be a better ally. *Harvard Business Review, 98*(6), 135–139. https://hbr.org/2020/11/be-a-better-ally.
Mignolo, W., & Walsh, C. E. (2018). *On decoloniality: Concepts, analytics, praxis.* Duke University Press.
National Museum of African American History and Culture. "Talking About Race." https://nmaahc.si.edu/learn/talking-about-race/topics/whiteness.
Nkrumah, K. (1965). *Neo-colonialism, the last stage of imperialism.* London: Thomas Nelson & Sons, Ltd.
Pon, G., Phillips, D., Clarke, J., & Abdillahi, I. (2017). Who's protecting whom? In D. Baines (Ed.) *Doing anti-oppressive practice: Social justice social work* (Chapter 4). Halifax, NS: Fernwood.
Schiele, J. H. (1994). Afrocentricity as an alternative world view for equality. *Journal of Progressive Human Services, 5*(1), 5–25.
Simmons University Library. (2025, July 30). *Anti-Oppression: Anti-Transmisia* [LibGuide]. Simmons University. https://simmons.libguides.com/anti-oppression/anti-transmisia
Sloan, L., Joyner, M., Stakeman, C., & Schmitz, C. (2018). *Critical multiculturalism and intersectionality in a complex world.* Oxford University Press.
Turner, F. J. (Ed.). (2017). *Social work treatment: Interlocking theoretical approaches.* Oxford University Press.
United Nations. "Treaty Bodies." www.ohchr.org/en/treaty-bodies.
Watson-Singleton, N. N., Lewis, J. A., & Dworkin, E. R. (2023). Toward a socially just diversity science: Using intersectional mixed methods research to center multiply marginalized Black, Indigenous, and People of Color (BIPOC). *Cultural Diversity and Ethnic Minority Psychology, 29*(1), 34.
Walumbwa, F. O., Avolio, B. J., Gardner, W. L., Wernsing, T. S., & Peterson, S. J. (2008). Authentic leadership: Development and validation of a theory-based measure. *Journal of management, 34*(1), 89–126.
Winship, J. (2002). *Social Work Department.* Infusing Spirituality and Religion into Social Work Practice. (n.d.). www.nacsw.org/AudioConf/042902Handouts.htm
Wright, E. D., Jones, K., White, G., Harper, R., & Alhassan, M. (2018). *School of social work handbook.* Clark Atlanta University.
Young, I. M. (2000). Five faces of oppression. In M. Adams, W. J. Blumenfeld, R. Castañeda, H. W. Hackman, M. L. Peters, & X. Zúñiga (Eds.) *Readings for diversity and social justice* (pp. 35–49). Routledge.

Further Reading

Anti-Oppressive and Decolonial Resources Unlocked
Nathaniel L. Currie

Resources Unlocked: Readings, Materials, and Tools for Anti-Oppressive Decolonial Work

The intention of this text is to be interactive and comprehensive for supervisors and supervisees, leaders, and professionals across the helping professions. There is an endless supply of readings, tools, media, and activities available around the world that can assist you in creating and maintaining your anti-oppressive decolonial practice process. In this chapter, you will find some of the most important resources used by experts and scholars in this area of practice, including many used and provided by the scholar-practitioners that have contributed to this text. This is not a complete list but a beginning offering to assist your journey.

Key Texts on Anti-Oppressive Practice and Clinical Supervision

Baines, D. (2020). *Doing anti-oppressive practice: Social justice social work.* Fernwood.

Berger, R., Quiros, L., & Benavidez-Hatzis, J. R. (2018). The intersection of identities in supervision for trauma-informed practice: Challenges and strategies. *The Clinical Supervisor, 37*(1), 122–141.

Bussey, S. R. (2024). Skills to enhance the efficacy of anti-racist supervision. *Journal of Social Work, 24*(3), 397–414.

Constance-Huggins, M. A., & Pate, E. C. (Eds.). (2025). *Critical race theory in action: Knowledge and application in social work practice.* Cambridge University Press.

Dominelli, L. (2017). *Anti-racist social work.* Red Globe Press.

Edwards, J., & Bess, J. (1998). Developing effectiveness in the therapeutic use of self. *Clinical Social Work Journal, 26*(1), 89–105

Goggin, E., Werkmeister Rozas, L., & Garran, A. M. (2016). A case of mistaken identity: What happens when race is a factor. *Journal of Social Work Practice, 30*(4), 349–363.

González-Prendes, A. A., & Brisebois, K. (2012). Cognitive-behavioral therapy and social work values: A critical analysis. *Journal of Social Work Values and Ethics, 9*(2), 21–33.

Kaushik, A. (2017). Use of self in social work: Rhetoric or reality. *Journal of Social Work Values and Ethics, 14*(1), 21–29.

Mullan, J. (2023). *Decolonizing therapy: Oppression, historical trauma, and politicizing your practice*. W. W. Norton & Company.

Sakamoto, I., & Pitner, R. O. (2005). Use of critical consciousness in anti-oppressive social work practice: Disentangling power dynamics at personal and structural levels. *The British Journal of Social Work, 35*(4), 435–452.

Wilcox, M. M., Winkeljohn Black, S., Drinane, J. M., Morales-Ramirez, I., Akef, Z., Tao, K. W., DeBlaere, C., Hook, J. N., Davis, D. E., Watkins, C., & Owen, J. (2022). A brief qualitative examination of multicultural orientation in clinical supervision. *Professional Psychology: Research and Practice, 53*(6), 585–595.

Key Texts on Practice, Agency, and Community Social Change

Aguilera, R. V., Rupp, D. E., Williams, C. A., & Ganapathi, J. (2007). Putting the S back in corporate social responsibility: A multilevel theory of social change in organizations. *Academy of Management Review, 32*(3), 836–863.

Alase, A. O. (2017). The task of reviewing and finding the right organizational change theory. *International Journal of Educational Leadership and Management, 5*(2), 198–215.

Battilana, J., & Casciaro, T. (2013). Overcoming resistance to organizational change: Strong ties and affective cooptation. *Management Science, 59*(4), 819–836.

Cohen, C. J. (2009). *The boundaries of Blackness: AIDS and the breakdown of Black politics*. University of Chicago Press.

Currie, G., Lockett, A., & Suhomlinova, O. (2009). Leadership and institutional change in the public sector: The case of secondary schools in England. *The Leadership Quarterly, 20*(5), 664–679.

Currie, N., Simmons-Horton, S., Burke, J., Farley, R., & Olson-Kennedy, A. (2024). Gender and orientation diversity in the family courts: A guide to terms and present issues. *Family Court Review, 62*(3), 615–634.

Green, M. P. & LCSW-R, A. E. (2007). Beyond diversity and multiculturalism: Towards the development of anti-racist institutions and leaders. *Journal for Nonprofit Management, 11*(1), 9–17.

Jenkins, J. J., & Dillon, P. (2012). "This is what we're all about": The (re)construction of an oppressive organizational structure. *Southern Communication Journal, 77*(4), 287–306.

Jimmieson, N. L., White, K. M., & Peach, M. (2004). Employee readiness for change: Utilizing the theory of planned behavior to inform change management. *Academy of Management Proceedings*, C1–C6.

Katombe, M. (2018). The effect of leadership on the resistance to change in an organization. *OD Practitioner, 50*(3), 47–55.

Owusu, N. (2020, January 28). Hiring a chief diversity officer won't fix your racist company culture. Catapult. https://catapult.co/stories/women-of-color-chief-diversity-officers-cannot-fix-racist-company-culture-nadia-owusu

Roberts, D. C. (2017). Transitions and transformations in leadership. In S. R. Komives & W. Wagner (Eds.), *Leadership for a better world. Part 1: Understanding the social change model of leadership development* (2nd ed., pp. 5–16). Jossey-Bass.

Ruggs, E., & Avery, D. (2020, June 10). Organizations cannot afford to stay silent on racial injustice. MIT Sloan Management Review. Retrieved from Coursepack.

Shelton, J., Kroehle, K., & Andia, M. M. (2019). The trans person is not the problem: Brave spaces and structural competence as educative tools for trans justice in social work. *Journal of Sociology & Social Welfare, 46*(4), 97–123.

Skendall, K. C. (2017). An overview of the social change model of leadership development. In S. R. Komives & W. Wagner (Eds.), *Leadership for a better world: Understanding the social change model of leadership development* (2nd ed., pp. 17–40). Jossey-Bass.

Sondaitė, J., & Keidonaitė, G. (2020). Experience of transformative leadership: Subordinate's perspective. *Business: Theory and Practice, 21*(1), 373.

Varma, V. (2020). Developing change readiness: A video-based classroom exercise. *Management Teaching Review, 5*(1), 20–31.

Wagner, W. (2017). Examining social change. In S. R. Komives & W. Wagner (Eds.), *Leadership for a better world: Understanding the social change model of leadership development* (2nd ed., pp. 233–260). Jossey-Bass.

Supplementary Resources for Continued Learning and Curriculum Building

Equal Justice Initiative – www.Eji.org
Just Associates. (2006). Making change happen: Power – www.racialequitytools.org/resources/act/strategies/community-engagement
Othering & Belonging Institute – https://belonging.berkeley.edu/
Poverty & Race – A publication of the *Poverty & Race Research Action Council* – www.prrac.org/poverty-and-race/
Racial Equity Tools – www.racialequitytools.org
Speak Up: Responding to Everyday Bigotry – *Southern Poverty Law Center* – www.splcenter.org/20150125/speak-responding-everyday-bigotry#everyday-bigotry

Key Texts on Anti-Oppression for Continued Learning and Curriculum Building

Beck, E. (2019). Naming white supremacy in social work curriculum. *Journal of Women and Social Work, 34*(3), 393–398.

Breaux, H. P., & Thyer, B. A. (2021). Transgender theory for contemporary social work practice: A question of values and ethics. *Journal of Social Work Values and Ethics, 18*(1), 73–89.

Burke, B., & Harrison, P. (1998). Anti-oppressive practice. In *Social work* (pp. 229–239). Palgrave.

Campbell, E. (2018). Critical race theory: A content analysis of the social work literature. *Journal of Sociological Research, 9*(1), 50–60.

Dupré, M. (2018). Critical social work practice addressing disability: Social work education in the future. *Canadian Social Work, 20*(1), 124–138.

Ferreira, S. B., & Ferreira, R. J. (2019). Fostering awareness of self in the education of social work students by means of critical reflectivity. *Social Work, 55*(2), 119–131.

Gray, M., Coates, J., & Hetherington, T. (2007). Hearing Indigenous voices in mainstream social work. *Families in Society, 88*(1), 55–66.

Pulliam, R. M. (2017). Practical application of critical race theory: A social justice course design. *Journal of Social Work Education, 53*(3), 414–423.

Simon, J. D., Boyd, R., & Subica, A. M. (2022). Refocusing intersectionality in social work education: Creating a brave space to discuss oppression and privilege. *Journal of Social Work Education, 58*(1), 34–45.

Strier, R., & Binyamin, S. (2014). Introducing anti-oppressive social work practices in public services: Rhetoric to practice. *The British Journal of Social Work, 44*(8), 2095–2112.

Tamburro, A. (2013). Including decolonization in social work education and practice. *Journal of Indigenous Social Development, 2*(1), 1–16.

Taylor, E. (1998). A primer on critical race theory: Who are the critical race theorists and what are they saying? *The Journal of Blacks in Higher Education, 19*, 122–124.

Thomas, R., & Green, J. (2007). A way of life: Indigenous perspectives on anti-oppressive living. *First Peoples Child & Family Review: A Journal on Innovation and Best Practices in Aboriginal Child Welfare Administration, Research, Policy & Practice, 3*(1), 91–104.

Varghese, R. (2016). Teaching to transform? Addressing race and racism in the teaching of clinical social work practice. *Journal of Social Work Education, 52* (Suppl. 1), 134–147.

Media and Activities for Curriculum Building and Group Learning

Crenshaw, K. (Host). (2018, November 4 2024–2025, Janaury 29) [65 Audio podcast episodes]. In Intersectionality Matters!. American Policy Forum.

Hannah-Jones, N. (Host). (2019, September 13). The Birth of American Music (No. 3) [Audio podcast episode]. In 1619. New York Times.

(Host). (2019, September 13). The Economy That Slavery Built (No. 2) [Audio podcast episode]. In 1619. New York Times.

(Host). (2019, September 13). The Fight for a True Democracy (No. 1) [Audio podcast episode]. In 1619. New York Times.

(Host). (2019, September 13). How the Bad Blood Started (No. 4) [Audio podcast episode]. In 1619. *New York Times*.

(Host). (2019, September 13). The Land of Our Fathers, Part 1 (No. 5) [Audio podcast episode]. In 1619. *New York Times*.

(Host). (2019, September 13). The Land of Our Fathers, Part 2 (No. 5) [Audio podcast episode]. In 1619. *New York Times*.

Holding Ground Productions. (1996). *Holding ground: The rebirth of Dudley Street* [Film].

Holding Ground Productions. (2013). *Gaining ground: Building community on Dudley Street* [Film].

Jhally, S. (Director), & hooks, b. (Speaker). (1997). bell hooks: Cultural Criticism & Transformation [Film]. Media Education Foundation.

This American Life. (2018). Episode 656, "Let me count the ways" [Audio podcast episode]. Available at: www.thisamericanlife.org/656/let-me-count-the-ways

University of Houston. "Critical Concept: Anti Oppressive Practice" [Video]. YouTube, uploaded by UH Class OET, 5 March 2018, www.youtube.com/watch?v=yX7Oz7ir-IE

Index

Please note that a number in bold denotes a box or table, *and italics* refer to a figure, while ***bold italics*** mean a figure inside a box.

Aarons-Cooke, S. M., xii, xvi, 263–288
  Black case worker seeking anti-oppressive supervision, **268–271**
ableism, 48, 49, 51, 305
  glossary, 313
Abrams, L. S., 112
abstract liberalism, 111
academia, 25, 63
academics, 14–15, 63, 192
accountability, 137, 146, 162, 166, 167
accreditation programs: anti-oppressive leadership, 302–304
acculturation, **97–98**
ACP. *See* Afrocentric perspective
ADDRESSING model (Hays), 151
administrative supervision, 13–14
ADORE model, 89
advocacy, 46, 242
  mental health practice (psycholegal setting), 193–194
affect, **297**
  definition, **295**
African Americans, 45, 47, 95, 121, 240, 244, 275
  subjugation perpetuated, 187
African children: sold into slavery, 188
Africultural coping strategies, 275–276
  cognitive and emotional debriefing, 275
  collective coping, 276
  ritual-centered coping, 276
  spiritually-centered coping, 275, 277
Afrocentric perspective, xi, 47, 239
  concepts, **246**
  glossary, 313
  social work, 244–245
  social work supervision, 42
  underpinnings, 245–247
  use within social institutions (key features), 242, 247

Afrocentric principles, 43, 44
  anti-oppressive supervision, 44–46
  application in clinical supervision, 44–46
  reflection questions, 47
  social institutions (decolonization), 239–248
Afrocentric principles (praxis in decoloniality), 44–46
  advocacy, 46
  collectivist orientation, 46
  community engagement, 45
  critical consciousness, 46
  cultural awareness, 45
  cultural humility, 46
  culturally-relevant interventions, 45
  ethics, 46
  holistic approach, 45
  language and communication, 45
  social justice, 46
  spirituality and religion, 46
  strengths-based focus, 45
Afrocentricity, 43, 244–248
  social work, 244–245
agency, 84, 134, 208
  key texts, 339–340
agency leadership, 293, 294, 301
Ahmed (2017), 58
AIDS Coalition to Unleash Power (ACT UP), **297**
Aldana, A., viii, xvi, 106–126
Allston, L.: *Community II* (artwork), *294*
allyship, 145–148, 260
  clinical work, 146
  definition, 145
  glossary, 314
  merger with leadership, 146–147
alternative response investigations (ARI): case vignette, **279–280**
"alternative schools," 192

American Psychological Association (APA): Code of Ethics (2017), 182
anti-Black racism, 82, 88, 89, 94, 254, 258, 263, 273, 283
anti-oppressive clinical supervision, 268
glossary, 314
history (family separation system), 265-266
language, 265
"manifestation of anti-Blackness," 83
multilayered, 265
unique and vicious, 265
anti-Blackness, xi, 82-83, 88, 89, 254, 255, 257, 258, 282
continuation of family separation system, 266-268
definition, 82
dimensions (helping professions), **261**
anti-miscegenation, 251
anti-oppression, 251-260
definition, 162
key texts, 340-341
resources, 342
training, 214
anti-oppression research: community-based, 231-237
principles, 232
anti-oppressive decolonial supervision, ix, 17, 19
anti-oppressive lens (social work supervision), viii, 32-72
Afrocentric perspective (social work supervision), 42
Afrocentric principles (importance), 43
Afrocentric principles (praxis in decoloniality), 44-46
cognitive linguistics (implications), 35
commitment to ongoing education, 70-71
critical disability theory, 48-49
cultural competence (enhancement), 43
cultural humility, 68-69
decentering oneself, 70
decolonization lens, 32
empathy, 69-70
empowerment (promotion), 43
empowerment theory, 66-67
framing (empowered by clinical supervision), 41
framing and metaphor, 33-35
gender studies and critical transgender theory, 50-51
language, 33
Latino critical perspective, 49-72
linguistic self-reflexivity, 35-36
people living with HIV (criminalization), **38-39**
power imbalances, 71
practice guidance (Dudley Street Initiative), **67**
queer theory, 60-66

reflection questions, **39**, 41, 72
social justice (advancement), 44
social justice (practice and policy), 36-41
spirituality (incorporation), 44
summary, 32
transgender, 50-60
transgender theory (application), 57-58
transgender theory (overview), 51-57
transgender theory (supervision practice), 58-60
anti-oppressive practice (AOP), ix, 1, 3-4, 136
application (family separation system), 271-279
call to action, 174-175
definition, 162
development, 172
foundational principles, 162-163
glossary, 315
implementation, 171
importance, 161
integration into supervision, 165-170
intersectionality (role in leadership and supervision), 163-164
key texts, 339-340
leadership and supervision, 161-176
mental health practice (psycholegal setting), 180-196
power dynamics in supervisor relationships, 164-165
practice activity, 176
practice guidance, **16**
reflective questions, 175
'social justice orientation to identify root causes', 161
anti-oppressive practice (challenges and opportunities), 173-174
barriers to implementation, 173
growth and innovation, 174
resistance, 173-174
anti-oppressive practice (self-reflection and professional development), 170-174
challenges and opportunities, 173-174
continuous improvement and adaptation, 172
critical self-reflection, 171
cultural self-awareness, 170-171
equity and inclusion, 172
anti-oppressive principles, 165-170
addressing implicit bias and microaggressions in supervision, 166-167
co-creation, 280-282
confidentiality and intersectionality, 169
cultural competence, 165
culturally-affirming leadership, 167
equity and social justice, 167
ethical considerations, 168-169

inclusive environment, 165–166
power dynamics (ethical navigation), 169–170
structural changes within organizations, 167–168
anti-oppressive social work (AOSW), 141
intersectionality with supervision, 142–143
anti-oppressive social work (key principles), 141
challenging oppression, 141
collaboration, 141
intersectionality, 141
power awareness, 141
reflective practice, 141
anti-oppressive supervision (AOS), 142. *See also* anti-racist and affirming supervision and leadership
definition, 142
anti-oppressive supervision (principles), 141
awareness of power and authority, 142
collaboration and empowerment, 142
cultural sensitivity, 142
ethics and social justice, 142
reflective practice, 142
anti-oppressive systems: glossary, 315
anti-oppressive work, xii, 9, 15, 23, **156**, 260
anti-racism
"can be ordinary," 109–118
definition, 302
DEIPAR, 87–89
education, 214
glossary, 316
higher education, 251–260
training, 214
anti-racism heuristics, 106–126. *See also* if-then anti-racism heuristics
CRT tenets and practice implications, **109**
theoretical foundations, 106–108
therapeutic treatment, 116–117
anti-racism praxis, viii, 108, 122, 124, 126
anti-racist and affirming supervision and leadership, 137–141. *See also* clinical supervision
anti-oppressive social work, 141
conversations (difficult and vulnerable), 138
critical reflection, 139
curriculum development, 139
emotional responses, 138
learning strategies (active), 140
oppression and decolonization, 139
principles and practices, 137
professional boundaries, 138
race and racism, 139
resistance, 140–141
anti-racist clinical practice, 106, 108, 116, 122, 126
anti-racist practices, viii, 115, 123, 124, 136

Anti-Racist Style Indicator, 272, 277, 278
apartheid, 244
appearance, 16, 52, 57
appearance-reality contrast, 57
Arao, B., 171
art as social justice
affect and effect, **295–296**
affective effect, effective affect, **296**
Bordowitz, G., 297
case vignette, **295–298**
Cullors, P., **297**
entanglement, **296–297**
interpretation, **298**
reflective questions, **298**
Tourmaline, **298**
art as social movement, 294
artivism, **295**
Asakura, K., 10, 167, 169
Asante, M.: *Afrocentricity* (1980), 244
Ashley, W., 121, 169
Association of Family and Conciliation Courts (AFCC): *Guidelines for Parenting Plan Evaluations* (2022), 189
Association of Social Work Boards (ASWB)
examination pass rate (2022) analysis, 194
licensing examination, 148
Atlanta, 26–29, **307**
Atlanta University, 240
School of Social Work, 245
Atlanta: Positive Impact Health Centers, **236**
attention deficit hyperactivity disorder (ADHD), **269**
attorneys: profession more than 80 percent white in US, 184
Authentic Family Engagement and Strengthening (AFES), 281
authentic leadership, 150, 170
glossary, 316
authenticity, 150
key quality (social work practice), 19–20
autonomy, x, 64, 66, **246**, 330
awareness: oppressive systems (dismantling), 211–215

Bailey, G., vii, xvi, 1–5
Bailey, Z., 332
Baltimore, **307**
Baylor School of Social Work, 315
Bell, D., 260, 267
Permanence of Racism (1992), 252
Benavente, G., 63
Bess, J. M., 20
best practice, 2, 183
mental health models, 183–184
Bettcher, T. M., 57

bias, 24, 46, 131, 137
bigotry, xi, 114, 156
binary structures, 64
BIPOC, xi, 188, 192, **228**, 239, 321
   children, 191
   Civil Rights Era (consequences), 240–241
   glossary, 316
   neo-colonialism (impact), 241–242
   servant leadership, 242–244
   social workers, 194
   transactional leadership style, 242
   tremendous success, 243
   under-representation, 193
Black American liberation movement, 223
Black Americans, 207, 223
Black children, xii, 188, 189, 254, 255, 256, 271, 278
   experience worst parts of society, 255
Black codes, 266
Black critical theory (BlackCrit), xii, 251–260, 264, 282
   anti-Blackness (family separation system), 266–268
   helping professions, 256–261
Black families, xii, 188, 189
Black feminism, 85
Black GBMSM, **235**
Black history, 191
Black leaders: family separation system, 263–288
Black lesbians, 181
Black Lives Matter, **297**
Black mothers, 265, **269**
Black Power Movement, 245
Black same-gender-loving (SGL) community, **306–311**
Black students, 255, 257
Black women, xxi, 85, 86, 119, 212, 278, 282, 284
Black, Indigenous, and People of Color. *See* BIPOC
BlackCrit: same as 'Black critical theory' (*qv*), 266
Bolden, C., **215**
Bonilla-Silva, E., 111
Bordowitz, G., 297
Boston, 293
Boston Redevelopment Authority, **67**
Boston: Dudley Street Neighborhood Initiative, **67**, 301
Bowleg, L., 66
Brace, C. L., 266
brave space, 17–18, 171, 300
   definition, 18
Breshears, E. M., 299
bricke, s., xii, xvii, **295–298**

Brooks, W. K., 181
Brown v. Board of Education (1954), 184
Brown, E., **26**
Burke, J., viii–ix, xvii
   anti-oppressive lens, 32–72
   case vignette (empowerment across lifespan), 152–157
   decolonization (supervision and leadership), 131–157
burnout, 187, **269**, 278

California, 264
Camp Wediko, *153*
   case vignette (empowerment across lifespan), 152–157
   funding structure, **156**
   guiding principles, **153**
capacity-building, 233, 234
capitalism, 205, 211
   core, 207
   dismantling, 207
   misguided values, 146
   perpetuates inequality, 212
carceral logic, 283, 284
   glossary, 317
carceral state, 186, 211, 266
Carn, R. H., **26**
case vignettes, vii–viii, x–xii
   alternative response investigations, **279–280**
   art as social justice and liberation movement, **295–298**
   Black case worker seeking anti-oppressive supervision, **268–271**
   Camp Wediko (empowerment across lifespan), 152–157
   children (inequity and oppression), **195–196**
   CRT-informed heuristics, 124–126
   CRT-informed praxis questions, 125–126
   DEIPAR in community practice, **96–100**
   family separation system (Hazel), **287–288**
   military-based social work, **226–228**
Center for Artistic Activism, 295
Centers for Disease Control (CDC), **39**
ceremony, 11
charisma, 21, 90
Chaudhry, V., 63
child abuse, **16**, 189, 269, **279**, 281
child custody, 189–191
Child Protective Services, **287**
child welfare, 188–189
child welfare system: same as "family separation system" (*qv*), 263
children, 273–274
   inequity and oppression, **195–196**
children of color, 255, 256

cisgender, 23, 51, 273
cisgender heterosexual community, 187
cisgenderism, 53, 54, 59, 333
　definition, 23
　glossary, 317
cisheteropatriarchal ideals, 113
cisheterosexism, **110**, 119, 123, 326
cisnormative binary gender categories, 64
cisnormative binary structures, 64
cisnormativity, 182
cissexism, 51, 54, 333
　glossary, 317
Civil Rights Act (1964), 257
Civil Rights Era, 245
　unexpected consequences, 240–241
Clark Atlanta University, **28**, **67**
classism, 3, **110**, 119, **123**, 207, 209, 326
Clemens, K., 171
clinical practice
　DisCrit (application), 48–49
　LatCrit, 49–72
clinical praxis: incorporation of CRT, 106–126
clinical supervision, 11, 13. *See also* social work supervision
　anti-oppressive, 268
　application of Afrocentric principles (importance), 43
　CRT-informed, 123
　dual relationships, 24–26
　family separation system, 263–288
　framing (empowerment), 41
　key texts, 338–339
　linguistic self-reflexivity, 35–36
clinical supervision (decolonization), beginning process, vii, 9–30
clinical supervision and leadership
　anti-oppressive practice, 3–4
　decolonization, 1–5
　necessity of now, vii
　practice interventions, 4–5
clinical work: allyship, 146
clinicians: advanced, 14
co-conspirator, xix, 146, 260
　glossary, 318
co-creation
　anti-oppressive principles, 280–282
　glossary, 318
codes of ethics, 25, 26, 65, 70, 182
cognitive behavioral therapy (CBT), 117, 213
cognitive linguistics, 33, 34
　implications, 35
cognitive structures, 34, 324
cognitive-behavioral therapy (CBT)
　trauma-focused, 186
Cohen, C. J., 60

collective action, 143, 213, 225, **297**
collective imperialism, 240
　glossary, 318
collective memory, 208
collective pain, 222–224
　interplay with individual pain, 222
collective view of self, **246**
collectivism, 43, 44, 46, 184, 241
colonialism, 87, 118, 180, 211, 218, 244, 265, 319
　historical roots of oppression, 206–207
　impacts on marginalized communities, 131
　pedagogies, 240
coloniality, 88, 94, 319
coloniality of power (Quijano), 86
colonization, 88
　glossary, 319
colorblind approaches, 184
colorblind racism, 111
color-evasive ideology, 115
communication, 45, 137, 162, 166, 170, 297
communities (supervision and leadership), 293–312
　anti-oppressive leadership, 302–304
　art as social justice (case vignette), **295–298**
　facilitative leadership, 299
　focused leadership, 304–305
　practice reflection (starting organization to save life), **306–311**
　preparing future leaders, 301–302
　reflection questions, 306, **311**
　social work 'pervasive', 305–306
　summary, 306
　transitional leadership and succession planning, 299–301
communities of color, 121, 215, 334
community, 274–277
community engagement, 45, 132, 144, 163
community social change: key texts, 339–340
community support, 220
　healing through collective action, 213
community trauma, 208–209, 210
community-based organizations (CBOs), **236**
　elevation with AOP, 26–29
community-based participatory research (CBPR), i, x, 231–237
　anti-oppressive, 232–234
　capacity-building, 233, 234
　future research, 235
　glossary, 319
　implications, 234–235
　power to perform research, 233
　power-sharing, 234
　reflection questions, 235, 237
　summary, 235
　welcomed in, 231–232

community-driven research, 236
  glossary, 319
complicity, **109**, **114**, 174
conduct disorder, 186
confidentiality, ix, **217**, **227**, **288**
  anti-oppressive principle, 169
Congo, 218
content knowledge and application, 196
  anti-oppressive lens (social work supervision), viii, 32–72
  AOP leadership and supervision, 161–176
  beginning process, 9–30
  clinical supervision (decolonization), 9–30
  decolonization (supervision and leadership), 131–157
  DEIPAR, 81–100
  if-then anti-racism heuristics, 106–126
  mental health practice (psycholegal setting), 180–196
  social work practice (decolonization), vii, 9–30
context, 41, 43, 45, 81, 83, 86
continued learning
  key texts, 340–341
  supplementary resources, 340
Council on Higher Education Accreditation (CHEA), 303
Council on Social Work Education (CSWE), 26, 65, 83, 302–304
counter-narratives, 124, 320
COVID-19 pandemic, **297**
Crawford, N. D., x, xvii, xxv, 231–237
Crenshaw Dairy Mart, **297**
Crenshaw, K., 68, 85, 119–120, 222
criminal justice reform, 215
criminal justice system, 185–187, 239
critical consciousness, 23, 182, 271, 272, 278
  core, 23
  family separation system, 284–285
  glossary, 320
critical consciousness-raising (CCR), 284
critical cultural competence, 165, 172
  glossary, 320
critical disability theory
  application to clinical practice, 48–49
  scholars, 111
critical race mixed methodology, 181
critical race psychology (CRP), 181
critical race theory (CRT), viii, xii, 49, 181, 232, 257, 267
  heuristics (case vignette), 124–126
  incorporation in clinical praxis, 106–126
  supervision considerations, **118**
  tenets (practice implications), **109**
critical reflection, 3, 139, 140, 163, 165, 167, 169, 173, 271, 299

critical reflexivity, 162
  glossary, 320
critical resistance, **298**
critical self-reflection, 21–23, **109**, 171, 285
  glossary, 320
  metacognition, 22–23
critical transgender theory, 50–51
Cross, W. E. Jr, 259
cross-cultural dynamics: trauma-informed community, 222–224
cross-cultural practices: empowerment, 224
cross-dressing, 52
cross-gender clinical work, 148–149
cross-racial supervision, 148–149
Crow Cruz, C., ix, xvii
  leadership and supervision (AOP), 161–176
  practice activity (holding supervisee accountable), 176
Cullors, P., **297**
cultural awareness, xi, 45, 134, 142, 190
cultural competence, 4, 46, **97**, 165
  definition, 183
  enhancement, 43
cultural curiosity, 69–70
  definition, 69
cultural erasure, 206, 208
cultural healing, 213
cultural humility, 68–69, 165, 183
  commitment to ongoing education, 70–71
  decentering oneself, 70
  empathy and cultural curiosity, 69–70
  intersectionality, 68–69
  power imbalances, 71
cultural identities, 4, 272, 274
cultural imperialism, 244, 264, 318
cultural norms, 98, 190, 220, **269**
cultural racism, 111
culture, **16**, 45, 220
  assumptions (pitfalls), 220
curriculum-building
  anti-racist leadership, 139
  key texts, 340–341
  media and activities, 341
  supplementary resources, 340
Currie, N. L., i, ix, xii, 1, 5
  anti-oppressive lens, 32–72
  case vignette (family separation system), **287–288**
  communities (supervision and leadership), 293–312
  decolonization, 131–157
  NAESM, Inc. (Atlanta), 26–29
  oppressive systems (dismantling), 205–228
  practice examples (criminalization of people living with HIV), **38–39**

Index

practice guidance (Dudley Street Initiative), **67**
resources (anti-oppression and decoloniality), 342
social work practice (decolonization), 9–30
cycle of socialization, 132, *135*
   client-centered approach, 133
   components, 133
   disruption, 133, 134, 136
   ethical challenges, 136
   impacts (profound), 136
   leadership, 136–137
   social work supervision, 134–136
   two parts (beginning and core), 132

Davis, A., 186
Davis, L. S., x, xx, 180–196
   case vignette (children: inequity and oppression), **195–196**
de Vries (2015): eight-plane prism, 55, *56*, 58, 60, 64
decentering oneself, 70
decision-making
   inclusive, 137
   participatory processes, 4
decolonial process, ix, 22, 300
decoloniality, xi, 239
   Afrocentric principles (application), 44–46
   definition, 9
   glossary, 321
   resources, 342
decolonization
   anti-racist leadership, 139
   clinical supervision and leadership, 1–5
   definition, 9
   preparation of practice environment, 17–23
decolonization (supervision and leadership), 131–157
   allyship, 145–148
   anti-oppressive social work, 141
   anti-oppressive supervision, 142
   anti-racist and affirming, 137–141
   AOSW and supervision (intersection), 142–143
   case vignette (camp Wediko), 152–157
   cross-gender work, 148–149
   cross-racial supervision, 148–149
   cycle of socialization (leadership), 136–137
   cycle of socialization (social work supervision), 134–136
   discussion questions, 152
   dismantling racism, 143–144
   inclusive leadership, authentic supervision, followership, 149–151
   motivation (maintenance), 144–145
   reflective questions, 152, **157**
   relational cultural theory and supervision, 148
   social work practice, 131–135
   summary, 151
decolonization lens, 9–10, 32
decolonization movement: Africa, Asia, Caribbean, 240–241
decolonizing curriculum: glossary, 321
deep structure sensitivity, 180
   glossary, 321
   theoretical foundations, 181–182
dehumanization, 83, 88, 89, **196**, 225, 244, 245, 259, 266, 268, 280, 315
DEIPAR (components)
   1. diversity, 83–84
   2. equity, 84
   3. inclusion, 84–85
   4. intersectionality, 85–86
   5. power analysis, 86–87
   6. anti-racism, 87–89
DEIPAR framework, viii, 81–100
   anti-Blackness, 82–83
   application, 81–82
   background, 81
   community practice (case vignette), **96–100**
   expounding acronym, 83–89
   meaning of acronym (coined by Dyer), 81
   reflection questions, 96
   summary, 96
   supervision (leadership and power-sharing), 81–100
   supervision and leadership, 89–96
del Mar Fariña, M., 168
Delaware State University, **28**
demographics, 83, 194, **217**, 264, **309**
Diagnostic and Statistical Manual (DSM), 53, 186
difference, 59, 61, 83, 84, 91, 148
discrimination, 245, 257, **295**
DisCrit. *See* critical disability theory
dismantling racism, ix, 143–144, 145, 147
dismantling systems of oppression, 212, 234
   glossary, 321
distal stressors: definition, 182
diversity, x, 82, 84
   categories, 83
   DEIPAR, 83–84
   justice-based efforts, 84
   literature, 83
   performance-based efforts, 84
diversity, equity, inclusion, 35, 302, 303
   legislative assaults, 194
Doctor of Social Work (DSW), 81
Dollarhide, C. T., 93
domestic violence, 59, **124**
dominance, 50, 85, 86, 87, 265, 272, 277, 280, 318
dominant group, 145, 184, **280**, 314, 322

dominant narratives, 211, 296, 320
  glossary, 322
Dorriz, A. A. R., 297
Du Bois, W. E. B., 282
Dudley Street Neighborhood Initiative (DSNI, Boston), **67**, 301
Duggan, L., 61
Dumas, M. J., 257, 258, 267
Duncombe, S., **295**
Dyer, J. T., viii, xviii, 81–100

economic inequality, 143, 212, **295**
economic oppression, 209, 245
economic system, xi, 239, 328
education, 239
  achievement gap, 191
  interdisciplinary work, 191–192
  opportunity gap, 191
  oppressive systems (dismantling), 211–215
  structurally-racist system, 241
education supervision, 12–13
Educational Policy and Accreditation Standards (EPAS), 26, 302
educators, 14–15
Edwards, J. K., 20
effect: definition, **295**
Egan, R., 169
Einbinder, S. D., 168
Ellison et al. (2017), 55
Emancipation Proclamation (1863), 266
emotion, 34, **246**, **295**, 327
emotional harm, 18, 205
emotional labor, 52, 135, 170
emotional responses, 138, 176
empathy, 19, 69–70, 71, 138, 214, 333
employment, xxiii, 25, 184, 215, 332
empowerment, xii, 152–157, **176**, 272, 278
  across cultural boundaries, 224
  key to anti-oppressive work, 305
  power over (replaced by power to or with), 243
  promotion, 43
  servant leadership, 242
empowerment theory
  glossary, 322
  supervision practice, 66–67
endemic racism: glossary, 322
Engram, F. V. Jr., xi, xviii, 251–260
  Black Liberation (2023), 254
environmental justice, 143, 193, **295**
equal pay, 211, 215
equality, 61, 84, 144, 163, 240, 302
  definition, 84

equity, 167
  DEIPAR, 84
  distinguished from 'equality', 84
  evaluating progress, 172
  ethics, 46, 182–183
  leadership and supervision, 168–169
ethnographic interview: glossary, 322
ethnographic narrative: glossary, 323
ethnoracial cultures, 191
ethnoracial differences, 92
ethnoracial identities, 180
ethnoracial: glossary, 323
eurocentrism, 11, 118, 120, 131, 188, 240, 241, 244, 245, 275, **280**, 321
evidence-based practice: mental health models, 183–184
Exonerated Five, 253
experiences of oppression, 2, 28, 54, 86, 92, 170, 173, 222, 305

facilitative leadership, xii
  definition, 299
Fairey, S., 294
fairness, 84, 136, **246**, **295**, 302
families of color, 188
family, 220, 274
  hegemonic view, 188
family court systems, 187–191
  child custody, 189–191
  child welfare, 188–189
family policing system
  glossary, 323
  same as "family separation system" (*qv*), 263
family separation system, xii, 263–288
  anti-Black racism (history), 265–266
  anti-oppressive clinical supervision, 268
  anti-oppressive principles (application), 271–279
  Black case worker seeking anti-oppressive supervision, **268–271**
  call to action, 285–286
  case vignette (Hazel), **287–288**
  co-creation, 280–282
  continuation of anti-Blackness, 266–268
  critical consciousness, 284–285
  discussion questions, 286, **288**
  glossary, 323
  questions for reflection, **270**
  race-explicit strategy, 282
  racial disparities (alternative response investigations), **279–280**
  restorative justice, 282–283
  supervision and leadership (integrated model), 286
  sustainable change, 284
  systemic analysis, 283–284

Index 351

family separation system (application of anti-oppressive principles), 271–279
  children and youth, 273–274
  community, 274–277
  family, 274
  self-awareness and positionality, 272–273
  supervisees, 277–278
  systems, 278–279
Fanon, F., 1, 271
  Black Skins White Mask (1952), 244
feminism, 9, 42, 50, 51, 85, 119, 182, 195, 212, 303, 315
femmephobia: glossary, 323
field: slavery connotations of term, 12
Florida, 303
Floyd, G., **297**
followership, 151
folx, xiii, 148, 149, **216–217**
  glossary, 324
foster care, 188, 189
framing, 33–35, **39**, 41
  glossary, 324
  implications, 35
Freire, P., 271
  Pedagogy of Oppressed (1970), 1
French, B. H., 121
Furman, G., 93

Garran, A. M., ix–x, xviii, 271
  decolonization (supervision and leadership), 131–157
  traumatizing systems (dismantling), 205–228
Gaza, 219
Geiger, J. M., 281
gender, **16**, 85
gender diversity, 264
  glossary, 324
gender dysphoria, 53
gender identity, 51, 52, **156–157**, **176**, 190, 328, 332
gender identity disorder, 53
gender minorities, 147, 206. *See also* sexual and gender minorities
gender nonconforming (GNC), **28**
gender norms, 182, **196**, 334
gender studies, 50–51
gender-based oppression, 58, 211
genocide, 206, 219
George (2019), 53
Georgia State University, **28**
Gill-Peterson, J., 63
Global South, 239, 240, 325
glossary, xiii, 334
gold standards, 183
  mental health models, 183–184

Gonzalez, D., **96–100**
Goodyear, R. K., 172
Green (2002), 62
group learning: media and activities, 341
group supervision, 12, 13, 14, 15, 19, **28**, **287**
Grzanka, P. R., 61, 66, 85

Haiti, 218
Hall, J. C., 92
Harro, R. L., 132
  cycle of liberation, 326
Hastings, M. E., 186
Hays, P. A., 151
health outcomes, 231, 232, 236
healthcare, **37**, 87, 147, 180, 183, 207, 211, 214, 255, 279, 332
healthcare racism, 215
hegemony, **109**, 111
  glossary, 325
helicopter research, 193
helping professions, xi, 256
  anti-Blackness (dimensions), **261**
  BlackCrit, 256–261
  inherently anti-Black, 257
  listed, 254
Hendricks, M. L., 182
heteronormativity, 62, 182
  glossary, 325
heterosexism, 24, 51, 283, 305
heuristics. *See also* if-then anti-racism heuristics
  CRT-informed, 106
  definition, 108
  glossary, 325
hierarchical structures, 2, 136, 205, 235
hierarchy
  adverse effects, 161
  misguided values, 146
higher education: liberation as praxis, 255–257
Hispanics, 260, 264
  terminology, 72
historical contexts, 218–219, 221
historical oppression, 175, 245, 247
historical trauma, 210, 245, 247
HIV-AIDS, **26**, **28**, 61, **235**, 297, **306–311**
  criminalization, **38–39**
  racial inequities, 233
Holder, R., **153**
holistic approach, 44, 45, 47, 122, 146, 284
homeless shelters, 59, 64
homonormativity, 61, 62
  glossary, 325
homophobia, 206, 211
hooks, b., 256, 271
housing, **27**, 59, 180, 212, 215, 274, 332
Howard University, 240

human-centered design (HCD), **237**
humanistic principles, **246**

if-then anti-racism heuristics, viii, 106–126
    case vignette, 124–126
    CRT-informed clinical praxis, 108
    reflection questions, 112, 118, 123
    summary, 123–126
    supervision, **114**
    supervision considerations, **123**
    theoretical foundations, 106–108
if-then anti-racism heuristics (examples)
    if oppression intersectional, then liberation intersectional, **109**, 119–123, **126**
    if race socially-constructed, then deconstruct race, 109–113, **109**, **125**
    if racism ordinary, then anti-racism can be ordinary, 109–118, **109**, **125**
immigrants, x, 39, **40**, 97, 99, 266
imperialism. *See also* collective imperialism
    historical roots of oppression, 206–207
Implicit Assessment Test, 277, 278
implicit bias, 24, 107, 113, 166–167, 173, 272
incarceration, 180, 186, 206, 259, 266
inclusion, 82, 302
    DEIPAR, 84–85
    monitoring progress, 172
    "step beyond diversity," 85
inclusive leadership, 151
    definition, 150
inclusivity, 2, 136, 141, 144, 212
Indigenous Americans, 181
Indigenous children, 280, 283
Indigenous communities, 121, 131, 132, 206, 208
Indigenous knowledge, 118, 131, 137
Indigenous ways of knowing, 240, 245
individual pain, 222–224
    interplay with collective pain, 222
individual supervision, **287–288**
individual trauma, 209, 210
indoctrination, 256
inequality, 84
    structural and cultural roots, 211
inequity, 10, 48, 186, 251
    children (case vignette), **195–196**
institutional racism, 87, 89, 206
instruction: dual relationships, 24–26
interdisciplinarity
    education settings, 191–192
    mental health in psycholegal setting, 180–196
intergenerational trauma, 116, 208, 210, 212, 274
    glossary, 326
internalized racism, 115

International Monetary Fund, 319
intersectional identities, 22, 50, 148, 149, 169, 190, **216**
intersectionality, viii, 24, 51, 54, 64, 65, 82, 106, **109**, 181, 305
    anti-oppressive practice, 163–164
    anti-oppressive principle, 169
    application, 85
    cultural humility, 68–69
    definition, 68
    DEIPAR, 85–86
    glossary, 326
    mental health practice in psycholegal setting, 180–196
    oppressive systems (dismantling), 210–211
    role in leadership and supervision, 163–164
    role in understanding pain, 222–223
    term coined by Crenshaw (1989), 85
It Gets Better campaign, 61

JMAC For Families, 281
Johnson, M., 34
Johnson, M. P., 298
Jones, J., xii, xviii, 293–312
journals, 193
Judy support: glossary, 334

Kendi, I. X., 265

labeling, 181, 256
Ladson-Billings, G., 183, 184, 191, 257
Lakoff, G., 33, 34
Lambert, S., **295**
language, 32, 45
    power, 35
Latine, 72, **96**, 100
    glossary, 326
Latino critical perspective, 49–72
law, 52, 87, 107, 181, 188, 205, 211, 251, 253, 257, 263, 285, 322, 330, 333, 335
law enforcement, 192, 266, 281
leadership, 89–96, **280**
    anti-racist and affirming, 137–141
    culturally-affirming, 167
    cycle of socialization, 136–137
    "destructive," 90
    integrated model, *286*
    merger with allyship, 146–147
    "not neutral," 282
    paradigm shift needed, 242–243
    "relational," 90
    task-oriented, 242
    time-sensitive role, 300
    training programs, 4

leadership and supervision
  anti-oppressive practices, 161–176
  ethical considerations, 168–169
leadership and systems practice, 312
  community-based participatory research, 231–237
  family separation system, 263–288
  liberation as praxis, 251–260
  oppression and trauma (dismantling), 205–228
  social institutions (decolonization), 239–248
  supervision and leadership, 293–312
Lebanon, 220
Lee, C., 183
LeFrançois et al. (2022), 62
legal system: collaboration with mental health professionals, 184–185
Lenox (Massachusetts), 293
LGBTQIA+, 182, 187, 188, 189, 190, 207, 212, **216**, 326
  history, 191
  youth of color, 192
liberation, vii, **67**, **110**, 119, 146, 162, 181, 195
  glossary, 326
liberation as praxis, xi, 251–257
  application (higher education), 255–257
  BlackCrit, 256–261
  discussion questions, 260
  helping professions, 256–261
  liberation movements, 253–254
  racial standing (rules), 252–253
  spirit murdering, 254–255
  summary, 260
liberation health theory, 146
liberation movements, 10, 253–254
  art, **295–298**
liberation psychology, 146, 182
liberation work: preparation of practice environment, 17–23
liberatory consciousness: glossary, 327
liberatory models, xii, 263–288
liberatory movements, 254
  glossary, 327
licensure, 148
linguistic self-reflexivity, 35–36
Lipscomb, A. E., 169
Lisenbee, R., ix, xix, 131–157
listening, 69, 138
lived experiences, 3, 54, 59, 64, 184, **217**, 234, **246**, 247, 267, 273, 282, 284, 299
logic, **246**
Lopez-Littleton, V., 89
Lorde, A., 148, 181
Los Angeles Times, **38**
Love, B., 327
Lusk, M., 320

Maine Wabanaki State Child Welfare Truth and Reconciliation Commission, 283
Major, Ms., **298**
Make America Great Again (MAGA) Insurrection (2021), 254
Maldonado-Torres, N., 88
managerial supervision, 13
mandated supporting, 281
marginalization, 36, 54, 68, 119, 205, 247, 267, 272, 305, 326, 333
marginalized backgrounds, 70, 71, 135, 136
marginalized communities, 1, 39, 45, 63, 68, 70, 107, 118, 131, 133, 137, 139, 143, 146, 183, 193, 215, 305, 314
  economic disenfranchisement, 215
marginalized groups, 136, 141, 206, 209, 211, 247
  glossary, 327
marginalized identities, 55, 58, 119, 166, 186, 208, 257
marginalized individuals, 207, 212
marginalized people, 193, 195, 196
marginalized populations, xi, 134, 145, 194, 205, 246, 314, 321
Marrow (2023), 52
Martinez, G., viii, xix
  DEIPAR in community practice, **96–100**
masculinity, 53, **196**
Massachusetts, 52
Massachusetts General Hospital (MGH), **152**
Master of Social Work (MSW), **67**
matrix roles, **246**
Maurer, K., 10, 167, 169
Meade, G., viii–ix, xix
  anti-oppressive lens, 32–72
  case vignette (Camp Wediko), 152–157
  decolonization (supervision and leadership), 131–157
Meaningful Involvement of People with HIV-AIDS (MIPA), **309**
Measure (data activism organization), 284
media, **38**, 40, 67, 132, 186, 211, 293
men who have sex with men (MSM), **26**
Menkel-Meadow, C., 283
mental health, 59, 116, **124**, 287
  military, **216–217**
  military-based social work, **226–228**
mental health practice (psycholegal setting), 180–196
  case vignette (children: inequity and oppression), **195–196**
  collaboration in legal system, 184–185
  deep structure sensitivity, 181–182
  discussion questions, 195, **196**
  family court systems, 187–191

mental health practice (psycholegal setting) (cont.)
  gold standards, 183–184
  justice system (criminal and juvenile), 185–187
  professional ethics, 182–183
  recovery and empowerment, 182
  research, advocacy, public policy, 192–194
  summary, 194–195
mentorship, 134, 136, 145, 214, 300, 302
metacognition, 22–23
metaphor, 33–35, **39**, 41
  glossary, 327
  implications, 35
  questioned, **37**
Meyer, I. H., 182
microaggressions, 116, 166–167, 180, 181, 214
Miller, J., 271
mindfulness, 117, 321
mindfulness-based stress-reduction (MBSR), 213
Minnesota African American Family Preservation Act (2024), 282
minority stress theory, 181
  glossary, 328
misogyny, 53, 54, 206, 324
mobile health (mHealth), **236**
Moio, J. A., 112
Moms for Liberty, 255
Moradi, B., 85
moral authority, 243–244
  definition, 243
motivation (maintenance), 144–145
  adaptability, 145
  celebration of milestones, 144
  collective action, 145
  creative engagement, 145
  highlighting change, 144
  inspiration and role models, 145
  mentorship, 145
  personal commitment, community, support, 144
  public engagement, 145
  reflection and growth, 145
  self-care to prevent burnout, 144
  support networks, 144
  tracking progress, 144
  visible impact, 144
motivational interviewing (MI), 183
Mulhall (2020), 61

NAESM, Inc. (Atlanta), 26–29
narrative therapy, 117, 186
Nasser, J-É., viii, xx
  anti-oppressive lens, 32–72
  oppression and trauma (dismantling), 205–228

National AIDS Education Services for Minorities. *See* NAESM
National Association of Social Workers (NASW), 183, 302
  Code of Ethics, 65, 70
National Institutes of Health (NIH), 236
National Survey of Child and Adolescent Well-Being (NSCAW II, 2011), 264
Native Americans, 181, 188
nativism, 50
naturalization, 111
neo-colonialism, xi, 239, 240, 241, 328
New York City, 197, 253, **269**, 293
New York Times, **38**
Nkrumah, K., 318
nomenclature: glossary, 328
non-binary, 51, 58, 147, **176**, 324
non-governmental organizations (NGOs), xi, 239
normality, 23, 53
"nothing about us, without us," **67**, **237**
nuclear family, 188
  cisheteropatriarchal ideals, 113
  Eurocentric ideology, 252

O'eil, P., 168
Obama, S., 294
Oh, H., 183
Oklahoma Supreme Court, 253
Olivas, N., **297**
Olson-Kennedy, A., viii, xx, 32–72
opportunity gap, 328
  definition, 191
oppositional defiant disorder (ODD), **269**
oppressed communities, 182, 185, 194
oppressed groups, x–xi, 184, 239, 240, 315, 320
oppressed individuals, x, 184
oppression, 44, 119, 148, 149
  affirming supervision, 139
  children (case vignette), **195–196**
  historical patterns, x
  historical roots, 206–207
  if-then heuristics, 119–123
  modern-day, 219
  psychological impact, 207–208
oppressive practices, xii, 65, 162, 268, 271, 272
oppressive structures, 4, 131, 139, 143, 164, 180, 185, 305, 321
oppressive systems (dismantling), 205–228
  case vignette (military-based social work), **226–228**
  community-level trauma, 208–209
  comprehensive approach, 205–206
  discussion questions, 225
  economic and social harm, 209–210

education and awareness, 211–215
historical roots, 206–207
multi-faceted, intersectional approach, 210–211
psychological impact, 207–208
reflective questions, 225, **228**
summary, 224–225
trauma (country-specific or culture-specific), 218–221
trauma-informed community (cross-cultural dynamics), 222–224
United States Military, **215–217**
organizational culture, 2, 47, 136, 150, 166
glossary, 329
orientation-diversity: glossary, 329
othering, 251, 252, 253, 256, 258, 259, 315

pain, 214, 224, **261**, 288, 296
collective and individual (interplay), 222
intersectionality (role in understanding), 222–223
Palestinian liberation movement, 223
Panfil, V. R., 60
parenting plan evaluators (PPEs), 190
patriarchy, 205, 206, 211, **280**
peer reviews, 193
People of Color (POC), x, 109, 113, 115, 185, 213, 329
personal biases, 132, 133, 170, 171, 173, 182
personal experience, 220, 221, **246**
police, 189, **261**, 274, 279, **288**
police violence, 206
policing, 211, 215, 256
policy reform, 64, 208, 211, 224
addressing systemic racism, 215
Portugal, 88
positionality, 24, 113, 131, 272–273, 274
glossary, 329
post-traumatic stress disorder (PTSD), 207
poverty, 190, 207
power, 82, 90, 254
definition, 86
issues in supervision, 91–93
social, 53, 161
power analysis
definition, 87
DEIPAR, 86–87
glossary, 329
power differentials, 30, 92, **109**, **125**, 164, 166, 170, 242
glossary, 330
power dynamics, ix, 18, 71, 86, 87, 92, 131, 134, 137, 141, 144, 164, **176**
ethical navigation, 169–170
supervisor relationships, 164–165
power structures, 1, 168, 211, **296**

power-sharing, 234
supervision, 94–96
practice activity: holding supervisee accountable to AOP, 176
practice environment, 4, 27, 32, 49, 167
liberation work, 17–23
practice environment (preparation for decolonization work), 17–23
authenticity, 19–20
critical self-reflection, 21–23
safe and brave spaces, 17–18
supervision goal planning, 18–19
use of self, 20–21
practice example: people living with HIV, **38–39**
practice guidance
anti-oppressive practice, **16**
Dudley Street Initiative, **67**
military hope, healing, harm, **215–217**
social work licensing, **16**
practice interventions: strengthening clinical leadership, 4–5
practice reflections
community-based organizations (elevation with AOP), 26–29
NAESM, Inc. (Atlanta), 26–29
THRIVE SS, **306–311**
practicum, **28–29**, 60
dual relationships, 24–26
supervision, 12–13
praxis
definition, 62, 168
glossary, 330
processing, 14, 16, 23, 33, 155, **156**, 316
glossary, 330
professional boundaries, 26, 90, 138
professional development, ix, 70–71
anti-oppressive practice, 170–174
professional ethics, 182–183
pronouns, xvi–xviii, xxi–xxii, 58, 120, **125**, 156, **157**
proximal stressors: definition, 182
pseudo race-based fear, 259
psychodynamic perspective, **153**
psychoeducation, 117
psycholegal setting: AOP and mental health practice, 180–196
psychologists: profession more than 80 percent white in US, 184
psychology, 243, 245
public engagement, 145
public health, **308**
public policy, 193
harmful metaphors, 40

queer activist movement, 61
queer histories, **298**

queer methodology: glossary, 334
queer theory, 60–66, 182
  social work practice, 64
  supervision practice, 65–66
  uses, 62
queer: glossary, 334
queering, 65, 193
  glossary, 334
Quijano, A., 86

race, **16**, 85
  anti-racist and affirming supervision and leadership, 139
  "collective hallucination," 110
  definition, 87
  glossary, 330
  "not biological reality, but classification system," 110
  social construction, viii, 106, **109**, 109–113, **114**, 123
  social deconstruction, 109–113
racial disparities, 107, 111, 116, 211, 215, 216
  alternative response investigations, **279–280**
racial gaslighting, 113
racial inequities, 231, 233, 265, **279**
racial justice, 106, 108, 111, 211, 212, 214
racial profiling, 215
racial standing (rules), 252–253
racial trauma, 186, 207, 208, 213, 214
  healing "societal responsibility," 224
  macro-level, 210
  mezzo-level, 209
  micro-level, 209
racialization, 87, 89, 124, 272
  definition, 112
  glossary, 330
racially-minoritized populations, 231, 232, 233, 234
racism, 44, 46, 82, 87, 190, 206, 244
  anti-racist and affirming supervision and leadership, 139
  definitions, 265
  dismantling, 143–144
  minimization, 111
  "ordinary," **109**, 109–118, **118**
  pervasiveness, 232
racism is ordinary, viii, 106
  glossary, 330
racist structures, 106, 233
radical healing, 121
rape, 88, 251
recovery and empowerment (models), 182
redlining, 180, 210, 255
Reed, M., **26**
reflective practice, **176**
reflexive self-awareness: glossary, 330

reflexive self-awareness: glossary, 331
refugees, x, 69
relational cultural theory (RCT) supervision, 148
religion, 46, 83, 190, 325, 327, 335
research, 66
  community-based, 231–237
  everyday application, 231–237
  findings (dissemination), 193
  importance, 65
  mental health practice (psycholegal setting), 192–193
research methods, 65
researchers, 14–15
resistance, 140–141, 173–174
Resnicow, K., 180
restorative justice, 212, 214, 215
  family separation system, 282–283
  glossary, 331
Riley Foundation, **67**
Roberts, D., 263, 266
Roberts, S. O., 193
Robinson Findlay, M., x, xx, 180–196
  case vignette (children: inequity and oppression), **195–196**
Rogerian theory, **154**
Rogerson, C. V., 171
Rollins, T., xii, xx, 263–288
  case vignettes (racial disparities alternative response investigations), **279–280**
root-cause analysis (RCA)
  definition, 284
Ross, K. M., 257, 258, 267
Rutgers University, **236**
Ryan (2020), 61, 62
Ryan White funding, **27**

safe space, 17–18, **28**, 213, 300
  definition, 18
safe-enough space, 17, 137
sanism, 52, 53, 57
  glossary, 331
Schelbe, L., 281
scholar-practitioner, i, xix, 14, 27, 338
  glossary, 331
schools of social work, 12, 66, 294
  anti-oppressive leadership, 302–304
schools: trauma-informed, 214
school-to-prison pipeline, 192, **196**, 256
  glossary, 331
Scott-Walker, L., xii, xxi, 293–312, *310*
  "All of Us," 311–312
  practice reflections (starting organization to save life), **306–311**

Index

segregation, 64, 111, 139, 180, 207, 244
self-awareness, 42, 272–273
   cultural, 170–171
self-determination, 20, 43, 45, 99, 184, 185, 235
self-efficacy, 150, 242, 330
self-knowledge, 57, **246**
self-reflection, 22, 42, 46, 68, 106, 113, 114, 133, 164, 167, 272, 315. *See also* critical self-reflection
   anti-oppressive practice, 170–174
Seneca Village, 298
seroversary, **308**
   glossary, 332
servant leadership (SL), 242–243
   BIPOC, 242–244
   glossary, 332
   moral authority, 243–244
   outrage, 243
   power (social construct), 243
   principles, 242
Sex Offender Risk Appraisal Guide (SORAG), 187
sexism, 53, 190, 209, 211, 305
sexual and gender minorities (SGM), x, 61, 187
sexual assault, **124**, 206, 253
sexual assault shelters, 59, 64
Shepard, B., 63
Simmons University School of Social Work, **28**, 81
Simmons-Horton, S., xii, xxi, 263–288
skin color, 88, 94
slavery, 82, 212, 244, 251, 263, 265
   afterlife, 266, 267
   laws, 266
Sloan, L, 69
Smith, J. C., xi, xxi
social determinants of health, 181
social discourse, 40, 41
   harmful metaphors, 40
social exclusion, 207, 209
social institutions (decolonization), xi, 239–248
   Afrocentric perspective (key features), 247
   Afrocentric social work, 244–245
   Afrocentricity, 244–248
   Civil Rights Era (unexpected consequences), 240–241
   leadership (need for paradigm shift), 242–243
   neo-colonialism (impact on BIPOC), 241–242
   power over versus power with, 243
   reflection questions, 248
   servant leadership (moral authority), 243–244
   summary, 247
   task-oriented leadership (implications), 242
social justice, 10, 46, 82, 85, 167
   advancement, 44
   art, **295–298**
   definition, 93
   glossary, 332
   practice and policy, 36–41
   variations, 93
social justice supervision, 93–94
social location, 22, 24, 85, 112, 121, 162, 168, 174, 175, 181, 329
social media, 143, 299, **309**
social structures, 49, 107, 132, 141, 206, **246**, 321. *See also* societal structures
social work
   continuous learning and professional growth, 42
   embedded nature of whiteness, 255
   metaphors, **37**
   military-based ~ (case vignette), **226–228**
   roots, 183
   training, 183
social work language: oppressive roots, 33
social work licensing: practice guidance, **16**
social work licensure, 15
social work practice, 5
   decolonization, 131–135
   queer theory, 64
   transgender theory (application), 57–58
social work practice (decolonization)
   beginning process, 9–30
   community-based organizations (elevation with AOP), 26–29
   critical consciousness, 23
   dual relationships, 24–26
   positionality, 24
   reflection questions, 29, 30
   summary, 29
social work supervision, 9–15. *See also* supervision
   Afrocentric perspective, 42
   anti-oppressive lens, 32–72
   ceremony, 11
   core, 10
   cycle of socialization, 134–136
   decolonization lens, 9–10
   goal planning, 18–19
   key stakeholders, 10
   models, 10
   sine qua non of social work practice, 10–11
social work supervision (types), 11–15
   administrative, 13–14
   advanced clinicians, 14
   clinical, 13
   educators, 14–15
   groups, 15

social work supervision (types) (cont.)
  licensure, 15
  practicum, 12–13
socialization. *See* cycle of socialization
societal structures, 48, 107, **118**, 144, 209, 210, 329
socio-political debt, 191
Socrates, 313
solidarity, 143, 144, 209, 210, 212, 213, 223, 224, 225, 313
Soloman, B., 271
source domains, 34, 327
spirit murdering, 254–255
  definition, 254
spiritual balance, **246**
spirituality, 46
  glossary, 332
  incorporation, 44
stewardship, 85, 242, 243
stigma, **38**, 181, 186, 247, **310**
strengths perspective, 117, **246**
  glossary, 332
Stroebe, W., 193
Strömberg, A., **280**
structural oppression, 54, 168, 174, 267
structural racism, xi, 87, 118, 120, 124, 239, 240, **270**
  glossary, 332
structural vulnerability, 119, 120
students of color, 111, 214, 256, 257
succession planning, xii, 299–301
Sudan, 219
Sue, D. W., 172, 183
suicide, 208, 227
supervisees, 277–278
supervision, 89–96. *See also* anti-oppressive supervision (AOS)
  anti-oppressive practices (integration), 165–170
  anti-racist and affirming, 137–141
  critical self-reflection, 171
  CRT-informed, **114**, **118**
  equitable, 134
  equity and social justice, 167
  if-then anti-racism heuristics, **123**
  implicit bias and microaggressions, 166–167
  inclusive environment, 165–166
  integrated model, *286*
  intersectionality with AOSW, 142–143
  power issues, 91–93
  power-sharing, 94–96
  process-based, 90
  relational cultural theory, 148
  social justice perspective, 93–94

supervision and leadership, xii
  challenges and opportunities, 173–174
  decolonization, ix
  impact and overlap on communities, 293–312
supervision practice
  empowerment theory, 66–67
  queer theory, 65–66
  transgender theory (supervision practice), 58–60
supervisors
  etymology of term, 94
  special case, 92, 170
  three aims, 277
supervisory relationship, 3, 13, 14, 20, 91, 94, 95, 96, 116, 134, 142, 150, 161, 169, **270**, 299
  power dynamics, 164–165
support groups, **26**, 213, 334
Supreme Court, 252
surface structure adaptations, 180
surveillance, 188, 266, 273, 274, 278, 282, 284, 323
survival thrust: definition, 276
Sylvia Rivera Law Project, **298**
Syria, 219
systemic analysis, 286
  family separation system, 283–284
systemic barriers, 137, 143, 193, 302
systemic inequality, x, 4, 136, 205
  glossary, 332
systemic inequities, x, 3, 136, 161, 165, 175, 195, **280**, 304
systemic injustices, 1, 143, 149, 163, 165, 169
systemic oppression, 93, 106, 114, 121, 132, 135, 136, 141, 144, 163, 168, 210, 211, 212, 218, 278, 305, 333
  trauma, 185
systemic racism, 87, 116, 139, 143, 209, 210, 263, 264, 267
  policy reform, 215
systemic violence, **109**, 206, 208
systems, 278–279
  traumatizing and oppressive ‐ (dismantlement), 205–228
systems of oppression, **110**, 119, 120, 122, 123, 132, 143, 168, 170, 172, **176**, 206, 207, 231, 265, 267, **280**, 282, 315, 323, 327, 333
  brick-by-brick dismantlement, 40

Tanzania, 240
target domains, 34, 327
Tarshis, S., 122
task-oriented leadership: implications, 242
Tate, W. F., 257

Index 359

Taylor, A. N., ix, xxi, 131–157
  case vignette (military-based social work), **226–228**
  United States Military (practice guidance), **215–217**
teacher assistantship (TA), 25
Testa, R. J., 182
Texas, 264, 284
Texas Community Engagement Model (TCEM), 281
Tham, P., **280**
therapeutic treatment (antiracist approach), 116–117
  cognitive restructuring, 117
  mindfulness, 117
  narrative therapy, 117
  psychoeducation, 117
  safe environment, 116
  strength-based approaches, 117
THRIVE SS (practice reflection), **306–311**
tokenism, 165, 166, 212, 281
Tourmaline, **298**
transgender, 50–60
transgender activists, **298**
transgender and gender-diverse (TGD), 186, 187
transgender theory
  overview, 51–57
  social work practice, 57–58
  supervision practice, 58–60
transitional leadership, xii
  crucial feature, 300
  importance, 300
  key element, 300
  successful, 301
transmisia: glossary, 333
transmisogynoir, 54
  glossary, 333
transmisogyny, 53
transparency, 3, 19, 136, 137, 174, 304, 316
transphobia
  glossary, 333
  healthcare, 147
trauma, xi, 149
  community-level, 208–209
  country-specific or culture-specific, 218–221
  historical contexts, 218–219
  personal reflections, 220–221
  twofold (psychological and material), 205
trauma (country-specific or culture-specific), 218–221
  cultural assumptions (pitfalls), 220
  historical contexts, 218–219
  implications for practice, 221
  modern-day oppression (impact), 219
  trauma (personal reflections), 220–221
  trauma responses (nuances), 219–220

trauma bond: glossary, 333
trauma porn, 281
  glossary, 333
trauma responses (nuances), 219–220
trauma-informed community (cross-cultural dynamics), 222–224
  cross-cultural practices (empowerment), 224
  inclusive spaces for healing, 223–224
  individual and collective pain (interplay), 222
  intersectionality, 222–223
  solidarity through shared struggles, 223
trauma-informed therapy, 213, 224
traumatizing systems (dismantling), 205–228
  comprehensive approach, 205–206
truth-telling, 89, 212
Tuck, E., 2
Tulsa race massacre (1921), 253
Tutu, D., 54

Undetectables Support Model, **309**
  glossary, 334
unhiding, **295**
Uniform Code of Military Justice, **227**
United for Families (case vignette), **96–100**
United States, 88, 206
  social-work students (125,000), 304
United States Military
  hope, healing, harm, **215–217**
  mental health (system within system), **216–217**
use of self, 20–21, 24
  definitions, 20
  'formal, professional, modality', 20
  practice voice, 21
Utsey, S. O., 275

Vakalahi, H. F. O., 293
Van Der Kolk, B.: *Body Keeps Score* (2014), 293
Versey, H. S., 115
violence, 58, 209, 259
Violence Risk Appraisal Guide (VRAG), 187
Volker, R. D., 299

war, 36, 88, 153, 219, 220, 335
web of resistance, 143, 144
Weber, K., 283, 284
WEIRD (western, educated, industrialized, rich, democratic), 180, 192
West, C., 272
western culture, 60, 182
white children, 189, 191, 255, 256
  wealthy, 256
white men, 251
  cisgender, seemingly heterosexual, wealthy, 251

white people, 149, 252, 253, 260, 335
  cisgender heterosexual dyad, 188
white privilege, 112, 113, 115, 181, **196**, 251, 273
  poor beneficiaries, 252
white supremacy, xi, 51, 114, 118, 180, 192, 206, 254, 263, 265, 266, 282, 285
  colonial patriarchy, 110
  culture, 264
  embedded nature (higher education and social work), 255
  glossary, 334
  most violent aspect of whiteness, 254
white teachers, 254, 257
white women, 206, 251
white: use of lower-case 'w', 100
white-centered perspectives, 258, 259
whiteness, 254, 256, 259
  alignment with humanness, 267
  as system, 251

creation (1681), 251
  destroys everything in wake, 252
  determines humanity of oppressed, 252
  embedded nature (higher education and social work), 255
  glossary, 335
Wilcox, M. M., 10
Wolfe, A., viii, xxi, 32–72
women, 51, 119, 206, 207, 273
Woodson, C. G., 271
World Bank, 319
Wright, D. E., viii, xxii
  anti-oppressive lens, 32–72
  social institutions (decolonization), xi, 239–248

Yang, K. Y., 2
Yemen, 219
Young, R. A., **152**, 153

Zaragoza, M., viii, xxii, 106–126
zero-tolerance policies, 191

For EU product safety concerns, contact us at Calle de José Abascal, 56–1°, 28003 Madrid, Spain or eugpsr@cambridge.org.

www.ingramcontent.com/pod-product-compliance
Ingram Content Group UK Ltd.
Pitfield, Milton Keynes, MK11 3LW, UK
UKHW020139090326
468786UK00019B/1631